Roads in the Sky

Conflict and Social Change Series

Series Editors
Scott Whiteford and William Derman
Michigan State University

Roads in the Sky

The Hopi Indians in a Century of Change

Richard O. Clemmer

Westview Press

BOULDER • SAN FRANCISCO • OXFORD

Conflict and Social Change Series

Copyright © 1995 by Westview Press, Inc.

Published in 1995 in the United States of America by Westview Press, Inc., 5500 Central Avenue, Boulder, Colorado 80301-2877, and in the United Kingdom by Westview Press, 12 Hid's Copse Road, Cumnor Hill, Oxford OX2 9JJ

A CIP catalog record of this book is available from the Library of Congress.
ISBN 0-8133-8538-5 (HC) — 0-8133-2511-0 (PBK)

Printed and bound in the United States of America

The paper used in this publication meets the requirements
of the American National Standard for Permanence of Paper
for Printed Library Materials Z39.48-1984.

10   9   8   7   6   5   4   3   2

Contents

Tables and Illustrations

Photo section faces p. 124

Tables

Figures

Maps

ix

Preface

I first went to the Hopi Mesas in the summer of 1968 to gather oral histories for a project funded by Doris Duke and sponsored by the University of Illinois Department of Anthropology, where I was a fledgling graduate student. I returned the following summer for the same purpose. Although little of that early research is reflected in the following pages, they do reflect much of the work that I did in the subsequent two years for a Ph.D. dissertation dealing substantially with cultural change.

Although I was able to spend little time on the Mesas after 1973, the Sekaquaptewa family's excellent weekly newspaper, *Qua' Toqti*, in the 1970s and 1980s kept me abreast of developments. My relocation to Santa Fe, New Mexico, in 1979 and subsequently to Colorado, as well as service on the American Anthropological Association's Navajo-Hopi Land Dispute Committee since 1990, made more frequent visits of longer duration possible.

Over the last quarter-century much has changed. Some changes were predictable; others were not. Issues such as the land dispute, generated in outline nearly three centuries ago and etched in concrete, so to speak, by a series of U.S. Government actions and inactions beginning in 1882, might well have festered indefinitely with little expectation of even minimal resolution. On the other hand, Peabody Coal Company's strip-mining of coal and deep-mining of artesian water became an issue for Hopis in 1969 and continues to be worrisome. While the rest of North America experienced an acceleration of social problems such as family conflicts, ideological factionalism, and substance abuse, it would have been folly to assume that Hopis would not experience these problems as well, and they soon did. While telephones were virtually non-existent in 1968 and piped water and electricity were seldom encountered, it was predictable that telephones, televisions, VCRs, and computers would become commonplace, as they now are.

But the waning of Christianity; the strengthening of the importance of oral tradition and ceremonialism; the persistence of matrilineality and clan ownership of lands at First and Second Mesas (re-affirmed in a court case in Hopi Tribal Court as late as 1983); the preservation of Walpi as a Tribal historic site; and the development of proprietary interests on the part of Hopis in cultural property -- religious and non-religious -- prior to passage of the Native American Graves and Repatriation Act might not have been predicted a quarter-century ago. In fact, I recall an official of the Bureau of Indian Affairs in Keams Canyon telling me quite conclusively in that first summer of 1968 that one day, the Hopi Reservation would cease to exist. It would be divided up into individually owned plots; the villages would become little cities or would cease to exist politically; the Tribe would be legally abolished; and Hopis would become just ordinary U.S. citizens, just as would all Indians, differing from other citizens only in their difference of heritage and perhaps customs.

No Hopis I talked to believed for an instant that such a situation would come to pass. Hopis would resist "termination" to the bitter end. And within two years U.S. Indian policy had indeed changed and the termination idea was shelved. But the overall issue of assimilation, acculturation, and cultural homogenization -- increasingly a worldwide phenomenon brought about by easy access to communication and internationally circulated durable goods -- remained trenchant and prominent. Would Hopis, and other Indians, simply become politically, economically, and ethnically enclaved as a rural proletariat, with little control over their destinies? Such predictions were, indeed, made.

Yet early on in my Hopi experiences I had encountered the "Traditionalists," a political group that continues to be poorly understood even by those who are familiar with the Hopi. It seemed to me that the vehemence of reaction to them portended something a little more complex than merely political factionalism over acculturation. The "Traditionalists" advocated a platform of sovereignty, self-determination, and international recognition that has now come to be recognized as common to many indigenous peoples throughout the world. They are not, strictly speaking, either nativists or cultural conservatives. In fact, they belong much more to the modernist traditions of critique and dissent than they do to the anti-modernization forces of conservatism, other-worldly exclusionism, or back-to-the-land agrarian communalism, despite displaying some aspects of these social movements.

Hopi Traditionalism has become incorporated into Hopi politics and society to the extent that Traditionalism can be said to be undergoing institutionalization. When I realized that this institutionalization was happening, much of the confusing rhetoric that surrounds the Traditionalists became clear in terms of its impetus: no modernization ever takes place without some kind of ideologically constructed struggle, and Hopi Traditionalism is merely part of Hopis' version of that struggle.

Thus I see the Hopi not as some formerly isolated population thoughtlessly appended to the destiny of the United States. Rather, I see the Hopi as a culture and society with a history stretching back more than a thousand years and with a future that will have been shaped by the struggle with modernity which has framed much of the last century-and-a-half of the world's history. What follows is my effort to understand the uniquely Hopi aspect of that struggle with modernity.

Richard O. Clemmer

Acknowledgments

I am most grateful to the National Institute of Mental Health, the American Anthropological Association, Doris Duke, and John R. Wilson, all of whom provided financial support at various times over the last three decades that made it possible for me to conduct research on the Hopi Mesas. Many thanks go to Garrick Bailey of the University of Tulsa, to Ben Priest of Parker, Colorado, and to Dean Birkenkamp, my editor at Westview Press, for providing critical review of the manuscript and helpful suggestions for its revision.

Thanks also to Elmer R. Rusco of the University of Nevada, who made available to me copies of important documents on the Indian Reorganization Act from the National Archives, as well as to Robert Rhodes, Dan Budnik, and David F. Aberle, all of whom kept the Hopi in my focus during long periods when I could not get to the Mesas. For preparation of the book I am exceedingly grateful to the staff of the Faculty Computing lab of the University of Denver -- Nichelle Hart, Jennifer Moore-Evans, and especially Carol Taylor, for her indefatigable persistence and skill in typesetting the final product, and in drawing the maps. I am also grateful to John R. Wilson for provision of the photographs taken by Joseph Mora, and to Christopher McLeod for permission to use two of his fine photographs.

Most of all, I express appreciation to many Hopi individuals over the years, a few of whom are mentioned in this book and many of whom have passed on, without whose assistance, cooperation, and patience I could not have proceeded or gotten this far. For what I have gotten right, I credit their guidance; for errors, I assume full responsibility.

R.O.C.

A Note on Orthography

While several orthographies of Hopi exist, including those developed by Heinrich Voth in the 1890s and much later by Carl and Florence Voegelin in the 1950s, Roy Albert and David Shaul in the 1960s and 1970s, and Ekkehart Malotki in the 1980s, and the Hopi Dictionary Project (in press), each of them is slightly different in use of characters and spellings, and until the Hopi Dictionary Project is published, there is no single source that contains spellings of all Hopi words that occur in the anthropological literature. Therefore, in the interests of accessibility and consistency, I have chosen to use the spellings that are most predominant in the anthropological literature in writing Hopi names and words. For spelling of village names, I have used the Hopi Tribal Constitution, since readers are much more likely to encounter those spellings than the admittedly more linguistically correct ones that have been used in recent works on the Hopi.

1

Hopi Prophecy, the World System, and Modernization

Prophecy and Events

Hopis have lived in their desert stronghold in northeastern Arizona for more than a thousand years. Yet as the world approached the millennium mark in the Twentieth Century, the same profound changes affecting the rest of humanity were also affecting Hopis. These changes, say Hopis, however, are no surprises; they were prophesied, as were others before them.

Late in the 19th century, several elderly Hopis prophesied that one day, roads would sweep across the sky, people would communicate through spider webs crisscrossing the land, and Pahaana -- the Hopis' lost white elder brother -- would return to help the Hopis overcome their problems. Decades later, airplanes flew over the reservation and telephone lines crisscrossed the land. Pahaana did not return. And a half-century later "Pahaana" had also become the term applied to all "white" people -- Euro-Americans -- despite the fact that none of them seem to have been the fulfillers of the Prophecy.

Roads in the Sky?

When I was a boy, down in the field, my father said someday, something pick you up, take you, drops you right at your door. And someday, there'd be roads in the sky.

---Corn Clan man, 72, Shungopavi
(Clemmer, Field Notes, 1968)

1

All this is known from prophecies: taxes, the road in the sky -- that's airplanes -- even the landing on the moon and the atomic bomb was prophesied. We know what is going to happen.
                                                    ---Badger Clan man, 48, Hotevilla
                                                    (Clemmer, Field Notes, 1968)

Our forefathers...told us that...there would be a road in the sky. How could anyone build a road in the sky...? When we see airplanes going back and forth over us we know what they were talking about.
                                                    ---Sun Clan, ca. 90, Hotevilla
                                                    (Kochongva 1956)

Hopi culture features prophecy as an important part of the ideology of tradition, and tradition as an important part of modern Hopi life. *"What the whiteman calls 'prophecy,'"*...said a Hopi teacher in 1982, *"I call the Hopi Life Plan. This life...was planned at some point in time. The Hopi call this tingavi. In Hopi, you set forth on a mission. This was how it was done at the beginning of this current life of the Hopi. A hard life, a life of confusion, turmoil, is predicted for the Hopis"* (Hopi Health Department 1983:35-38).

Some of the confusion and turmoil are evident in issues of modern life that all Hopis must confront: pervasive factionalism; endemic political dissent; continuing controversy over a Tribal Council that sometimes loses its quorum for weeks at a time; "the evils of the white man (alcohol and drugs)" taking hold (Hopi Health Department 1984:20); quandaries over how to determine the appropriate role for tourists, anthropologists, missionaries, and partisans in the Hopi world. But modern Hopi life also features more measurable successes and tangible easing of life's hardships: the return of more than 1,000,000 acres of Hopi land; the return and repatriation of culturally and religiously significant art objects; achievement of increased control over mineral leasing; conquest of debilitating diseases and high infant mortality; demographic expansion and technological change.

The issues that Hopis confront in their everyday lives are part of a more global contest. This contest involves strategizing, battling, and negotiating for control over territories, resources, populations, and loyalties. It is a contest of politics, economics, and culture, full of unexpected outcomes, played out through the latest phase of human history -- the phase of modernism and modernization. Despite apparent isolation, Hopis have been participants in this contest for 150 years.

This book documents the ways in which Hopis have collectively used their culture and their sociopolitical structures to deal with changes. I focus on six major events in Hopi history: a factionalist schism that split the largest Hopi village, Oraibi, into first three, then ultimately six separate villages; the impact of the federal Indian Reorganization Act of

1934; the rise of a political movement known as "Traditionalism"; the story behind far-reaching oil and coal leases of the 1960s; settlement of the Hopi-Navajo land dispute; and the disappearance of ceremonial objects into private collections and museums. I emphasize the role of ideology, but also the importance of a context formed by the world system, modernization, and political economic processes.

A Brief Introduction to Hopi Culture, History, and Context

Occupying the tops and escarpments of three mesas and a plateau to the south and east of the Grand Canyon, the Hopi are limited by legislative fiat and population pressure from neighboring Navajos to 1,500,000 acres. Descended from a mixture of prehistoric peoples loosely known as "Basketmaker" and Uto-Aztecan-speaking groups that migrated through the Colorado Plateau area sometime around 800 A.D. These immigrants contributed their language, "Hopic", which is related to Takic and Numic languages spoken by Cahuillas in southern California; Utes and Paiutes in Utah, Nevada, Oregon, eastern California, and northern Arizona; and Shoshones in Utah, Nevada, Wyoming, and eastern California. Among all of these linguistically related groups, the Hopi are the only people that have a distinctly Puebloan culture.

Puebloans share distinctive diagnostic cultural characteristics among themselves such as nucleated settlements built of two- and three-storey apartment complexes arranged in straight rows with streets and plazas; calendrical, collective ceremonies performed at specific times of the year; a pantheistic religion; and a subsistence strategy based heavily in horticulture. Puebloans were once widespread on the Colorado Plateau and the Rio Grande and San Juan River drainages, but population shrinkage and settlement nucleation resulted in Puebloans becoming concentrated in the Rio Grande and Pajarito Plateau areas of what is now the state of New Mexico by 1400. A few Puebloan groups settled to the west, however: at Acoma, Laguna, Zuni, and Hopi. Known as the western Pueblos, these peoples probably absorbed other Puebloans from abandoned settlements such as Mesa Verde, Chaco Canyon, the Mimbres River area, and even as far as Casas Grandes (Paquime') in northern Mexico. Hopis undoubtedly absorbed groups of Puebloans from Walnut Canyon, the Little Colorado River (Homolovi), and Sunset Crater (Wupatki, Wukoki) to the south as well as small Puelboan settlements in the Grand Canyon to the northwest and the Painted Desert area to the east. Therefore, Hopis' claimed aboriginal territory historically encompassed the San Francisco Peaks near Flagstaff, the Grand Canyon, all of Black Mesa, and areas south of Interstate 40 which cuts through northern Arizona -- more than thirteen million acres.

In 1540, when first contacted by Spaniards, Hopis probably numbered between 5,000 and 6,000.[1] When the United States formally extended jurisdiction into the Hopi area in 1870, several smallpox epidemics and famines had reduced the Hopi population to fewer than 2,400 (Dockstadter 1979:524-525; Simmons 1979:221.) Since then, villages have increased in number from seven to thirteen in the last 150 years, and the population has grown threefold to just over 9,000. Although mining and cattle grazing have come to dominate economically, many Hopis still regard earth and land as a sacred, rather than a secular, resource.

The Hopi are not only one of several hundred Native American "Tribes" enclaved on reservations, but also qualify as an "indigenous nation" within the scheme of international law and politics. Within this international scheme, indigenous nations began to assert collective rights to some degree of sovereignty, autonomy, and self-determination in the last quarter of the Twentieth Century. As one of these indigenous nations on the international stage as well as an American Indian Tribe with federal recognition, the Hopi are participants in a world-wide political and economic system in which efforts at modernization and attempts to maintain cultural pluralism often clash. Therefore, the Hopi provide a good case study not only for how a modern Puebloan group is handling the tensions of modernization and cultural preservation, but also of how a small indigenous nation is faring in the complex forces of world-wide modernization within the U.S. political and economic framework. Some of the problems that have confronted Hopis in the last century -- such as those stemming from ecological and demographic events and even from population pressure from neighboring tribes -- may be viewed independently from the impact of the world system; but other events and processes, such as the search for oil and coal; questions of cultural property; the spread of industrial technology; and the streamlining and rationalization of political forms and processes along Anglo-American and Eurocentric lines are being played out in an international arena. To the extent that the Hopi are affected by these processes and events -- and thus are participants in them -- their culture and history are as much products of forces originating well beyond the borders of Hopiland as much as they are products of historical traditions and trends that have been unfolding within Hopiland itself since time immemorial. Before focusing more specifically on the Hopi, then, a brief look at the concept of the "world system" and the parameters of the "modernity" that is taken as its hallmark, will provide a worthwhile perspective.

The World System, Modernization, and Cultural Pluralism

The concepts of a political economic "world system" and modernization provide the motivation for this study. World systems theory begins from the premise that identifiable social, political, and economic systems extend beyond individual nations, communities, and populations. Political and economic relations link and lock smaller social subsystems into larger ones. Production and distribution of goods, services, and people with the goal of maximizing profit and gaining economic advantage hold the system together. The world system started to form at least as early as the 15th century (Braudel 1981, 1982, 1984; Wallerstein 1974) and may have had its beginnings as early as the third century B.C. (Frank and Gills 1992).

Central to world systems theory are the concepts of core/periphery and metropolis/satellite. These pairs of concepts are similar. Cores are geographic areas where the most efficient production technologies are developed; where people have easy access to material goods and to the flow of money; where political and economic power-brokers hatch strategies for moving people and goods on a large scale, whether for military purposes or to develop new markets and products. Peripheries are geographical areas that provide labor and buyers of products, but have only small, dependent centers of commerce, money, and production. These small centers turn parts of peripheries, better termed semi-peripheries into little satellites of populations that work, buy, spend, and produce in response to the needs or whims of the power-brokers in the very centers -- the metropoles -- of the core areas (Jorgensen 1971:84-90; 1972:9-11). The core metropoles of the world system are generally acknowledged to have been in Germany and the United States during most of the 20th century; in England and France for the 18th, 19th, and early 20th centuries; and in Spain and Portugal in the 16th and 17th centuries, although Thornton (1992) has modified the picture somewhat by documenting the important role of competition from African states in the Dutch, Portuguese, and Spanish struggles for monopoly over the 15th-century world system.

Several general aspects of the world system are important to establish from the beginning. One is that the system has been spreading out from cores to peripheries for centuries, and in that spreading out, it has incorporated all or parts of pre-existing systems of trading, bartering, and marketing. These pre-existing systems, or parts of them, continue to function, often with relative autonomy, as subsystems of the world system. The linkage and locking of parts into the system has changed those parts, but the system itself is constantly being changed as well, by the specific cultural and social patterns which those parts bring to the system. The result is a trend toward homogenization, on the one hand, and pluralism on the other.

Secondly, there is a good deal of flexibility in the system, which usually benefits the power brokers most of all, but sometimes benefits participants in the subsystems at the expense of the power brokers. This flexibility stems from what might be called the "plug-in" factor. Populations and areas are sometimes connected by a very thin "wire" of distribution that either transmits labor and goods into the system or out. Whoever has the power to "pull the plug," so to speak, has the power to determine the relationship of the particular population and area to the entire system. But pulling the plug might result in merely greater autonomy for the isolated subsystem, following an adjustment period. Thus the "world system" is a system only in the sense that it has relatively few, but standardized, driving motivations: money, profit, valuation of material things, and the capacity to turn human labor and raw materials into money, profit, and material things. The question is whether those standardized, driving motivations of producing and selling things are pushing the world toward a single, homogenized cultural system.

The idea of a one-world, homogenized cultural system was introduced as the basis for the original concept of modernization back in the early 19th century. In the 1970s, some observers began to suggest the idea once again. One aspect of modernization is that political units have become larger while at the same time becoming fewer in number. Some observers took this trend plus the worldwide spread of such things as Pepsi- and Coca-cola, transistor radios, McDonald's hamburgers, Western-style clothing and music, and the world system's general commitment to constantly increasing production and maximizing economic advantage, as indications that a homogenous world culture was indeed emerging. They saw the idea of a homogenized world culture, with agreed-upon, shared values and attitudes, as a necessity if humans were going to solve problems such as warfare, famine, overpopulation, nuclear proliferation, runaway energy consumption, global warming, the hole in the ozone layer, pollution of the oceans, and desertification.

But other observers noted just the opposite trend. Many peoples around the world have resisted various aspects of modernization, whether rightly or wrongly, and for a diversity of reasons, just as strongly as others have embraced them, and formerly large empires are currently undergoing "balkanization."

Indigenous Autonomy

Some of the strongest sources of that diversity continue to be the 5,000 or so indigenous peoples -- some of them with shrinking populations -- that anthropologists called "primitive" until not so long ago and studied intensively because they thought they were going to disappear. Many did (cf. Bodley 1989). But many did not. The Hopi are among those that did not disappear. They show no signs of doing so.

The most pressing questions embedded in the ideas of a world system, modernization, and cultural pluralism concern political and economic autonomy. Does cultural pluralism imply, or require political and economic pluralism? How likely is it that cultural distinctiveness can be pursued by a population unless it has territorial integrity, political autonomy, and control over its economic resources?

Some observers say it is very unlikely (Morris 1986; 1992; Robbins 1992). Yet few indigenous people have any degree of guaranteed territorial integrity or political autonomy within the nation-states that encompass them. Many have economic independence only to the degree that they are poverty-stricken and limited to a subsistence economy. Those in the United States -- the 300 or so Indian Tribes -- are virtually unique in that regard. And the degree to which the territorial integrity and political autonomy is real or illusionary is debatable (cf. Morris 1992; Robbins 1992; and Clemmer, Aberle, Jorgensen and Scudder 1989 with Washburn 1989).

Sills (1992) has suggested some measures of indigenous peoples' autonomy, largely in terms of a struggle against influence by the dominant nation-state. I suggest additional measures: (1) the degree to which an indigenous nation expands its territorial base; (2) the degree to which it bends the nation-state's political apparatus to its own political objectives; (3) the degree to which it is able to assert determining control over production and distribution of goods and services; and (4) the degree to which it successfully asserts its own cultural rules, norms, attitudes, values, and institutions as the basis for collective decision-making, problem-solving, and interaction with other indigenous nations as well as with the nation-state and with international bodies.

Against these measures of autonomy, and within the context of the world system, the six events taken for discussion raise some significant questions.

- Was the factionalist schism of 1906 a product of purely Hopi internal dynamics -- a self-induced reshuffling of political relationship within an autonomous indigenous nation? Or a disintegration brought about by the imposition of U.S. rule?

- Did the Indian Reorganization Act implement a "prevailing system of colonial governance" (Robbins 1992:97) on behalf of the U.S.? Or did it grant Hopis' a relief from domination?
- Did the "Traditionalists" help to maintain Hopi cultural and political autonomy? Or did they just get in the way?
- Did oil and coal leases grant Hopis economic control? Or were they mere giveaways to multinational corporations?
- Did Hopis achieve a victory in a long-standing, on-going contest with Navajos? Or were they manipulated by outside interests, duped into internecine competition that benefitted third parties?
- Is the return and repatriation of ceremonial objects primarily a guilt-motivated good-will gesture to a Tribe whose ritual structure was meant to die? Or does it signify the impact of a minority's culture on the majority's thinking?

Some tentative answers lie in an analysis of Hopi culture and history at the points where they intersect Euro-American history and culture. Such an analysis must take into account the pressures and constraints, but also the opportunities and possibilities, that the interaction has created.

The dialogic, two-way nature of American and Hopi relationships has been defined largely by political, economic, and cultural factors. Hopis have developed cultural and political ideologies that mediate this dialogue. After 100 years of contact with the dominant American culture, Hopi culture today maintains continuity with aboriginal roots, but also reflects the mutual impacts of Twentieth Century history and Hopi culture on each other, within the contexts of the world system and modernization.

The Two Modernities

The First Modernity

Although we may have encountered "post-modernism" and "post-industrialism" some time in the 1970s, the Twentieth Century was nothing if it was not the apogee of modernization and modernism: the technological, economic, artistic, and political age of wonderful things and scientific creations. Modernism[2] is more than just "everything that is happening now" and "everything that is not old fashioned." Modernity and modernization constitute a set of agendas, states of being, moral orders, ideologies, and assumptions, as well as styles, methods, and techniques. This set has two opposite poles: the pursuit of progress and opposition to it. These two salient, juxtaposed hallmarks of modernization characterize Hopi history in the Twentieth Century as much as they do the history of the Western World.

On the one hand, modernization constitutes social change in a particular society that tends toward increasingly greater dependency on industrially-manufactured goods, services, and energy from distant areas; loss of political, economic, social, and cultural autonomy; increased use of cash instead of barter and socially-determined reciprocity; "rationalization of the ways social life is organized and social activities performed;" and "the pragmatic use of fact and logic in the achievement of various identified goals" (Moore 1979:1). Modernization's advocates assumed that applying standardized methods of observation and comparison would yield a base of knowledge so that social planners could preserve "good social habits" and "mark the bad ones for destruction" (Matthew Arnold and E.B. Tylor quoted by Stocking 1968:85). Thus modernization is more than just a certain kind of change. It is planned and implemented according to a set of goals and an ideology of values.

Some modernizing goals are: increasing economic output; improving health and life expectancy; educating the population; increasing technological innovation and invention; developing a reliable administrative governmental bureaucracy staffed by a civil service. Modernizers value punctuality, objectivity, hard work, discipline, fair competition, success, standardization, predictability, future orientation, saving for a rainy day. Many modernizers' goals, values and methods are contained in the concept of progress: "a sense of moral satisfaction with certain evolutionary trends" (Harris 1968:37). The idea of progress originated in the 18th-century European period called the "Enlightenment" and contained "the notion of a model type of individual living in a model society and operating with model thoughts and values." The model society itself would arrange its parts in a rank order so that the parts "fall into a natural or functional (and frictionless) balance" (Voget 1975:74, 87). It would curb deviations and aim for harmonious equilibrium. Friction, factionalism, and dissent would mark a failure to progress. Throughout most of the Twentieth Century, progressing was something that industrial nations considered themselves to be doing automatically and something that non-industrialized nations were supposed to try to be doing.

Progressive modernists counterposed themselves to conservatives, reactionaries, and traditionalists largely by embracing factual and technical solutions to all problems. "The technical state of mind is secular," wrote sociologist Wilbert Moore (1979:7), "having scant patience with Fate, Divine Will,...tradition, the wise teachings of the founding fathers, or the shared but unexamined wisdom which 'everybody knows.'" The opposition of modernity and tradition is the basis for theories of social change: modernity will be realized "when tradition has been destroyed and superseded" (Rudolf and Rudolf 1967:3).

Modernity is supposed to supersede tradition. Because traditionalists in general are supposedly frozen in time, their outlook hardened into a lifeless quiescence, and therefore easily outdistanced over time by the march of progress. In one of the few analyses that directly challenged modernist assumptions during their heyday, Rudolf and Rudolf (1967:3-4) summarized some of the heuristic contrasts between modernity and tradition as follows:

> "Modernity" assumes that local ties and parochial perspectives give way to universal commitments and cosmopolitan attitudes; that the truths of utility, calculation, and science take precedence over those of the emotions, the sacred, and the non-rational; that the individual rather than the group be the primary unit of society and politics;...that mastery rather than fatalism orient attitudes toward the material and human environment; that identity be chosen and achieved, not ascribed and affirmed; that work be separated from family, residence, and community in bureaucratic organizations

But they also pointed out that this dichotomy is false for several reasons, among them: (1) Modernity does not necessary supersede tradition; and (2) Tradition can, and often does, grow and attain increased ideological power along with progress, becoming entwined with it.

The Second Modernity

Tradition constitutes part of the "second" modernity: the modernity of challenge, criticism, dissent, exceptionalism. In this sense, tradition and traditionalism are not mere conservatism. Traditionalists want to maintain an anchor in the past. But unlike mere conservatives or reactionaries, who may agree with progressivists on the importance of individualism in modern life, traditionalists maintain the role of human agency by masking it with an invocation of instructions from powers beyond the control and understanding of individual persons. Traditionalism is not mere conservatism because it relies on collective acknowledgment (if not complete agreement) on what is important to be remembered, and thus must constantly be constructed and created.

This critical modernity, with its romantic, traditionalist flavor, arose in mid-19th century Europe and later in the Americas. Its expression is best seen in literary and artistic forms, but it can also be seen in social and cultural ones: utopias, communal experiments, manifestoes of opposition and dissent. This strong critical expression declared itself against industrial technologies, against the dampening of emotions, against the narrow pursuit of rational objectivity at any cost, against narrow individualism, against standardization and conformity, against crass materialism; and for intuition, for the unconscious, for the uncalculated and spontaneous, for "rebellion, anarchy, and apocalypticism," for communalism, for spiritualism (Cantor 1988:6-11; Calinescu 1977:41-42). It rejected one-dimensionalism and embraced the paradoxical. One well-known example of critical modernity can be found in the Surrealists. In the 1920s, Surrealist writers and artists articulated and translated this aspect of the "second" modernity into the most pronounced and intensive artistic, literary, social, cultural, and political critique of the modernist era (Marcus and Fischer 1986:123). Claiming inspiration from cosmic forces, they produced forms of critical artistic and social expression that nearly overcame the industrial, standardized expressive motifs epitomizing progress (Nadeau 1965).

Thus there are two modernities: one that exalts that which it defines as individualistic; industrially technological; factually technical; rationally secular; and cosmopolitan. And there is the other modernity that lauds that which it defines as collective and communal; handcrafted and natural; intuitive and fatalistic; prophesied and paradoxical; local and parochial. Traditionalisms of all kinds are aspects and products of modernization. "Traditionalism" is a kind of modernism. It is an ideological and cultural concomitant to "progressivism."

The Hopi provide an example of this modernist dichotomy. Traditionalism and progressivism among the Hopi have resulted from Hopis' differential interpretations of their history and culture, and they represent two broad metaphors, rather than actual behavior patterns. The Chairman of the Hopi Tribe made the following remark about the importance and pervasiveness of prophecy; "Prophecy is all around us, whatever we do -- we're the prophecy in motion" (Hopi Health Department 1984:2). Hopis still take prophecy and its communication very seriously, maybe more seriously than ever before, and Hopi prophecy is not limited to religious contexts. It is intertwined with "progressivism." It embeds political ideology, expresses cultural belief, and contextualizes social interaction. Its subject matter ranges from the religiously apocalyptic to the economic and technological. It anticipates changes and events on a global, cosmopolitan level as well as on a local, parochial level.

The actual behavioral patterns associated with "traditionalism" and "progressivism" are to be seen in the daily patterns of social and political relations and activities; the economic constraints and reactions to them; the seizing of opportunity and the coping with unpredictability that history brings; and the changing material conditions of a society engaged by the periphery of a whimsical world system.

2

An Introduction to Hopi Society and Material Conditions

Modern Hopis and Their Culture

Clustering in 13 villages and settlements around and on three steep-sided mesas and a low plateau to the south and east of Grand Canyon, Hopis number about 10,500 (Robinson 1988). They claim an aboriginal territory encompassing Tusak Choma (San Francisco Peaks); Po ta ve taka, Polungaoihoya, and Nei yavu wash (Lolomai Point and Grand Canyon); all of Black Mesa, Navajo Mountain, and Betatakin Ruin (Tokonavi and Ky westima); Nah meetoka (Lupton Canyon), and areas to the south of Interstate 40 (old Route 66) bounded by Zuni Salt Lake (Ma'k'yanne) (Ferguson and Hart 1985:50-51, 126); Tsi mun tu qui (Woodruff Butte); Yoche Ha-hao-pi (Apache Descent Trail); and Honoapa (Bear Springs) (James 1974:104; Hopi Health Department 1984:22). By 1943, administrative fiat had shrunk their land to 650,000 acres. But by 1992 Hopis had recouped an additional 900,000 acres.

Hopi daily life at the end of the Twentieth Century hardly resembled the daily routines at the end of the Nineteenth. Nonetheless, some of the social and political anchors of nineteenth-century Hopi life persist. Hopis continue to determine descent, inheritance of certain kinds of non-moveable property such as houses, and clan affiliation through the female line, that is, matrilineally. Hopis continue to accomplish religious functions as well as social ones by activating rights and obligations coordinated through the traditional social structure of clans, matrilines, sodalities, and marriage links. Symbolic rights, privileges, and duties continue to reveal a cultural hierarchy superimposed over the popular

14

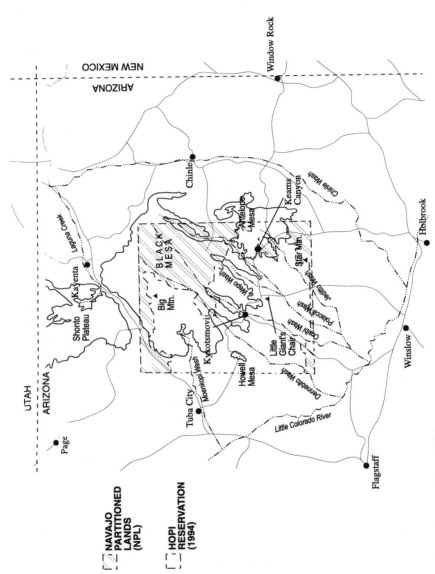

Hopi Reservation: 1994

NAVAJO
PARTITIONED
LANDS
(NPL)

HOPI
RESERVATION
(1994)

culture of a world linked by satellites, air travel, automobiles, computers, and television.

Hopis and Their Land

Much of this continuity is reinforced by Hopis' conviction that their ancestral ties to their material surroundings that stretch back in time not merely for generations, but for centuries of generations. Their material surroundings, their land and the sandstone which still furnish building materials, owes its character to the action of processes that are aquatic, meteorologic, volcanic, tectonic, biologic, and mythic. A couple of hundred million years ago, a vast inland sea began receding, leaving a soft, muddy world. Hopi myth tells of two brothers, Pukunghoya and Polongahoya, who hardened mud into the folded and faulted sedimentary sandstones, mudstones, and shales of Hopi country by spraying the mud with medicine given to them by Gogyang Wuuti, Spider Grandmother. Not far from the contemporary village of Moenkopi, dinosaurs walked through the mud before it hardened, leaving their footprints. Could their prints have been interpreted as those of giants and monsters that Hopi myth says the two brothers had to slay before humans could emerge into the world?

Later floods left marshes and lagoons farther to the north, before the entire Colorado Plateau was raised by unrelenting geologic upheaval. These wetlands were eventually compressed into the carboniferous shales and bituminous coals of the Fruitland and Wepo Formations by layer upon layer of sand and mud that became deposited on top of them and gradually compressed into sandstones and shales. These coal deposits are found throughout Hopi country:in Coal Canyon, in Keams Canyon, on Coal Mine Mesa, in the Oraibi Valley, and on Black Mesa. Hopis and their ancestors have mined some of them since the 600s. By the 1900s they would become important to three interest groups: to Hopis for economic stability; to energy companies' for strategic development plans and profit; and to Euro-Americans as one of the motors of a modern lifestyle.

It was only in late Tertiary times, 15 to 20 million years ago, that the forces of the Colorado River began attacking the hard sandstones and shales of the Colorado Plateau to form the Grand Canyon. Hopi mythology says that the brothers Pokunghoya and Polongahoya also made this and other watercourses as well as the mountains, the innumerable scattered mesas, buttes and spires, and the many canyons that cut the southern part of the Colorado Plateau. They did it by throwing lightning bolts around and piling mud up in great heaps and scored the earth as they played a game of stick ball (*nahoydadatsia*) (Courlander 1971:26).

The high volcanic mountains such as the San Francisco Peaks and Tokonavi Mountain (10,000-13,000 feet) eventually sprouted stands of spruce, fir, pine, and aspen, and became the home of the Katsinas (also spelled Katchinas, Kachinas, Katcinas and Catsinas), spirits who bring rain and come to the Hopi villages to dance. Shrines are secreted at various places on the Peaks and their slopes as well as on Tokonavi, and shrines also dot the Grand Canyon and the trail down into it. Hopis have gathered salt, a sacred as well as a secular resource, from a natural deposit in the Grand Canyon since time immemorial; legend has it that an adventurous lad once floated down the Colorado River, through the Grand Canyon on a raft. With the help of Spider Grandmother, he brought prayer offerings to the island home of Huru'ing Wuuti, shell-and-turquoise woman, where the River used to pour into the Gulf of Mexico. In return, Huru'ing Wuuti promised the Hopi a consistent supply of hard things -- shells, turquoise, coral -- for making jewelry (Courlander 1971:27).

Aside from the Grand Canyon and the San Francisco Peaks, Hopi country varies uniformly in elevation from 4,500 to 7,000 feet and can be described primarily in terms of sand and sandstone; shale and alluvium. The sand and the stone from which it weathers give the country a range of gold, bronze, and scarlet hues varying from pink through vermillion and from vanilla to sepia, owing to varying concentrations of hematite, a kind of oxidized iron (Baars 1972:25). Floods and intermittent streams and rills carry silt off the mesas, buttes, plateaus, and mountains onto the broad valleys formed by the Little Colorado River and its tributaries. Some of this silt remains on the valley floors as alluvium. This alluvium provides one of the keys to Hopi survival over the centuries: the layer of well-drained sandy soil is 20 feet thick or more in most places; is rich in organic matter; and holds important supplies of ground water that make farming viable (Hack 1942:12). Where the land has not been recently cleared or grazed, grasses and sagebrush, squawberry, greasewood and other native shrubs, in later years increasingly crowded by Eurasian tumbleweed as a result of overgrazing, hold the soil in place. Above 6,000 feet, interspersions of pinon and juniper take over from the grasses and shrubs, giving some parts of the country a forested appearance.

The Modern Seasonal Round

Hopis still consider themselves primarily agriculturalists, although close to half of all households have some livestock, for the most part cattle, and nearly all have cash income from wage labor or craft sales. Planting season arrives in April, often accompanied by a bright, glaring sun that burns but does not warm, and by fierce winds that blow sand into dunes and piles against the sides of mesas and even into the dry streambeds. Alternately, in some years, farmers must scrape away an inch or two of late snow and break a thin crust of frost with their planting sticks to drop a few kernels of seed-corn into the silty soil. Craftspersons prepare their winter's work for the dozens of arts, crafts, and jewelry wholesalers that come on buying trips nearly constantly in March, April and May or for placement in one or more of the dozen, Hopi-owned local craft shops as well as for the two big marketing events of summer: the Museum of Northern Arizona's "Hopi Show" and Santa Fe's Indian Market. The handful of well-known, full-time artists are far outnumbered by part-time craftspersons who supplement household incomes based on wage work that is sometimes intermittent or seasonal.

Just a small amount of corn is planted in April; this corn is early corn, to be harvested for *Nimankatsina*, "Katsina Home-going," a ceremony celebrated in late July. Most corn as well as beans, squash, melons and other crops are planted a month later, in mid-May. Only occasionally do gentle rains and melting snows send the right amount of moisture at planting time. Working against an average growing season of 130 frost-free days, Hopi men have attuned much of village life to marking the season with ceremonial rituals that ensure timely clearing and planting. Although women are the guardians and keepers of the seed-corn, they do not plant it; their crops are usually onions, peppers, tomatoes, cabbage, carrots, and other crops that need constant care and watering, planted near village springs and irrigated from them. Every inch of land is tenured, even if unplanted, or claimed for grazing, even if apparently untenanted.

Some of the more permanent dunes are good for planting melon vines or fruit trees (Hack 1942:12). The short, stubby varieties -- many disfigured with unpruned dead branches killed by frost or drought -- are occasionally arranged in near open rows but more often cluster anonymously in small batches. By June, their identity as apple, pear, peach or apricot is revealed in foliage, blossom, or fruit. Everything by that time is in leaf, bloom, or sprout. Tourist season also starts in June.

18

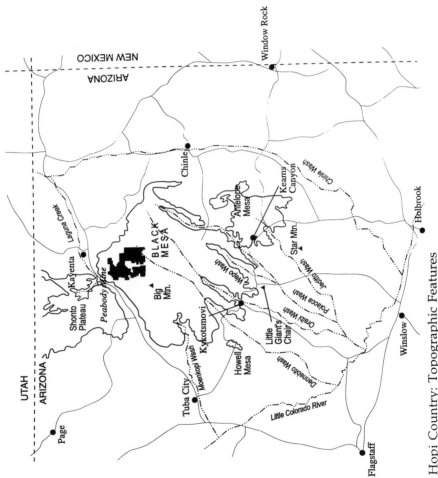

Hopi Country: Topographic Features

UTAH
ARIZONA

Page

Tuba City

Moenkopi Wash

Howell
Mesa

Dennebito Wash

Little Colorado River

Flagstaff

Winslow

Little
Giant's
Chair

Orabi Wash

Polacca Wash

Jeddito Wash

Kykotsmovi

Wepo Wash

Big
Mtn.

Shonto
Plateau

Kayenta

Laguna Creek

Peabody Mine

BLACK
MESA

Antelope
Mesa

Star Mtn.

Keams
Canyon

Chinle

Chinle Wash

Holbrook

NEW MEXICO
ARIZONA

Window Rock

The Katsinas, the human-like spirits of the dead who start coming to the Hopi villages after winter solstice to dance, return to their home in Tusak Choma and other shrines in the San Francisco Peaks in late July. By the time their return is celebrated, rains should already have started. In Hopi belief, the religious symbology expressed in ritual accomplishes the proper arrangement of energy forces for generating crops of corn, beans, melons, squash, and fruit, and for persuading the Katsinas to leave their homes to the south and travel to Hopiland as moisture-laden clouds. Cloudbursts in July often send sheets of rain every afternoon. Hopis pray for these rains to be the gentle, female kind; but more often than not, they descend in torrents, turning one or more of the six streambeds that course through the broad, steep-walled valleys separating the Hopi mesas into flood channels. An inch of rain can fall in less than an hour. These washes -- the Jeddito, Wepo, Polacca, Oraibi, Dinnebito, and Moenkopi -- are usually dry and choked with tamarisk and willow. But during summer storms, they can carry huge quantities of sand, silt, rocks, boulders, and debris, overflowing their banks in some places, gullying fields and cutting up to a foot of new channel in the streambed itself.

Gray days often pile up in August until once more, following Snake and Flute ceremonies at full moon, hard-blued days sting fingers and face with dawn cold and end with warm, yellow sunsets that make the mesas and their sandstone villages look like the fabled golden cities of Cibola. Cattle sellers prepare for the annual livestock auction and the last community-wide sets of dances are held.

These dances are "girls' choice" courtship dances and used to come in a rush in late August, featuring colorful costumes and lively steps celebrating harvest in each village. Now that a permanent, accredited high school finally (1987) has been built in the Hopi homeland, these social dances -- with butterfly, corn, and quadrille motifs -- have assumed a more leisurely scheduling, with some occurring over the labor Day holiday. By staggering the scheduling and holding some in September, villages diminish the tourist crunch.

The height of tourist season is mid-summer. Tourists have been coming to the Hopi villages regularly since the 1890s. Yet nothing in Hopiland is specially set up for tourists, despite the fact that tourism is a multi-million-dollar industry, except for a couple of very small campgrounds and a Cultural Center complex consisting of restaurant, motel, craft shops, museum, and restrooms with flush toilets and hot water. But the tourists seem to be led by an invisible pied-piper, peering earnestly at shapes and glitterings above an escarpment, wondering aloud if they are looking at a village or a merely a pile of stones, and inquiring about dances. The more sensitive visitors also know that most religious dances are off-limits, as are some entire villages, and know that cameras are to be kept locked up in cars, since photography is generally against the law in Hopiland. Partisans, individuals who feel a special affinity for the Hopi, also tend to come in summer, lately finding disappointment in being barred from experiencing Katsinas "pounding the earth with their dancing feet" and of encountering "thoughts and beliefs" that they believe to have been "everyone's only yesterday, uninterrupted from the depth of humanity's past" but are now "on deposit" solely within Hopi rituals and sacred ceremonies (Boissiere 1986:21). Partisans obey the same restrictions as tourists, but perhaps with more willingness and understanding (cf. Rivera 1990).

By October, tourists' and partisans' numbers have thinned. Women's dances are in preparation. November brings the first dustings of snow, as well as the most powerful, important, and secret religious ceremonies, and the end of the old year. The return of the sun following the solstice brings a collective relief reflected in boisterous night dances in the kivas, and in February the sprouting of beans planted in flats indoors and the cooking of bean sprout stew ushers in the climatic contractions and expansions of March. March turns summer's dust and winter's ice to puddles and mud by day and into intractable ruts by night. But within a month people will think about planting again; Katsinas will be seen dancing on weekends in the village plazas; and another seasonal round will have been completed.

Hopis' "First" Modernity:
"Progress" and Material Conditions
in the Twentieth Century

In the 1940s there was no Tribal Council; there were no mineral leases; Hopis were limited to exclusive use of 650,000 acres of land; and they still had a largely subsistence economy minimally supplemented by wage work and sale of livestock products. By 1986, Hopis had a wage-labor economy, minimally supplemented by horticulture, livestock and craft sales. The Hopi Tribal Government provided about 45% of the jobs, with 470 employees, with the Bureau of Indian Affairs and Indian Health Service providing 25% and 10% of the employment respectively (Robinson 1986). Hopis seem to have surmounted the depressing statistics of Native American ethnicity in raising their per capita incomes from $2,232 in 1986 (Robinson 1988) to $4,865 as reported by the U.S. Census Bureau in 1990. They reduced their unemployment rate from 37% in 1986 (Robinson 1988) to 28.7% in 1990 (compared to 55% for all Native Americans). Their median household income has risen from $7,470 in

1980 to $13,750 in 1990. The number of families below poverty level has been reduced from 50.5% in 1980 to 45% in 1990. And Hopis have reversed the population drain from reservations to urban areas that has placed more than 60% of Native Americans in cities. In contrast, as of 1986, close to 90% of Hopis maintained residency on the reservation (Robinson 1988). Conditions in Hopi communities were by no means depressing: More than 80% of all homeowners owned their homes outright, free of mortgage, and 90% had electrical appliances, often including television sets and VCRs, and the expansion of the Hopi land base has already been mentioned: from 650,000 acres in 1974 to more than 1.5 million acres in 1992.

These improving material conditions were not mere accidents of history or due solely to U.S. Government intervention. They resulted at least in part from the rational pursuit of goals that were carefully calculated by the Hopi Tribal Council. By the 1980s, through partial incorporation into U.S. political and administrative structures, the Hopi Tribal Government was getting about $800,000 annually in transfer payments for its citizens, based on eligibility criteria of people serviced through U.S. Government contracts and programs. Most tribes are heavily dependent on such transfer payments. But more than 60% of the Hopi Tribal Government's revenues came from private sources. Six to seven million dollars annually came into Tribal coffers from lease income from mineral development.

The Tribal Government used much of the mineral royalty income in the 1960s to pay some of the fees and expenses of drafting lawsuits, various legal actions, and pieces of legislation aimed at regaining lost land. These legal and political actions aimed not only at evicting 10,000 Navajos, but also at gaining ownership in the Anglo-American legal tradition.

Ownership in the Anglo-American legal tradition requires patents, deeds, and binding agreements. In the land tenure system evolved through two centuries of Native Americans' dealings with the Anglo-American legal tradition, collective, tribal land ownership was subsumed under what is called the "trust relationship" (Deloria and Lytle 1984:16-24; Deloria 1992:271-273). The U.S. Government legally holds all Indian-owned land "in trust" as the international, independent guardian for Tribes, which the U.S. regards as having only domestic, dependent sovereignty (Deloria 1974:113-160; Morris 1986, 1992). This unique definition of sovereignty and land ownership grants Tribes one advantage among many disadvantages: their lands cannot be taxed by any state, county, city, or other local government or mill-levy district. Among the disadvantages are the prevention of recognition in international law except as "minorities" within the U.S. nation-state (Anaya 1990) and the necessity for congressional recognition and approval of Tribal land claims and ownership rights.

The U.S. Government has confused itself and Indians alike, time and again, in trying to reconcile legal precedent favoring the Tribes with economic and political priorities favoring U.S. business, industry, and citizenry. In trying to impose Anglo-American legal principles wherever possible, it has encouraged development and maintenance of exclusive use and access as a hallmark and prerequisite of ownership. Tribes can lease portions of their land, but only with approval of the U.S. Secretary of the Interior. The Secretary of the Interior has nearly always required that a lease for any particular plot be negotiated between the respective Tribe and *one* lessee, even if the actual users are multiple in number. Leases are binding agreements. In their absence, the U.S. Government would prefer to simply ignore any problems.

The U.S. would prefer to ignore any problems stemming from claims, use, and occupancy of the same land by two or more tribes. That is exactly the situation that Hopis and Navajos found themselves in by the end of the Nineteenth Century. Throughout the Twentieth Century, Hopis found their land increasingly used and occupied by Navajos, until the U.S. Department of the Interior unilaterally restricted Hopis to using *only* the land that Navajos were *not* using and occupying. Land that is claimed to be owned by one party but is occupied and used by another quickly slips into the legal nebulas of "squatters' rights;" "adverse possession;" and "clouded title" in the Anglo-American legal tradition. This legal slippage becomes especially a problem when neither deeds, patents, leases, nor other binding agreements in the Anglo-American tradition exist. In cases of Indian lands, the problem is resolvable only by Congress. Establishment of a reservation and a Government administrative agency with jurisdiction over a particular Tribe grants a certain exclusivity with regard to indian ownership as opposed to non-Indian ownership, but even if non-Indian squatters can be tossed off a Tribal reservation, other Indians cannot. This is precisely the situation that Hopis faced for a hundred years: Navajos occupied first 10%, then 30%, then 60%, then finally 75% of the "Hopi Reservation." The prospects of reversing the situation looked very unlikely indeed.

Thus, the reversal of the situation in the last half of the Twentieth Century -- with Hopis getting congressional recognition of title to first 25%, then 63%, then 75% of the original "Hopi Reservation," is virtually unprecedented and merits attention as well as explanation.

Hopis' "Second" Modernity:
Dissent and Critique

Throughout the latter half of the Twentieth Century, at every strategic juncture of decision-making and action, counter-proposals, opposition, and dissent emanated from a group known loosely as "Traditionals" of "Traditionalists." At times, the group included a number of men and women who held key positions in the politico-religious hierarchy of various villages. But the Traditionalists' ideology more closely resembled that of a modern social movement than it did the ideology of aboriginal Hopi culture. Its proponents advocated political sovereignty long before (1949) the concept was introduced into international legal circles (1973) (cf. Ortiz 1984:29-46; 101-111). They seemed to ignore economic realities and pursue utopian principles. They invoked the symbology of Hopi myth and prophecy and placed the wisdom of the elders and "founding fathers" into service for sweeping, cosmopolitan goals formulated on a global scale. They visited European capitals and large American cities to proselytize their message, and sought alliances with social reformers and other members of other indigenous nations from the Andes to Lapland. They conducted their ideological push-pull with their Hopi adversaries on a universal scale and in an international forum.

This ideological push-pull has made the Hopi appear hopelessly factionated to the non-Hopi world and frequently consternated non-Hopi partisans. History reinforces this factionated image: at the turn of the Twentieth Century, many of the Traditionalists' fathers, mothers, aunts, uncles, grandparents, great-aunts and great-uncles had directly opposed forced schooling and other "progressivist" Government policies. They had been instrumental in the split at Oraibi in 1906. There is no doubt that the parochial, locally-anchored "Hostiles" of 1906 furnished much of the strategy and prophetic ideology for the "Traditionals" of a half-century later.

The "Traditionals" also seemed to have largely parochial concerns: they opposed the Indian Reorganization Act; called for abolition of the Tribal Council; kept anywhere between four and six villages out of the Tribal Council for 50 years; almost blocked the filing of a claim with the U.S. Indian Claims Commission; filed a lawsuit to void strip-mining contracts with Peabody Coal Company; and testified against the Navajo-Hopi Land Settlement Act of 1974. How then, did they reach across these apparently insular, domestic issues to appeal to non-Hopi interests? Part of their strategy lay in cultivating ties with Euro-American, European, and Tribal partisans among the dissenters, critics, and exceptionalists throughout the modern world: environmentalists, human rights activists, religious ecumenicalists, New Age alchemists, college professors. They involved the Congress on Racial Equality; the Native American Rights Fund; the Sierra Club; and the Indian Law Resource Center in Hopi concerns. They became regular participants in conferences of various United Nations' Non-Governmental Organizations in Geneva and especially in the Working Group on Indigenous Populations and (cf. Ortiz 1984:50-57). They inspired the Fourth Russell Tribunal on the Rights of the Indians of North and Latin America in Rotterdam in 1980 (cf. Ortiz 1984:62-63). And they provided testimony to the UN Subcommittee on the Prevention of Discrimination and Protection of Minorities in 1987 (cf. Rosen and Weissbrodt 1988). Hopi individuals' participation in these forums put them into discussions initiated by the movement for self-determination for indigenous peoples, whose leaders see their societies as "community-based, egalitarian, and close to nature, and are intent upon maintaining them that way" (Haviland 1990:449). And on December 11, 1992, Thomas Banyacya, virtually synonymous with the Traditionalist Movement in the eyes of many followers of indigenous politics, addressed the General Assembly of the United Nations in celebrating the "Year of Indigenous Peoples," as hurricane-force winds and torrential rains buffeted the building and the East and Hudson Rivers rose to flood stage and flooded the waterfront.

Thus, Hopi traditionalism is an aspect, a product, and a producer of modernization. The two modernities, "progressivism" and "traditionalism," entwine each other. Hopis have created their own versions of the "two modernities" by combining technical, secular, factual knowledge and goal-orientation with an ideology that stresses Fate, tradition, and the wise teachings of the founding ancestors and ancestresses to promote social and economic change on the one hand, and to deal with it on the other. The impetus for much of that change has come from outside Hopi life in some periods, while in others, Hopis have generated the impetus themselves. The resistance and receptiveness to changes from the outside, as well as the initiation of change from the inside against resistance from the outside, have been strongly conditioned by three sets of constraints and pressures: (1) those generated by Hopis themselves; (2) those generated by Navajos; and (3) those generated by Euro-Americans. Euro-Americans have garnered the distinct advantage in many of these situations. Their economic, territorial, and nationalist ascendancy has been supported by a powerful government with an armed force and an administrative bureaucracy that has always been able to pursue its policies with utmost rational efficiency, no matter whether those policies were woefully inappropriate and fraught with hopeless confusion, or inspired by accurate insights and pristine clarity of purpose.

Hopi Culture and History in the Twentieth Century

The following discussion aims for an analysis of modernization through an examination of the six discrete topics mentioned earlier. I do not propose a complete explanation of either modernization as a phenomenon; or of Hopi culture; or of Hopi history. Modernization and modernity have been dealt with exhaustively in general by a myriad of scholars. Analyses of Hopi culture abound (cf. Laird 1977), as do good introductions to Hopi history (i.e., Dockstader 1979, 1985; Spicer 1962; James 1974; Rushforth and Upham 1992). Only five writers (Yamada 1957; Nagata 1968, 1978, 1979; Cox 1970; Buschenreiter 1983; Kaiser 1989, 1990; Kaiser and Clemmer 1989) give anything but scant attention to why, or how, Hopi traditionalism has played a role in modernization, and there is also scant attention in any of the scholarly literature to law and politics in the Hopi world. Nagata (1970, 1978, 1979); Sekaquaptewa (1972); Whiteley (1987); and myself stand almost alone in our interests in that direction. Nagata (1970) is virtually the only scholar to initiate a study of the economic and political context of Hopi culture change, and Nagata completed his analysis long before any possible resolution of the Hopi-Navajo land dispute was in sight and before the full political and economic impact of mineral leasing had been felt.

Therefore, this study is an update. But it also establishes a context for discussing the above issues in terms of world systems theory and in terms of the interplay of culture, history, economics, and politics. This is why I want to reel in several other topics that previously have been handled in very restricted and isolated contexts: the cloning of five new villages from other mother village of Oraibi; the adoption of the Indian Reorganization Act (IRA) and formation of the Hopi Tribal Council; and the rise of the "Traditionalists." These issues appear on the surface to have very parochial, localized significance. They appear to have little to do with a worldwide system of politics and economics. But they do. While Peter Whiteley (1988a, 1988b) has dealt most recently and most thoroughly with the Oraibi split, his analysis amounts to a revisionist historical reconstruction. While my pervious discussions of the IRA, the Tribal Council, the Traditionalists, and mineral leasing constitute the only systematic discussion of these issues to date (Clemmer 1969, 1978a, 1978b, 1986, 1988, 1989) they focus much too narrowly on participatory democracy and decision-making, as do others (i.e., Washburn 1979, 1984, 1985) thus skirting the larger scope of modernization and the world system which provided the economic and political context for such issues. By discussing mineral leasing, return of sacred objects, the land dispute, traditionalists and traditionalism, the IRA, the Oraibi split, and the "two modernities" together, I hope not only to show the historical connections among these issues and events, but also to show the points in history where culture, ideology, politics, society, economics, nationalist interests and land-based resources intersect, and why they intersect.

Prelude: Hopis, Spaniards, Mexicans, Navajos, and Mormons. Nearly 300 years of interactions among Hopis, Spaniards, Mexicans, Mormons, and Navajos set the stage for the Twentieth Century. Thus the following chapter briefly summarizes the period between 1540 and 1880. These interactions are a prelude for what was to come later. While Mormons and Navajos continued to be important ethnic groups in the Hopi world after 1880, their positions and roles change radically with concerted efforts by the U.S. Government to intervene in Hopi life. Although Hopi history does not begin with the Spaniards' intrusion, their involvement with the Euro-centered arm of the world system did.

3

Spaniards, Navajos, Mormons: 1540-1875

> When the Spaniards came, the Hopi thought that they were the ones they were looking for -- their white brother, the Pahaana, their savior.
> ---Sun's Forehead Clan man, 55, Shungopavi (Nequatewa 1936:42)

Even though Americans and American culture have framed Hopis' contacts with non-Indians in the Twentieth Century, Americans and their culture did not intrude upon a "pristine" cultural-historical situation by any means. Americans constituted the fourth major political, economic, and cultural force that had entered the Hopi realms in recent historical times. The Spaniards were the first; Navajos the second and Mormons the third. While it could be argued that Mormons are merely a variety of Americans, in fact, the Mormons saw themselves as armed with a distinctly different set of values, attitudes, and mores from those of the Americans, and they deliberately set out to establish a political and economic utopia that would be separate from the United States. Much of the early contact between Americans and Hopis was conditioned by Hopis' earlier experiences with Mormons and with a long history -- nearly two centuries -- of contact with Navajos. Because Spaniards were the first to bring the Euro-centered arm of the world system into Hopi country, it is worthwhile to consider some of the impacts of Hopis' experience with the Spaniards, especially since the Hopi are one of the few groups to have endured prolonged domination by the Spaniards -- more than 50 years -- without being influenced even a little bit by Spanish culture, unlike their Puebloan cohorts to the east, who were influenced to some degree.

1540: Hopis Encounter Spaniards

When General Francisco Vazquez de Coronado, at his camp in the half-ruined and abandoned Zuni village of Hawikuh more than 100 miles southwest of the Hopi villages instructed that the Spaniards' presence be announced to all nearby realms, "the natives (Zunis) immediately carried this message to those localities that had communication and commerce with them" (Castaneda 1940:213). Coronado's presence hardly needed to be announced. Hopis had undoubtedly heard about the wide swath the Spaniards had cut in their journey northward since trade and cultural exchanges between Hopis and Zunis were a regular part of Hopi life. Zunis had provided the first military resistance to the Spaniards. Warriors from Hawikuh, one of the six (or possibly seven) (Ferguson and Hart 1985:29) Zuni Pueblos, attacked Coronado and his men as they made their way northward, probably near the confluence of Concha Creek and Zuni River, on July 6, 1540. Coronado's men rallied, overcoming the ambush, and invaded Hawikuh, killing and scattering its inhabitants and confiscating the meager supplies of food saved from the previous harvest.

Thus the appearance of Coronado's lieutenant, Pedro de Tovar, with seventeen cavalry, a priest, and three or four foot soldiers could hardly have been a big surprise to Hopi residents of a town that went unnamed, but which was probably near Awat'ovi.[3] Hopis may have harbored an ambivalent curiosity about the Spaniards and the meaning of their intrusion, but they probably anticipated them as much as traders as they feared them as raiders and destroyers. Hopi warriors appeared. They impressed upon them the necessity of behaving like guests by drawing lines in the earth to separate their lives from those of the Spaniards. Centuries later, "drawing the line" would once again become an important symbolic act, in the context of Twentieth Century factionalism.[4]

The details are unknown, but within that boundary, the Spaniards started some sort of negotiations. At some point the Spaniards transgressed the line and the troops attacked. Immediately the Hopi warriors scattered. According to the Spaniards' official scribe the Hopis thereafter "offered their towns openly, permitting the soldiers to go there in order to buy, sell, trade" (Castaneda 1940:214-215).

Because Hopi country -- which the Spaniards called "Tusayan" -- had no permanent streams, Spanish settlers confined their colonizing to the Rio Grande Valley, establishing Santa Fe as their colonial capital 300 miles to the east in 1610. The Spanish never garrisoned any troops anywhere near Hopi Country. But between 1628 and 1633, Franciscan missionaries persuaded Hopis to build three large stone churches at

Awat'ovi, Shungopovi, and Oraibi. Hopis furnished all building materials and labor, hauling huge trees from Tokonavi and the San Francisco Peaks for beams. These three mission villages also probably had schools and village functionaries on the Spanish model: sheriffs, governors, sacristans, catechists, church wardens. The priests also probably tried to make the missions into production centers by introducing cattle, sheep, goats, donkeys, and fruit trees.

Ramon Gutierrez (1991:63) speculates that, in apparently conjuring rain; claiming to cure the sick and to wield enormous spiritual power; bringing sources of meat, such as domestic sheep, goats, and cattle right into the villages; and claiming vows of chastity, the priests had initially successfully placed themselves above chiefs, spiritual leaders, shamans, and even witches.[5] But in 1655, one of these missionaries, cast out to the fringes of the Spanish colonial frontier, vented his rage and frustration on sought-after converts. Other abuses followed (Spicer 1962:191). By 1659 a severe famine gripped the entire province of New Mexico. Things improved the following year, but by the mid-1660s, Hopis were feeling the effects of a prolonged drought. In 1621 Hopis had been exempt from tribute (Spicer 1962:190) but by 1662, Spanish provincial rulers in Santa Fe were extracting woven cloth and buckskins (Kessell 1979:186-188; Montgomery 1949:217-219). In 1670, famine again swept the land. Persecuted for maintaining their religion, exploited for their labor and products, and living under increasingly adverse material conditions, Hopis became less and less tolerant of the demanding Spaniards.

The Pueblo Revolt, 1680, and the Destruction of Awat'ovi, 1700

Thus when Rio Grande Puebloans proposed a rebellion in 1680, Hopis wholeheartedly participated. They summarily killed the four missionaries. The rebellion was successful and kept the Spaniards out of the region for 12 years, until 1692, and out of Hopi country until 1700.

Hopis destroy Awat'ovi. When Hopis killed the missionary priest at San Bernardo de Aguatubi (Aguatubi or Awat'ovi, meaning "place of the bow," is also written Ahua-tuyba; Aguato; Awatobi; Acuatubi; and in Navajo, Tallahogan) in 1680, they pulled out the huge, long beams of Douglas Fir supporting the church's roof, thereby collapsing it. They remodeled the convent-school and friar's quarters, subdividing them into small residence and storage rooms, and sheep pens. When they heard that a Franciscan missionary had reopened the mission at the Zuni village of Halona in 1699, however, Awat'ovi's residents sympathetic to Christianity or to the Spanish or both again remodeled the quarters, taking out the interior walls and remodeling it back into a make-shift church. Two Franciscan missionary priests visited Awat'ovi in October or November, 1700, baptized a lot of people, said a mass, and preached.

But leaders of other Hopi villages asserted a position at odds with that of Awat'ovi's Christians. In the last days of 1700 or the beginning of 1701, Hopis from all the other villages attacked Awat'ovi, burned it, killed nearly all the men, and distributed some of the surviving women and children among the other Hopi villages. Espeleta of Oraibi probably led the attack (Brew 1949:22). Common consensus among Hopis and non-Hopi scholars alike, is that "Awat'ovi was destroyed because its citizens perpetrated a defilement of traditional Hopi principles and ethical standards" (Rushforth and Upham 1992:104). This defilement included the young taunting elders, old men pursuing young women, and mature women pursuing boys, the desecration of shrines, and general public violence. The Catholic priests were held responsible for inspiring these lawless violations of cultural norms (Courlander 1971:177-178). Hopis told U.S. Army captain John H. Bourke (1884:900) in 1881 that Awat'ovi "was full of 'singing men,' whom the Moquis (Hopis) did not like."

Archaeological investigations confirm the Hopi version of events (Brew 1949). The people and village as well as church and mission seem to have been quite brutally destroyed. Hopis told anthropologist J.W. Fewkes (1895a) that captives were taken from Awat'ovi and later killed and their heads cut off. In 1964, archaeologist Al Olsen dug up the burials and trundled them off to the Museum of Northern Arizona. One of them yielded the "crudely dismembered, violently mutilated..." remains of 30 individuals, including eight children. In 1968, anthropologists Christy Turner and Nancy Morris examined the burials. Hopis told them about several mounds some distance from Awat'ovi that they said contained yet more burials of these dismembered captives (Turner and Morris 1970).

Hano-Tewa

Tewas, also called the Tanos or sometimes the Thanos and Tiguas or Thanos and Teguas in Spanish documents, are non-Hopi-speaking Puebloans from the Rio Grande area, 350 miles to the east and were only one of the groups that sought refuge from the Spaniards following their reconquest of the Rio Grande in 1692. Tewas participated in the successful destruction of Awat'ovi and may have even instigated it. Thus they were able to establish a permanent and important position in Hopi life. It is said that Hano-Tewas were among the most incensed when Awat'ovi accepted Spanish missionaries again in 1700, and they certainly contributed warriors who were among those that fell upon Awat'ovi and destroyed it. Although they would later prove important in repelling Ute, Comanche, Apache, and Navajo raids (Dozier 1966:13-14, 17-18), they were initially important in discouraging the Spanish in 1701 and again in 1716 (Twitchell and Bloom 1931).

The Spanish Era Concludes with Many Changes But Few Impacts on Hopi Culture

Spain's presence had impacts in three areas of Hopi life: cultural ideology; the regional balance of political power; and material conditions. Hopis from Shungopavi established Shipaulovi as an "innocent town," that would be spared by the Spaniards when they returned to find the "guilty" parties who had killed the priests (Nequatewa 1936:46). But the new village of Shipaulovi was also "to be a place for ceremonial paraphernalia where it could be most securely kept from falling into Spanish hands" (Spicer 1962:192). Walpi was moved from the foot of the mesa to the top, as were Shungopavi and Mishongnovi. When Escalante visited in 1776, he found Hopis constructing a village on First Mesa, a few hundred yards from Walpi, next to Hano-Tewa; the women were just putting the finishing touches on the outside mud plaster. This village was Sichomovi. Thus, although Awat'ovi had been destroyed, the number of distinct socio-political units -- the villages -- had increased from five to seven.

Material Conditions

Spanish colonists unleashed material forces whose long-term consequences they could not have predicted. Horses provided nomads from the north -- Athapaskan-speaking Navajos and Apaches; Shoshonean-speaking Comanches; and Numic-speaking Utes -- with mobility and consequent raiding ability and potential for migration. Cattle, sheep, and goats provided something to raid and also replaced native ungulates such as deer and antelope (Adams 1989:85) as a steady supply of meat that reproduced itself and had a potential for migration equal to that of their human owners. But their foraging also changed the desert ecology. By 1700 Hopis were already corralling sheep in pens close to their homes (Brew 1949:54), herding them to grazing areas during the day and bringing them back to the corrals at night. By the mid-1700s some Hopis had combined cattle herding and farming with seasonal transhumance; residents of a summer farming settlement near the present-day Moenkopi kept herds of cattle nearby (Nagata 1970:31). In the area of architecture and food-processing the Spaniards contributed the concept of the chimney; Hopis capped them with upside-down pots with the bottoms punched out.

In contrast, Navajos used their animals' migratory tendencies to explore and expand into new territory. Keeping and breeding horses, Navajos combined herding with trading and hunting and later with temporary summer residence in one location where they farmed and pastured their stock for a season or two. Navajos were soon combining a cycle of migration, settlement, splitting of households and herds, subsequent migration, and settlement, thereby creating a cycle of increasing demographic and territorial expansion with increasing sophistication in farming, animal husbandry, and horse-keeping. These patterns would grant Navajos a sociopolitical and geographical flexibility that would eventually bring a downturn in Hopis' circumstances that would endure for nearly a century and a half and completely overturn the regional balance of power.

Hopis and the Balance of Political Power, 1680-1820

The boundaries of the Hopi *techqua* -- their aboriginal lands -- are more than just the outline of wistful nostalgia marked by mythically-sanctioned religious shrines. They actually designate real political boundaries, an area within which Hopis maintained considerable success in pursuing their own distinct cultural ideology and within which Hopi political and economic priorities were salient, if not dominant. Hopis maintained their independence during the post-Spanish reconquest era not by remaining isolated from political events, but rather by getting involved in them. Throughout the 1700s Hopis seem to have acted with impunity against developments that were not in their self-interest. They set upon a band of Havasupais in 1754 and had no trouble moving en masse to Zuni country after a drought between 1777 and 1780, despite the hostilities of three generations earlier. During the 1700s and even before the Pueblo Revolt in the mid-1600s, Hopis made and broke commitments and alliances with Navajos, Utes, Havasupais, Zunis, Tewas, Tiwas, and Spaniards. While Hopis at Walpi resisted the Spanish in 1716, Hopis at Shungopavi and Oraibi complied with Spanish requests and allowed a few priests to escort several hundred Rio Grande Puebloans from Payupki, Tikovi, and Hukovi between 1742 and 1747. In 1745 at least one Hopi village maintained such close alliances with Navajos that a Spanish missionary actually thought he was preaching to Hopis, when it actually turned out that he had baptized Navajos -- he claimed, 5,000 of them! (Spicer 1962:194). Yet in 1661 Hopis at Walpi had turned over nine

"Apache Navajos" to the Spaniards for enslavement (Correll 1979 I:35) and by 1754 Hopis were actually requesting Spanish intervention against the Navajos.

Hopi-Navajo Relations
in the Mexican Era, 1823-1848

In the 1700s, Navajos were just one of many small indigenous groups on the fringes of the Spanish colonial empire. Their proper name -- the name they use for themselves -- is Dine', but because they are known in the anthropological literature equally well as "Navajos" because that is what Hopis call them, I will continue to refer to them as "Navajos." The story of their success is a story of horses, sheep, cattle, desert, and global trade. Since the earliest Athapaskan archaeological sites date from 1525, it is reasonable to assume that Athapaskan-speaking Navajos and Apaches entered the upper Rio Grande and Cimarron River drainages no earlier than 1525 (Gunnerson 1979:163) but no later than 1590 (Bailey and Bailey 1986:11-12). Navajos and Apaches obtained horses in the Revolt of 1680. By 1691 the first Navajos had settled on the Kaibito Plateau, about 75 miles northwest of Oraibi (Adams 1963:37-38; Aberle 1974:326-327), but they were probably in the vicinity as early as 1686 (Bandelier 1892:383; cf. Brugge 1983) and were certainly visiting the Hopi villages as early as the 1660s (Correll 1979 I:35). Spanish documents from 1706, 1775, 1776, and 1781 clearly indicate Navajos living on the Kaibito Plateau (Adams 1963:37-38) but there are neither Spanish documents nor archaeological evidence indicating any Navajos or Apaches anywhere near Hopi territory before the 1680 Revolt.

The first record of Navajo-Hopi conflict is 1754 (Twitchell and Bloom 1931) when Hopis actually appealed to the Spanish for military assistance against the Navajos. But most of the time, it seems that Hopis did little to prevent Navajos from using Hopi country as a safe haven following Navajos' raiding of Spanish settlements. Trading, visiting, and intermarriage probably characterized Hopi-Navajo relations more than raiding or armed conflicts.

But the situation changed when Spanish power began to weaken (Bartlett 1936). By 1812 Navajo harassment was a standing problem for Hopis, Zunis, Rio Grande Puebloans, and Spaniards alike. By 1818 Hopis and Zunis asked for Spanish military help against Navajos. Severe drought beginning in 1818 and not ending until 1825 exacerbated the competition for territory and resources. A letter between Mexican officials in 1819, accompanying a treaty of peace between Navajos and Mexicans, mentioned the Hopis as a protectorate people whose property the Navajo were enjoined to respect as a term of the treaty. The treaty was short-lived. Hopis asked for Spanish intervention against Navajos again and in 1820 newly-appointed Governor Facondo Melgares responded by marching against Navajos with 200 soldiers. Hopis and Hano-Tewas managed to detain some Navajos in Walpi and sent word to Melgares. Camped nearby, Melgares sent a detachment that attacked the Navajos, killing some and driving off the rest.

Mexico officially brought the Spanish era to an end in 1824 when Spain recognized Mexico's independence. Hopis nominally became part of the Mexican Republic. But the colonial government in Santa Fe had really come under the direct control of Mexican officials by 1820. Nonetheless, Hopi and Navajo oral traditions reflect ambivalent and fluctuating relationships between Hopis and Navajos (Stephen 1936:1016). Relationships were apparently cordial or even friendly, but could turn hostile at any time. Oral histories recount at least one pitched battle at Oraibi that ended disastrously for Hopis (Voth 1905a:258-266; Nequatewa 1936:52-59; Hill 1936:3-6). The year is uncertain: 1832 (Young and Morgan 1954); 1837 (Spicer 1962:213) or 1840 (Stephen 1936:1002).

Navajos' coupling of nomadism with herding developed in response to Spanish political policies and Ute raiding. Navajo raiding and slave-trading developed within a few short years, probably between 1800 and 1830, as a result of far-flung political and economic developments bringing wealth stratification to the Navajo polity. In Hopi country and in much of Navajo country as well, matters were not helped by a drought between 1818 and 1825. Hopis' loss of political power happened quickly and steadily, but was neither complete nor irrevocable. Hopis would occasionally garner the advantage and hold it for a time. A Navajo oral history probably captures the real situation quite well:

> When the Navaho were hungry they went to the Hopi country. The Hopi would treat them well ... When the Navajo had been fed the Hopi would throw them off the mesa. In revenge the Navajo would organize a war party. After the attack ..., the Hopi would prepare a return attack in the Navaho country. Then ... a treaty would be made which would last until some one was thrown over the mesa, or until a Navaho killed a Hopi in the cornfields. The Navajos were usually the ones who broke the treaties (Hill 1936:3).

This Gilbert-and-Sullivan-type see-saw of contretemps and avenge-harrying fits a pattern of blood-feuding and revenge warfare that is well known and documented throughout the world (Rosman and Rubel 1971; Carrington 1971:73-98; Vayda 1974; Wilson 1988; Kuschel 1988). But like the "potato wars" of the Haida, Tlingit, and trading post operators on the

Northwest Coast at about the same time period (Grumet 1975:308-309), Hopi-Navajo skirmishes of the 19th century were part of a regional context of economic and political competition. As political and economic stratification intensified among the Navajo, the less affluent among them were pushed further to the margins of the "Navajo province" and into Hopi territory. Attacks became more brutal and daring as competition among Navajos for economic advantage and political prestige became more heated and pressures for sharing wealth among kin mounted.

It was in this free-for-all, laissez-faire economic context that clever individuals, whether Indian or non-Indian, amassed wealth on Mexico's northern frontier (Quintana 1991:61). Wealth was amassed not only by trading and cheating, but also by raiding. The raiding was not done just by Indians, but raiding did offer horse-mounted Indians opportunities for amassing wealth that they had not had before. Cattle and sheep became wealth on the hoof. The growth of large herds invited more raiding and rustling.

Hopis, along with most of the Rio Grande Puebloans, seem to have been disadvantaged in this new economy on two counts: not only were they the victims of raids, but also they were not in the raiding-rustling-selling-trading loop that linked Utes, Comanches, Navajos, Mexicans, Yankees, and perhaps some Puebloans.[6]

In contrast, Navajo herds swelled during this period.[7] Much of the increase was at the expense of others. Even after Americans had established a military presence, following the surrender of Mexican troops in Santa Fe during the Mexican-American War. Navajos continued to raid, taking an estimated 400,000 - 500,000 sheep from Spanish-Americans between 1847 and 1851 (Bailey and Bailey 1986:18).[8] Yet raiding possibilities cut both ways for virtually every community in the region. In 1853 explorer A.W. Whipple's guide told him about some years earlier, perhaps in the 1830s, joining a party of Mexicans and Hopis bent on slave-raiding that were turned back by "Yampais," probably Utes (Whipple 1941:158).

The American Era

In 1846 Acting Governor Bent documented a far more unremitting situation for the Hopi to his commanding officer. The Hopis, he wrote, had formerly been "a numerous tribe in the possession of large stocks and herds but have been reduced in numbers and possessions by their more warlike neighbors and enemies the Navajoes....They number about 350 families or about 2,450 souls" (Abel 1915:7). He undoubtedly underestimated, but by 1853, the estimate might well have been accurate:

by then a smallpox epidemic had hit the Hopi villages. While the explorer Antoine Leroux had given A. L. Whipple a figure of 6,720 for the year 1851, in 1853, Whipple, surveying a possible railroad route to the Pacific, gave the Hopi villages a wide berth because three Zunis he chanced to meet told him the Hopis were dying "by the fifties per day" from the epidemic (Whipple 1941:157). All figures between 1861 and 1882, even if they are underestimates by 50%, indicate that Hopi population *dropped* by more than 30% from 1775 (Donaldson 1893:28). In contrast, Navajo population soared during the same period, from 4,000 to 11,000 (Bailey and Bailey 1986:19-20), an *increase* of 175%.

On October 6, 1850, Indian agent James S. Calhoun received a "deputation" of four Hopis in his office in the Governor's palace at Santa Fe. "They complained bitterly," wrote Calhoun to his superior in Washington, "of the depredations of the Navajos." The deputation included the "chief" of Oraibi and "the Cacique of *all* the (Hopi) Pueblos" from "Tanoquevi," that is, from Hano-Tewa. Calhoun characterized each of the seven village as "an independent Republic, having confederated for mutual protection" (sic) (Abel 1915:262-265). While the confederation may have been short-lived and very loose, its apparent leadership under a Hopi-Tewa from "Tanoquevi" highlights the persistence of Hopi-Tewas' military importance from Spanish times.

On August 28, 1851, thirteen Hopi men visited Calhoun to "ascertain whether their Great Father" would do anything for them, again complaining that "the Navajos had continued to rob them, until they had left them exceedingly poor, and wretched" (Abel 1915:415). Thus by 1852 not only did officials of the United States Government know about Hopis' problem with Navajos and have reliable information about it, but also, they had in hand a formal request for action from Hopi leaders. This point is an important detail for considering the Government's efforts, and non-efforts, at resolving the Hopi-Navajo land dispute, in Chapter Ten.

The United States built Fort Defiance and garrisoned troops there specifically to deal with the Navajo threat. Sometime between 1853 and 1856 (Eggan 1967:35-40) a group of Hopis from Walpi and Hano-Tewa went to Fort Defiance. The soldiers gave them knives and some clothing for a visit and on their return journey, Navajos killed four of the Hopis and took their burros and the soldiers' gifts. In retaliation, Hopis mounted an expedition "to the north," where they killed "many Navajo" and drove home many sheep. Old Djasjini, recounting the incident in 1892, was part of this expedition. "We helped the American soldiers" after that, he said; "We waylaid the Navajo wherever we found them, and we killed many of them" (Stephen 1936:1018-1019).

But the alliance between Hopis and U.S. troops did not deter all the Navajos. In 1860 Navajos attacked Fort Defiance, and when Brigadier

General Carleton suggested rounding up Navajos along with Apaches and placing them on a reservation at Fort Sumner, New Mexico, higher authorities sanctioned the plan. General Carleton authorized a bounty for captured livestock, and a "scorched earth policy" in which "troops destroyed cornfields, peach trees, hogans, water holes, animals, and people" (Roessel 1983:511). Nearly 8,000 Navajos went to Fort Sumner with no resistance.

Kit Carson took charge of ferreting out Navajos west and north of Fort Defiance, including Canyon de Chelly and Shonto. He went to all the Hopi villages and wrote to Carleton on Dec. 6, 1863, that he had succeeded "in obtaining representatives from all the villages -- Oribi excepted -- to accompany me on the war path....They were of some service, and manifested a great desire to aid us in every respect." The Hopis were supplied with powerful rifles and used them effectively (Nibley 1944:300). Hopis also lured 35 Navajos into Walpi on the pretext of serving them a meal. While they were eating, Hopi women armed with large corn grinding stones took their places behind each eating Navajo and at a given signal, the women clouted them on the head. The Navajos were then finished off and their bodies dumped over the cliff. Hopis showed Mormon missionary Jacob Hamblin and geologist-explorer J. W. Powell their bodies in 1870 (Nibley 1944:300). But in 1936 Hopis expressed regret at their treachery (Bartlett 1936:35).

Carson was given to understand that Oraibi had an alliance with nearby Navajos and apparently to ward off any joint attack by Navajos and Hopis from Oraibi, he took the Oraibi "governor" and another of their "principal men" prisoner, keeping them on the march for several days before releasing them (Kelly 1970:75-77). More than a hundred years later, in the heat of the Hopi-Navajo land dispute, elderly Hopis from Oraibi as well as Navajos at Big Mountain would speak of a "treaty" between Oraibi and nearby Navajos giving them permission to live on Hopi land in return for the Navajos' agreement to abide by certain conditions. Did this "treaty" date from Carson's visit? or from just prior to it? It is impossible to say. But Carson's experience at Oraibi emphasizes the ambivalent and variable nature of relations between different groups of different Navajos and different Hopis.

By March, 1865, more than 9,000 Navajos occupied the Bosque Redondo Reservation at Fort Sumner (Roessel 1983:515). But several thousand more had escaped Carleton and Carson by retreating into the Kaibito Plateau; Black Mesa; Navajo Mountain; Grand Canyon; Monument Valley; and the Henry Mountains. Estimates range from 1,000 to 5,000 (Aberle 1966; 15; cf. Roessel 1983:514).

Upon release in 1868, Navajos were given seeds, farming implements, 15,000 sheep, approximately two for every adult, and annuity goods not to exceed $5.00 per person per year for a period of ten years. In 1872, the annuities were delivered in the form of 10,000 more sheep (Aberle 1966:30; Bailey and Bailey 1986:27). Their headmen signed a treaty agreeing to be peaceable and to stay within the boundaries of a 3,414,528 acre reservation. The reservation was located far to the west of Dinetah, the Navajos' southwestern homeland near the headwaters of the Rio Grande, and included less than 10% of the land they had formerly owned and used (Roessel 1983:520). Nearly 50% of it was land claimed by Hopis.

The signing of the 1868 treaty turned Navajo-U.S. relations inside out. U.S. politicians had been justifiably horrified at the treatment meted out to the Navajos at Bosque Redondo and Navajos rightly garnered a great deal of public sympathy. Pressured by white settlers in the San Juan Valley and Spanish-American settlers to the south and east, Navajos moved increasingly westward and northward (Bailey and Bailey 1986:74). For the following 60 years U.S. policy would favor Navajos with restoration of nearly 3 million acres of their old lands east of the 1868 reservation and north of Hopi territory, and would add another 9 million acres, mostly carved out of lands claimed by Hopis, Zunis, Paiutes, and Utes. Navajos' way of life developed in a distinctive direction. Raiding became negligible, then ceased altogether.

These differences reflect not only the different directions that Hopis' and Navajos' economies were taking, but also the fact that Navajos had greatly increased their land area at the expense of Hopis, and were also using the land much more intensively. The situation was exacerbated by drought and famine so severe in 1865 that "people in great numbers left from all the Hopi villages and went to the villages on the Rio Grande and to the Mexican villages ... to find food" (Stephen 1936:1022). Sichomovi was nearly deserted; the drought hit the entire west and did not break until 1869. Following their return from Ft. Sumner in 1868, Navajos went on an orgy of raiding Utes, Jicarillas, Mescaleros, Hopis, Puebloans, Spanish-Americans, and Mormons (Bailey and Bailey 1986:38-39); in so doing, they were able to increase their herds from several thousands to several hundreds of thousands in less than a dozen years. Between 1868 and 1933, the year that the U.S. Government began mandatory livestock reduction, Navajos' sheep had increased by nearly 2850% and Navajo people by 285%; in contrast, Hopi livestock had increased by only 285% and Hopi people by barely 25%.[9]

Mormons

Although nominally Americans, Mormons -- adherents to the Church of Latter Day Saints -- deliberately sought religious, political, and economic independence from the United States and from American society (Leone 1979:4,18; Hansen 1981:127-128). Therefore, early Mormon dealings with Hopis and their impact on them must be considered in an historical context separate from that of the American era. When Mormons entered the Hopi scene, they came hard on the heals of the disastrous Mexican era and constituted a political-economic force that juxtaposed itself to Navajos as well as to Americans. In fact, American intentions were probably as opaque to Hopis in 1857 as were Mormon goals (cf. Abel 1915:262-265). It is therefore not surprising that Hopis were friendly toward Mormons. They may have seen them initially as a wedge that could be driven between them and their persistent Navajo neighbors.

Mormon religious ideology dovetailed with Mormon geopolitical goals. Published in 1830, the Book of Mormon claimed to tell the story of the New World from its first settlement by people who had crossed the sea from Palestine sometime before 400 B.C. The story picks up where the Bible leaves off concerning the escape of ten Tribes of Israel from Jerusalem in advance of the invading Babylonians. These people were led by the Hebrew prophet Lehi. Lehi had two sons: Nephi and Laman, who marry and produce descendants - Nephites and Lamanites. The story ends with the last of the Nephites writing their story on metal plates which he then buries near Palmyra, New York, fearing death at the hands of the Lamanites. The religion's Prophet, Joseph Smith, claimed to have been guided to the tablets by the angel Moroni, but after he read them and translated them into the Book of Mormon, the tablets disappeared (Leone 1979:12).

Common interpretations of the times supplied the link between the "Lamanites" and the Indians of North America. The idea of the American Indians being the ten lost Tribes of Israel was widespread in the 1820s (Hansen 1981:11). The idea neatly solved an existential and theological dilemma: How could the American Indians truly be human if God had revealed nothing about the existence of them or their continents in either the Old or New Testaments? And how could the Bible, as the Word of God, truly be taken as a source of all relevant knowledge and a guide to practical living if it entirely omitted an entire branch of the human race? The dilemma was solved by the interpretation of American Indians as the descendants of the Ten Lost Tribes of Israel. The Bible, then, was not flawed after all; it merely needed updating. And the Indians just needed re-incorporation into the Christian fold.

Mormonism formed part of a larger 19th century American search for primitive Christianity, a quest for simple origins and shelter from the Industrial Revolution that was beginning to clutter the landscape of America's yeoman agricultural ideals. Between 1847 and 1890, Mormonism offered an alternative, a place where traditional society was restored and where "the economy was regulated in behalf of the larger interests of the group even if this entailed individual sacrifice (Hansen 1981:126). Mormonism above all sought order, logic, and rational decision-making by a divinely-inspired patriarchal elite. Anthropologist Mark Leone (1979:168-169) summarizes the relationship of Mormon ideology to practical life as "handling the material world with an immediateness, skill, and effectiveness that are crucial to the success its people enjoy. There is a dynamic relationship between a concept and a given situation. They form each other. Neither concept nor life is allowed to develop any hint of inappropriateness in the face of the other." In other words, Mormon doctrine abides no contradictions, even if they exist.

Mormons founded Deseret, a "full-blown religious state" in what is now Utah in 1847. There they established "an entire social environment, complete with schools, courts, irrigation systems, exchange networks, price controls, systems of weights and measures, a monetary system including specie, a network of roads, maps, an exploration plan, land, timber and water rights management, printing facilities," and an administrative structure with all roles filled by churchmen. Headed by a male religious hierarchy with Brigham Young, the eldest male and Joseph Smith's son-in-law, filling the role of Patriarch, even after American "conquest," this religious empire continued to be "more independent from the United States than the South was before and during the Civil War" until Congress declared Utah a state in 1890 (Leone 1979:18).

Believing Indians to be the descendants of the Lamanites, and perhaps in some fashion, the heirs to the formerly great Nephite civilization, Mormons not only tried to convert them to Mormonism, but also pressed the tribes of Utah into economic and political alliances. Revelations inspired Mormons' belief that their continual contact with the fallen Lamanites would eventually turn them back into the "white and delightsome" people they had once been. Shortly after Deseret came into armed conflict with the United States in the "Mormon Wars" of the mid-1850s, a diaspora of Mormons set out from Salt Lake City to Arizona, Sonora, and southeastern California. Accompanying this diaspora was an effort to seek possible allies among the indigenous nations to the south.

1858: Hopis Encounter Mormons

In 1858, Brigham Young "called"[10] Jacob Hamblin to found a new colony in southern Utah, Santa Clara, and to go to the Hopi villages and to look for good places to settle in the vicinity. Young urged Hamblin and the Latter Day Saints to extend "every help possible" to Indians that were willing to accommodate the "Saints" (Leone 1979:22). He counseled

Hamblin "not to infringe upon their rights in any particular, thus cultivating honor and good principles in their midst by example as well as precept." He predicted that "the hour of their redemption draws nigh, and the time is not far distant when they will...begin to rise and increase in the land" (Nibley 1944:308). In 1858, an exchange of products, ideas, and even people began between the Mormon settlements of southern Utah, which was Hamblin's home, and Hopis. In the fall of 1858 Hamblin and ten others set forth. The emissaries were totally unfamiliar with the territory and its landscape, and thus were fully dependent upon their Paiute guide. Not until they were nearly at the foot of Third Mesa did they realize how close they were to Oraibi. Their guide identified an unfamiliar series of sounds as the song of a Hopi man, coming down the face of the mesa along a path of toe-holds cut into the sandstone. "On his way to his field," said the guide. Fields of green corn plants broke through the expanse of desert sand at frequent intervals. The guide went ahead and announced them. On November 1, 1858, they entered Oraibi.

Oraibi in 1848. Oraibi was a large place. It had five rows of houses, most of them three, four, or five storeys, separated by streets. Led up a gently-winding trail that ascended the 300-foot-high mesa sometimes sharply in steep staircases cut into the stone and short pieces of switch-back trail, the Mormon visitors wound their way to the southwestern edge of the village and into one of the long, narrow streets. Cats and dogs abounded. Children clustered warily around the eleven strangers, sometimes running up ladders to the second-storey terraces of the stone houses. The walls of the houses were made of alternating layers of large stones, mud mortar, and small stones, which allowed more movement when frost got into the mortar in winter and thus gave the walls more stability.

A Hopi man named Tuba (actually Tuuvi), announcing himself as chief of the Corn and Water clan, greeted them in Ute (probably actually Southern Paiute). Hamblin reported Tuuvi as having heard of Mormons as well as Americans and as remarking that Americans killed Hopis. The remark might refer to an incident in 1834 in which American trappers killed fifteen or twenty unarmed Hopis in cold blood. Tuuvi might also have referred to the deaths from smallpox in 1852-53, which might well have been attributed to Dr. Ten Broeck's visit a few months earlier.

Hamblin was "convinced the Hopis were the last living reminders of the once mighty people,...the greater Nephite culture which had now vanished" and believed "that the Hopi fathers had once been white and delightsome, were Israel, and had come out of Israel" (Bailey 1948:204).[11] Hopis treated the Mormons cordially. They were housed in the second storey of a house, reached by a ladder, which had a corner fireplace and chimney. The chimney drew well and did not smoke. Skins, bows and arrows, quivers, antlers, blankets, and clothing either hung on ram-horn hooks in the walls or were piled on stone benches that lined the wall. They were served water in gourds and boiled mutton with hominy corn (*noqkwivi*) in shallow earthenware bowls with pottery ladles for spoons and folded sheets of paper-thin piki bread, which women made by spreading cornmeal paste by hand on a basalt stone griddle greased with watermelon seeds, cooking the sheets for less than a minute and then peeling them off and folding them. The piki and mutton were followed by thick, sweet dumpling-like corn pudding (apparently *somiviki*, made of yellow cornmeal, but the pudding can also be *hurzurziki* of purple cornmeal or *pikami* of blue) fermented with dropseed or wild buckwheat and baked overnight with hot coals in slab-lined ovens dug into the sides of the mesa and smothered in dirt. Tamales of goat meat, crumbled piki, and wild potatoes all tied up in corn husks and boiled, rounded out the meal.

After a couple of days, Hopis took the Mormons to a large room. The room, entered by ladder from above and measuring 30 by 40 feet, was probably an ordinary kiva, a square chamber used for religious ceremonies and as a kind of clubhouse by men. But Hamblin was given to understand that it had been prepared for them years earlier in anticipation of their arrival and it was there that Hamblin spoke about Mormon prophecy and teachings through the Paiute interpreter. Later, Hamblin was told "by a very aged man that when he was a young man, his father told him that he would live to see white men come among them, who would bring them great blessings, such as their fathers had enjoyed, and that these men would come from the west. He believed that he had lived to see the prediction fulfilled in us," wrote Hamblin in his diary (Nibley 1944:259-263).

Hamblin left four missionaries there and departed. But within two months, the missionaries had to leave, unsuccessful in their missionization efforts, "owing," said the men, "to a division among the people as to whether we were the men prophesied of by their fathers" (Nibley 1944:259-263). The missionaries' presence may well have been an unwanted intrusion; Hopis had to feed them as well as tolerate them. But we can also imagine a good deal of exchange of ideas and information taking place. November is a time when stories, myths, and legends were told and when there was generally a lot of visiting and talking in the Hopi villages. With harvests over and spring preparation not yet possible, winter was a slow time, devoted to weaving, basket-making, and other indoor pursuits. The Mormons' intentions to plant agricultural colonies to the south might well have provoked a keen interest in Hopis' techniques for success at dry-farming and use of flood waters. For their part, Mormons had made some strides of their own in channelling the turbulent runoff from spring snow-melt and summer downpours with dikes, dams, and ditches.

Was there an exchange of such technical information? We will never know. But the continual exchanges of products and back-and-forth visiting between Mormons and Hopis over the following half-century, and even into the Twentieth Century, economic contexts argue for a basic dialogue having been established that kept some individuals on both sides sufficiently interested in each other to endure beyond the subsequent intrusion of much more powerful influences.

Eight Mormons returned to Hopi in October, 1859. Hopis traded blankets, pottery, piki, and peaches for various things offered by the Mormons. Hopis insisted they be given farm tools outright because American soldiers had just been there and given them farm tools (Bailey 1948:214, 218-219). This distribution may actually have been in 1856, when troops from Fort Defiance gave Hopis spades, axes, hoes, plows, and hatchets. Troops may have visited again in 1859; Tuuvi told Hamblin American troops were expected, but in fact they never arrived. Two missionaries stayed, but only a few weeks. This time Hopis insisted the Mormons supply their own food, especially meat, and may have given them the cold shoulder; upon return, the missionaries said they left because they could not stand the solitude. Hamblin returned to Santa Clara and planted Hopi peach pits, which produced trees (Bailey 1948:219).

In December, 1862, Mormons were again at Hopi, where a severe drought had resulted in the deaths of 24 men and 22 women at Oraibi. The drought continued through 1868, and may have been followed by another bout of smallpox in 1866-7. Hamblin preached in the kiva in 1862 and he and other Mormon missionaries followed Hopi instructions and planted prayer sticks for rain. Three Hopis, including Tuuvi, accompanied him back to Santa Clara; they were there three months, returning to Hopiland in April, 1863 (Bailey 1948:252-253) Mormons again visited Hopis in 1869 and 1870. Hamblin guided American explorer John Wesley Powell, who would later found the Bureau of American Ethnology, to the Hopi villages in October, 1870. Powell and party were able to return to Oraibi in November, remaining there for about three weeks, trading for items that would go to the U.S. National Museum. In November, 1870, Tuuvi and his wife accompanied Hamblin back to southern Utah, where they stayed until September, 1871, when Hamblin accompanied them back to Oraibi.

Altogether between 1858 and 1873 the Mormons sent fifteen expeditions to the Hopi; Jacob Hamblin went on every one of them (Peterson 1971:181). On orders from Brigham Young, Hamblin laid out a wagon road in 1873 from Kanab to Lee's Ferry and there to Flagstaff

(McNitt 1962:104). By their own account, the Mormons tried to enlist Hopis' help as technical advisors in their colonization of the desert south and west of the Colorado River, offering the Hopis riverfront farmland in exchange! Perhaps trying to phrase things in a way the Mormons would understand, Hopis politely declined the invitation by citing traditions, revelations, and prophets. They must not cross the Colorado River, they said, until the three prophets who in ancient times had taken them into their present country, should appear and lead them forth again. But the Mormons were not those prophets.

Starting in the 1870s, Mormons built seven towns on the Little Colorado River and its tributaries. The settlements were supported by agriculture irrigated by a system of more than three dozen dams. They resembled the prehistoric water-control devices built by Puebloan inhabitants of the area, and had the same problem:they washed out regularly in spring and summer floods and had to be regularly rebuilt (Leone 1979:88-92). In 1874 Tuuvi, the "Corn and Water Clan Chief" of Oraibi gave Hamblin permission to settle on 12 acres of his clan land at Moenkopi (Bailey 1948:349). Mormon families, including John D. Lee of Lees' Ferry, later indicted for complicity in the "Mountain Meadows Massacre" of 1857, homesteaded near Moenkopi permanently in 1876, and the alliance yielded two side-by-side settlements: the Hopi village of Moenkopi and the Mormon colony of Tuba City. Mormons and Indians alike irrigated crops from Moenkopi Wash; some Hopis may have even cultivated fields near Leupp or Holbrook under Mormon protection.[12]

The Mormons' presence provided Hopis with a buffer between Moenkopi and surrounding Navajos. The Mormons were constantly negotiating with Navajos throughout the 1860s and 1870s. With their far-flung network of missionary-diplomats among Utes, Paiutes, and Navajos, the Mormons might well have been able to partially restore the "balance of power," disrupted with the Spaniards' withdrawal, until the clear ascendancy of the U.S. Government in the region after 1890. They also provided Tuuvi with a status and role that had not previously existed in Hopi society: that of secular chief and primary liaison between a Hopi community and a community of non-Indians. It appears that alliance with Mormons may have been the catalyst that kicked off suspicion and later hostility to Americans; special agent Crothers reported Oraibi's chief as hostile in 1872 (Titiev 1944:72). Agent Mateer (1878) also encountered less than a friendly welcome in 1876.

Worsening Environmental Conditions: 1884-1905

How much technical guidance the Mormons may have gotten from Hopis in implemented their system of water control through dams, dikes, and ditches remains unknown. But the same worsening environmental conditions that caused arroyo-cutting in the channels of stream beds of the Moenkopi, Oraibi, Dinnebito, Polacca, and Jeddito washes beginning between 1884 and 1910, also affected the Mormon settlements (Hack 1942:58-64; Leone 1979:88-92). Mormons' strategy of water control may even have accelerated environmental deterioration along these streams and thus upstream in Hopi country itself. A dam traps silt behind it. As silt accumulates, the level of the stream rises. On streams with gentle gradients, the level of the stream bed might be affected for miles upstream. As the river bed rises with deposition of silt, a pond stretches out further and further, becoming shallower with distance. Such a process creates conditions ideal for farming until a downpour cuts a new channel around the dam or washes it out (Leone 1979:92). If a new dam were not built immediately, the resulting cascade of debris and volume of water might well gouge the channel with such force that the velocity of water also increased, quickly causing arroyo-cutting. Arroyo-cutting appears to have started in Moenkopi Wash in 1884 and in Oraibi Wash by 1902, accelerating yearly until by 1937, the Wash's channel had deepened by 70 feet (Hack 1942:58, 64).

By 1879, the Mormons were proving to be more of a bother than an asset; Tuuvi had already submitted a complaint to Agent William Mateer about Mormon expansion (Wyckoff 1990:39). By 1897, the Mormons had become truly unwelcome. Competition for the small amount of irrigable land along Moenkopi Wash had strained relations among Mormons, Hopis, and Navajos alike. The U.S. Government had awarded allotments to Hopis and Navajos, not to Mormons, and over Mormon protests. In 1898, Hopis planted fields newly repatriated from Mormon claims. Fearing Mormon attack, Hopis used their power-balancing strategy to enlist Navajos' assistance. As Hopis planted the fields, a line of 40 armed Navajo guards followed them on horseback, assuring a lethal response to an anticipated Mormon attack that never came (Johnston 1972:79-82). By 1902 Congress had created the Western Navajo Reservation and courts had decreed eviction for the Mormons.

The Mormons entered Hopi history at an important juncture. It is that historical juncture that explains their apparent acceptance by Hopis despite their proselytizing and brazen assumptions that they could colonize Indian land. Even through Paiute or Spanish translations, Mormons' divulgence of their revelations and theories might have intrigued Hopi ceremonial leaders, whose traditions produce a predilection for intellectualizing. Hopis might well have responded with carefully-constructed explanations of their philosophy, religion, and revelations of their own. For Hopis, the encounters might have provided an opportunity as well as a necessity to enlist allies with a kind of verbal persuasion that might obviate a military presence which Hopis could not generate, in the same way that Hopis had dealt with Navajos, who borrowed some elements of Hopi and Pueblo religion.

Only a dozen Hopis joined the Church of Latter Day Saints during this early missionizing period. But the Mormons constituted, however briefly, a new and potentially important political and economic force in the region. Their actions and ideology were consistent and predictable. Despite the Americans' victory over the Mexicans and their disciplining of Navajos, only the hindsight of history could have foretold the Mormons' replacement with Americans from the Hopi perspective. The Mormons provided new flux in the crucible of Ute, Paiute, Navajo, and American interests that vied for influence and stability in the region. And one of their converts, Hopi-Tewa Tom Polacca, proved an important influence in countering the resistance of First Mesa's politico-religious leaders to government-imposed eduction as well as a kingpin in the growing trade in prehistoric and contemporary pottery during the 1890s and early 1900s.

4

Hopi Culture on the Edge of the Twentieth Century

Hard on the heals of missionaries (1858); the U.S. military (1863); U.S. Indian agents (1869); and traders (1875) came anthropologists. The first was Major John Wesley Powell, one-armed Civil War veteran and head of the U.S. Geological Survey. He visited briefly in 1870 and returned in 1879 as head of the newly-formed Bureau of American Ethnology, accompanied by anthropologists Frank Cushing, Matilda Coxe Stevenson and her husband Colonel James Stevenson. Frank Cushing returned briefly in 1881 and 1882; Alexander Stephen made a brief visit in 1881 and in 1883 took up more or less permanent residence; the Stevensons made another visit in 1886; and Jesse Walter Fewkes arrived in 1890, taking up more or less where Stephen left off after Stephen died in Walpi in 1894. From nearly the very beginning of interactions between Hopis and citizens of the United States, then, anthropologists were part of the resulting cultural, social, and political dialogue. Therefore, these early anthropologists are of interest to a discussion of Hopi ethnography for two reasons: first, they established the schematic "baseline" picture of Hopi culture and society which has formed the starting point for nearly all anthropologists who had followed them; and second, they played active roles in constructing the social field within which Hopis and Americans interacted in the waning years of the Nineteenth Century and the early years of the Twentieth Century.

Anthropology and Ethnography

The Dialogic Nature of Anthropology

Anthropology is by nature "dialogic" in that much insight, information, and interpretation comes to the anthropologist through in-depth conversations with a distinct group of people that are his or her key consultants. (Conrad Kottak [1991:25-27] calls them "well-informed informants".) At the point in time that a particular anthropologist engaged Hopi culture and society, he or she did so with a specific methodological framework and a particular set of research goals. The outcome was a product of what people told the anthropologist plus what the anthropologist observed and experienced plus the paradigm, or methodological framework, which the anthropologist used for making sense of the information. Thus, a good many anthropologists' understandings were actually produced by the "natives" in the first place. These understandings "went into dialogue," so to speak, with the methodological concepts of the discipline ("clan;" "religion;" "hierarchical rankings," and so forth) when they are published, as well as with the *cultural* and *linguistic* categories peculiar to the anthropologist's own society.

While anthropologists pursued their own particular research goals and following the trails along which their observations and experiences led, the society and culture in question -- in this case Hopi society and culture -- continued to exist independently the anthropologists were experiencing, and writing about. The probability that the "natives" were not always of one mind about the meaning of some event or concept is evident from the compendium of anthropological materials on the Hopi, and thus the likelihood of complete correspondence between what anthropologists say about Hopis (or any other group of studied people) and the multiplicity of *Hopis'* experiences and perceptions, is slight indeed. Hopis have always taken an active role in constructing different anthropologists' pictures of Hopi culture is a more active one than anthropologists would like to credit to them. Hopis have more often than not seized the opportunity presented by anthropologists to get across a point or to hone a "native" perceptual category of which anthropologists may or may not have been aware. In some cases, the point may have been purely personal; in other cases we find the bias of clan, village, or ceremonial affiliation. The dialogic nature of anthropologists' production of knowledge about Hopi culture and society is, then, *historically-conditioned* (cf. Marcus and Fischer 1986:96).

This chapter therefore has two purposes: to introduce a historically-conditioned "baseline" picture of Hopi culture and society and to sketch a short history of early anthropological work among the Hopi. Scholars began reconstructing "aboriginal" Hopi culture in 1882 but were still at it over a hundred years later (Schlegel 1973, 1992; Geertz 1987a; Loftin 1990; Whiteley 1988b; Rushforth and Upham 1992). An annotated bibliography of works on the Hopi runs to nearly 700 pages (Laird 1977); thus my review of the anthropological literature cannot be exhaustive. But I go into somewhat detailed descriptions of the work of early ethnographers if only to clear up some confusion about Hopi social organization caused recently by interpretations of later scholars (e.g., Rushforth and Upham 1992, Whiteley 1988b).

Frank Cushing: Collector-Ethnologist

Ethnologist Frank Hamilton Cushing found himself participating in a very dicey dialogue in Oraibi in December, 1882. Cushing had set out from his base at Zuni with three other men including a half-Navajo/half-Hopi (described as an adopted Zuni) as interpreter (Hinsley 1989) on a collecting expedition for the Smithsonian Institution. He was headed for Oraibi specifically, where he planned to exchange pots, pans, needles, and other items for pottery, blankets, and other.craft items, much as Powell had done more than ten years earlier. Oraibi's village chief, Loololma, welcomed Cushing cordially, but when he tried to set up his little roadside shop in the plaza, Cushing encountered opposition. Surprised to find opposition at Oraibi to his museum collecting efforts and to Washington in general, Cushing (1883:17) was frightened and outraged at being bluntly told that he stank like a white man; was nothing but a pile of shit; and should leave (cf. Cushing 1923; Parsons 1922). He was up until 3 AM on December 21, engaged in a very confrontational conversation. When finally released, he woke up his companions and told them he wanted to leave immediately, although they did not. As dawn broke and the day advanced, virtually everyone in the pueblo treated them with sullenness, throwing angry glances at them. In the afternoon, they departed.

Cushing was not amused. In his report to John Wesley Powell, Director of the Bureau of American Ethnology and Cushing's boss, he asserted that "sorcerer priests of the tribe" had, "by means of a reckless effrontery, unparalleled by anything I have else known of other Indians" (Cushing also worked among the Zuni and Seneca), boldly attacked the "regular chief" (Loololma). "They go so far to threaten the life of the highest priest-chief of the tribe" (sic) Cushing 1883 quoted in Titiev 1944:76).

"As we throw dung out of the plazas"

Cushing's reception at Oraibi was totally unlike his reception at the other villages. He had first gone to the Hopi villages in October, 1879, with the photographer John K. Hillers and two fellow ethnographers, Colonel James and Matilda Coxe Stevenson, later made famous by the *Illustrated Police Gazette* of March 6, 1886 which pictured her shaking her fist in the face of an angry Hopi about to kick her in the shins to deep her from forcing her way in a kiva (Green 1990:228). Cushing returned on June 22, 1881, where he met Tom Polacca (also Pulakai, Pulakaia, Pulakaka, and Pu-la-ka-kai), a Hopi-Tewa who had lived at Zuni, presumably when many Hopis sought refuge there following smallpox epidemics and droughts. Polacca accompanied Cushing to Zuni and on to the Hopi villages at First Mesa and to Oraibi on June 28, 1881. He was said to speak six Indian languages as well as Spanish and English; was characterized as "wealthy;" had been "religiously adopted by the Cacique of the Walpis;" and had been to San Bernardino and Santa Barbara, California (Green 1990:7, 18-19; 166-168; ARCIA 1877:160), probably to obtain shells no longer obtainable through native trade routes, and possibly in the company of Mormons, who later established colonies near both towns. Polacca was a Mormon convert (Peterson 1971:193). and lived in a large house with a portico. Cushing hired Polacca as an interpreter in 1881 at $1.00 a day. In 1882 Polacca helped Cushing as best he could in his debacle at Oraibi (Green 166-8, 388-9).

Cushing went on to camp in the arroyo below Mishongnovi and Shipaulovi, where he made collections of "more than twelve hundred specimens," noted Moqui folk-lore and tradition, and studied "the considerable collections of antique pottery gathered." Whether this was prehistoric pottery he dug up or items he bartered for, is uncertain. But he obviously made a haul. Thus Cushing initiated the museum market for Hopi material culture; Thomas Keam, a trader, and Alexander Stephen, an ethnologist like Cushing, would initiate the commercial market for Hopi material culture, but would intertwine it so thoroughly with the museum market that one of the collections that Keam and Stephen jointly assembled -- the Hemenway collection -- would remain "lost" for nearly a hundred years (Wade and McChesney 1980).

Cushing was never to return to the Hopi villages, and this report is the extent of his "fieldwork" there. But three other ethnographers, Alexander Stephen; Jesse Walter Fewkes; and Heinrich Voth (with George Dorsey) would complete baseline studies and undertake activities that would establish the anthropological picture of Hopi culture and also have consequences reaching far into the future, into the Twenty-first Century.

Anthropological Thinking
in the Nineteenth Century

The major figures in the ethnology of the Hopi prior to 1930 were Adolph Bandelier, John W. Powell, Alexander M. Stephen, J. Walter Fewkes, Heinrich Voth (with George Dorsey), Robert Lowie and Elsie Clews Parsons. J.W. Powell wrote little about the Hopi except what amounted to a travel diary and Bandelier relied heavily on two sources: reports of travelers and explorers and reports from the Mindeleff brothers, Cosmos and Victor, who documented some ruins in the Hopi area and made connections between ancient sites and contemporary Hopi and Rio Grande Pueblo culture largely on the basis of architecture. Bandelier's work combines some truth with many errors.

A brief look at early anthropological approaches reveals how they may have influenced these and other anthropologists' interpretations of Hopi culture between 1880 and 1925. Two schools of thought dominated American anthropology during this time period: unilineal evolutionism and historical particularism.

Unilineal Stage-Sequence Evolutionism[13]

The unilineal evolutionists outlined a "line of progress" through three stages: savagery, barbarism, and civil society. The unilineal stage-sequence evolutionary scheme was blatantly ethnocentric and empirically wrong. The unilineal evolutionists did their utmost to ignore facts that did not fit, or to distort them to make cultures and societies "fit" the scheme. Unilinealism also fostered a kind of romantic patronizing of native societies, whose members ostensibly did not know the value of industrial items (because they did not produce them) and would have no concept of private property (because they were communal).

A good deal of romantic naivete accompanied the unilineal evolutionary viewpoint. This romantic naivete closely resembled the "noble savage" idea of American Indians that characterizes various periods of American popular and artistic thinking (Berkhofer 1978:71-104). The idea was basically this: although American Indian culture had many fine qualities to it, it was basically doomed to be engulfed by Anglo-American civilization. In the words of one ethnologist: "Whatever may be the faults or foibles of the Pueblo, or of the Indian in general, whatever his aspirations, his incongruities, his strength, or his weakness, as a type of man he is destined to disappear under the irresistible influences of a mightier race. His social life become enfeebled by attempts to put into practice half-understood conventionalities borrowed from the white man. The Indian will live, but his existence will come to be a memory in place of a reality" (Fynn 1907:258-61). Of course, nothing could have been farther from the truth.

Historical Particularism

Historical particularism is associated with Franz Boas and his students, particularly Alfred Kroeber and Robert Lowie. The historical particularists saw any particular culture as being an assemblage of distinct traits -- clusters of behavior patterns, values, attitudes, knowledge, skills, material items -- that could run into the thousands and that could be conceptualized logically in categories. Traits were "ideal types:" they consisted of generalizations about behavior, action, beliefs, etc. that were repeated sufficiently often by enough people that the participants could recognize them and summarize them to an ethnographer, or the ethnographer could recognize the patterns straight off. Much of the baseline ethnography on the Hopi was done by historical particularists.

For the historical particularists, cultures were not tightly-bonded, rigidly coherent entities. They were the results of people interacting with one another in particular places, in particular time periods. They were as flexible as they were unpredictable. They did not necessarily make sense. Cultures also slopped over their supposed boundaries in all directions, so that a researcher might have to look far outside the geographical boundaries of any particular society to determine the real significance of any particular cultural trait, element, form, pattern, or configuration. Just discovering how one particular element -- say a myth -- was functionally connected with another element -- say, a clan -- would tell the researcher little about either myth or clan. Finding a similar myth and a similar clan concept in a neighboring culture, however, would tell the research a lot. The researcher would be less likely to be consternated or confused by trying to reconcile, say, four different versions of the same myth told by four different people from four different clans within the same society (Goldfrank 1948) and would also be less tempted to favor one at the expense of the other three.

The historical particularists rejected the idea of developmental sequences and staunchly opposed unilineal evolutionism. They regarded it as scientifically naive at best and as ethnocentric and racist at worst. They saw unilineal evolutionism as scientifically naive because the methodology tried to fit every single culture and every single cultural fact into predetermined categories: the supposed "stages" of sociocultural progress. Boas especially saw it as racist because it was so easily used to bolster the belief that certain "races" -- Blacks, American Indians -- deserved second class citizenship because they were evolutionarily inferior, naturally the products of the barbaric or savage stage, not the civilized stage (Hyatt 1990:18-22; 84).

The Naturalist Descriptive Convention

Despite their vast philosophical differences, the unilineal evolutionists and the historical particularists shared something in common: a commitment to a descriptive, comparative, natural-science methodology. Virtually every investigator doing research among American Indians prior to the late 1920s -- with the exception of Edward Sapir -- was either an evolutionist or a historical particularist. Cushing, Stephen, Fewkes, and Voth, along with Dorsey, were all evolutionists; Kroeber, Lowie and Parsons were historical particularists.

The assumption that drove the naturalist convention was that careful and systematic observation would yield insight, understanding, and eventually, rock-bottom truth. The tools of the naturalist were a quick eye and ear, plenty of paper and a pen, and an ability to conceptually split and lump categories. They all strived for accuracy and for correspondence among agreed-upon, logically positivistic categories. The phrase, "clan ownership of lands" would mean the same thing to an evolutionist as it would to a particularist. "Ceremonial chieftaincy" would constitute a descriptive category that investigators from both conventions could recognize when they saw. Evolutionists and historical particularists alike also treated theoretical speculation with skepticism; noted native interpretations with caution; relied heavily on detailed recordings of observations; and sought empirical, representations of native categories within the broad framework of the larger descriptive categories of natural science.

With descriptions and comparisons, the naturalist scientist would construct an edifice of inductive facts, whether the ultimate goal was to stuff them into the evolutionary chimera or leave them lying in piles of particularist history. Thus, evolutionists and historical particularists alike produced voluminous studies packed with descriptive detail sprinkled with native terms such as "*tiponi*"; "*wuya*" and "*monwi*" that defied good translation; particularly to be avoided was any speculation that was not empirically grounded. Thus Alexander Stephen, for example, castigated fellow BAE ethnographer Matilda Stevenson for "ethnologic villainy" for indulging in speculative interpretation and tried "to avoid forming conceptions from Hopi suggestions, unless presented to me in tolerable completeness and some authority" (Wade and McChesney 1980:4-12).

J.W. Powell, Collector-Ethnographer

Cushing, Fewkes, and Stephen all worked for the U.S. Bureau of American Ethnology, founded by geologist John Wesley Powell in 1879 and directed by him until his death in 1902. Powell was familiar with the Hopi scene. He had stayed in Oraibi in 1870 long enough to record observations on architecture and on one ceremony at Shipaulovi, probably Lakon, a ceremony owned by women but involving men as well and to collect ceremonial and technological items.

Powell's collecting technique clearly placed him in the superior bargaining position. After several weeks, Powell unpacked his trade items and put them on display for a day: knives, needles, awls, scissors, paints, dyes, leather, and machine-made fabrics "in gay colors." Then he meandered through people's houses noting items that he liked. Retreating like a pasha to his temporary quarters, he then received people, one after another, bringing their trade items: baskets, pottery, stone, bone, horn, and shell implements, homespun cotton garments, ceremonial headdresses, Katsina dolls. For what he did not want, he offered nothing; for what he did want, he set the terms and refused to bargain. Some people were undoubtedly disappointed. Nonetheless, Powell reported the barter as being "carried on with a hearty good will," with "jesting and laughing" (Powell 1895:342-344).

Stephen, Fewkes, Voth: Romantic Evolutionists in Search of Clans, Ceremonies, and Secret Societies

Alexander Stephen's Baseline Ethnography

Alexander M. Stephen produced the first full ethnographic account of Hopi life, at least the male side of it. Trader Thomas Keam first brought Stephen to Walpi in 1881. They approached the top of the 300-foot-high bluff, by a steep, winding, narrow horse trail from which numerous footpaths and steps cut into the stone led up along even steeper inclines. All three villages still consisted of two and three storeyed sandstone buildings, usually faced with mud plaster, with ladders leading to second-storey terraces facing streets and plazas. Terraces were used for shucking and drying corn and peaches; for making baskets and pottery; for washing and bathing with yucca root soap; and for visiting in good weather. The terraces, not the plazas, constituted the public space of a village. Entrances were only off these terraces; ladders through floors and ceilings led to a family's single-room third story and down to first-floor stories that were generally sleeping or storage quarters. Ten years later, Stephen would rent one of the houses, although by the 1890s Hopis had begun extensive remodeling jobs, putting in doors and windows and sealing off second stories from rooms below.

Low ceilings made rooms six to eight feet in height; the short length of available poles of pinon wood limited rooms to rectangles about 50 feet square. Often the short, thin pinon rafters needed support from a center pole; smaller poles crossed the rafters, fitted tight together, and were covered with a thick later of brush and mud to support a floor above. Small doorways, three to four feet in height, connected rooms within a house, and at this time, one could still occasionally find three generations of a single matrilineage living in one three-storey set of connected rooms. From rafters hung Katsina dolls, *tihu*, of which Stephen would later publish the first public description, and sometimes dried meat and peaches. Walls and floors were plastered with mud and the walls generally had a coating of kaolin, white clay. The few windows were made of gypsum. Interior niches and ram horns protruding from walls provided storage spaces and clothes racks. Low stone seats running along one or two sides covered with goat or sheep skins served as divans. Small corner fireplaces served cooking and heating needs; coal was the usual fuel.

Stephen returned in either 1883 or 1884 for a year or more, and spent portions of 1887 and 1889 either in Sichomovi, on top of First Mesa, or at Keam's ranch a few miles away in the canyon. He lived his three years straight in a house on the mesa beginning in 1891, dying there in 1894 of either influenza or tuberculosis. He publicly referred to the Hopi as "the remnants of a waning race" and privately, in bouts of depression, "would chastise his Hopis as decadent members of a barbarous race incapable of following the white man's road" (Wade and McChesney 1980:14, 10). Yet he was accepted and even invited into most of the men's secret societies to observe their ceremonies.

Stephen expressed reluctance to rely on "native theorists," and sometimes found "native" explanations mutually contradictory (Stephen 1936:713, 718, 767). Stephen apparently never learned to speak Hopi fluently, since he consistently worked through interpreters, but he did compile a short glossary of Hopi words. He also made over 500 careful line-drawings; catalogued nearly 500 items for the Hemenway collection shown in Madrid at the Columbian Exposition of 1892; and wrote down nearly 30 tales, legends, myths, and oral histories. He paid potters to make replicas of ancient forms and designs, and interpreters to make translations for him, although he could not have paid them very well on his meager $50 monthly salary. He seems to have concentrated most on what he initially understood the least: ceremonies and social organization. He felt that ceremonialism was fundamental to Hopi life.

The Villages. In 1880, Hopi society consisted of four population centers: The easternmost of "First" Mesa, "Middle" or "Second" Mesa; the westernmost, or "Third" Mesa; and the growing settlement of Moenkopi, populated at least as early as 1870 (Powell 1895:341) and well-established in alliance with Mormons by 1876. First Mesa had three villages: Hano-Tewa, Sichomovi, and Walpi. Second Mesa also had three villages: Shungopavi, Shipaulovi, and Mishongnovi. Third Mesa just had one village: Oraibi, with Moenkopi, 40 miles distant, also being a "Third Mesa" village. Although there were local variations, Stephen's work reveals a similar political form and process at all three mesas. One village at each mesa exercised political leadership totally independent of the other two mesas. A second village constituted a "daughter village" whose political form and process was dependent on and subsidiary to the primary village. At First Mesa this daughter village is Sichomovi. At Second Mesa, it is Shipaulovi. At Third Mesa, it is Moenkopi. At Second Mesa, Mishongnovi constituted an "ally" or "guard village" (cf. Connelly 1979). At First Mesa this "ally village" was Hano-Tewa. Third Mesa had no "ally village." Stephen found that Tewas were initiated into virtually every one of the Hopi secret societies on First Mesa.

The Kikmongwi. Each primary village had a *Kikmongwi*, or "village chief." Each secondary village may or may not have had its own *Kikmongwi*. According to Stephen, Sichomovi had none, while Shipaulovi had a Kikmongwi who had to be installed by Shungopavi's institutional process. Hano-Tewa and Mishongnovi were largely politically independent, having their own leaders. Oraibi, of course, had its own village chief.

Marriage. Stephen distinguished marriage as one of the few social relationships established outside the ceremonial context. Social and economic activities were primary in marriage, rather than ceremonial ones. Involvement of nearly every relative on both sides of the groom's as well as the bride's family in the various steps of courtship and wedding, established social and economic bonds among a large number of people -- affines -- related through what amounted to an alliance between two different matrilineages. At the birth of a child, all women of both matrilineages had the privilege of bestowing a name on the child in a dawn ceremony six months or more after the child was born; one of the names would "stick" and become the child's common childhood name.

Matrilineality. Stephen documented women's ownership of houses, clan paraphernalia, and seed corn, as well as clans' ownership of separate plots of land. He documented clans as totemically named -- reed, bear, sand, lizard, "pikyas" ("sprouting corn"), coyote, Katsina, horn, flute, snake -- and matrilineally determined: clan membership was passed down only through females.

The Wuya. Stephen found clans to be rather vaguely constituted entities, tied to a specific *wuya,* that was both ancestor and object, either an effigy, a bundle, or a mask. But in reality, the owning entity -- the clan -- was actually an extended matrilineage *within* the clan. A matrilineal household's possession of the *wuya* established it as the most important of the matrilineages within the particular clan to one another. Each clan had a "clan house" where the *wuya* were kept, as well as the altars of the society performing the ceremony that the clan owns, and the Katsina masks. The women of the house fed the masks and *wuya* every day, and thus the clan's ceremonial paraphernalia were really in the custody of the eldest woman of the clan who headed the female membership of her lineage. The matrilineage constituted the mechanism for transmitting rights, duties, land, houses, and ceremonial knowledge, and thus was vital with respect to status, residence, and economy.

Clans and Ceremonies. Stephen found clans to be the owners of ceremonies and the places in which many of them are performed, the chambers which he first called *estufas* (Spanish for "steps," because many of the kivas in the Rio Grande Pueblos are entered by first ascending steps to the roof and then descending a ladder through a roof-top entrance) but later switched to the Hopi word, *kiva.* Each kiva was dedicated to one particular ceremony. But any one kiva was also used for other ceremonies and as a kind of clubhouse for men who "belonged" to it. They went to the kiva often to smoke, talk, card and spin cotton, and weave sashes, belts, blankets, robes, and other clothing out of cotton. During Katsina and Powamu initiations, every kiva was filled, including those of Sichomovi and Hano-Tewa.

In response to the question, "What happens to a ceremony if the clan's last lineage dies out?" Stephen was told that another lineage of the same clan might take responsibility for its obligations. This process accounted, for example, for the Coyote Clan also being known as the Cedarwood Clan. In extreme instances, a ceremony and paraphernalia might be offered to any individuals who would take the responsibilities and privileges of leadership. Because ceremonies were the responsibility of men but the masks, *wuya*, and other paraphernalia were the responsibility of women, the transfer of ceremonial responsibilities had to involve agreement between a brother and a sister, either related through having identical parents or related through extensions of kinship, that is, by membership in the same clan. Stephen found that when the last Bear Clan woman died at Walpi, thereby presaging the extinction of the Bear Clan entirely, the Patki (Water) clan took over the Soyal ceremony, owned by the Bear Clan, but the office of town or village chief, the *Kikmongwi*, which was supposed to go with it, actually ended up with the Horn clan. Thus Stephen documented flexibility in Hopi social organization.

The Secret Societies

Each ceremony is performed by a secret society, or sodality. Stephen called them fraternities, but also documented the existence of at least two women's secret societies, and thus the term "fraternity" is somewhat erroneous. Stephen determined that there were between 20 and 28 secret societies. Some of them were "paired" with others, while others had overlapping memberships that were nearly identical. Those that were "paired," fell into three groups: the Snake-Antelope and the two Flute societies; the Powamu and Katsina societies; and the "men's." The latter were the Ahl (Horn); Kwan (Agave cactus, or One-Horn); Taw (Singers) and Wuwutsim (no translation). These men's societies initiated new members once every four or five years; initiations brought men into adulthood. Three Women's Societies, the Maraw, Oaqol, and Lalakon encompassed nearly all of the adult women in the three villages, but also included some men, and were paired, more or less, with the Wuwutsim. The women's societies were not mutually exclusive.

The Snake and Antelope societies performed two different parts of the same ritual and thus had mutually exclusive memberships. They alternated their ceremonies every other year with those of the Flute society, which also had two mutually exclusive groups that performed different parts of the ceremony. The Powamu and Katsina societies were also mutually exclusive with respect to one another, but every child was initiated into either one or the other at around age six. Because the initiations all took place at the same time, the Katsina society was, in effect, divided into eight different sections, one for each of the kivas in the three villages. The Soyal, Dawawympkiya (Sun-Watcher), Sumakolia, Poboshwympkiya ("Eye-Seeker"), Tcukuwympkiya (Coyehimci, or Goyemsi Clown), Paiakyamu (Tewa or "Koshare" Clown), and Keletaka (Warrior) societies were not mutually exclusive, but their memberships tended to be restricted. The Soyal society included all of the chiefs of the other societies plus other important ceremonial office-holders. The Sun-Watchers were a small and largely informal group. They monitored the sun's progress throughout the year and announced the passage of the months.

The Ceremonial Calendar

Except for the Sun-Watcher, Warrior, and Curing societies, each society had a particular time of the year when its major ceremonies took place. In addition, the "major" societies, as Stephen called them, that is, the Soyal, men's, women's, Powamu, and Katsina societies, all had minor ceremonies that occurred about six months after the major ones. Hopi religion is communal, pantheistic, dependent on community rituals and rites of passage, and calendrical in nature. The Sun-Watchers track the sun's movement so that when the sun's rays fall on a particular marker, preparations begin for a particular ceremony. Timing is crucially important; a ceremony might be performed a little ahead of time, but can never be performed after the proper time has passed. Thus in theory, the days and months would cycle one after another in a regular, predictable fashion, in the following yearly order:

<u>November:</u>
kindling of "new fire";
Wuwutsim;
Men's societies initiations every four to five years;
Morning after Wuwutsim: Coming of the Soyal Katsina
<u>December:</u>
Winter Solstice ceremony-Soyal society
<u>January:</u>
Winter Lalakon
Winter Snake or Flute
Night Katsina dances (kivas)
Buffalo dances (social)
<u>February:</u>
Winter Maraw
At new moon: Powamalyu (some years) and Powamu; Powamu and
Katsina initiations (some years)
Patcava, in years when there have been initiations into the men's
societies
Water serpent dance

Natackas and Soyokos ("ogres" or "bogeys") come
March through June:
Katsina dances and clown performances (daytime, plaza)
June:
Soyal society prayer offerings at Solstice
July:
Niman (Katsina Home-going)
Morning after Katsina Homegoing: Kiva ceremony by Katsina and
Powamu chiefs
August:
Snake-Antelope (even years)
Flute (odd years)
September:
Butterfly and other social and harvest dances
Fall Maraw alternating with Oaqol
October:
Lalakon

Society Chiefs

Each secret society had a "chief;" in some cases the chief was of the clan owning the ceremony performed by the society, but not always. Not all clans owned ceremonies, but each ceremony-owning clan also had a ceremonial "chief." Some clans also had the right and obligation to furnish someone to fill a specific role in a particular ceremony. Hopis referred to all these men collectively as *"monwi"* (*"mongwi"*) which Stephen loosely translated as "chief." Thus there were secret society chiefs, clan chiefs, and ceremonial chiefs. Society and ceremonial chiefs were installed by their fellow society members, but they were actually selected from among the sons of the eldest female of their lineage and clan. When the individual in question was to hold more than one office, the selection would be made by all the *monwi* together. Each society chief possessed a *tiponi*, a kind of "medicine bundle," containing items of ritual and symbolic importance collectively owned by the secret society or by the clan owning the ceremony which the society performed.

Medicine Men's Societies and the Warriors. The Sumakolia were a curing society composed largely of Tewas and centered at Hano-Tewa village, as were the Paiakyamu, a clown society. The Poboshwympkiya society was a curing society composed mainly of Hopis, and specialized in curing people who had been bewitched by sorcerers; they used crystals to "see" the affliction. Stephen found that the Warriors consisted mainly of the same membership as the Snake society, but he speculated that in past times, when warfare was active, it had probably included nearly all younger men.

Who Governs?

Stephen found political power to be diffuse and succession to chieftaincy a negotiable right. When Simo (also Cimo), "chief" of the Horn and Flute clan who was also *Kikmongwi, Soyal* society chief, and chief of the Horn and Flute society died in 1892, he was succeeded by one of the sons of the eldest of his sisters. It was she, of course, who held the clan's *wuya*. Clan women of the Kikmongwi's house were important; they had the duty of shelling the sweet corn to be distributed to the village people, who would plant it for the Katsinas as the first planting of the season (Stephen 1936:351). Thus the office of "clan chief" was somewhat illusory; the real power was held by the eldest female of the clan, who might be called the "clan chieftess," although neither Stephen nor any other researcher has used that term.

But the final decision as to *which* of the eldest sister's son was not up to the candidate's mother alone. Stephen (1936:951) found that the final decision would be made by all of the *monwis* -- the "village council" -- during the *Soyal* Ceremony at Winter Solstice. The village council consisted of the Kikmongwi; Bear Clan Chief; Flute Chief; Corn Clan Chief; Two-Horn (Al); One-Horn (Kwan); Wuwutsim; Singers (Taw) society chiefs; 3 Chiefs holding offices in the Soyal (Winter Solstice) Society; Powamu Chief; Katsina Chief; 2 Eototo Chiefs; the Badger Clan, who headed one of the two medicine societies (the other was Tewa); the Snake/Sand Clan, Antelope Society, and Snake Society Chiefs as well as the Chief of the Sun-Watcher society, apparently a Tewa (Stephen 1936:63, 82; 558; 955-56; 813-14; 1090; 1106; 1135).

Decision-Making. Decisions were made by informal consultation and consensus. The village council discussed a matter until unanimity was reached. Stephen witnessed a discussion in 1893 that proceeded from speaker to speaker in order of ceremonial hierarchy: "All spoke except Ka'ta ... uncle to Hayi (Flute Chief and Kikmongwi), not otherwise a chief, who merely expressed acquiescence with each speaker," wrote Stephen (1936:956); "Chiefs take precedence thus:

1. Flute Society Chief; Kikmongwi; Grey Flute Society Chief
2. Bear/Spider Clan Chief
3. Wuwutsim Chief
4. Singers Chief
5. Two-Horn Society Chief

6. One-Horn Society Chief
7. 2 Eototo Chiefs
8. Corn Clan Chief, Sun Watcher, Soyal Society Chief
9. Powamu Chief
10. Antelope Society Chief
11. Snake Chief
12. Crier Chief (Speech Chief) (Associate of every Chief)
13. War Chief. He travels in the rear in peace time, to see that all other chiefs keep true to the path. At the meeting he was the last to speak."

It was by following such ritual speaking protocols that consensus was reached; each speaker not only was assured of learning the full content of his predecessor's thoughts, but also was assured plenty of opportunity to either modify his own to dovetail with them, or think of how to carefully measure words so as to refrain from commitment until he assessed his constituency. Stephen determined that despite the ceremonial hierarchy, the chiefs engaged in the same work and led the same kind of life as other villagers.

Rankings. Stephen found that the various secret society chiefs were ranked with respect to one another; because the secret society chiefs were ranked, their respective clans were ranked with respect to one another. His data revealed ceremonialism as the basis for clan rankings, rather than the other way around. Stephen found that Hopi rituals, and therefore Hopi politics, were traditionally rooted in the clan system. Because clans own ceremonies, ceremonial ranking also reflects clan ranking. Hopis explained the clan ranking to Stephen in terms of the order in which each clan arrived in the village, ahead of or behind another clan.

Thus the clan and society chieftaincies, the specific roles that a ceremonial officer played, and the proprietary rights of a lineage over certain ceremonies or positions of responsibility, all defined the relationships of particular groups of individuals with regard to one another. The relationship between clans and ceremonies was one of stewardship, in which the clan held the ceremony in trust, so to speak, and maintained the responsibility to see that it was performed, even though its performance was done largely by members of other clans.

Ceremonial Parents. Stephen found that membership in the secret societies cross-cut the clan system. That is, nearly every secret society had at least one member of a majority of the clans in the village. For example, of the sixteen clans in Walpi and Sichomovi, Stephen found that in each of the four men's secret societies, at least ten different clans were represented. He also found that an individual was initiated into a particular secret society through his or her ceremonial father, usually selected from a clan that is neither the individual's mother's nor father's clan, and that the individual's mother had the primary privilege of selecting the ceremonial father for a boy and the ceremonial father and mother for a girl. A boy helped his ceremonial father farm; a girl helped her ceremonial mother grind corn. At puberty, she ground corn for her entire matrilineage; at marriage, for her mother-in-law.Men joined a secret society by being sponsored by their ceremonial father; women were sponsored by their ceremonial mother. Every child had a ceremonial father as well as a ceremonial mother. Stephen found that mothers had the right to choose a child's ceremonial father before the child was even born, although this prerogative was not always exercised.

Thus, membership in a secret society depended on a number of complex social relationships in which an individual was enmeshed, and although the *principle* of ceremonial stewardship was highly institutionalized, its sociological expression was highly variable in accordance with the motivations and social position of the persons within an individual's social web, as well as in accordance with the abilities and motivations of the individual in question. Ceremonialism not only perpetuated the thrust of Hopi culture, but also placed responsibility on individuals to be not merely a cogs in the system.

Jesse Walter Fewkes, Ethnographer and Collector

Fewkes used the old Spanish term, Tusayan, reintroduced by Thomas Keam and the Mindeleff brothers, to refer to the Hopi, their territory, and the ruins within it such as Wupatki, Sikyatki, Awat'ovi, and the ruins in Tsegi Canyon. He clearly showed that Hopis were the descendants of the inhabitants of the prehistoric Puebloan ruins of the area, the heirs to what some archaeologists were beginning to erroneously call the "Anasazi." ("Anasazi" is a Navajo word meaning "people of the past who are not us.")

Hopi ceremonies held no less fascination for Jesse Walter Fewkes than they did for Alexander Stephen. But Fewkes (1895b) first came to the Hopi villages as Director of the second Hemenway Expedition, relying heavily on Stephen after Cushing, Director of the first Hemenway Expedition, withdrew in 1888 owing to ill health. Along with Thomas Keam, Stephen had already been collecting Hopi pottery for some time, paying Nampeyo and other potters to make reproductions of ancient forms and designs. Fewkes gave no credit to either Keam or Stephen for stimulating the resurgence of Hopi pottery-making and putting it on a commercial basis. Instead he "advanced the now fabled account of

Nampeyo visiting his dig at Sikyatki and copying prehistoric motifs from discarded potsherds. His veiled inferences led subsequent writers to attribute the revolution to Nampeyo alone" (Wade and McChesney 1980:10-11).

Nampeyo.[14] Nampeyo was an accomplished potter by the time she was a teenager; William Henry Jackson photographed her making pots in 1875 or 1876 when she was about 15 years old. And undoubtedly she did visit Fewkes' archaeological excavation at Sikyatki, since her husband Lesou was a member of Fewkes' field crew. She also undoubtedly copies some prehistoric motifs from potsherds (cf. Fewkes 1919). But she had also undoubtedly been doing so before Fewkes arrived. Rather than doing the collecting himself, Fewkes had Mary Hemenway, the Expedition's sponsor, purchase Thomas Keam's collection for $10,000. Stephen had apparently already catalogued it; the collection was exhibited with his introduction and notes.

Intrusions. Like most of his contemporaries, Fewkes lamented that Hopi culture was doomed. "Hopi aboriginal life is fast fading into the past," he averred, "and the time for gathering ethnological data is limited" (Fewkes 1902a:510). Referring to the Hopis in a letter in 1891 as "the most primitive aborigines of the United States," (Wade and McChesney 1980:8-9), Fewkes nonetheless did not want Hopi ceremonialism to disappear. Citing the U.S. Constitution as reason enough that their children should not be forced into school "to root out of their minds their old belief and plant White men's beliefs in their place," he contrasted Hopi religion to Christianity and found the former infinitely superior. Thus, like Stephen, Fewkes also thought he was racing against time to record Hopi ceremonies before they disappeared and used the assumption to justify his intrusions into sacred ceremonies.

But some Hopis had begun to resent ethnographers' intrusions; Fewkes, Stephen, and Keam "tried in various ways to induce the Snake Chief, Kopeli, to allow us to see the Snake washing (in the kiva). We found Kopeli willing to admit us, but some of the older and more conservative priests strongly objected." Fewkes talked his way in anyway, along with a partner, J.G. Owens.

Katsinas and Tihus. Following Stephen's (1893) lead in the earliest published account of a Katsina doll, Fewkes distinguished between Katsina *dolls*, or *tihu*, and the Katsinas themselves. Men make the dolls for their daughters, sisters, nieces, and other female relatives for distribution to them by the Katsinas during dances. The dolls are educational as well as artistic; they represent the Katsinas, but are not Katsinas themselves. On the other hand, the actual Katsinas are ancestral spirits:people who have died (Fewkes 1897, 1901, 1921). They are not the ancestors of the Hopi alone, but are the ancestors of other groups as well

-- Puebloans, Navajos, Apaches, Utes, and even White people. He also described performances by the clowns, which they did from March through June during and in between dances. Fewkes omitted some data out of deference to his Hopi consultants as well as to his anthropological readers: the clowns performed "many obscenities which cannot be mentioned in this place" (Fewkes 1892:48).

Maasaw. Fewkes (1902b) also produced the first description of the Hopi deity, Maasaw, God of Fire, Death, Germination, and the Underworld. Stephen had written just a few weeks before his death, of Maasaw hacking at his chest with a dull stone axe blade, trying to pull him into the land of the dead (Wade and McChesney 1980:12). Eventually Maasaw succeeded. Fewkes became so interested in Maasaw that, say Hopis, Maasaw came to visit him. Fewkes returned to Walpi in November, 1898. Fewkes started taking notes on the beginning of the Wuwutsim ceremony. After taking notes in the kiva all day, he was asked to "go away and stay in his house for Maasaw was coming, and no outside person was ever allowed to see what was going on." Fewkes did go away. But Hopis say that Maasaw satisfied Fewkes' curiosity by entering Fewkes' house despite a locked door. Asking Fewkes for a cigarette, Maasaw lit it with the fire of his breath. Telling Fewkes all he wanted to know about Maasaw, the deity than placed a spell on Fewkes; convinced him to believe in Maasaw; and turned Fewkes into a little child for the rest of the night. When Fewkes recovered, he promptly departed, so the story goes (Nequatewa 1936:121-123). Fewkes himself cited the outbreak of smallpox as the reason for his sudden departure.

H. R. Voth: *Missionary, Ethnographer, Collector, Photographer, Intruder, Befriender of the "Hostiles"*

Henrich Voth was another matter entirely. Unlike Fewkes and Stephen, who came to the Hopi villages for specific ethnological purposes, Voth came as a Mennonite missionary. He established a mission at the foot of Third Mesa. His wife gave sewing lessons and held prayer meetings for Hopi women until her death in 1901 and Voth built a little church and school. Eventually another Mennonite, a Miss Collins, joined them and taught secular as well as religious subjects in the school.

Voth was enigmatic in more ways than one: having come to Oraibi as a missionary, he departed without having made a single convert. Ostensibly an agent of acculturation, he was befriended by one of the leaders of the "conservative" or "Hostile" faction, Yukiwma, who seems to have returned the friendship. Although he worked on a Hopi hymnal and a Hopi version of the New Testament, his most important work consisted in producing, word for word, Hopi prayers and chants, and in describing Hopi religious rituals in minute detail. He took hundreds of photographs; reproduced Hopi altars and ceremonial paraphernalia; amassed two large collections of material items, ceremonial as well as utilitarian; and made meticulous observations of ceremonies and transcriptions of Hopi prayers in Hopi language. He noted the ritual cross-dressing of women in men's clothing during Maraw, and the women's good-naturedly taunting the men with songs "of a phallic or even of an obscene nature" (Voth 1912:29-32).[15]

Hopis remembered Voth in the 1960s less as a missionary than as an intruder who barged into kivas and was constantly underfoot. Evidently his alliance with some leaders provided him with a certain entre, but his rapport was limited. He returned several times as a collector. He helped George Dorsey assemble a collection for the Field Museum's Stanley McCormick Expedition out of Chicago. One of his collections eventually went into the Fred Harvey Company's "Hopi House" at Grand Canyon; another went to George Heye in 1918 for the Heye Foundation's Museum of the American Indian in New York city, now divided between the Old Customs House in Battery Park and the new National Museum of the American Indian in Washington, D.C.

The Overall Sense of Hopi Ceremonialism

Stephen, Fewkes, and Voth discovered the overall sense of Hopi ceremonialism: the bringing of rain; production of fertility and fecundity; the passage of season so that cold would beget warmth; the invocation of assistance and approval from the shades of ancestor. But were Hopis hoping to achieve anything else besides favorable material conditions in the highly complex, colorful, symbolic interlocking rituals? Did the rituals seek to replace the wildness of undisciplined imagination and fear with the insight of controlled imagery and intentional visualization? Was there a kind of revelatory series of levels, at which the initiate or participant attained ever greater knowledge of the physiological world and how it worked? Was there a point at which an individual broadened his or her sense of self to the point that "self" and "group" or "person" and "community" merged, at least in the mind? Could an individual feel and remember making the transitions from fledgling apprenticeship to stewardship of traditions to master of destiny? Did individuals progressively annul more and more of their own personal histories and "become" the essence of fate, destiny, and tradition through periodic rituals that abolished normal time and sought collective regeneration of humanity and nature in a kind of timeless sequence of repeatable processes? Did repetitions of rituals slowly but inexorably bring the participants from the shadowy, reflective non-reality of the world of the living into the "true," archetypical world of the eternal, that is, of the non-living, the ancestors, where primal forces hold sway and replace the confusion of the shadowy world of the living? Would the minds of high ceremonial officers become more highly integrated and entwined with each other than would the minds of ordinary initiates? Did the high ceremonial officers conducting a ceremony actually experience feelings of mind-body integration different from those felt by mere observers? Would they see themselves as not only the primary guardians of, but also responsible for, the configuration of cosmic energy forces causing not only chemical and physical processes of nature such as rain and growth of crops, but also the psychic order of human existence, Hopi or otherwise? Neither Fewkes nor Stephen nor Voth ever said. Or perhaps they never were told, or never asked.

Lowie and Parsons: In Pursuit of Clans

Robert Lowie (1917, 1929a, 1929b) concentrated on establishing Hopi social institutions within larger regional cultural patterns. He observed that the Hopi bore almost no cultural resemblance to their nearest linguistic neighbors, the Shoshone, Paiute, and Ute. Rather, the Hopis were unmistakably Puebloans: not only did they live in permanent villages organized around plazas, like the Puebloans, but also their religion had many of the same deities as Puebloan religion. They used kivas for certain esoteric rites and preparations; they had secret societies that performed them; and many of the rituals themselves were similar to those of Zuni, Acoma, Laguna, and the Rio Grande Pueblos. It was to be expected that their social organization would also show Puebloan traits.

Rotation in Politico-Religious Office. Lowie discovered that at Mishongnovi, on Second Mesa, the Gray Flute and Blue Flute societies leaders were of completely different clans than they were on First Mesa. There was also something else important about Mishongnovi: the town chieftaincy, that is, the position of Kikmongwi, rotated among the Bear, Cloud, and Parrot Clans, a specific man from each taking a four-year term. This pattern may have reflected the demographic differences between Mishongnovi and the First Mesa villages; the latter's population numbered four to five times that of Mishongnovi.

Clan Exogamy. Lowie concluded that the concept of clan exerted a deep influence on how Hopis perceive their relatives, even though Hopis used Uto-Aztecan kin terms that are close to those of Shoshonean languages that do not have the term or concept, "clan." Hopis' emphasis on clans constituted a distinguishing feature of Hopi life. Hopis not only practiced clan exogamy, that is, forbidding marriage between members of the same clan or people whose clans were in the same "clan cluster" but also they classed many relatives and affines together on the basis of clan. All members of spouse's clan, for example, were *mowi*. For another example, all of a person's father's sister's female's descendants in the female line would be called "aunt," even after the father's sister had died and the person in question was very old. An octogenarian would call his aunt's great-great-granddaughter, that is, the daughter of the aunt's granddaughter's daughter, who would be the age of his own granddaughter, "aunt," because she was not only his aunt's direct lineal descendant, but also was of her clan and thus stood in the same clan-defined relationship to him.

Clan Splittings and "Phratries." Lowie suggested that the concept of clan defined most of what Hopi social organization is all about. He reflected on the fact that not only were clans ranked with respect to one another, but also, they seemed to wax, wane, combine, split, and recombine into clan clusters. Thus, in this ranking system, mobility upward was possible, as was mobility downward. A clan might die out, but memory of the original clan was maintained by maintaining knowledge of the clan name. Conversely, a clan might split, necessitating a new clan name for the new segment.

For examples, Hopis at Walpi told him that the reason for the existence of a Cloud-Corn clan, that is, a single clan with two names, was *not* that they were "two originally distinct clans that have become joined, but *one* clan with two names" (Lowie 1929b:309). "This is the native conception of the matter as repeatedly impressed on me on the First mesa," he noted. In other words, the clans were in the process of fissioning, of splitting, of segmenting. Thus, the different clan clusters (which Titiev and Eggan later somewhat misleadingly would call "phratries"), had resulted more from splitting than from lumping. Lowie found that this segmentation process went through an initial stage of multiple lineages. After several generations, when these matrilineages had become large, each would embrace a separate name, and would eventually become, conceptually, separate clans. But Lowie also reported a "lumping" situation in which one clan adopted another when its members had dwindled to just one or two men.

Thus, there were two processes that might result in Hopis remembering and naming more clans than were represented by actual matrilineages or even persons in a particular village: one was the process of a large clan fissioning; the other was the process of one or more smaller clans merging and thus taking over the shrinking clan's ceremonial offices. Once the shrinking clan was extinct, its memory would be kept alive by its name being linked to the name of the succeeding clan, and by that clan's maintenance of stewardship of the extinct clan's *wuya* and ceremony.

Elsie Clews Parsons: Historically Particularistic Reconstructor of the Grand Scheme of Hopi and Pueblo Clans, Lineages, and Ceremonialism

Elsie Clews Parsons was the last of the great historical particularists to do research on the Hopi. An independently wealthy clinical psychologist and author of several books on feminine socio-psychology, Parsons earned a Ph.D. in Anthropology under Franz Boas and set forth on a new career as an ethnologist in 1919. Although some of her more speculative suggestions have not held up over time (Brew 1949; Eggan 1950:77) she vigorously pursued the historical particularist concern with cultural elements or traits, took up the unilineal evolutionists' enchantment with ceremonialism and folklore, and also continued investigations of kinship begun by Lowie. Much of her contribution to Hopi ethnology lay in her comparisons between Hopis and Zunis.

She did virtually the first complete study of Zuni witchcraft, comparing it to Hopi, and concluding that it was not very prominent in Hopi concerns (Parsons 1927), at least not in comparison to Zuni, where witches were punished with public floggings following a tribunal (cf. Roscoe 1991:100-105). Less than two decades later, however, Titiev (1943:557) would conclude that "no one can study the Hopi or any other Pueblo tribe without reaching the conclusion that the fear of witches plays a vital part in their patterns of culture. The highest officers in a pueblo may be accused of witchcraft," he said (Titiev 1943:553) "sometimes for no better reason than that they hold positions of such extraordinary importance. "A witch, *powaka*, literally "spirit" (Voegelin and Voegelin 1957:44), is thought to have the power to affect people from a distance. Witches are feared because of this power and are thought to cause misfortune. They use magic to influence human behavior, circumstances of the natural world, or the outcome of an event at a distance from the event, circumstances, or person.

Clans, Lineages, and Wuyas

Relying heavily on Stephen's field notes, eventually organizing, editing and publishing them in two volumes 40 years after Stephen's death, and relying equally on Lowie's work, Parsons used comparative methodology in the naturalist convention to produce an overall picture of Puebloan social organization and ceremonialism (Parsons 1921, 1923, 1926, 1932, 1933, 1939). Taking up the question of clans and their splittings and their relationships to ceremonies, she clarified the disposition of the clan *wuya* if a clan split.[16] The clan's ceremonial objects stayed at *the* clan house, even after a clan split. The eldest female assuming the female leadership of the original clan continued to be the custodian of the *wuya* and continued to *the* clan house continued to serve as the clan house for the "new" clan.

Parsons suggested that Hopi clans originally developed from lineages, citing as evidence the fact that Hopis had no word for "lineage," but that the term *wuya* more or less designated the *concept* of clan, even though it was not necessarily the same as the social scientist's *descriptive sociological picture* of the clan as being a social category filled with people. *Wuya*, she said, means much more than the object of the totemic concept and what it symbolizes. It also conveys the clan's ancestral purpose and tradition; the collective motivation that all members of the clan should have, in theory, to each other and to fulfill the clan's purpose, destiny, responsibility, and obligation; and the concept of stewardship. Stewardship is also summarized in the words *nawis*, "must, irrespective of consequence, take some action;" and in the phrases, *tina:tyaw-yingwa*," they guard, look after, take care of" (it) and *nawistota*, "they are willing to obliged to" (Voegelin and Voegelin 1957:41, 42, 53). Parsons found that clan members may personify their *wuya* by addressing it by a kinship term, giving it offerings of food from time to time, and even praying to it for guidance, protection, and good crops.

Parsons found several important cases at First Mesa and Shungopavi in which leadership of several secret societies had changed radically from one clan to another, and in which the ceremonial responsibilities of one particular secret society were taken over nearly completely by the members of another. Thus it was not only clans which provided the Hopi social fabric with strength and flexibility; it was also the ceremonial structure as well. She also (Parsons 1933) confirmed the hierarchical nature of Hopi leadership.

In *Pueblo Indian Religion* (Parsons 1939), she completed documentation of a regional grand scheme that showed the functional and structural equivalents and parallels among all Puebloan religious concepts, deities, and ceremonies, including those of the Hopi, Navajo, Apache, and other southwestern cultures. For example, she found that the concept of elder-and-younger-brother was linked to that of the two "war gods," as well as to that of two brothers prominent in myth and folklore and to two powerful deities that figure in the Soyal ceremony of the Hopi and other equivalent ceremonies of other cultures. She documented a large number of spiritual entities aside from Katsinas and *wuyas* that definitely merited the label "pantheistic" for Hopi religion. Not only did Hopis address prayers to a number of different Gods and Goddesses, but also, most of the secret rituals of the secret societies involved prayers and offerings to spiritual entities personified in effigies, many of them comprising components of altars or sand paintings. The only Hopi deity she found that had no equivalent in any of the other Pueblos was Maasaw.

Structural-Functionalism: A Key to Analyzing Hopi Society

A new generation of anthropologists followed hard on the heels of the historical particularists. Structural-functionalists Mischa Titiev and Fred Eggan participated in an ethnographic field school taught by Leslie White in Hopiland in 1932. Although White would later coin the concept of "universal evolutionism," basing the concept on an "energy" theory of history, he did not publish his initial article on the topic until 1943 (White 1943) and cannot be considered an evolutionist at this time. In 1932, White used a naturalist convention that was perfectly compatible with historical particularism. So did Titiev and Eggan.

But they would eventually use a very different set up assumptions to analyze their data: the assumptions of structural-functionalism. The English anthropologist A.R. Radcliffe-Brown set the tone for such research by defining the social system as a set of "parts" working together with a sufficient degree of harmony and internal consistency to keep the society together. Looking at structural functionalism in 1953, Meyer Fortes (1953) called its impact "revolutionary. It enabled social anthropology to throw off the bonds of evolutionary historicism and to recognize itself, once and for all, as a separate discipline concerned with 'mechanism and function.'" For the structural-functionalists, ethnological research was a search for mechanical order, for the well-oiled parts of society that kept people in their places and kept the whole organism functioning, for the latent and hidden services that customs performed without their practitioners being aware of them.

The structural-functionalists searched for comparisons in order to establish scientific laws that would be generally predictive regarding human behavior and social institutions, laws that would say, "Because we find custom x, we will undoubtedly find custom y because x is functionally related to (or dependent on) y." Like the evolutionists and the historical particularists, the structural-functionalists continued to use the naturalist method and to strive for detailed descriptions.

Just as the unilineal evolutionists had a blind spot about "progress," and the historical particularists about "speculative explanation," so too did the structural-functionalists have their blind spots. They tended to ignore cases in which people circumvented the rules; in which conflict dominated over solidarity; and in which a set of historical events over which the participants had little control and which might have originated largely outside the society itself completely changed the way a society functioned. Above all, they had a blind spot when it came to social and cultural change. Because their goal was to produce a picture of how a particular society functioned, they tended to collapse time periods and describe life in kind of stable never-never-land, in which the way things were, constituted the way things would always be. Thus they saw no problem in combining their own observations with reconstructions of life-as-it-had-been on the basis of what their consultants remembered. Just as long as it all fit, and as long as it all made sense.

Mischa Titiev in Old Oraibi: 1932-1934

Mischa Titiev's (1944) *Old Oraibi: A Study of the Hopi Indians of Third Mesa* does not give a good, easy read. Its organization is whimsical. Its style is turgid. Its narrative bristles with arcane details. But its messages are clear; its authoritativeness is unmistakable; and its author's involvement with his subject is unassailable.

Titiev came to the Hopi villages in the summer of 1932 along with Edward Kennard, Fred Eggan, Jess Spirer and George Devereaux. The participants in White's field school made their headquarters in a small, newly-built house in Kykotsmovi, a village that had been established at the foot of Third Mesa around 1900. White had already begun his series of comprehensive studies of five of the seven Keres-speaking Pueblos (Acoma, Sia, Santa Ana, San Felipe, Santo Domingo) and tried to reconstruct Oraibi's social organization using W.H.R. Rivers' (1910) genealogical method. His results were dubiously successful.

Titiev returned in August, 1933 and lived in Old Oraibi through March, 1934. He returned for the summers of 1937 and 1940, and began writing his ethnography in 1941. Known as "Mischhoya" (Little-boy-Misch), he became a "participant-observer," being invited to weddings; helping in harvest and planting; and even being pulled into a dance line during a Katsina dance along with Fred Eggan. His primary consultants were Don Talayesva, soon to gain fame as "Sun Chief"; Tawakwaptiwa, the Kikmongwi; Tawakwaptiwa's son and daughter; and their spouses.

Like Stephen, Fewkes, Lowie and Parsons before him, Titiev was fascinated with how Hopis had created their unique pattern of kinship, clans, households, secret societies, and ceremonies and tackled nearly a complete inventory of ethnographic subjects: social organization, politics, economics, religion. Structural-functionalism dominated Titiev's analysis[17] but he seems to have been influenced by behavioral psychology, speculating and marveling on what he called the "Group Mind" that guided much of Hopis behavior: "a group of individual minds all of which have been culturally conditioned to react in patterned ways to certain stimuli" (Titiev 1972:260). Titiev was particularly interested in split of 1906 and in Oraibi's pre-1906 social organization.

Reconstructing a Picture of Oraibi's Social Organization

His work was a reconstruction. He combined his observations at Oraibi with data from long, intensive interviews, welding together "digests of the literature published by many other investigators" with "as much fresh material as I have been able to gather in the field" in order "to present the reader with a single comprehensive picture of Hopi life" (Titiev 1944:4) as it had functioned between about 1880 and 1910.

Titiev started building his comprehensive picture with the system of kinship and marriage, then moving to households, lineages, clans, and clan-clusters, which he called, "phratries," and a discussion of what mechanisms, if any, integrated clans and villages together. "One thing was clearly demonstrated by the summer's work at Oraibi in 1932," said Titiev, "and that was that the genealogical approach alone would not solve the problem of Hopi lineages, clans, and phratries" (Titiev 1944:49). In other words, Hopi society was not held together by kin ties alone. By using White's data; house plans and censuses done by Mindeleff and Stephen in the 1880s; and his own interviews with several informants on the clan affiliations of each household's members, Titiev achieved a picture of Old Oraibi's social organization as of 1890 of which he was reasonably confident. The various informants and sources of information agreed with one another within a degree of statistically reliable accuracy - - 1.9% (Titiev 1944:51).

The "Order of Closeness." Working from this data base, he determined that extensions of kinship, real and fictive, as well as households formed by marriage and affinal ties, operated like a series of concentric circles, moving outward from the individual in a kind of spiral.[18] This "order of closeness" more or less corresponded to the strength of the individual's loyalties to particular categories of persons. Kin groups and the secret societies -- also based on fictive kin ties -- operated as task groups that assembled for specific, often temporary and expedient purposes. They did not constitute discrete, mutually exclusive groups.

Titiev (1944:13) worked out what he called the "order of closeness" for any particular individual: (1) immediate family, but especially children or spouse or siblings of opposite gender; (2) Mother's Sister and Mother's Sister's children; (3) Others of the household, often elderly uncles, a grandparent, a niece or nephew, or cousins; (4) Own clan; (5) Father's household; (6) Own phratry (i.e., clans linked to one's own in the same clan-cluster); (7) Farther's Sister, other members of father's clan, and father's phratry; (8) Ceremonial father and ceremonial father's clan and phratry; (9) Doctor father and doctor father's clan and phratry, if the individual in question had been treated by a medicine man.

Clans, Water, Land, and Households. Clans had greater solidarity and commanded more loyalty than the village since they owned water rights as well as land and *wuyas* (Titiev 1944:69) But the basic feature of Hopi social organization was really the matrilineage: a "woman, her daughters, and occasionally a granddaughter" (Titiev 1944:7), in theory all bringing up their children under the same roof, but in reality beginning to set up their own households, separately, when possible even as early as the 1890s. Thus time and succeeding generations -- straightforward demographic processes -- resulted in the splitting of lineages into separate, named clans (Titiev 1944:46-48).

Demography and "Phratries." Parsons and Titiev independently came up with the idea of how Hopi phratries developed: the phratries were not at all isomorphic with regard to one another, but rather, developed unevenly, also as a result of demographic processes. As a lineage got large enough to split into clans, one or both of the clans, or one lineage within one of the clans, might in turn undergo the same process. The phratries, then, might have anywhere from one to half a dozen clans at any point in history. Although Titiev (1944:46-48, 57) hypothetically pictured phratries arising from the splitting of a large clan into several extended lineages, he also acknowledged the possibility that phratries could "collapse" again into one clan with several names. Such an event might result from demographic shrinkage due to a lower survival rate for women than for men. Demographic shrinkage had been happening since the 1850s. Without women, a clan or lineage would die out. In order to keep its memory alive, members of a related clan -- descendants of persons who at one time were closely related, matrilateral cousins or maybe even sisters, but whose exact ties with one another had been forgotten -- might recombine with the clan to which it was linked. Thus one clan could acquire several *wuyas* and different clan names, and a single individual might be identifiable under several clan names. For example, one man was Parrot clan in one context and Katsina clan in another (Titiev 1944; 52-54). Titiev also noted a case of a woman "jumping" from one phratry to another: from Sun's Forehead to Reed, because she had quarrelled with her own clan mates (Titiev 1944:57).

Thus it was really the female-centered household that constituted the most important social organizational unit of daily life.[19]

Ceremonialism and Hopi Social Structure

Even most Hopis did not have full picture of Hopi religion for several reasons. Each secret society had rituals to which only its members were privy, arguing for Hopi ceremonialism being just what many Hopis said it was: a collection of rituals thrown together as a result of their having been brought by various clans at different times.[20] Titiev (1944:96, 100) sought to make sense of Hopi ceremonialism as a "coherent picture" because it "buttressed" the other parts of Hopi social organization. Titiev noted that the real building blocks of Hopi society were the matrilineages, headed by females, that owned the house and in some cases, the *wuyas*. These matrilineages, consisting of 3 or 4 generations at best, were necessarily small in size and only weakly connected with other matrilineages of the clan and other clans of the clan-cluster, or phratry. This weakness, Titiev felt, would endanger the coherence of any single village to the point that some other social "glue" or "buttress" was necessary.[21]

The Dead and the Underworld. Titiev (1944:107) found the single driving motivation for all ceremonies to be "a belief in the continuity of life after death." The Underworld preceded, superseded, and mirrored earthly life, with elements of hell and purgatory as well as limbo, but with little corresponding to heaven (Titiev 1941). The distinction between "this world" and the "Underworld" was replicated in the changes marked by sunrise and sunset -- day is the "Upper World" of the living, and night is the "Lower World" of the Dead -- as well as by division of the ceremonial year into the world of the ancestors -- the Katsinas (December-July) -- and the world of earthly life (July-December). "The entire complex of Hopi religious behavior stands revealed," he said, "as a unified attempt to safeguard Hopi society from the danger of disintegration and dissolution" (Titiev 1944:178), by a refusal to admit death as a finality to life, as is the case in all religions incorporating ancestor veneration.

Men's Initiations: Rebirth and Emergence. The men's initiations, which Titiev called "Tribal Initiations" were "the most complicated and among the most vital of all Hopi ceremonies." But by 1934 the initiations had lapsed in Oraibi. They had never been performed in Moenkopi, Kykotsmovi, or Bacavi. Thus Titiev was forced to rely on interviews with a few old men; observance of the few public aspects of the ceremonies at Hotevilla; and the incomplete descriptions provided by Fewkes and

Stephen from First Mesa. The deity Maasaw featured prominently in some of the rights, as did his female counterpart, Tawapongtumsi ("Sand-Altar Woman") as did Alosaka, a Sun God; Muyingwa, god of fertility; Mocking Bird, who figures prominently in a version of the Origin myth; and Talautumsi, goddess of childbirth, who is regarded as the mother of the initiates, who are likened to helpless little birds. The initiations accomplished a "rebirth" of the men and a renewal of contacts between the living and the dead, that is, between the people of the previous world and the people of this world. "Emergence" and "rebirth" provided the metaphors for the initiation ceremonies and their significance.

Warfare, Warrior Sodalities, and Warrior Rituals

Men, Women, Momtsit, and Maraw. Warfare had previously been far more important than was evident in 1934. Warfare and its significance had been abandoned quite quickly. But formerly, every male had been expected to join the *Momtsit,* Oraibi's equivalent to Walpi's *Kaletakwimkya.* Two clans owned the Momtsit jointly: Kookop and Spider, whose members were among the few complete clans to vacate Oraibi wholesale for Hotevilla and Bacavi in the split of 1906. In his field notes, Titiev (1972:282) had originally hypothesized that the coming of the whites and the consequent extinction of the Momtsit as a functionally meaningful secret society had something to do with the Kookop and Spider clans leading the "Hostile" faction into a state of rebellion. (See Chapter Five.) But he never followed up on this hypothesis.

Momtsit functioned with four levels: the ceremonial officers; the *real* warriors who had openly acknowledged killing an enemy and scalping him and had undergone a special ritual; the Nakwawimkyam (Stick-Swallower Society members); and the ordinary Kaletaka, the warrior who may or may not have killed anyone in battle. The Momtsit appear to have venerated many of the most important deities: Pukonghoya, the elder brother, in this case known as the elder war twin; Palongahoya, the younger war twin; Maasaw; Gogyang Wuuti (Spider Woman); Sotukinangwu'u, the main Sky deity; either Alosaka or Tawa, the Sun; and Songwuka, the Milky Way deity. They constructed an altar with the six directions -- the four cardinal points plus zenith and nadir, starting with north and moving clockwise, represented by Mountain Lion, Wolf, Wildcat, Bear, Kwatoko (Vulture?) for above and Snake for below.

Hopis appear to have gone "on the warpath" regularly every fall, following harvest, until the 1870s. They would celebrate their return by dancing with scalps. Women, especially unmarried girls, would also dance, choosing for their partners those returned warriors that caught their fancy. The warriors distributed booty gotten from the warpath, and the girls' parents would also distribute presents. In fact, the distribution became so prominent in later years that the dance came to be known as "Market Dance," and some of its aspects may have been absorbed by the "women's choice" Butterfly and other social dances now done in August and September and into the Lalakon, the "Basket Dance," done by women in October, when they throw presents to the men. Was the Momtsit crucial in keeping any single village together? The answer is not immediately evident. All of the villages had let their warrior societies atrophy. But Momtsit's inclusion of all adult men in a village must have had a galvanizing effect that no other secret society could have had.

The women's societies must have had a similarly equivalent integrative function. The Maraw included nearly all adult females in a particular village and had overlapping memberships with the Lalakon and Oaqol. In fact, Oaqol (Owakult) appears to have been developed "late" (Titiev 1944:169) at First Mesa and to have diffused from there to Second and Third Mesas. If the "women's choice" of partners in the Butterfly and other social dances of the 20th Century really were transferred from the Momtsit and Kaletakwimkya rituals, the maintenance of that custom plus the persistence of one or more of the women's societies in all but two villages may reflect an interesting case of the coalescence of women's solidarity in the face of the tendency for men's to splinter in the latter half of the Nineteenth Century.

Law and Political Control: "Who Governs" Reconsidered

Titiev concluded that seven villages functioned independently of every other; Shipaulovi (Shungopavi's daughter village), Sichomovi and Tewa (Walpi's daughter and ally villages) and Moenkopi(Oraibi's daughter village) were subordinate to the main three, but the new villages, Bacavi, Hotevilla, and Kykotsmovi ("New Oraibi") were as independent as Walpi, Shungopavi, Mishongnovi, and Oraibi. No single village dominated all the others, and even within the various villages, the hierarchy of chiefs in the village councils varied from village to village, as did the chiefs' clan affiliations. Even the hierarchy within a particular village varied over the years.

Titiev could discover neither legislative nor judicial structures. Instead, the phrase "*pi um i*," "it's up to you," seemed to characterize the limit of direct sanctions. "It is most startling," noted Titiev (1972:80), "to learn that even the performance of an important ritual is left entirely to the will of its owner." This bent toward individuality seemed to be balanced, however, by "the power of public opinion." "The known fact that 'people will talk,'" noted Titiev (1972:43) "is an ever-present deterrent from wrongdoing." Gossip, criticism fear of criticism, and anxiety at the possibility of others' jealousy, thought Titiev, constituted powerful mechanisms for social control as well as secrecy (Titiev 1972:27, 43-44, 56, 81): what people did not know about, they could not gossip about.

Anthropologist Harold Colton (1934) at the Museum of Northern Arizona had put together a brief summary of Hopi law and Titiev did discover some enforcement mechanisms: the war chief and certain Katsinas. The war chief could punish miscreants and might be aided by a Katsina. However, the Katsina could also punish miscreants independently. War chiefs' powers had diminished considerably since U.S. troops had begun enforcing the *Pax Americana* successfully in the 1870s. But the position of war chief was still being filled well into the first half of the 20th Century. And Titiev witnessed a confrontation between a war chief and an enforcing Katsina during a communal work party, called by the Kikmongwi. The war chief refused to perform a certain task. The Katsina confronted him. But the war chief defied the Katsina and got his way. Finally, the Kikmongwi dismissed the war chief from the work party.

This particular war chief had one additional aid in 1934: appointment as judge from the U.S. Indian agent. As we shall see, such an appointment virtually doubled the degree of authority which the war chief might have already had, and indicates the importance of the Anglo-American in the reconfiguration of Hopi culture.

Titiev also noted an important prerogative held by two of the four men's secret societies: Kwan (One Horn) and Ahl (Two-Horns) that seemed to parallel or even surpass those of the war chief, the Kikmongwi and the punisher Katsinas as village policemen. No initiations can proceed until the Kwan men had garnered at least one candidate for their initiation, and Kwan and Ahl men patrolled the village during initiations, enforcing the secrecy ban, symbolized by a line of corn meal drawn across the entrances to the village and on the road leading to it. People are forced to remain indoors without glancing outside, and if the Kwans catch an intruder, they have the right to beat him or even to put him to death. It is the Kwans who have the sole power to install the village chief and other "high officers" (Titiev 1944:139).

The importance of the Kwans' role, and especially that of the chief of the Kwan society, would become important at Bacavi and Hotevilla in later years in a way that Titiev would not have predicted. But Titiev would not speculate very long on what he could not demonstrate. He suggested only (Titiev 1944:66, 55) that perhaps legislative functions had at one time been "more pronounced," referring to Franciscan missionary Silvestre Escalante's last visit to the Hopis in 1776. Escalante had written to his superiors that this "rebellious province" maintained "formidable penalties against those who were found to have been talking with the fathers in the matter of religion." Six years later, another Franciscan friar, Father Morfi, had even referred to Oraibi as being "like the capital of the province the largest and best arranged of all" (Titiev 1944:69). Nonetheless, Titiev (1944:68) concluded that there was no such thing as a "Hopi state" because "never has a leader arisen to mould the autonomous villages into la co-ordinated unit worthy of being called a tribe."

Had the Spaniards perceived a system of domination and enforcement where there really was one, simply because their own empire had been arranged that way? Could one read too much into the authority of the war chief, the Katsinas, the Kikmongwi, the Kwan and Ahl chiefs, the village chiefs' hierarchy? Or was Titiev overlooking a part of the system he was trying to reconstruct? Could it be that the combined impacts of Navajo and Mexican raids; severe and rapid depopulation; radical shifts in the balance of power; and imposition of U.S. hegemony had virtually destroyed an internal legislative system that had formerly granted power to some and denied it to others? Titiev did not confront these questions directly, although his research obviously made him aware of them. Sidestepping the question of power and authority in Hopi society would lead subsequent ethnographers to portray the Hopi as functionally an egalitarian society with only minor authority vested in the village chief (Hieb 1979:181). But unequal access to political power and economic resources was very real, and was exacerbated by material conditions preceding the Oraibi Split.

The Oraibi Split of 1906

Titiev wrote what was then the most comprehensive account of the Split of 1906, attributing it to an inherent tendency of Pueblo societies to factionate (Titiev 1944:99). The idea was not without its detractors: Leslie White pointed to the role of foreign cultural influences and disputes over their acceptance or rejection as a likely determining variable. Titiev's perception of the split as well as that of other researchers fifty years later will be covered in Chapter Five.

The Clan as Lineage: Fred Eggan's Functionalist Research[22]

Fred Eggan's research paralleled that of Titiev. Eggan (1950) placed Hopi social organization in a regional context, systematically comparing the Hopi with the Hopi-Tewa at Hano; the Zuni; and the Keres-speaking Pueblos of Acoma and Laguna. He drew further comparisons with the Eastern Pueblos along the Rio Grande and in general with other north American Indian tribes. He relied heavily on the works of Stephen, Fewkes, Voth, Lowie, and Parsons,[23] and on Titiev's data and analysis.

Eggan viewed society as a group of individuals who have adjusted their interests sufficiently to co-operate in satisfying their various needs. Eggan concluded that the Hopi rested on one end of a continuum. On the Hopi end, he saw -- as did Titiev -- the primary unit of social organization as the matrilineage, that is, the group of people related to each other over four or five generations through female descent, who were born in the same house and at one time were members of that household, and the children of the female members of that household. "In Hopi thinking," he noted, "the 'clan' and the 'clanhouse' are the important units" (Eggan 1950:337 n17). But while Hopis might generalize lineages as clans, they clearly differentiated the various "households" -- actually lineages -- within a clan. A clan could encompass anywhere from one to six separate extended lineages. The *lineage,* said Eggan (1950:119) is of primary importance because it contains the *mechanism* for transmitting rights, duties, land, houses, and ritual knowledge, and thus assumes vital importance with respect to status.

Clan Names and Lineage Stewardship. A Hopi clan did not necessarily correspond to standard definitions of "clan" in anthropological literature. For one thing, the Hopi clan is a kind of corporation, holding land, houses, and ceremonial knowledge and property "in trust" for future generations (Eggan 1950:110), but does not have either residential unity or any cohesion in terms of economic production.[24] For another thing, Eggan documented the fact that one lineage's stewardship of clan-owned ceremonies could result in its being called by a different clan name from another lineage; such was the case at Shungopavi, where a new Kikmongwi had been chosen from one lineage which now called itself the "Black Bear Clan" and thereby distinguished itself from its cousins, the "Gray Bear Clan"! Eggan documented instances of lineages and clans, switching phratries in historic times. At First Mesa, such a process had occurred between 1880 and 1944, when the village chieftaincy - the role of Kikmongwi - shifted from the Bear to the "Millet"[25] and finally to the Flute clan, each of which is in three separate phratries at other villages (Eggan 1950:98-99; 66-67). The "Millet" clan, while formerly grouped with the Maasaw, Kookop, and Coyote clans, had recently come to be grouped with the Horn and Deer clans, because it took over stewardship of the Flute ceremony from the Flute clan, which had been grouped with the Horn and Deer clans before it died out. The Rabbit clan, while constituting its own phratry at First Mesa, had recently joined Parrot and Katsina clans at Third Mesa, for similar reasons (Eggan 1950:63-79). He also found varying conceptualizations of *wuya*; "Where the *wuya* is of interest primarily to the clan it is usually called by the kin term for 'mother's brother,' but where it is of interest to all Hopi it may be called 'father,' 'mother,' or 'grandmother'" (Eggan 1950:114).

Hopi Social and Ceremonial Organization: Summary[26]

Four researchers -- Lowie, Parsons, Eggan, and Titiev -- using two different methodological approaches, historical particularism and structural-functionalism, came to the same conclusions about Hopi social organization. These conclusions affirmed the earlier observations of Stephen, Fewkes, and Voth. Hopi society was divided in 1890 into five maximal socio-political units: Walpi/Sichomovi; Hano-Tewa; Shungopavi/Shipaulovi; Mishongnovi; and Oraibi/Moenkopi. Following the Oraibi split, Bacavi, Hotevilla and Kykotsmovi were added. A similar kind of social organization was replicated in each of these units to greater or lesser extents. Secret ceremonial societies, most of them controlled by male "chiefs" and two to three headed by female "chiefs," cut across and integrated the various minimal parts of each maximal socio-political unit.

Only occasionally voluntary alliances among these maximal units could unite all Hopis in a single organization. No integrative mechanisms connected these units with one another otherwise. Within each maximal socio-political unit, clans and clan-groups regulated marriage through exogamy. Clans owned land, water rights, houses, and ceremonies. Clans were ranked with regard to one another, and these rankings were expressed through religious ceremonial ideology. Clans were flexible units, varying in size and composition in accordance with social and demographic variables. The basic units of the clan system were matrilineages that either constituted the entire entity of a particular clan by owning the clan lands, ceremonies, *wuyas*, and clan house, or had variable access to political and economic powers and privileges within a clan-group, or "phratry." Such variable access defined the matrilineage's relative rank within the particular socio-political unit. Although certain clans were ideologically associated with certain ranks and ceremonial statuses, in reality the particular clans and matrilineages occupying particular statuses varied greatly from one socio-political unit to another, and even *within* a socio-political unit over time. Within the clan-and-matrilineage system, the minimal unit was the female-headed household.[27]

Women's Power and Men's Ambivalence

Because Hopi clans, matrilineages, and households played a pivotal role in the topic of the next chapter -- the Oraibi Split of 1906 -- and because an understanding of women's roles is absolutely crucial for understanding how and why the clans, matrilineages, and households played that pivotal role, a review of men's and women's relationships on the cusp of the 20th Century rounds out this chapter. The review is based on Titiev (1944); Eggan (1950); Stephen (1936) and Parsons (1921, 1926, 1932).

Under no circumstances, could men have dominated Hopi society completely at the expense of women. Women owned the houses, even if it was their husbands that built them. Women owned the clan land. Women owned the produce from the land (Forde 1931:379-371). Women owned the seeds that were planted and even controlled the rights to particular varieties of crops. A man depended on his mother to give him seeds that he planted in the first year of residence in his wife's household, and thereafter depended on his wife's lineage's seeds (Whiting 1937). A woman reinforced her claim to land and its produce by having her husband farm it. A woman who was a clan's eldest member would have several fields at her disposal and would distribute them to her daughters upon their marriages. She would also have the right and the responsibility to settle any disputes concerning land use.

A clan's eldest female was known as the "clan mother" and also, of course, held the *wuya*, the "mother" or "heart" of a ceremony. If her husband happened to be chief of the secret society performing "her" ceremony, an elderly lady might well be the locus of a great many potential loyalties, even if those loyalties were not all of a personal nature. As Schlegel (1977:254) has noted, in Hopi society, "women usually get their way."

Several developments in the last quarter of the Nineteenth Century began to create conditions under which a rise in the power of men and a change from matrilineality to patrilineality might be predicted (Martin and Voorhies 1975): growth in the importance of large herd animals; political influence from a larger society of more hierarchically organized neighbors, the Americans; permanent invasion of the ecological niche by communities of Navajos; and the possibility for men to acquire economic wealth independently of women through selling labor, crafts, livestock, and wool. Deterioration of climatic conditions and consequent threats to men's livelihoods as farmers accompanied these developments and formed the context within which Oraibi split and disrupted not only relationships between the genders, between men and women, but also upset the delicate balance in which the ceremonial system had held male solidarity in Oraibi. It is to the split and its context that we now turn.

5

The Oraibi Split of 1906 and the Great Transformation

Conflict

On a hot and windy summer's day in June, 1891, seven cavalry, a school teacher, and a government bureaucrat waited uneasily outside Oraibi. Inside the village, 300 men held bows and shields, waiting to train arrows on the little band of intruders. Five deities associated with war, and rarely seen publicly in recent years, appeared in the plaza. But the war never happened. The incident was the second of several confrontations between Hopis and the U.S. Government. These confrontations come to a boiling point in the Split of 1906. But the split would not culminate what had been begun; rather, it would institutionalize it.

Although they have been attributed by various authors to a host of mutually exclusive variables including population pressure on scarce farmlands (Bradfield 1971); a conspiracy to fulfill Hopi prophecy (Whiteley 1988a, 1988b; Krutz 1973); and the structurally factionalizing components of Hopi social organization that rests on balancing the disintegrative principles of the lineage against the integrative principles of sodality and village (Titiev 1944), ruptures in the social fabric of Oraibi between 1895 and 1910 were strongly conditioned by political factors revolving around Hopis' relationships with the U.S. Government. The events are well documented; their significance remains prismatic and multifaceted.

One curious feature of the Split is the role played by attitudes of hostility toward Americans on the part of Oraibi's residents. It was in 1858 that Mormon missionaries had to leave Oraibi owing to a dispute among clan leaders as to whether or not they matched the prophesied

Elder Brother. The leaders apparently lined up on opposing sides: some favored embracing the strangers, while others favored throwing them out. But the dispute seems to have been settled in the Mormons' favor. The explorer Ives regarded Oraibi's chief as "surly" in 1858. Kit Carson encountered anti-American and pro-Navajo sentiment in Oraibi in 1863. In 1872, special agent Crothers reported hostility by Oraibi's chief. In 1878 the "Oraibis refused to be enrolled" (ARCIA 1878) in agent Mateer's census. Cushing encountered hostility in 1882.

Another curious feature is the position of Loololma, Oraibi's village chief. Loololma probably became chief around 1880. Titiev (1944:72) reported that he reversed his predecessor's anti-American stance as the result of a trip to Washington with trader Thomas Keam in 1880. But the trip did not occur until 1890 (Yava 1978:157-164).[28] In 1882 Loololma kept assuring Cushing that the hostiles were nothing but trouble-makers. But the question is whether or not *anyone* at Oraibi was truly "friendly"; Cushing's companion Metcalf felt that the entire village was anti-American. Levy (1992:92) suggests that even Loololma was not really a "friendly," but rather, was simply trying to stall the government with vague promises. There is, in fact, no evidence that, until the mid-1890s, Oraibi had *any* substantial faction of "friendlies." Their existence derives directly from the American political ideology of assimilation.

The Political Ideology of Assimilation

The Nature of Political Things

"Political" describes, or refers to, the ways in which people organize to maintain social control internally and relationships between themselves and others, externally. Politics involves relations among people that speak directly to their personal interests, goals, and agendas, as individuals and as groups of individuals. People use politics to chink gaps in their self-esteem; to gain material advantage or present others from gaining it; to manipulate people into doing things that they would into doing things or to prevent them from doing so. Politics can be revolutionary or equilibrium-maintaining; political actors can be pathfinders or dispensers of psychological bromides. In relationships that Hopis had with Americans, politics attained a heightened degree of importance at points where general U.S. Indian policies were brought to bear on daily Hopi life; where these policies intersected with Hopis' internal political relationships, social and economic changes of great magnitude often resulted.

There could not have been "friendly" and "hostile" factions in Oraibi without something to be "friendly" or "hostile" toward. These metaphors acquired political content within Hopi society and became part of Hopi political activity and relationships, even though Hopis had not initially developed the metaphors. Americans generally regarded Indians as falling into one of two categories -- hostile, fearsome, and brutal, such as Comanches and Apaches; or friendly, industrious, and peace-loving, and thus admissible into the Anglos' own self-image of themselves as pioneer gardeners in a trackless wasteland (Hinsley 1989:173). Indians that were offered the opportunity to become gardeners in the wasteland and rejected the offer were perforce regarded as being in the other category: "hostile."

The Intent of Congress

Some close attention to U.S. Indian policy around the turn of the century is appropriate. The intent of Congress during the last quarter of the 19th century was to turn "hostile" Indians into "friendly" ones and to integrate Indians into "the national life as independent citizens, so that they may take their places as integral elements in our society, not as American Indians but as Americans, "enjoying all the privileges and sharing the burdens of American citizenship" (ARCIA 1891:4). Grant's second administration (1873-1877) saw successful lobbying on the part of Protestant churches engaged in missionary work; human rights advocacy groups such as the Indian Rights Association, formed entirely by U.S. citizens; and the liberal wing of the Republican Party toward this end. The result was a uniform policy implemented on every reservation. Its cornerstones were: (1) Day schools (later boarding schools) staffed with teachers; (2) one or more resident missionaries; (3) a resident agent (special agents were employed where residencies were not established;) (4) one or more resident or visiting technicians, usually farmers, and (5) a resident physician. The purpose of such a staff was to administer the Reservation so that its inhabitants would eventually become either rural yeoman or rural proletariat, differing only in the color of their skin and knowledge of their heritage from surrounding populations of American homesteaders. The policy took no account of the diversity of lifestyles, cultural heritage, or economies of American Indian communities, nor did it accommodate the possibility that, if given a choice, many American Indians would have preferred to remain who they were.

Agents were authorized to form squads of all-Indian police; to set up either courts of Indian offenses or Tribal courts; and to designate one or more "chiefs" or "captains" as both the Indians' official representative to the agent, and the agent's DE JURE appointee in keeping the lid on dissent and unrest. Thus reservations became not just places, but also distinct, and separate administrative units of the U.S. Government. Agents set up systems of distribution, loan, or sale of farming implements to Indians; outlets for marketing of crops; freighting contracts in which Indians were encouraged to purchase wagons for a modest down-payment and then were paid to haul freight for the BIA and crops for reservation farmers.

Education was probably the most important component of the allotment policy. Education was crucial to implementing the policy's general goals to "relieve the government of the enormous burden" of operating the reservations, and also to "settle the Indian question within the space generally allotted to a generation. "By forcing children to attend school, the Indian Office sought not only to enhance literacy but also to 'civilize' the 'natives' by removing them from tribal influences and to stamp out Indian languages by forbidding children to speak anything but English under threat of corporal punishment. Vocational courses of study with emphasis on agriculture, technological skills, and homemaking would integrate Indians into the rural proletariat" (Fuchs and Havighurst 1972:6, 8-9).

In 1887, Congress passed the Dawes Allotment Act, intended to accomplish the division of collectively-held tribal land into privately-owned, individual family allotments of 640 acres or less and the confiscation of remaining lands for distribution to U.S. citizens. The assimilationist ideology was strengthened after the Act's passage and the goals of suppressing Indian religious ceremonies and social dances that missionaries found offensive and, after 1892, compulsory education, were pursued more vigorously.[29]

Indians at this time were not in a position to participate in developing policies affecting them. No system of representation of Indians in the U.S. Government existed. Indians were not citizens. They had been purposely isolated from U.S. citizens by Government policy. Until 1871 they had been treated as citizens of separate, sovereign, "domestically dependent" nations (Deloria 1974:113-160), with all of the liabilities of small foreign nations surrounded by a much larger and more powerful one, and few of the privileges. Under the assimilation/allotment policy, each Indian reservation became a "small department of the federal Government" (Spicer 1962:349).

Implementing the Ideology at Hopi

Officially established in 1869, the "Moqui Pueblos Agency" had no agents until 1871, when temporary "special agents" were assigned to it on a year-to-year basis. They operated out of the Navajo Agency until 1874, when a permanent agency was established at Trout Spring, 15 miles northeast of Walpi in 1874. In 1875 agent Truax started a tiny school, staffed with a missionary teacher, and published a short-lived school magazine. In 1876 William Mateer took over as agent, but shortly thereafter, the entire enterprise had been abandoned due to lack of funds.[30] Mateer was succeeded by an agent named Fleming.

Trader Thomas Keam arrived at about the same time. Keam had battled Navajo agent William Arny for a trading license starting in 1871; Arny was eventually dismissed under suspicions -- probably well-founded -- of embezzlement. Keam gave up on the Navajo situation when his marriage to a Navajo woman fell apart but finally obtained a long-sought trading license in 1875, filing a patent on 640 acres in what is now Keams Canyon, and started trying to initiate changes in the lives of First Mesa's residents (McNitt 1962: 145-149). Keam's ranch eventually included a trading post, house, and seventeen out-buildings, all constructed of dressed native sandstone. When agents were re-assigned in 1878 but continued to operate out of Fort Defiance, Keam offered one of his buildings to Agent J.H. Fleming in 1880. But Fleming was less than pleased with being agent to a tribe that had no reservation.

Creating the 1882 Reservation

Keam and Fleming seem to be the persuasive forces behind the "Moqui Reservation," but more likely than not, it was simply an idea whose time had come. In 1876 Truax had urged that a Hopi reservation be established. Perhaps Keam urged the reservation because he feared losing the Agency if he could not persuade Fleming to stay at the proffered headquarters at his ranch. Fleming wanted jurisdiction over a reservation, not just over a tribe. Fleming insisted on a reservation because he said two former agency employees were going through the Hopi villages ostensibly stirring Hopis up against the Government and the idea of sending children to a boarding school. Fleming wanted to arrest them, or at least to oust them. He could not do so unless there were some reservation boundaries from which to oust them.

Fleming wrote the Commissioner of Indian Affairs, asking how to proceed. The Commissioner told him to recommend boundaries of a reservation which would include "all Moqui villages and agency and

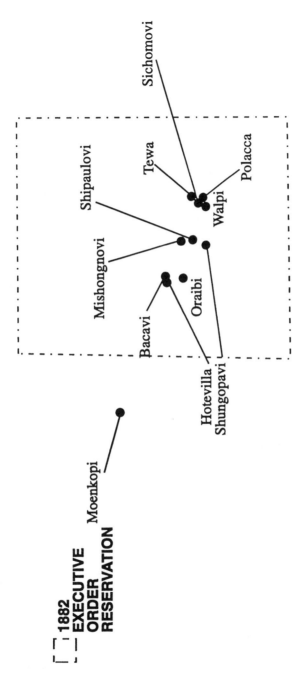

Hopi Towns and Reservation Boundaries: 1882

large enough to meet all needful purposes and no larger." Fleming replied with a map and description which did *not* include all the Hopi villages. The Commissioner forwarded the materials to President Chester A. Arthur, who had granted an audience to Cushing, the five Zunis and the Hopi-Zuni-Navajo Nanahe just a few months earlier. The Commissioner requested an executive order creating the reservation in order to (1) vest title to the Moqui in the lands they occupied; (2) afford them U.S. protection; and (3) permit the agent legal authority to evict "unprincipled whites" and "arrest and punish mischiefmakers" (Stephens 1961:70-74).

As part of a general policy, Congress authorized the U.S. President to create reservations by "executive orders" that followed the same formula in all cases: "for the _____ Indians and such other Indians as the Secretary of the Interior shall settle thereon." Thus, the executive order establishing the "Moki Indian Reservation" contains this wording. That little phrase would create irreparable confusion in years to come. Its boundaries were quite arbitrary: the 2.45 million acre parcel conformed neither to the Hopi use area; nor to topographical features; nor to Hopis' wishes (they were not asked). It was a perfect rectangle, 70 miles by 55. Its boundaries included 300 Navajos, and excluded the 100 Hopis living in Moenkopi. A distance of 20 miles separated Moenkopi from its western boundary.

Establishment of the reservation benefitted Thomas Keam most immediately. Keam seems to have been a proselytizer for progress and the modern life. He wanted Hopis to "live like white men;" to move down from the mesas to the valley; and to be educated in the English language and the industrial arts. It was Keam who pushed hardest for schools for the Hopi. He wrote a letter ostensibly on behalf of "Cimo, tribal chief of Mokis" (actually Kikmongwi of Walpi and Sichomovi) plus the "chiefs of Mishongnovi, Shipaulovi, and Shungopavi" and 15 "religious leaders" requesting a school accompanied by a petition with each man's name and clan mark (ARCIA 1886:LXXX). But Cimo was also known to oppose schooling (Yava 1978:11). Ostensibly in response, a "Moqui School Reserve" was established, in 1885, but without any school buildings. Keam offered some of his buildings for an "Indian industrial boarding school" and in 1886 the Government agreed to lease 19 buildings for $100 a month, opening the "Moqui Boarding School" in September, 1887 after persuading as many parents as possible to send their children to it (Miller 1907). Many Hopi, especially at Oraibi, showed little interest, or actively opposed it. In 1889 the Government bought the buildings outright, including the 640 acres on which they sat, for $10,000.

In 1890 presidential authority was granted for surveying the Hopi Reservation preliminary to making allotments (ARCIA 1890:XLVII). The allotments were on the desert floor, below the mesas, where Hopis had their fields. Despite some tradition of individual usufruct, Hopis interpreted these moves as hostile acts. In 1891, the Government sent a party of surveyors to survey the Reservation. All village chiefs opposed the scheme (Titiev 1944:76; Parsons 1922). But the surveyors returned in 1894 and this time Keam and Stephen drew up a petition from Walpi's men opposing allotment. The petition requested "one continuous boundary ring enclosing all the Tewa and all the Hopi lands" and including enough land for their flocks and herds as well as fields" and was signed by 123 men with their clan marks from all villages. The petition went unacknowledged (Yava 1978:123-4, 165-7). Men from Oraibi pulled up surveyors' markers and openly threatened to burn the school at Keam's ranch (Spicer 1962:203).

Not more than a few hundred Hopis moved off the mesas and only those at Moenkopi took allotments. Attempts to allot land were ended in 1912 when agent Crane recommended against allotment, noting that the water supply was too small, the people did not want allotment and were not ready for it, and a growing land controversy with the Navajos had not been settled. But the allotting efforts precipitated two confrontations between Hopis and troops at Oraibi, and the policy of compulsory education was the source of innumerable confrontations at Third Mesa and at Second. Yet another source of conflict arose when the Agency implemented its "hair-cutting order" in 1901-02. Superintendent Burton ordered all men to have their hair cut. Such humiliating treatment emphasized the power of the American nation-state, but also drew fire from Hopi partisans such as Charles Lummis in Los Angeles and one of the teachers, Belle Axtell Kolp, niece of a former territorial governor of New Mexico, who resigned her position in protest. They formed the "Sequoia League" and enlisted such heavyweights as Phoebe Apperson Hearst and Theodore Roosevelt (Lummis 1968). Kolp filed a long affidavit of mistreatments in Los Angeles in 1903. Burton was reprimanded, but not removed.

There is much evidence that Hopi men were not against the principal of allotment, as we shall see. In fact, they may have even favored it, but they wanted to do it their own way, not to have it done for them. The reasons for Hopis' opposition to allotment may not be immediately obvious but they become so when the nature of Hopi farming is taken into consideration. On reservations where farming was not very important or virtually non-existent, people could be expected to be somewhat ambivalent. But Hopis were absolutely dependent on agriculture, even as late as the 1930s, and they had a keen awareness of how important flexibility was. *Assigned* allotments would destroy that flexibility, preventing a man from shifting the location of his crops from year to year and also preventing him from farming several plots in several locations. Many men did this and continue to do it as a kind of practical insurance against climatic disaster, which might result in one field being washed away in a flood while another simply gets a good dose of moisture.

The Great Transformation: Economy and Demography

I have borrowed the title of Karl Polanyi's (1957) well-known study of the development of market capitalism in western Europe because it captures the essence of what modernization is all about: a change in world view from maintaining "habitation" to "improving" the utility of land; a shift in population from countryside to city; an increase in mortality due to introduction of new diseases, followed by a population explosion; intervention by governments to insure the interests of private property; changes in the pattern of work, from maintaining subsistence to earning wages and making profits, thus making labor into a commodity; a development of situations in which profit and loss, rather than kin relations, are the basis for social interaction; and the secularization and democratization of ideas. All of these things began to happen to the Hopi when Mexico abolished mercantilism, embraced laissez-faire capitalism, and opened its northern frontier to American changes. These changes began slowly and haphazardly, and certainly they did not happen all at once. But they accelerated after the American take-over, and despite some successful resistance to them, these historical processes quickly began to frame the context of everyday Hopi life. Not all of them were initiated by the Euro-American intruders; Hopis initiated some of them as well, adding to, rather than replacing, pre-existing Hopi social and economic institutions. But many Hopis also resisted the changes, and it is the resistance as much as the embracing of the Great Transformation that characterizes modernization in general, and Hopis' modernization in particular.

Cash income: farming, livestock, wage labor, contract freighting

Ratios between farming, livestock, and wage labor income seem to have been well established by 1890 and remained stable for the following 40 years. Agent Fleming furnished three wagons to "Moquis for farming and freighting" in 1880 and 1881, (ARCIA 1880:XIII; 1881:XXXII). By 1884, the Agent was hiring Hopis to haul supplies to and from railhead and loaning money for Hopis to buy freight wagons and mules as well as cattle, reporting that "a few of the principal men" among the Hopi were "beginning to gather herds of cattle." Hopis still depended on trading "surplus melons and peaches" with Navajos for sheep, which regularly overran Hopi gardens, especially at Wepo and Tallahogan springs (ARCIA 1884:136-138). But Hopis' sheep herds were beginning to increase and by 1886 they numbered 25,000, yielding a "wool clip" of "6,000 lbs., of which 3,000 was manufactured into blankets" (ARCIA 1886:LXXX, 402, 432-3; 420; 444-45). The following year, the wool clip was 20,000 lbs, of which half was sold at eight cents a pound, and the rest "fabricated into wearing apparel and blankets for their personal use;" the corn yield was estimated at 40,000 bushels. The agent estimated Hopis grew 32,000 melons, pumpkins, and squashes (ARCIA 1887:177-8; 358).

In 1888, the corn harvest was estimated as equally as good as in 1887, although Hopis had either sold (or lost to rustling and raiding) more than a quarter of their sheep (ARCIA 1888:420, 439). In 1890 Hopis again grew close to 40,000 bushels of corn, storing about a quarter of it for use during the year, selling about 200 bushels to traders, bartering a third of it for about 300,000 pounds of mutton, and grinding the rest into cornmeal or consuming it on the spot. For the first time Hopis were reported as selling horses and mules, for a total of $1,000, and 50 cattle at $18 for $900.00. Sale of blankets, cotton fabrics, rugs, and basketry brought $3,500, and Hopis did $5,000 worth of freighting, probably mostly for the Agency but likely for Keam as well (ARCIA 1890:167-170). In 1889 and again in 1890 the corn harvest was a whopping 70,000 bushels, and in 1891, the "value of products sold to others" (not the Government) was again around $5,000 (ARCIA 1891 I:310-311; II:72, 92-93), including 26,000 pounds of wool sold at $.08-09 per pound (Donaldson 1893:46).

While some of these estimates may be a little high, figures for the decade 1880-1890 point out six important aspects of the Hopi economy: (1) the slow but steady growth in prosperity; (2) the importance of neighboring Navajos as a source of meat and outlet for surplus agricultural products; (3) the growing importance of cattle; (4) the growing importance of the market for raw wool and craft items, a market that could only have been created by Keam on one end, and the Mormons on the other, since Keam was the only licensed trader for miles around; (5) the growing importance of cash; (6) the continuing importance of agriculture.

The year 1892 promised some improvement, by the account of the agent as well as by that of Alexander Stephen. "Until about a year ago the Moquis were considerably troubled by the Navajoes," reported agent David Shipley. "However, about one year ago, with the cooperation of Special Agent Parker, I issued a decree prohibiting the Navajoes from entering within a radius of 15 miles of the village of Me-shung-ne-vi. Since this time the Moquis have more ground for cultivation." (ARCIA 211-21). Stephen (1936:954-955) estimated 1,200 acres planted in corn at "East Mesa;" 800 acres of corn at "Middle Mesa;" and 1,600 acres of corn at Oraibi. He figured another 2,000 acres, total, planted in vegetables, beans, melons, squash, pumpkin, gourd, chile, onions, amaranth, sunflower, cotton, wheat, and buckwheat, with 1,000 acres of orchards, primarily peach and apricot. On the basis of the previous year's harvest, Stephen predicted a yield for corn of 12 bushels per acre, for a total of 43,200 bushels, with 200-300 bushels being sold or traded to traders and 7,500 bushels bartered to Navajos for 5,000 sheep, each weighing 30 lbs, and another 300 or so bushels traded to them for blankets and other items. He figured between 20,000 and 25,000 consumed, ground into cornmeal, and fed to animals, and about 10,000 bushels stored. But the numbers of Hopis' sheep had diminished drastically, from 20,000 to 8,000, and cattle had decreased from 800 to only 500 (ARCIA 1892:211-212, 789, 802-803), and the corn yield turned out to be much less than Stephen had predicted: only 25,000 bushels. By 1893 the agent reported only 2,000 sheep and goats (Donaldson 1893:46; ARCIA 1893:694, 710-711). It is clear that the decade of the 1890s brought a steady economic deterioration.

Wage jobs were available, but not abundant. By 1899 U.S. Government Indian agents were acting as contractors for the Santa Fe Railway, assembling work gangs of Hopis as well as Navajos; the relationship continued through 1907, when the Railroad laid off its Indian workers due to "retrenchment." Between April, 1906 and February, 1907, between 48 and 210 "companies of Indians, mainly Hopis, Mohaves, Navahoes and Pueblos, were kept at work on the Santa Fe railroad" for gross earnings of $25,101.61, and the agent also regularly hired out several hundred Hopis, Navajos, Pueblos, and Apaches for seasonal work in the beet fields of southern Arizona and Colorado (ARDOI,AI 1907 II:13). Some Hopi men went to Winslow for jobs at the Santa Fe roundhouse, hauling ashes out of the locomotive fireboxes (Yava 1978:20). Missionaries hired Hopi men for casual labor, paying them $.50 a day (Qoyawayma 1964:53). The Agency at Keams had one regular interpreter on staff at $20 a month, and three Hopis had the Keams-Fort Defiance mail carrying contract (Yava 1978:13, 21).

Trading Posts. Frederick Volz ran a store in Canyon Diablo and opened a store near Oraibi Day school around 1898, installing his brother William, "a Mexican" as clerk. Volz bought Katsina dolls, weavings, basketry, and even some pottery from Hopis, paying probably less than a dollar for the Katsina dolls, and sold the collection to George Heye in 1901 (Harvey 1963:38-49, 48). (Eventually the collection went into the Museum of the American Indian in New York.) Hopis reportedly derived "considerable income from the manufacture and sale of pottery and baskets, purchased more, perhaps, for their novelty than for practical use" (Indian Rights Association 1898). But much of Volz's trade was with Navajos who went through Hopi cornfields to get there, letting their burros and ponies eat Hopis' produce. Hopis complained about Volz to agent Burton, not only due to his trading practices but also because he apparently had a violent temper (Whiteley 1988a:102-103). In 1901 Hopis sold nearly $13,000 worth of products to traders and to the Government agency, coal, wood, and beef as well as craft items. Some crafts were apparently marketed through a man named Douglas Graham who "began a long trading career" at Hopi in 1878 (ARDOI,IA 1901, I:686, 708-709). Graham may well have been the middleman between Keam and other buyers. In 1902 Lorenzo Hubbell extended his business when he bought Keam's old "Tusayan Trading Post." Keam moved back home to England.[31] Hubbell immediately began marketing Navajo and Hopi crafts by mail order: $2.50 - $4.00 for sashes woven by Hopi men; Hopi baskets and plaques woven by women at $.50 to $2.50 each; Katsina dolls at $.75 to $2; pottery from $.25 to $5.00, $2.50 to $10.00 for prehistoric pottery. Hubbell eventually may have taken over Volz's trade, but not his store; Volz's store "on the road to Oraibi" (Babbitt 1973:40) had been abandoned by 1906 (Whiteley 1988b:103).[32]

Burton, the same Agency superintendent who had ruthlessly enforced school attendance and the hair-cutting order, encouraged Hopi traders. By 1905 two traders, Naquiestewa and Thomas Tawakwaptiwa, younger brother to Wilson Tawakwaptiwa, the Kikmongwi, opened stores in Oraibi, and a "Sam Pawiki" had opened a store in Kykotsmovi by 1908 (Nagata 1970:198). Thomas later moved his store to Moenkopi, where he also developed a thriving cattle herd and worked as interpreter for the Tuba City agency which opened in 1903. By 1910 a total of three Hopi-owned stores were operating in Moenkopi. Hopis got jobs at the boarding school, opened in 1899 in Blue Canyon and moved to Tuba City in 1903 and perhaps also at the three missions nearby. But freighting at Tuba City had always been in the hands of Mormons, who shipped out Navajo wool and pinon nuts, and operated a general merchandise store for dealing with the Indians (Nagata 1970:32-37).

Disaster: Drought, Depression, Deprivation, and Arroyo Cutting

The year 1894 is a telling one. Freighting is down to $1,457. Products sold amount to only $2,000. Hopi are down to 5,000 sheep, 3,000 goats and 500 cattle. The corn harvest is 40% of 1893's harvest (ARCIA 1894:100-101; 566-7). Why? For one thing, the United States was in the depths of a rock-bottom depression. The West especially had been plunged into ruin when the U.S. Government declared the gold standard and let the price of silver "float" as any other commodity. The price floated downward. Wool and livestock prices were drastically lowered. The price of silver plummeted; silver mines closeddown. People were thrown out of work; half the populations of some towns pulled up stakes and departed. Two of these were Jerome and Prescott, about 150 miles to the south of the Hopi villages. The area was in the grip not only of a national depression, but also of a regional one.

Table 5.1 Economic statistics for selected years, 1886-1902

Year	# of sheep goats	# of cattle	wool clip, lbs.	corn, bu.	other veg.	sales $	freight haul $
1886-87[a]	25,000	[b]	20,000	40,000	32,000 count	1,600	
1888	18,000			40,000		5,400	5,000
1889	6,000	250		70,000	6,575 bu.		185
1891	8,000	500	26,000	43,200		5,000	
1892	8,000	500		25,000	1,500 bu.	2,720	1,325
1894-95	5,000s 3,000g	500		10,000	750 bu.	2,000 1,360	706
1902	5,600s 14,400g	1,365		20,000		5,500	2,500

[a]In some cases I have combined years in which the statistics were substantially the same in the interest of brevity and to show trends.
[b]Empty cells reflect lack of data in the agents' reports for that category in that year.

Water. A severe drought in 1893-1894 was followed by a severe winter in 1894-95 with heavy snowfalls. Warm weather in the spring and consequent heavy spring runoffs exacerbated arroyo cutting along all of the washes and their tributaries. Rainfall in spring and summer of 1893 would have made irrigating from the washes increasing difficult; spring deluges from snowmelt in 1894 would have changed difficulty to disaster.[33] The period between 1895 and 1904 was another period of drought, "broken by a series of great storms early in 1905" (Bradfield 1971:28) that gouged Oraibi Wash into an ever-deepening arroyo for ever. To top things off, Oraibi's spring had been drying up for years and continued to do so. Deepening it once hardly helped. Women stood for hours at a time waiting to fill their jugs from the water that seeped every so slowly up into the well's sandy bottom.

Navajos and Mormons. Navajos had begun to get the upper hand in the competition for land. Their sheep had increased to 1,000,000; goats to 250,000; and their population had expanded so that they accounted for nearly 45% of the population of the 1882 Reservation. In other words, there were nearly as many Navajos in Hopi country as there were Hopis. By the mid-1880s, every major population of Navajos had the opportunity for regular trade with Anglo-Americans (Bailey and Bailey 1986:38-39). By 1890 there were seven trading posts on the reservation, and 30-odd posts just off the reservation. Navajos began marketing wool at least as early as 1876, and by 1880, they were regularly marketing about 800,000 pounds per year (Aberle 1966:33). In 1889 the Navajo wool clip was 2,100,000 lbs. (compared to a some 20,000 lbs. for Hopis). Between 1903 and 1906, Navajos virtually monopolized the market on livestock, wool and blankets; the value of those items rose in just three years from $500,000 to $1,000,000. While Hopis also had some trading opportunities, they dealt with no more than one or two traders until well into the late 1890s, and had to traverse miles of Navajo country to get to any other posts.

Merino Sheep. Anglos' introduction of merino sheep in the mid-1880s brought another ecological disaster. Unlike the churros that had been introduced by Spaniards in the 1600s and had been adopted by Hopis and Navajos alike, the merinos yield a much heavier coat of wool. This characteristic meant a temporary boom in the wool trade for Navajos and Hopis alike, who also acquired the merinos. But also unlike the churros, they have very efficient eating patterns: they graze an area down to the nub before moving on. This grazing pattern could easily result in huge areas being nearly entirely denuded, and in 1893 and 1894 the drought would have packed a double whammy: not only would forage have been scarcer, but what forage there was, would have been grazed to the root, and would not have had a chance to resprout.[34] Denuded floodplains would have had topsoil swept away at an alarming rate, and the velocity of runoff would have initiated channelling and arroyo cutting.

Land Gridlock. Finally, competition among Hopis, Navajos, and Mormons at Moenkopi had placed resources into a kind of gridlock: there was no room for anybody to expand there. One hundred Hopis were living there at the time, but the Mormons had made Hopis into virtual share croppers on their own land. Navajos had also moved in (Nagata 1970:33, 37, 39; cf. ARCIA 1896:113). In 1892, troops had even been called out to investigate fatal conflicts between Navajos and Mormons and also complaints by Hopis that Mormons had dispossessed them (Stephen 1936:997-1001). When Hopis and Navajos were finally allotted the former Mormon lands in 1897, five Navajos received almost as much as the eleven Hopi allottees (Nagata 1970:39). Attempts by some Hopis to found a small colony along the Little Colorado River near Leupp (La Farge 1936a:48), possibly also under Mormon protection, had not met with success.

Busts, Booms and Smallpox. The year 1898 brought a very brief improvement in material conditions. The corn harvest was 50,000 bushels, and Hopis sold $8,000 worth of products to traders. But Hopi livestock continue to dip in numbers (ARCIA 1898:600, 616-617). Then disaster struck. A smallpox epidemic swept First Mesa and spread to Second Mesa before vaccine could be obtained. Vaccinations and fumigation of crops, houses and people checked its spread at First Mesa, where only twenty-four died, but the pestilence killed at least 163 at Second Mesa. Two-hundred-twenty people -- half the population -- , were not vaccinated due to refusals stemming from mistrust of the Government's intentions (ARCIA 80-81, 158-159). Certainly Hopis would have had no knowledge of how the principle of vaccination worked; it is possible that no one even explained it to them. Most vaccinations bring on a slight and short instance of the disease itself and thus some people may well have seen the vaccinated initially get worse after treatment. Those who did accept vaccinations would have had to surrender a large amount of trust to federal authorities. Those who refused seem to have seen it as another part of the resistance to U.S. authority. At Second Mesa, eight arrests were made of men who urged refusal; two of them were kept under police surveillance at the agency until 1900.

At Mishongnovi and Shipaulovi, bodies "piled up in the streets. "The Indian agent called in a detachment of African-American soldiers (the "Buffalo Soldiers") from Fort Wingate and ordered a mass cremation. A witness to the events, artist Louis Akin, reported that "the bodies were gathered and thrown into a crevice, covered with oil, and burned" (Babbitt 1973:41). Oraibi was spared only because Government officials managed to enforce a quarantine. The deaths resulted in Oraibi's population being 10% higher -- at 990 -- than that of First Mesa and Second Mesa combined (ARCIA 1899:80). Weakened from the disease and unable to plant fields, many Hopis from First Mesa went to the Mormon settlement of Joseph City, where they had on-going trading relationships, to glean Mormons' wheat fields (Yava 1978:13-14).

Somehow, Hopis were able to acquire about 50,000 sheep[35] by 1900, but corn harvests continued to run low (ARDOI,IA 1901, I:686, 708-709; ARDOI,IA 1904, I:138). In 1902, Oraibi's corn crop failed completely. Mennonite missionaries Voth and Epp had two carloads of corn shipped out from Kansas (Whiteley 1988a:43). The cash economy became even more crucially important.

Tourism: Boon, Curse, and Growing Source of Cash Income. The Santa Fe Railroad completed its line through Winslow and Flagstaff, linking Los Angeles with Kansas City, in 1884. In 1897 it specifically began advertising its routes using Indian themes, commissioning ethnographer Walter Hough (1898) to write a thick, meaty pamphlet on the "Moqui Snake Dance," profusely illustrated with photographs (cf. Forrest 1961).[36] The pamphlet contained explicit directions on how to get to the Hopi mesas for the famed Snake Dance, advising the travelers to hire horses, mules, wagons, or buckboards in Winslow, Holbrook, Diablo Canyon, or Flagstaff. In 1903 the Santa Fe hired artist Louis Akin to paint Hopi Indians specifically for an advertising campaign; Akin rented the upper floor of a two-storey house in Oraibi for 50 cents a week and experienced no difficulties living there for nearly a year, despite the factionalism (Babbitt 1973:8-9). Between 1879 and 1906, no fewer than 28 popular accounts of the Snake Dance appeared in articles and books, two of them in Europe (Laird 1977). The Harvey Company arranged with one of the Volz Brothers to provide transportation from the rail stop at Canyon Diablo (now "Two Guns," Arizona) to the Hopi villages for Snake Dances.

By 1904 the Santa Fe had bought a rail line originally run into Grand Canyon by a mining company and the Harvey Company, which had operated swank dining rooms and hotels along the route from its beginnings in Kansas, had built "Harvey House" hotels in Albuquerque, Holbrook, and Winslow, eventually operating a chain of 75 along the route all the way to Los Angeles. The company had begun its collection of Indian arts and crafts in 1899, opening its "Indian Room" in Albuquerque's refurbished Alvarado Hotel in 1903. The room featured one of H.R. Voth's replicas of Hopi ceremonial objects and an altar, similar to that which he had made for the Columbian Exposition in 1895 and which later turned up in the Field Museum. Hopis protested the sacrilege, but to no avail. Voth made three more altars for the Harvey Company in 1913 (Harvey 1963:34-40).[37]

In 1905, Congress placed Grand Canyon under the protection of the U.S. Forest Service, and the Harvey company opened El Tovar Hotel and "Hopi House" craft shop in the same year. Architect Mary Colter designed Hopi House to authentically resemble a two-storeyed cluster of rooms in Oraibi. The Harvey Company paid Hopis from Mishongnovi,

Shungopavi, and Shipaulovi a pittance to put on truncated social dances for the tourists, and encouraged them to sit in front of El Tovar and Hopi House and weave baskets and plaques. The famous potter, Nampeyo, from First Mesa, made pots in front of the entrance to El Tovar. Hopi men may also have done some work in silver at "Hopi House." Hopis had learned silversmithing from Zunis and were experimenting with it by 1890 (Spicer 1962:204), apparently not turning it into a paying craft until after 1900 (ARDOI,IA 1901). But Andrew Hermequaftewa, from Shungopavi, worked copper and brass before switching to silver and rode the rails all the way to Williams to trade his jewelry to Havasupais for their tanned buckskin. At least one of the ten silversmiths who learned the craft in these early days eventually also set up shop in Grand Canyon village, selling his jewelry along with other people from Second Mesa who sold crafts at Hopi House and El Tovar (Wright 1972:11-22).

Farming

But farming remained the mainstay of the economy even as wage labor and a cash economy were penetrating the Hopi and Navajo areas. Because this period is also the period of the Oraibi split, a more intensive look at Hopi horticulture is in order since economic factors cannot be separated entirely from any consideration of political events in this case.

C. Daryll Forde, Mischa Titiev, Alfred Whiting, Volney Jones (1938), and John Hack did studies of Hopi agriculture between 1929 and 1938. R. Maitland Bradfield (1971) summarized much of their findings and added some of his own from 1968-69, but it is the studies done in the 1930s that are most revealing since Hopis were demographically and economically substantially the same in 1936 as they had been in 1906. Even the climatic conditions were similar. The big changes in economy, climate, and demography all came before 1900. Thus the general description below applies as much to 1900 as it does to 1930.

Farming Techniques. By the 1930s, Hopi farmers were growing six distinct types of corn; between four and eight different types of beans; three kinds of squashes; pumpkin; gourds for rattles; jerusalem artichoke, at least two kinds of melon; chili; onions; cabbage; peach, apple, and apricot trees. Some farmers also grew tomatoes, carrots, cherries, almonds, pears, grapes, peas, beets, turnips, cucumbers, lettuce, radishes, coriander, wild potato, and amaranth, along with tobacco, sunflowers, devils claw, mint, Rocky Mountain beeweed, and other plants used as medicines and for dyes and in basketry (Whiting 1936, 1939:9; Forde 1931; Hack 1942:19-20). Wheat, introduced by the Spaniards, was quickly abandoned because it required too much water; Hopis only started growing it again when irrigation became available at Moenkopi, but Hopis were growing it at First Mesa, perhaps at Wepo or Tallahogan springs, in 1893 (Stephen 1936:955). Mormons had brought turban squash, sorghum, and safflower in the 1870s, and beginning around 1915, Hopi men began buying commercial seeds and experimenting with crops such as peanuts, hybrid yellow corn, and cauliflower, all of which were unsuccessful, but for different reasons. As of 1935, about a third of the crops were being planted from seeds purchased from mail order houses (Whiting 1937).

Bradfield (1971:19, 31) estimated a net decrease in farmland under cultivation from about 5,000 acres in 1882 to around 3,000 acres in 1970. But the amount of acreage planted in 1935 was probably about the same as that planted in the 1890s, and may have even been larger. A Hopi man told Richard Brandt (1954:256) in 1947 that "when the government stopped the clan holdings and said the Hopi can cultivate any land they want, now we farm more and plant more trees. I sell corn and fruit." The largest source of subsistence in 1937 was still agriculture, accounting for 54% of the total, with wage labor constituting 32% and livestock 10%. Statistics from 1891 indicate about the same proportion of income from wage labor, freighting contracts, and sale of sheep and mohair goat wool as in 1937: between 25% and 33%. Thus it seems that the major change between 1900 and 1937 lay in Hopis' shifting about 10% of their time and labor from horticulture to animal husbandry. It seems safe to infer that the material conditions of horticultural production identified by researchers in 1937 would have been substantially similar to those operating in 1900: access to good, rich land; to reliable water supply; and to good, robust, fertile seeds. The main difference would have been that in 1900, nobody was ordering seeds from mail catalogues.

The difference between horticultural products in 1890 and horticulture in the 1930s was in variety of crops and seeds; *not* in the degree of importance of crops and *not* in the *material conditions* under which Hopis had to pursue horticulture.

Rushforth and Upham (1992:34-8,112,132,201) have called the Hopi system of farming a "hedge-your-bets" system of environmental adaptation and that is a good name for it. But they have also called it an "enormously successful" system. That is not a good characterization of it. Hopis enjoy a relatively long growing season of 130 frost-free days but due to a scanty water supply, crops mature slowly and are often damaged by frost. A field might be located in a spot where the frequency of heavy rains is very high but rainfall is erratic and most fields receive scant precipitation (Hack 1942:21). Hopis plant their corn to a depth of ten to fifteen inches, where the sandy soil holds some moisture. Many Hopis plant in shallow drainages, but even special planting measures and the seeds' special adaptability does not make up for the low mean precipitation of eleven or twelve inches. Special methods need to be employed. These special methods are flood-water farming and irrigation. Flood-water farming works best where fields will benefit from sudden downpours, but will not be washed away by powerful floods.

The best and most common location for fields is at the mouth of a small tributary arroyo where the arroyo ceases to be a channel and the water starts to spread and forms an alluvial fan (Hack 1942:26-28). Since the alluvial fan changes from season to season, so does the location of a field. Farmers build small earthenware dams to prevent channelling or washing out of the crop during floods. But nearly every flood used to bring Hopi farmers out during the growing season to divert water to the plants or prevent it from washing crops away. Broadening natural terraces right below the mesas and buttes so that runoff spread out gently and evenly, is another technique.

A kind of dry-farming is also possible. Dry farming limits the kinds of crops that can be planted to corn, fruit trees, and beans; melons "are conspicuously absent " from dry-farmed fields. Dry farming is done on sand dunes. It works because water becomes trapped in the bottom of the dune by a layer of shale; seeds are planted deep; and the loose surface of the sand acts as a dry mulch which prevents evaporation (Hack 1942:32). "The largest development of this kind of agriculture is the village of Hotevilla where according to U.S. Soil Conservation statistics (1937) over 60 percent of the cultivated land is watered by rainfall only, and thus is farmed by the method of sand dune agriculture. This figure is in great contrast to the figure for the whole Hopi country" (Hack 1942:42-43). Hack noted that in 1893 the inhabitants of Oraibi diverted water from the main wash for flood-water farming. He speculated that, when arroyo-cutting started some time after that date, deepening the arroyo by ten feet, making flood-water irrigation impossible, crowding of farmers might have led to the quarrel and split of 1906. Lorenzo Hubbell, Jr., a trader there at the time (since 1902) and Hopi Edmund Nequatewa both assured him it had not.

Only three areas have actual irrigation agriculture: Moenkopi; First Mesa; and Second Mesa. More than twenty-five owners irrigated crops on the south side of Tallahogan Canyon, close to Awat'ovi, by diverting water flowing from natural springs. In addition to fruit trees, corn, and squash, farmers had onions, cabbage, turnips, carrots, chile, and tobacco. Wepo spring, also on First Mesa, is the only spring near the Hopi villages allowing sustained use for irrigation; its flow is over thirty gallons per minute, better than many wells (Hack 1942:36-37). More than a dozen families had gardens there (Forde 1931).

Third Mesa has only one "contact" spring: at Hotevilla. In contrast to Third Mesa, the First Mesa villages have eleven "contact" springs where Hopis used water seeping out of breaks in the escarpment to irrigate gardens. The Second Mesa villages have thirteen of these springs, four of which are used to irrigate gardens, and 70% of the farmland belonging to clans of the six First and Second Mesa villages is located along Wepo and Polacca Washes and their tributaries. The rest of the fields took advantage of gravity: the accumulation of surface drainage from higher elevations (Forde 1931:60-61). First Mesa's farm lands were laid out in sixty square and rectangular plots owned by eleven different clans. Arroyo cutting had deepened all the washes by about thirty feet starting around 1900. Second Mesa villages had seventy plots but deviated markedly from First and Third Mesas in having 120 small plots owned by the men's societies and kiva groups. At Moenkopi, farmers diverted water from Moenkopi Wash, which flows most of the summer, to fields planted largely in corn.

Clan Lands. Fields are cleared of weeds and brush by end of winter, usually in February. Men plant, but often women and children help. "In former times, while the clan system of land tenure was universally in vogue, it was customary for each group to plan and harvest as a unit" (Titiev 1944:184). Titiev heard accounts of communal planting and harvesting on behalf of the Village chief "and other high officers." "The chief was formerly relieved of all farming cares," Hopis told him, "wood was hauled to his house by all the villagers, and garments were woven for all the members of his family." One of Titiev's Hopi consultants told him (Titiev 1944:61-63) that Oraibi's Bear Clan formerly had a large tract traversed by the Oraibi Wash, "so shallow in those days that its flood waters were a great boon to nearby fields." Stones marked its boundaries. The Bear Clan leaders, some time in the remote past, had given smaller plots to the War Chief; the Patki (Water) Clan head men; the holder of the "Aholi" ceremonial position in the Katsina society; and to the Greasewood, Rabbit, Spider, and Parrot Clans. The chief awarded all of these lands, Titiev was told, as rewards for the assistance of individuals from these clans in ceremonial duties.

Only the fields of two other large clans appear to have been located sufficiently near the Oraibi Wash to be irrigated by diverting water from it; those of the Piikyas (Sprouting Corn) and Eagle clans holding ceremonially important posts. Levy (1992:8) found "an almost perfect correlation" between the importance and number of ceremonies controlled by a particular clan and the quality of land it controlled. "The system of clan ranking by ceremonies," he concluded, "is nothing more than a translation of economic reality into the realm of the sacred, serving to sanctify the exalted position of a limited number of clans."

A "free area" at Oraibi was left unassigned where any resident could lay out a farm, but only with the chief's consent. Conditions for the Kikmongwi's consent included frequent participation in Katsina dances, particularly the Niman dance; hauling wood to the kivas in preparation for the Soyal ceremony, owned by the chief's Bear Clan, and for subsequent winter ceremonies; promptness in responding to calls for farming for the chief; cleaning springs or other communal work; and willingness to occasionally sponsor a dance (Titiev 1944:63). Thus, at least at Oraibi, a tangible association linked ceremonial ranking with access to material benefits, and mobility upward and downward was possible.

Actual farming is a solitary occupation (Titiev 1944:184-7). Land could not and cannot be bought and sold. An unmarried man farms his own clan lands, turning the produce over to his sisters and mother. A married man's produce stays in the household into which he is married, being shared by wife, children, and perhaps other members of wife's lineage. "In any general account of their agriculture," wrote C. Daryll Forde in 1931 (pp. 370-371), "the Hopi will explain that the fields belong to the woman and that they receive them from the clan. The mother of each family has several fields at her disposal. When her daughters marry she hands them one or more, or parts of several, and on her death her female matrilineal relatives assume control of the land, the direct descendants having prior claim." A woman reinforced and maintained her claim to land and its produce by having her husband farm it. But several Hopis told Forde that an "individual could not in practice refuse demands should occasion arise for a share in the crop from fellow clanswomen. The clan mother, senior woman who usually keeps the clan fetish and ceremonial paraphernalia, would intervene in any dispute as to land or houses and would settle the matter after discussion. These statements tend to reinforce the central idea of ultimate clan ownership of land as indicated by the marking stones (kalalni)."

Variations in Land Tenure

But one Hopi lady from First Mesa told Forde (1931:378) she gave two fields to her two brothers, who planted those fields and also those of their wives' clans, and Forde as well as Lowie also documented possession of fields by men and even cases of men passing plots within their own clan lands onto their sons, daughters, nieces, or nephews. "Where a man had no son or daughter," Forde (1931:383-4) was told, "his land was usually claimed by his relatives of *his* own clan." Thus a man might farm his father's clan lands if there were no bidders for them from the owning clan. This possibility depended upon permission of father's clan, however, and if the fields went fallow, they automatically reverted to father's clan's ownership. Nagata (1970:108-111) was told in the early 1960s that, just prior to the American era, Hopi rights of usufruct and disposal of land were starting to change at Third Mesa, so that farming plots were held by individual men, although formal ownership was still by clan. Thus a man might designate another man of his own clan to inherit rights to his field, or a man might put new land into cultivation if it was not already within the boundaries of another clan's land. These lands would not, of course, be in the best areas.

Although clan land is localized, clan members are not. Membership in a clan is a guarantee only the necessity to abide by exogamic marriage rules; it does not automatically grant access rights to land owned by one's clan, one's father's clan, or a phratry-linked clan. A woman and her children might share in the produce from her brother's or matrilateral cousin's field, but she might just as easily share in the produce from her husband's or her father's field. The kin link and the personal relationship between the two people are the determining factors. Hopis told Titiev in the 1930s that formerly, a clan (or a lineage) had planted and harvested lands together. Titiev even witnessed a communal planting party, but the participants were of several different clans. Forde (1931:396-7) was given a transcript of a description of a planting party in 1912: the old men smoked; the boys and girls planted; and two Maasaw Katsinas enforced the labor.

Haves and Have-Nots. Titiev (1944) noted quite clearly that not all clans had their own lands, and clearly, some clans had better lands than others. Thus, participation in a planting party was a way of ensuring a family of some of the produce, even from some one else's lands. This situation could well result in what was described to Titiev as some people being "slaves" for others. Brandt (1954:24-25; 339n.2) noted in 1946-47 that high-ranking groups formerly had a favorable position with respect to land rights," and that even in the 1940s, some people continued to "fear chiefs because of their associations with ceremonies and ceremonial objects, which renders them supernaturally dangerous." A man describing himself as Christian and progressive told a Government investigating team in 1955 that "in the old days when the Hopi government was intact those of us who are common did not have as much fertile land to farm. Anything the Kikmongwi says we are servants unto him. He stays in command. Springtime comes, all the people plant his fields." And Helen Sekaquaptewa (1969:8-10, 38-40, 44), a Hotevillan who left Oraibi as a child in 1906, stated that the Oraibi Kikmongwi always formed a work group in the spring to irrigate and prepare his fields for planting before other fields were prepared, and that men were also expected to help plant, maintain, and harvest the Kikmongwi's crop.

The Kikmongwi always had a large store of corn and in times of famine he and his family ate well while others starved. His clan, the Bear Clan, had the best lands along the Oraibi Wash.

Other situations of some Hopis working for others might result from demographic processes. Good land in terraces and floodplains is limited, and a clan or phratry whose population grew too rapidly due to the vagaries of demographic probabilities would be in real trouble after a couple of generations. A man could alleviate pressure on his own clan lands by farming his wife's clan's land, but only if there were no candidates for its use. Population imbalances could result in a clan running out of farming alternatives quickly. The establishment of Moenkopi was an effort to alleviate pressure on the farmland of five phratries from Oraibi (Nagata 1970:37-44), but pressure from Mormons and Navajos almost immediately limited the possibilities there.

Clans that experienced the opposite process and risked becoming "empty" due to a lack of women, could "import" women of linked clans from other villages, but would more likely merge with linked clans in the same village. The merging process could also involve two different phratries, as noted earlier. These instances are ones in which the principle of ceremonial stewardship, as interpreted by particular individuals who were willing to assume its burdens, could result in actual, tangible, material benefits. As long as there were no other bidders, ambitious and energetic persons might rise higher in the hierarchy by taking on ceremonial responsibilities. An entire lineage, and thereby a clan, might do the same, thereby slipping into better agricultural lands to which they could now legitimately lay claim. Such a process is well documented at Walpi between in the early 1900s when the Stick Clan went extinct (Forde 1931) and between 1880 and 1944, when the village chieftaincy -- the role of Kikmongwi -- shifted from Bear to Millet and finally to Flute clan, each of which is in three separate phratries at other villages (Eggan 1950:98-99; 66-67).

A Summary of Economic and Political Context

Between 1893 and 1906 the following processes were equally at work at all Hopi villages: (1) government pressure for children to attend school; (2) a cycle of drought, deluge, and arroyo cutting; (3) increasing competition for land from Navajos; (4) steady influx of tourists and anthropologists; (5) general acculturative pressures; (6) development of silversmithing as a viable source of income; (7) missionization. Between 1893 and 1906 the following processes affected *First Mesa and Second Mesa only*: (1) an epidemic; (2) consequent depopulation.

The following processes affected First Mesa, Third Mesa, and Second Mesa *un*equally and differentially: (1) increasing population pressure on a decreasing amount of arable land plus competition from either Navajos or Mormons or both: *Third Mesa only*; (2) a history of intellectual debate concerning fulfillment of prophecy by Mormons and Americans: *Third Mesa only*; (3) a history of opposition to the U.S. Government since 1872: *on a sliding scale, with First Mesa with the least and Third Mesa with the most*; (4) a history of contacts and interchanges with Mormons: *on a sliding scale, with Second Mesa with the least or none at all and Third Mesa with the most*; (5) agency employment and freighting contracts: *on a sliding scale, from First Mesa with the most through Third Mesa with the least, where "wage-work opportunities were remarkably limited"* (Levy 1992:112) *to Second Mesa with none at all*; (6) wool, livestock, and coal sales: *on a sliding scale from First Mesa with the most through Third Mesa with less to Second Mesa with the least*; (7) pottery sales: *on a sliding scale, from First Mesa with the most, due to women selling pots to Stephen and Keam, through Third Mesa with less to Second Mesa with the least*. In fact, First Mesa potters were beginning to exert exclusive control of the Anglo-American pottery market, which would ultimately result in potters having access to this market only if they were from, or had kin on, First Mesa (Wyckoff 1985:1-2, 81); (8) jewelry and basketry sales: although begun at First Mesa, silversmithing seems to have been *exclusively associated with Second and Third Mesas* by 1900, as was basketry; (9) Competition for decreasing arable land, phrased in terms of competition for ceremonial functions and roles controlled by the Kikmongwi in the face of increasing population: *Third Mesa only*.

Thus, with equally low populations, First Mesa had the greatest economic alternatives and Second Mesa had the least. With a population 10-20% greater than that of the other two Mesas combined, Third Mesa and Moenkopi had only slightly better economic opportunities than Second Mesa and nowhere near the opportunities that First Mesa had. An interesting economic connection bound Second and Third Mesas together: while Hopi men learned silver smithing from one man in particular at First Mesa, Sikyatala, the majority of silversmiths were at Oraibi and Shungopavi: 4 in Oraibi and 3 in Shungopavi. With the exception of Bert Fredericks, brother to Tawakwaptiwa, Oraibi's "Friendly" Kikmongwi, all of the silversmiths were "Hostiles" who ended up in Hotevilla. Two of these included Dan Kochongva and Andrew Hermequaftewa, prominent figures in the "Traditionalist Movement" forty years later, and another was Tawahongnewa (Wright 1972:12), leader of the Second Mesa "Hostiles" who would challenge Tawakwaptiwa in 1906. (See below.) With this assessment in mind, we turn now to the events of the Split themselves, which began long before 1906.

The Events: 1890-1909

Trader Thomas Keam persuaded the Commissioner of Indian affairs and the Chiefs of four of the five villages that filling the school with children would get them an all-expenses-paid trip to Washington, D.C. (ARCIA 1890; Yava 1978:157-164). They met the Commissioner of Indian Affairs and the Secretary of the Interior, but they did not get to meet the President. It was on this trip that the chiefs were asked to select missionaries, and apparently they did: the First Mesa and Second Mesa representatives selected Baptists and Loololma selected the Mennonites, who arrived a year later in the persons of Rev. H.R. Voth and wife. Loololma's trip to Washington must have emphasized his ties to the Government in the eyes of many of his villagers. Upon his return, Loololma's opponents gave him a hard time. At one point, he was even made a prisoner in his own kiva; clearly he could no longer command respect. His opponents refused to allow Oraibi's children to go to school and apparently they had the backing of nearly the entire village. This defiance, of course, put Loololma in violation of his agreement. It must have also put him into a position of some embarrassment, as it did Keam, who had persuaded the Government to buy his ranch buildings for the school in the first place. In 1892 Congress made Indian education compulsory. Opposition to schools persisted at all three mesas, but at First Mesa, Tom Polacca's insistence on schools may have dampened resistance from political ceremonial leaders because of Polacca's pivotal economic position (Yava 1978:10-11).

Between November, 1890 and August, 1906, troops were called out to Oraibi four times and once to Shungopavi. Arrests were made and altogether forty-nine men were jailed. Exacerbating and complicating the situation were the surveyors sent out to allot land in severalty in spring of 1891. Intentions of arresting the ringleaders of the resistance to allotment led to the confrontation related at the beginning of this chapter. The force of 300 armed Oraibi men was probably the entire Momtsit Society, warriors reconstituted after more than two decades of inactivity, since several of the Momtsit patron deities also appeared: Kwatoko (Kuatu-ku-e), Maasaw, Spider Woman, and the War Twins. War was averted when the troops judiciously withdrew, but they returned with reinforcements, accompanied by trader Keam and anthropologist Fewkes, and a Hotchkiss cannon in July. They halted outside the village and were met by six leaders, one of whom showed commanding officer Corbin a stone tablet, with markings on it, documenting the Bear Clan's right to control Oraibi and all the land around it. The six leaders then led Corbin, Fewkes, and Keam up the trail. On the way they encountered the

Momtsit chief, who told them the fight was off. The warriors were ready, they said, but the rest of the people did not want a war. Corbin arrested the nine leaders, including Patupha and Loololma, and took them to Fort Wingate. They were later released.

On November 29, 1894, troops arrested nineteen men and confined them at hard labor for nine months in the new maximum security military prison on Alcatraz Island in San Francisco Bay. An army captain with the Seventh Infantry was assigned to the "Moqui" Agency as acting agent (Spicer 1962:203; ARCIA 1895:96-97, 118-119; 1896:113). Upon their return, the "Hostile" leaders consolidated their position and the ruptures were finalized between 1896 and 1897. "Hostiles" also appeared at Mishongnovi and Shipaulovi, and after the 1898-99 epidemic, moved to Shungopavi (Whiteley 1988a:47). The "Hostiles" began holding their own ceremonies at Oraibi, making their own ritual paraphernalia and persisting in their opposition to the schools. Lomahongiwma of the Spider Clan even started holding his own Soyal ceremony, supposedly the property of the Bear Clan and thus owned by the Kikmongwi's sister. These actions amounted to creating a separate village within the village. In 1899, parents in Oraibi -- with over 1,000 people -- still maintained a successful 90% boycott of the boarding school in Keams Canyon as well as a day school and mission school at the foot of Third Mesa. The Agency regularly called out Indian police -- primarily Navajos -- to search houses for truant children and, if finding them, haul them off to school.

Loololma died in 1904. One of his eldest sister's sons, although not the eldest of those sons, Tawakwaptiwa, succeeded him. Tawakwaptiwa was locked into a "Friendly" stance by his social situation, although there is some evidence that in his convictions, he may have leaned more to the "Hostile" than to the "Friendly" position. In 1905 the "Hostiles", instigated by Yukiwma, challenged the new Kikmongwi by bringing 30 sympathizers under the leadership of Tawahongnewa from the Second Mesa villages into Oraibi. Tawakwaptiwa had little choice but to oust them. The U.S. Indian Agency supported him in this endeavor, but Yukiwma went to Shungopavi and urged the "Hostiles" to withhold their children from the little day school which the Agency had established at Toreva, near Mishongnovi, in 1897. Agency personnel attacked the dissidents with ammonia and a pickaxe. Finally things settled down and the agency personnel encouraged Tawahongnewa to build a village for the Shungopavi and Oraibi "Hostiles" to live together. This second effort at consolidating the "Hostile" contingent succeeded. On March 1, 1906, Oraibi's "Hostiles" ceremonially admitted Second Mesa's 52 "Hostiles" led by Tawahongnewa.

Tawahongnewa was probably trying to usurp Tawakwaptiwa's position as Kikmongwi (Whiteley 1988a:47-48) and thus, along with

Lomahongiwma, Yukiwma, and Kewanimptewa, who would become chief of Bacavi, was one of at least four contenders for the Kikmongwi's position and at odds with Tawakwaptiwa. There also may have been other contenders such as Charles Fredericks, one of Tawakwaptiwa's four brothers (see Chapter Six), as well as competition from men in the Yayaat and Poboshwimpkya curing societies, to which Patupha, who challenged Cushing in 1882, probably belonged (Levy 1992:104, 130-31). These curing societies were shamanistic in nature, providing guarantees of health, invulnerability to attack, manipulation of supernatural powers, and elimination of famine. When drought, famine, and disease struck anyway, their power probably was threatened. A switch to the secular realm of politics might be expected; shamans "frequently play an important role in mobilizing public opinion" (Harris 1991:176).

The following fall, on Sept. 7-8, 1906, the "Hostile" faction's leaders proposed a pushing contest between the two factions on the outskirts of the village. The "Friendlies" eventually won and pushed the "Hostiles" out of Oraibi (Titiev 1944:86; Nequatewa 1936:131). But apparently not even all of the ostensible "conspirators" were completely prepared on the particular day; According to Whiteley (1988a) Lomahongiwma was working for the Mennonite mission on the morning of the split.

The Government's Role

Throughout the affair, Government officials were by no means disinterested onlookers. Shortly after the split, Francis Leupp, Commissioner of Indian Affairs, made a special trip to the Hopi Reservation to review the situation and talked personally with the Oraibi Chief and the "Hostiles." Upon returning to Washington, he authorized the reservation Superintendent to ascertain how many "Hostiles" would be willing to "cut loose from the leadership of the chief agitators" and pledge to accept U. S. government suzerainty. In consultation with the President and the Secretary of the Interior, Leupp drew up a plan which included sentencing the "Hostile" leaders to a year imprisonment at hard labor; sending the Oraibi Chief away to school; and sending troops to "preserve order" (Leupp 1907).

Troops reached Third Mesa on October 27, 1906. Commissioner Leupp selected Reuben Perry, Superintendent of the Navajo Reservation at Fort Defiance and later principle of Albuquerque Indian School, as "special agent" to put his plan into effect. With police and troops under his command, Perry fanned the flames of hostility by proposing a duel between Oraibi's chief, Tawakwaptiwa, and Yukiwma (Nequatewa 1936:70-73). Whiteley (1988a:53) says that "Perry arranged the duels when he learned of the prophecy that the Oraibi leader who departed from the Hopi would agree to have his head cut off by Pahaana. This act of self-sacrifice would purify conditions and enable people to live and flourish in the Hopi way." This is not, of course, exactly what Yukiwma had said (cf. Voth 1905b), but perhaps Whiteley is right that Perry would have interpreted it that way.

Thirty years later, Edmund Nequatewa (1936:70-73) recalled the events as he and others remembered them:

> The captain said he (Tawakwaptiwa, the Oraibi Chief), still had a chance to kill Yukiwma (the primary leader of the "Hostiles," later to become Hotevilla's Kikmongwi), but Tawakwaptiwa said it was all over now. The captain said that the next morning at sunrise he would give him a chance to do his duty. So about dawn the captain, Tawakwaptiwa, and two Hopi policemen and a guard came to Hotevilla and at the sand dune the captain gave automatics to Tawakwaptiwa and his interpreter.
>
> Yukiwma was waiting for them on top of the sand dune. They slowly moved upon on the hostile chief who stood on the top of the sand dune, waiting for his time to come. He was all by himself, but behind the sand dune his men were hidden with all the weapons they could find. They intended to kill Tawakwaptiwa if Tawakwaptiwa killed Yukiwma.
>
> When the sun came up the captain told Tawakwaptiwa to walk up to Yukiwma, but he refused to move. The chief said that he would not do it because he said Yukiwma must be right and that he himself had made mistake in thinking of doing away with him. So right there he told him that he was under arrest and that he was going to be taken away some place to serve his term in prison.
>
> After a few days Chief Yukiwma was called again and all the men followed him to Kiakochomovi (Kykotsmovi). The captain asked him again if he had changed his mind or decided to surrender. He said, "No." Kewanimptewa stepped up and said that he was ready to surrender and that there were some others that would follow him. Chief Yukiwma was put to one side and Chief Kiwanimptiwa on the other. The captain said, "Take your choice." All who went on Yukiwma's side were under arrest and would be taken away. All that went on Kiwanimptewa's side were to be sent back to try to make up with Tawakwaptiwa at Oraibi.

Perry arrested 101 "Hostile" men, sending eleven younger men to Carlisle Indian School in Pennsylvania, and sentencing seventeen to one year at hard labor and seventy-one to hard labor in Keams Canyon. Two were released when they signed agreements acknowledging the U.S. Government's authority. Police took the prisoners out daily in chain gangs of six to a chain and set them to work building a road from the canyon up the slope of the mesa, which eventually connected with the Holbrook Road. Tawakwaptiwa was sent with his wife and two children to Sherman Indian Training School in Riverside, California, "until he has fitted himself by acquiring enough knowledge of English to be able to speak and understand fairly the language of the Government of our country and the laws, for the instruction and guidance of the people he aspires to rule" (Leupp 1907). Troops escorted the Shungopavi people back home.

The "Hostiles" who did "cut loose" went back to Oraibi under the leadership of Kewanimptewa, but then left Oraibi again in 1909 and founded Bacavi, just across the road from Hotevilla. The Government "rewarded" the capitulating faction and its leadership in two ways. First, the Agency superintendent made Kewanimptewa a judge with a salary of $10 a month. Second, when Kewanimptewa insisted that he and his people could no longer live in Oraibi, the Government agreed to Kewanimptewa's request for tools, doors, and windows for houses in the new village.

Consequences of the Events: Summary

The following consequences resulted: (1) replication of some sociopolitical units, that is, villages, village chiefs, and some ceremonial positions; (2) shifts in the political balance and a playing out of political rivalries; (3) destruction of most, although not all, of Third Mesa's ceremonial order; (4) consolidation of the U.S. Government's power and authority over peoples' children; (5) establishment of myth, prophecy, and "tablets" as idioms for political ideology, activity, and legitimacy; (6) redefinition of the Kikmongwi's role in terms of strengthening his position as a secular leader; (7) a loosening of the ceremonial bonds binding men together; (8) a "freeing up" of men's time from ceremonial pursuits and a re-allocation of it to craft work (especially silversmithing and weaving), off-reservation wage labor, and various entrepreneurial pursuits; (9) the changing of two productive springs from clan-owned to community-shared resources; (10) the abolition of inequities in access to better quality land; (11) changes in the land tenure system from communal to individual ownership; and (12) an end to the pattern of some Hopis without land working for other Hopis with land. But exactly why did the split happen? Explanations fall into three categories: conspiracy theory, anthropological theory, and "human agency" theory.[38]

Explanations I: Conspiracy Theory

Commissioner of Indian Affairs Leupp (1907) was the first to suggest, in print, that the split resulted more from a contrived conspiracy among the leaders than from ideological disagreements:

It is believed by not a few persons who know these Indians well that their division grew wholly out of the internal political dissensions of the tribe; that one of the factions conceived the device of declaring itself friendly to the United States Government not because it felt so especially, but because it believed that by such a declaration it could win the favor of the Government and obtain an invincible ally in its struggle with the other faction, and that the tactical effect of this move was to force the opposition into an attitude of hostility toward the Government by way of keeping up something to quarrel about.

Leupp's suggestion is so close to Nequatewa's (1936:131) assessment that it seems difficult to dismiss it. Nequatewa said that the split was contrived by the Oraibi Chief -- presumably Loololma -- and the "Hostile" leaders because Oraibi was becoming too large to operate as a single village under traditional Hopi social structure and because the Oraibi chief had been urged in Washington to get his people to move off the Mesa and establish settlements a few miles away. Hopis at Moenkopi told Oliver La Farge (1936a:49, 50) substantially the same thing, although La Farge dated the urging to 1865 and attributed it to a commanding officer at Fort Defiance. This suggestion was on the agendas of some government officials, notably agents Burton in 1899 and Mateer in 1878. But Hotevilla and Bacavi are right on top of the mesa, not below it. Only Kykotsmovi is actually off-mesa.

Polingaysi Qoyawayma (1964:47), in her autobiography, also said that the split was "planned from the beginning." But Albert Yava (1978:112-115), in his autobiography denied it. In 1973, I wrote (Clemmer 1973:15) "The element of strategy is definitely present, and the fact that the Government's strategy did not result in Oraibi coming under Government influence lends credibility to interpreting the split as having strategical elements."

But what is at issue are the *reasons* for the split and the conspiracy, if there was one, and the *process* by which it was accomplished. Was there only *one* reason? or several? Was the process one of *manipulation* by leaders; *choice of alternatives* by persons; or a combination of the two? Following Sekaquaptewa (1972), Peter Whiteley added weight to the conspiracy interpretation by learning from his Hopi consultants that the split was a "deliberate plot," brought into operation by Oraibi's active ceremonial elite, "via the subtle machinations of Hopi political action." Prophecy ostensibly played a crucial role: "The years prior to the split were recognized as fulfilling the conditions set forth in the prophecies as appropriate" for Oraibi's destruction. These conditions were "severe transgressions of ritual propriety" (still too sensitive to discuss in the 1980s) that ostensibly occurred during Loololma's tenure as *kikmongwi* and for which he was therefore responsible. "Such corruption is regarded as critical to the desire to bring the ritual order to an end," avers Whiteley (1988b:269, 283). "Thus it was resolved to bring the corrupt way of life in Oraibi to an end." "By splitting the village, the leaders could simultaneously solve the symptoms of corrupt ritualism -- that is, the land, water, and population problems, of which the were well aware." "The education program and the general issue of acceptance or rejection of the white man's way were chosen as the necessary catalyst. The leaders could move toward their ultimate aim unbeknown to the common people, who were unwittingly carrying out the plans."

How would the leaders have managed this deception? Whiteley called it nothing less than a "revolution from above."[39] "Traditionally, the *pavansinom* ("important people," but literally, "people of force, strength, or might" [Albert and Shaul 1985:61; Voegelin and Voegelin 1957:45, 20]) made the political decisions," such as the "destruction of the third world, or of Awat'ovi." They manipulated the people along certain lines, sometimes creating ruses in order to get people to act in a certain way. Often only the leaders knew the real reasons behind the decisions and actions. Whiteley's consultants told him, "It's called plotting, but it's actually faking it for the *sukavungsinom* ("common" people, literally, "other" people), disguising it from them" (Whiteley 1988a:142).[40] Their deliberate purpose was to radically change the political-religious order, "the central axis of the social system." The result was effective abolition of the Third Mesa 'class system'" (Whiteley 1988b:283, 274).

Explanations II: Anthropological

Whiteley (1988b:244-254) summarizes and dismisses three kinds of anthropological explanations, which he identifies as "determinisms:" sociological, material, and acculturative. I will not repeat those summaries here. Whiteley likes the conspiracy theory in which leaders manipulate followers because it injects "a deliberate, decision-making element with specifiable sociocultural consequences" which none of the anthropological explanations have (Whiteley 1988b:283). One assumption is that Hopi explanations are in competition and incompatible with anthropological explanations; apparently another is that only elites are capable of deliberate acts.

In contrast, Jerrold Levy (1992:3,156,8,53-54) offers the anthropological explanation that "a restricted resource base required that Hopi society structure itself on an inequitable distribution of land," and that this Hopi "system of social stratification" was "nothing more than a translation of economic reality into the realm of the sacred," with different lineages within a clan "defining the order of succession to the control of clan property." This system of social stratification "worked to manage scarcity," rather than abundance, and to restrict some individuals to fewer economic resources than others. The ceremonial system, with high-ranking lineages owning or performing important rituals, validated the economic inequalities. The Split resulted from efforts by low-ranking individuals to manipulate their leaders and dismantle the system of economic inequalities, not the other way around. This explanation, he says, neither invalidates nor competes with the Hopi explanations because their purposes are entirely different from each other. They are generated from different standpoints.

Explanations III: Human Agency

Standpoints and Motivations

One of these standpoints incorporates the concept of "human agency." The concept of "human agency" refers simply to the fact that persons, that is, "social actors," are "knowledgeable," that is, they are capable of initiating actions and changing the course of events according to their own agendas and are not mere "passive recipients of influences that irresistibly condition their conduct" (Giddens 1987:85). The 1906 Split indicated a shift: the ceremonial leaders could no longer make norms "'count'" (Rushforth and Upham 1992:239 quoting Giddens 1976:110) and thus new norms -- phrased in terms of prophecy and its interpretation -- were created. Claims, prescriptions, statements about what "ought" to be done, etc. constitute ideology, not fact, and thus must be "negotiated"; the various Hopi explanations of the Split constitute "negotiated" ideological statements reflecting the various actions of various "human agents."

Hopi explanations of the Split, like all other ideological statements, quite clearly do their work on the level of memory, logic, and metaphor. These explanations are generated from multiple standpoints and agendas and motivations; historical events never "register uniformly within any group of ethnographic subjects" (Marcus and Fischer 1986:107). Thus there is no single "native point of view." "You are going to get details that conflict with one another," Albert Yava (1978:114) warned folklorist Harold Courlander concerning the Oraibi Split, "because every clan interprets events according to how events are seen by them."

For example, Tawakwaptiwa told a version of the Emergence myth to Mischa Titiev (1944:72-73) in 1934 that also accounted for how and why the split occurred: it had occurred before in the previous world, precipitated by troublemakers from two particular clans, and thus pre-destined to re-occur because the witches had "escaped" into this world and returned to Oraibi to make trouble, thus being ousted to Hotevilla and Bacavi. These ostensible mischief-making clans were the Bow and Spider. Virtually all of the Spider Clan people were pushed out in 1906. But not all of the "mischief-makers" went to Hotevilla and Bacavi. In 1922 the custodian of the Bow Clan altar, which had been important in Oraibi's men' initiation ceremonies, publicly burned it. Tawakwaptiwa's story also has an implicit prediction that eventually, those led by the Spider clan -- meaning the people of Hotevilla and Bacavi -- would experience economic deprivation forcing them to return to Oraibi. Tawakwaptiwa did not tell Titiev that he and Yukiwma and Lomahongiwma had conspired to cook up a spurious issue concerning education and the "white man's way."

Hopis at Moenkopi and also Tawakwaptiwa told Oliver La Farge that everybody who left Oraibi was supposed to "stop dancing," but did not; Christians at Kykotsmovi told La Farge (1936a:47-49) that they were fulfilling the prophecy by not "dancing" and by converting to Christianity. But Dan Kochongva and leaders at Hotevilla told La Farge that the prophecy foretold the persecution of those who maintained them.

Hopis at First and Second Mesa told La Farge that the Oraibi-Kykotsmovi-Moenkopi idea that the prophecy foretold, or mandated, abandoning ceremonies was "silly." "There were major differences over the school question," averred Albert Yava (1978:113) from First Mesa. "Some families wouldn't talk to other families. There were fights in the streets, and some men took to carrying weapons."

Thus, *at least three different explanations by participants, based on three different interpretations of the prophecy*, purpo⁺ to explain the split, and a fourth interpretation of the prophecy *by non-participating Hopis* denies any correspondence between prophecy and the events.

It should be clear by now that any number of motivations caused people to take various actions in the Split and also to generate any number of explanations afterward; that there is no single "Hopi native viewpoint;" that there is not one prophecy, but many; and that several distinct political ideologies derive from it. Rather than manipulations of myth and prophecy being "the cynical products of politicians" to dupe the masses, myths are "adjusted and fashioned to suit changing social conditions." The "plotting" most likely came after the Split, not before it, and is expressed in purely ideological terms to in Levy's (1992:164-5) words, "provide acceptable justifications for disturbing events in a manner that allows the traditional social system to continue," if nevertheless altered to some degree.

Bondage and Freedom. In emphasizing the hierarchical nature of Hopi society, Whiteley makes it appear that the common folk would follow orders no matter what, especially if they thought their lives depended on sticking with their ceremonial leaders. But if we accept that assumption, we must credit most Hopis with very few critical abilities and assume unwitting reflex responses by less intelligent social organisms to uncomprehended and unquestioned orders by more intelligent authorities. Such behavior patterns may be attributable to a society with strong clans and lineages,[41] but not to Hopi social organization. It also does not accord with Hopi ceremonial organization; if it did, the dissident ceremonial leaders would never have been able to become dissident ceremonial leaders. Only one of them -- Lomahongiwma -- had been an accepted ceremonial leader before the ceremonies became divided into two mirror images of each other in 1896-97. People who live in perpetual ideological bondage to their ceremonial leaders do not follow new, self-proclaimed ones very easily. Surely, Hopis are not so different from the rest of the human race that they would form an exception.

Freedom is, on one hand, the right to refuse to behave, even if ultimately the right of refusal is not granted, and on the other, the right to take action in the face of disapproval. The fact that Bacavi and Hotevilla continued to hold ceremonies reflects the fact that not all participants wanted to see the demise of Hopi religion, or were even aware that the demise was supposed to happen, and that some persons had genuine convictions motivating them to refuse obedience either to Tawakwaptiwa or to the U.S. Government. "Ordinary" men might well have been motivated by a desire to get away from a situation that was becoming less and less tenable. That situation involved the power of the Kikmongwi and deteriorating material conditions.

Material Rewards. Here is where materialist explanations begin to make more sense than the conspiracy theory. Whiteley (1988b:245-254) summarizes some of the arguments against this materialist explanation, but the biggest one concerns advantage: what advantage would people have gained by moving? Hotevilla has the poorest farm lands: 60% of the fields in 1937 were located on dunes, the least reliable location in terms of water supply. Why would people leave a location with deteriorating farmland for a location with demonstrably poor farmland? Recall that the village chief -- or rather, the Bear Clan altogether -- did not work their fields. Other people worked them for them. The village chief used the ceremonial system to reward some men with good land, thereby denying it to others. The chief's family had wood chopped and brought to it; controlled others' labor; and parceled out land or withheld it at will. But with the beginning of arroyo cutting, probably in 1894, just two years before the ceremonial fabric ruptured, incentives to work for the Bear Clan would have begun to diminish. Some men, rather than having no material incentive to move, simply would have had no material incentive to stay.

Hack (1942) thought that the deterioration of farm land through arroyo cutting might have had something to do with the move, and Bradfield (1971) followed up on this suggestion, even though Lorenzo Hubbell, Jr. and Edmund Nequatewa, eyewitnesses to the Split, had assured Hack in 1937 that farmland had nothing to do with it. Terraced gardens were already being irrigated from Reed Spring (Bacavi) before the Split (Whiteley 1988b:102) and perhaps similar use of was being made of Cedar Spring (Hotevilla) as well. But the majority of the population had to make do with the "free area" dependent on direct precipitation, land of poor quality in need of lying fallow every few years. It was capable of supporting only about 65 people (Levy 1992:53). Thus, working for the chief either ceremonially or in his fields was an absolute necessity for many people, who might hope to be awarded with a non-inheritable segment of the chief's better lands. Others might cooperate in planting or hoeing parties in order to gain a share in the produce from a high-ranking clan's better lands.

But when arroyo cutting began making flood-water farming from the Oraibi Wash much more difficult or impossible, the advantage of working for others disappeared. The high-ranking clans would be expected to either have been among the first to colonize Moenkopi -- and they were -- or to have been in the "friendly" faction. And indeed, Levy (1992:95-103) found that "members of high- and middle- rank clans were friendly and those of low-rank clans were hostile significantly more often than would be expected by chance," although a few individual members of the Spider and Eagle clans were exceptions.

The Roles of Women. Titiev (1944:81-87) suggested that many if not most people were motivated by personal loyalties, largely to their households. He saw women as providing a crucial pivotal role, often swaying their husbands on the basis of *their brothers' or father's ceremonial loyalties, rather than* their *husbands' clan loyalties.* The ceremonial leaders discussed by Whiteley and by Titiev were nearly all men. But women, who *owned* the houses, who were stewards of the *wuyas* and *tiponis,* and who in theory *owned* the crops and the land, did not stand by idly and let the men manipulate them. Some women had motivations of their own. For example, Levy (1992:104) found rivalry among several women for the role of Clan Mother of the Bear Clan. He also found evidence that "high-status women were trying to produce heirs and tended to shorten birth spacing, thus displacing the older sibling from the breast and inadvertently exposing it to a variety of infectious diseases" that resulted in many early deaths of high-status children. Thus "in an effort to preserve their position, ... the prime lineages of the leading clans were engaging in a self-defeating practice" (Levy (1992:42-3).[42] Women's motivations to maintain their lineages by having children would have carried over to motivations for keeping the family of procreation, and thus the household, together.

Immediate Consequences: Anticipated and Unanticipated; Intended and Unintended

One immediate consequence was the arrest of the Hostile leaders. We can assume they might have anticipated something like that, based on the arrests of 1891, 1893, and 1894. A second consequence was the incarceration of Hotevilla's children in the Keams Canyon Boarding School until 1910. The third was the attendance of the children of Kewanimptewa's returnees at the Oraibi day school, although when they founded Bacavi, they did not go to school for four years, until a school was built and staffed in January, 1913 (Whiteley 1988a:102). A fourth was the founding of Hotevilla, and a fifth the founding of Bacavi. A sixth was the emergence of two strong chiefs: Yukiwma and Kewanimptewa. A seventh was a radical change in the definition of chieftaincy: no longer was it a ceremonially-defined and ritually-consecrated position; it was strongly secular. An eighth consequence was a change in land tenure: neither Bacavi nor Hotevilla has clan lands, and the fields are not owned by women. Individual men own the fields and may pass them onto whomever they choose. Finally, Bacavi obtained not only its own school, but also the Government's assistance in construction, and by 1914, Hotevilla also had its own school. The question is: how many of these other consequences were anticipated or intended?

New Villages: Government Strategy? The idea of new villages appears to have been encouraged by Government representatives Lemmon and Staufer who urged Tawahongnewa to establish a separate "Hostile" village with followers of Yukiwma. Furthermore, when Kewanimptewa proposed the idea, he immediately got the support he requested. The Government's strategy seems to have been to try to consolidate its influence and to leave Hotevilla to its own devices.

Superintendent Lemmon undoubtedly thought the Oraibi chief would return from Sherman a docile, cooperative, education, "progressive" leader. But the strategy backfired. Tawakwaptiwa returned embittered and resentful. Although he gave no opposition to the regular attendance of Oraibi's children at the day school at the foot of Third Mesa or the boarding school at Keams Canyon, the Chief made life uncomfortable for Mennonite converts and others who wanted to go their own way in one fashion or another. Increasingly more people moved to Kykotsmovi at the foot of the Mesa, where the government and mission schools and trading post were located. In 1923 Tawakwaptiwa decided that those who had moved to Kykotsmovi had abandoned him, and he deliberately cut the ceremonial ties binding them to him. Kykotsmovi thus became a separate, independent village, with no Kikmongwi.

Kewanimptewa planned a traditional village with "modern" accoutrements. He persuaded the Agency to supply lumber and glass for doors and window and to supply wheelbarrows, saws, hammers, nails, tools, and even the agency's carpenter. He told people to build houses in straight rows around a plaza so that later a sewer, water lines, and electricity could be installed easily (Whiteley 1988a:92). But this strategy may have been slow in hatching; Kewanimptewa did not make the requests until after Tawakwaptiwa had returned from Riverside and was making life difficult for the returnees. The deliberate and universal change in land tenure seems aimed at not only pleasing the Government, which was still trying to allot lands to individual men in severalty, but also at ending the economic bondage of some individuals to others and turning the two springs at Hotevilla and Bacavi into shared community resources, rather than restricted clan possessions.

Ironically, Hotevilla's obstinacy got it just what it ostensibly did not want: a school. Although Hotevilla's children were virtually held captive at the boarding school for four years starting in 1911, after 1915, children from other Third Mesa did not have to board at Keams Canyon. When the Hotevilla school opened, jobs materialized for matrons; janitors; grounds keepers; and other support personnel. Polingaysi Qoyawayma (Elizabeth White), the first Hopi to become a school teacher, taught there in the 1920s. Only one or two families continued to keep their children out of school; authorities made no moves against the truancies. Ultimately, Kykotsmovi became a community larger than Oraibi and Bacavi put together, although Hotevilla quickly grew to Third Mesa's largest village and has remained so.

Interpretation of the Historical, Political, and Economic Context

Oraibi's split was indeed a serious of deliberate acts for political and economic reasons. But why did Oraibi alone choose to split? Hopis knew quite well how to bud off population segments and mold them into new villages. They did it in the 1690s with Shipaulovi; in 1776 with

Sichomovi; and in the 1870s with Moenkopi. Why, then, did so much trauma, contention, conflict, delay, acrimony, and ideological justification surround the splitting process at Oraibi from 1897 through 1909?

To answer this question, we must return to the topic of political, economic, and historic context, and also consider culture, society and politics in the light of "human agency." Rivalry for the chieftaincy may have been going on at Oraibi for decades. Between 1880 and 1909, at least five and possibly six rivalries are apparent: Loololma/Patupha; Loololma/ Lomahongiwma/ Tawakwaptiwa/Yukiwma; Tawakwaptiwa/Tawahongnewa (from Shungopavi); and Tawakwaptiwa/ Kewanimptewa. Without Yukiwma, Kewanimptewa, and Tawakwaptiwa each having his own village, only Tawakwaptiwa would have remained a chief. Although Tawakwaptiwa maintained his claim to legitimacy by virtue of heredity, agent Lemmon and Commissioner Leupp obviously wanted to turn his office into quite a secular one, endowing him with qualifications "to rule" through education. Chieftaincy took on a distinctly secular character, whether intended or not.

Ambitious men at First Mesa had plenty of paths to prestige and material success: freighting, agency employment, working for Keam and later Hubbell. Ambitious women also had options: making pottery for Keam, Stephen, and Fewkes and working in the boarding school. Second Mesa people did not have these options available to them and would have felt the pinch when arroyo cutting started, just as the Third Mesa people did. But they had a few more springs and they were not drying up. Tragically, after 1899, smallpox had reduced the number of people to about half the population of Oraibi. Still, the fact that "Hostiles" developed there as well as at Oraibi tells us something.

Oraibi had progressively had its options truncated and thwarted. All parties were manoeuvering within a social field intersected by economic and political conditions that were becoming increasingly threatening. Opposition to Americans seems to have been nearly unanimous in Oraibi from 1872 on. As it became clear that alliance with Mormons had become a bad idea, and that alliance with Navajos was out of the question, what alternative did Oraibi have? Alliance with Americans, obviously. But the Americans had established their first agency far to the east in 1874, and by 1875, they had been cornered by Keam, whose ranch and trading enterprise attracted commerce, cash, and opportunity. In contrast, what did the Oraibi people get? Orders to ship their children off to the new local capital; encroachment on their lands not only by Mormons but also by Navajos; increasing limitation of Mormons' political power, on which Oraibi may have been counting heavily in its power-balancing attempts; little or no assistance from Americans in limiting the encroachments; missionaries committed to asceticism and convinced that the Hopis were a dying race; arbitrary and unilateral attempts to cut up their lands; and a failure of material conditions which the shamans could not cure (Levy 1992:131) and which, in many Hopis' minds, was directly linked with degree of ceremonial efficacy.

Surely most Hopis did not think that they could successfully oppose the U.S. Government by moving a distance of four miles and setting up new communities. I doubt that many, if any Hopis seriously considered moving to Kawestima. And the division between "Friendlies" and "Hostiles" seems to have been, so to speak, less than skin deep, at least in terms of most participants' commitment to all the institutions of the U.S. as opposed to all the institutions of Hopi society and culture. The Hostile leaders undoubtedly did plot and scheme; but whether they plotted and schemed with Loololma or against him remains a very open question, and whether Tawakwaptiwa was party to the full conspiracy also remains an open question. Whether Mormon influence was direct or merely in the background also remains a question. The Hostiles developed their stance within the context of Oraibi's uneasy political and economic alliance with the Mormons. Material conditions provided the context for the Oraibi Split; History set up the pro- and anti-American political ideology; and culture translated it into Hopi social organization.

Conclusion: Culture, Ideology, Politics, and Society

Culture is the system of shared meanings, symbols, behavior patterns, values, attitudes, and material items that give a group of people an identity, both to themselves and to others. Cultural ideology is the cognitive dimension of culture, a cognitive map, an intellectual, logical model of the world and its constituent parts which supplies thereby a model of the natural world, of the place of humanity within that world, and of the relationships physical and metaphysical, of the world to the cosmos. It also provides a model of the social world and its components which tells who a group is, how and why they differ from others, and which allocates members of the group to social categories constructed on the basis of age, gender, descent, marital status, wealth, occupation, skill, power and so forth. It provides the normative aspects of culture, a hierarchy of values for evaluating the components of the social world, and also motivates people and encourages them to put forth effort (cf. Worsley 1984:42). Culture becomes politicized in certain contexts when competing interest groups interpret the same cultural ideology in seemingly contradictory fashions.

Until 1906, much of Hopis' cultural ideology could be derived from religion and kinship. The ideology stressed the importance of "both commoners and ceremonialists," with ceremonialism being open to every individual on some level. But after 1906, myth, prophecy, and tradition assumed increasingly greater importance as sources of cultural ideology. And if the Split of 1906 did nothing else, it brought to the fore the political nature of cultural ideological interpretations.

The image of Hopis levelling ideological fusillades at each other in the name of "progressivism" and "traditionalism" clashes with the image of progress that well-meaning partisans, then and now, would like to savor. But the progressive-conservative, or friendly-hostile, or liberal-conservative idiom was not something entirely imposed by outsiders; Hopis assimilated the metaphor and used it within their own cultural, social, political context. Common-folk Hopi were no more manipulated by their upper-class betters than the ceremonial leaders were by the commoners. All changes in context produce human experiences that are qualitatively different from previous experiences. When there seems to be no flow of things, when the element of time seems to smash the promises and desires of the future one after another, than reality loses all freshness and seems unable to renew itself. When drought follows plague; troops follow missionaries; good farmland washes away or gets usurped; water in the well dries up; and new economic opportunities seem to rush away like filings toward magnets, out of people's direct control, then the little imps of cultural despair and social unrest begin to appear in the forms of disbelief, lack of commitment and enthusiasm, anger and discontent, gossip and quarrelsomeness.

The Contact Situation. Under material conditions of stress and duress, acculturative pressures are felt much more acutely than otherwise. When disaster, disease, and deprivation accompany the establishment of an administrative structure to implement certain specific policies or to establish different rules for a smaller, less powerful society by a clearly more powerful society such as the United States,, then ambiguous and ambivalent interfaces among individuals in potentially volatile social fields are created. These social fields, summarized under the rubric, "contact situation," consist of people, contexts, agendas, places, activities, and goals, contributed by both societies. The relationship between dominating society and dominated society establishes distinctive but unpredictable sets of social, political, economic, and cultural processes and institutions consisting of what the dominated imposed; what the dominated accepted; and what the dominated put in place to deflect the impositions that they wanted to resist. "Human agency," implying an ability by groups of individuals to influence events, also introduces some degree of unpredictability. Thus the Hopis eventually did accept schools and did deal with agents and missionaries. But they also generated new meanings for the new contexts.

One result of the Split was a lengthening of the curvature of lived experience along which people could arrange their political affairs and express political sentiments. No longer was it necessary to define politics in terms of religion; no longer would it be necessary to attain one or more ceremonial positions in order to travel a political road. People could be "free" from some of the ceremonial obligations binding them.[43] A universal political ideology had been put in place, replacing the ambiguity of the previous forty years with institutional metaphors: "anti-government" Hotevilla; "pro-government" Bacavi; the "progressives" of "New" Oraibi (Kykotsmovi) and the "conservatives" of "Old" Oraibi. Hopis undoubtedly treated these new metaphors as having a great deal of indeterminacy in terms of content; perhaps no greater number of "pro-government" individuals could be found at Bacavi than at Old Oraibi. But the metaphors quickly became established as social realities and as the basis for cultural and political ideological frameworks. Within the following three decades the import of these social metaphors and ideological frameworks would slowly permeate the entire Hopi polity.

Hopi children on a burro around the turn of the century.
SOURCE: Photo by Fay Cooper Cole. Photographic reproduction by Steven Ray
Pearlman.

Hopi country.
SOURCE: Photo by Richard O. Clemmer.

Kykotsmovi with fields in the foreground. The large, white structure is a
Mennonite church.
SOURCE: Richard O. Clemmer.

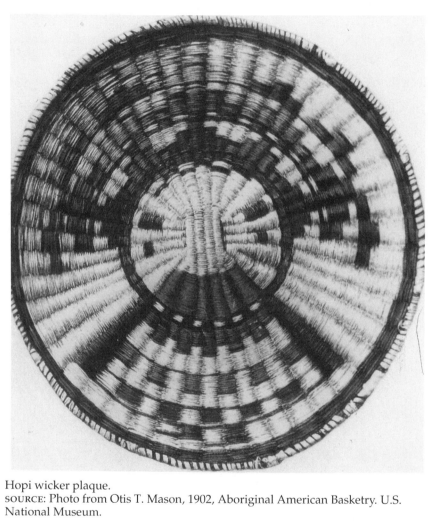

Hopi wicker plaque.
SOURCE: Photo from Otis T. Mason, 1902, Aboriginal American Basketry. U.S. National Museum.

Interior Hopi fireplace as J.W. Powell saw it in 1874.
SOURCE: Photo by John Wesley Powell, 1895, Canyons of the Colorado.

Tusayan milling stones as seen by J.W. Powell in 1874.
SOURCE: Photo by John Wesley Powell, 1895, Canyons of the Colorado.

A passageway in Walpi as seen by J. W. Powell. Sketch by H. Hobart Nichols, 1890. SOURCE: John Wesley Powell, 1895, Canyons of the Colorado.

A rare photograph of the four-story, mud-plastered dwellings in Oraibi, 1905, just before the split.
SOURCE: Photo by Joseph Mora, courtesy of John R. Wilson.

Hopi men, "hostile" prisoners on a forced march from Hotevilla to Keams Canyon, escorted by the 5th Cavalry, November 1906.
SOURCE: Photo by Joseph Mora, courtesy of John R. Wilson.

A Hopi girl in a temporary shelter at Hotevilla, October 1906. The "hostiles" set up make-shift shelters and camps before starting to build the new village.
SOURCE: Photo by Joseph Mora, courtesy of John R. Wilson.

Black Mesa Mine.
SOURCE: Photo by Christopher McLeod.

Sign of the Times, Oraibi, 1978.
SOURCE: Photo by Christopher McLeod.

6

Reorganization: 1910-1945

The 1930s were the era of reorganization in more ways than one. Congress authorized the "New Deal" and a special "New Deal for Indians." Initiation of the New Deal is said to be the beginning of the era of political modernization in America (Black 1966:90). Initiation of the *Indian* New Deal is said to have altered the means, but not fundamentally the end, of U.S. Indian policy: acculturation and some degree of assimilation. But it is also said to have reflected a conviction that Indian societies could be reconstituted as integrated units, functioning as political and economic pressure groups (Cornell 1988:95). Coming hard on the heals of nearly two decades of various assaults on culture, religion, and personhood by Government personnel and a brief period in which Government and missionaries cooperated on a campaign of religious repression, the New Deal also followed a period in which various non-Indian partisans had declared themselves on the side of Hopi culture and had established a tradition of involvement in Hopi life and politics. This involvement was curried and nurtured by many Hopis, who saw these non-Indian partisans as welcome allies in their struggle with missionaries and the Indian Bureau, and as increasingly important sources of markets for jewelry, weavings, basketry, and other artistic and craft items. Hopis gradually started switching from raising sheep to raising cattle, and an uneven, but overall improvement in cash flow encouraged more Hopis and non-Hopis alike to open stores and trading posts.

Thus in many ways Hopis had already begun their own reorganization, on cultural as well as on social and political levels, before 1930. A new cultural ideology had been introduced. Alterations in social organization were strengthening the village as the unit of identity and the power of the Kikmongwis as village leaders. Many villages had begun to give impetus to new directions in politics, economics, and social life. But Old Oraibi seemed intent on fulfilling its ostensible destiny of self-destruction. Arts and crafts, particularly carvings, weavings, basketry, and pottery were an early source of cash that replaced raw wool to some extent, and a kind of "Hopi Nouveau/Hopi Deco" decorative motif for pottery synthesized ancient Hopi designs with contemporary art styles to as a basis of growing public appeal for Hopi art.

Reorganization of the Sociopolitical Fabric

As the 1920s rolled on, Old Oraibi became nearly a ghost town. In 1917 Hopi converts and Mennonite missionaries finally completed a huge, magnificent dressed sandstone church, originally planned by Voth more than 20 years earlier, just outside the village to the southeast. Almost at the moment of its completion, lightning struck it, setting its wooden beams and interior afire and collapsing the roof. The missionaries reverted to using the small, white clapboard church in Kykotsmovi and its twin in Bacavi. By 1934 Oraibi was a mass of tumbled sandstone blocks, with only fragments of four rows of houses being occupied, plus a few scattered dwellings scattered on its outskirts. Only three kivas were being used, and only two of the four men's secret societies still functioned. Wuwutsim, Soyal, the Qoqol and Niman Katsina ceremonies, Powamuya and Lalakon were its only ceremonies. The last men's initiations, Maraw ceremony, and Snake Dance were held in 1912; the last Patcava in 1913; and the last Flute ceremonies in 1909. Oraibi's population had dwindled to 112 in 1933, and Tawakwaptiwa prophesied that soon, Old Oraibi would be completely deserted. But after that, the full ceremonial calendar would be revived! (Titiev 1944:94-95).

By the early 1920s, the Hopi socio-political situation had become quite complicated. The populations of Kykotsmovi and Moenkopi expanded. Kykotsmovi, also known as "New" or "Lower" Oraibi, at the foot of Third Mesa, given its "independence" in 1923 when Tawakwaptiwa declared that there would no longer be any official ceremonial cooperation between Oraibi and Kykotsmovi. By the 1930s, Kykotsmovi had "modernized" and was electing its governor. From 1910 to 1947, Bacavi was governed solely by its Kikmongwi, Kewanimptewa, feared by some as a witch and described by others as an impressive clairvoyant. Head of the Kwan Society yet unwilling to sponsor any men's initiations, he was powerful and respected, and seems to have asserted much more authority than other Kikmongwis (Whiteley 1988b:123, 205, 213-216). Part of this authority stemmed from that granted to him in appointment by the U.S. Government as Bacavi's judge/policeman in 1913. In this capacity, he enforced the school attendance order in Bacavi and Hotevilla and had the Agency's police force to back him up. His chosen successor never took up the office of Kikmongwi -- which came to be called "governor" some time in the 1930's -- but some time in the 1950's Kewanimptewa's son and his son's son held the office until "this became formalized into a two-year elected position in the late 1960's" (Whiteley 1988b:216). Kewanimptewa appointed himself representative to the Hopi Tribal Council in the 1930's and in the 1950's his apparent choice for that role continued to hold that position by consensus or default until the late 1960s. Bacavi abandoned its ceremonies when five knowledgeable older participants in Wuwutsim died, prior to 1917; abbreviated performances stopped in the mid-1920s. Oaqol stopped in the early 1920s, and stewardship of the Flute ceremony reverted to Lomahongiwma's brother at Hotevilla, after Lomahongiwma's death in 1919 (Whiteley 1988b:198-200).[44]

Hotevilla recreated many of the religious societies and much of the ceremonial cycle. Yukiwma, now the only leader of the "Hostiles" and member of the Fire or Kookop Clan, assumed the position of Kikmongwi but not ownership of the Soyal ceremony associated with the chieftaincy. When Yukiwma died in 1929, three candidates for the office of Kikmongwi emerged. Paliwuhiama, the Spider Clan nephew of Lomahongiwma and Chief of the Soyal Society as well as keeper of the Flute Clan altar, was "looked upon as Village Chief by virtually the entire pueblo" (Titiev 1944:211) in 1934, but by 1936, he had dropped out of the picture. Pongayawyma, Yukiwma's sister's son, came to be regarded as Yukiwma's most legitimate successor (Hopi Hearings 1955:285). But silversmith Dan Kochongva, Yukiwma's son and an important member of the Ahl (Two-Horn) Society that installs Kikmongwis (Nagata 1962:76; Titiev 1944:130ff), assumed the power if not the title of Kikmongwi, even though he was of a relatively low-ranking clan, the Sun Clan, which owns no ceremonies.

At Moenkopi, "educated Indians", people "similar to what Kluckhohn described as 'Agency Indians' (Kluckhohn and Leighton 1962:106)" (Nagata 1970:50), "challenged the traditional power structure of the village, which was based on allotment lands and sanctioned by the parent village of Oraibi" (Nagata 1970:49-50). In the late 1920s, some of these younger, educated villagers formed an informal "village council intended to mitigate factional differences by providing a group 'which did not discriminate by religion and which everybody in the village could join.'" It was meant not as a governing body, but rather, only as a discursive forum. However, by 1932 its membership consisted entirely of younger people from the geographically higher portion of Moenkopi that later became known as "Upper Moenkopi" (Nagata 1970:51-53). The "village council" could not maintain its mediating position and thus it dissolved (Nagata 1970:55). The growing progressive-traditional split ruptured the village politically. Eventually, the Upper District accomplished a ceremonial split similar to that in Oraibi in 1897 by holding its own Katsina initiations. When the Hopi Tribal Council was revived in 1950, "the Upper group of Moenkopi turned to New Oraibi (Kykotsmovi) and Keams Canyon, where most of the council activities were planned and executed" (Nagata 1970:59).

Politically, then, Hopis continued to present distinct socio-political entities with a well defined, but diffuse, system of leadership and no unity beyond the village level. Some Hopis tried to form a "Hopi Council" in 1924; reasons for its existence and its agenda are unclear. The agency superintendent opposed it, all but calling it a communist plot. When Hopis in Kykotsmovi formed a second "Hopi Council" which also included old Chief Tawakwaptiwa from Oraibi in 1931, however, to negotiate a solution to the Hopi-Navajo land question (Stephens 1961:127-129), a different superintendent supported it (Miller 1931). Short-lived and informal, this council came to be regarded as representing only Kykotsmovi. At First Mesa, bronc riders and horse-breeders formed the Rodeo Association and also started a "Rodeo Council." The Superintendent tended to treat this council, also informal, as a "true First Mesa council," even though "the chiefs absolutely refused to admit its existence" (La Farge 1936a:29).

The Reorganization of Culture

In a sense, the Split of 1906 had accomplished a reorganization of part of Hopi society, and the ideology that framed it -- acceptance or rejection of Americanisms -- began a reorganization of the range of possibilities in comprehending, organizing, and transforming peoples' experience of reality. Formerly, the world had been permeated with misery, toil, filth, disease, death, and hardships that formed the backdrop against which it might be said that a kind of libidinal peace and joy was achieved through religious ceremonies and in fulfilling social obligations. But this world was replaced by one in which the individual's social position and relations to others appeared determined not only by the mysterious and uncontrollable character of natural events, but also by two sets of overriding critical standards: first, those of all Hopi society, and second, those of the Euro-American institutions imposed on them. Various aspects of these Euro-American institutions, from missionization to schooling to wage labor, presented promises of success and material improvements for some individuals but clearly not to the same degree for all.

Men living in Oraibi, Moenkopi, Kykotsmovi, and Bacavi may have gained considerable autonomy by not being pressured into long, arduous ceremonial preparations during the busiest time of the year, July through December, since virtually all ceremonies occurring in these months had lapsed by 1925. They might prepare and plant their fields in February, March and April and go off to work for the railroad; at seasonal jobs in Grand Canyon; or as silversmiths in Phoenix, after their own crops were in. Because responsibility for Niman rotated among the kivas, a man might dance in only one Katsina dance a year, at Powamuya in February, and perhaps do Niman once every three, four, or five years.

But partially dismantling the collectivities of Hopi life -- clan land tenure plus most of the ceremonial secret societies operating for nearly half the year -- would also dismantle much of the social fabric holding Hopis together. No longer would the commonalities of initiation into men's societies in all villages give all men similar experiences. No longer did the warrior societies and warfare offer the possibilities of male solidarity and cooperation, if briefly, on a pan-village level. In fact, a consequence of the Split was to differentiate Hopis from each other, both in terms of actually *eliminating* certain possibilities in some villages -- in terms of ceremonies -- and also in terms of releasing the *specifically Hopi* constraints on behavior. In short, individuals were freer to go their own ways.

American Reformers and Liberals and Their Influence

At the same time, paradoxically, Hopis became on the one hand, more subject to the whims of their leaders, the Kikmongwis, since they emerged not only increased in number, but also more important in political life, and on the other hand, more subject to the whims of U.S. Government officials. The period from 1911 through 1924 can be called the era of repression and persecution; missionaries and bureaucrats flexed their muscles and used the reservation context to launch assaults on the internal logic and social fabric of Indian life. It was the era of super-patriotism, xenophobia, and reactionary conservatism in the United States in general, in which various groups tried to nationalize "Culture" in accordance with their own ethnic and religious values.[45]

Two broad categories of social activists fought against this reactionary conservatism. Women, who had just gotten the vote and become a new political force, played an active part in both groups. One was the "reformers;" the other was the "liberals." For a brief period, Indian country -- especially the Pueblos and Hopiland -- would be their battle ground. The reformers had gotten prohibition and universal suffrage enacted. Devoted to a platform of equality for all, they were generally integrationist, assimilationist, and thoroughly Christian. Their viewpoints dovetailed with those of the reactionaries in the effort to promote a nationalistic culture but opposed all extremist and illegal activities. The "liberals" also opposed extremism and the reactionaries, but they opposed the reformers as well. They promoted internationalism, rather than nationalism; took an interest in all social, artistic, and literary experiments; and supported cultural and social pluralism. The liberals sought a reorganization of society and politics on all levels to allow the expression of personhood to flower fully; the reformers, in contrast, sought a reorganization of personhood for all modern individuals on all levels.

The Reformers' Assault on Culture and Religion

Much of the Reformers' agenda was reflected in Indian country. It amounted to nothing less than an assault on Hopi culture and religion. "Transition" institutions were created that would ease the Indians, supposedly, into the "modern" world. One of these institutions was the Tribal Court, where the force of Indian agents' rule was made to be felt.

Political Forms: The Court. A "Tribal Court" had been established in the 1890s as a direct arm of the Agency Superintendent (cf. Hagan 1966:104). It operated much like the Courts of Indian Offenses that had been created in 1883 (cf. Hagan 1966:109-111), but was separate and distinct from the nearby Navajo Court of Indian Offenses which operated until 1959 (Hagan 1966:152). The Superintendent appointed three judges, one from each Mesa, who rotated monthly as presiding judge; one of these had been Bert Fredericks from Oraibi and the other, Kewanimptewa from Bacavi. Hooker Hongave from First Mesa was in office the longest. The Superintendent selected Hooker Hongave as Chief Judge, who more or less represented the Superintendent as an Appeal Judge.

As in cases tried before the Courts of Indian Offenses, cases could be appealed from Hopi Tribal Court to U.S. District Court, but cases were virtually never appealed beyond the superintendency level. While a village council might be called upon to settle disputes between individuals, this rarely happened. Hopis could and sometimes did bring disputes directly to the Superintendent or other government officials on the reservation for adjudication (Colton 1934:22).

But these courts and their procedures were nearly irrelevant to the real political process. Indian agents continued to rule the Hopi reservation with a dictatorial hand, as if it were their "Empire" (Crane 1925:124, 179), and troops were called out to capture children for the Keams Canyon Boarding School as late as 1911 (Crane 1925:157-174). Periodic arrests of individuals and attempts to discourage Hopi religion continued to impress the impact on federal jurisdiction on Hopi life (cf. ARCIA 1899:80-81; 158-159; Crane 1925:186; Talayesva 1942:189-190; James 1974:174-186; Duberman, Eggan and Clemmer 1979:103-124; Eggan, Clemmer and Duberman 1980). Leo Crane, a "lousy superintendent" who clearly despised Hopis but later "wrote some books making himself out to be just swell" (La Farge 1936a:1), re-instituted the procedure of taking troops to root out "dissidents" -- now concentrated at Hotevilla -- and to drag children to the boarding school in Keams Canyon. In 1911 he barged into dozens of homes in Hotevilla, dragging sixty-nine children out and piling them into wagons, which took them to the Keams Canyon School from which they were not released until 1915. Yukiwma was arrested. Crane followed the same procedure at Shungopavi. According to Whiteley (1988a:104-105) Yukiwma and Kewanimptewa supposedly agreed that a larger school would be built at Hotevilla to accommodate Bacavi's and Hotevilla's pupils. But when the school opened in 1916, Yukiwma opposed it. Agent Crane (1925:87, 186), describing Yukiwma as "now in the medicine man and prophecy business," imprisoned him in the guard house until 1919. There was no procedure for redress of these grievances: the Tribal courts and judges had no jurisdiction over the U.S. Government officials who appointed them; Arizona's courts had no jurisdiction over Indians; and Congress did not extend constitutional protection to Indians until it granted them U.S. citizenship in 1924.

The Seeding and Nurturing of the Partisans: 1921-1924

While agency superintendents cracked down in asserting their authority, and used the Tribal Court to reinforce it, Hopis appealed to the American public to oppose it. The result was the rapid development of individuals, formal organizations, and informal groups into a loose coalition of activists who were brought into Hopi life as "biased allies." They not only liked Hopis and their culture, but also willingly took action at Hopis' direction, sometimes even in opposition to other Hopis. These were the Liberals. This pattern of partisanship on the part of "outsiders" established a tradition in Hopi life that persisted for most of the Twentieth Century. These Liberals made the Reformers back off, clear out of Indian life forever.

The Bursum Bill and the Indian Defense Association. In 1921 the infamous Albert Fall, of "Teapot Dome" oil scandal renown, became Secretary of the Interior. "Teapot Dome" was only one of Fall's schemes; he tried continuously to accelerate the allotment process on Indian lands in order to get them released for him and his cronies to pounce on. In 1922 they got the Senate to pass something called the Bursum Bill; the House defeated it finally in 1926, following intense lobbying by partisans, romantics, leftists, and free-thinkers (cf. Laughlin 1982). The Bursum Bill would not have affected Hopis, but it would have cheated the Pueblo Indians of New Mexico out of much of their most valuable agricultural land (Kelly 1983:190-93, 269; Weigle and Fiore 1982:19-21).

Wealthy liberals who lived in New York but owned property in and around Santa Fe and Phoenix, visiting Indian country during the summer, formed the Eastern Association on Indian Affairs. John Collier formed the American Indian Defense Association when it became apparent that the already existing New Mexico Association on Indian Affairs (later the Southwestern Association on Indian Affairs), led by Nina Otero Warren, was sympathetic to the Indian Bureau. The New Mexico Association as well as the Eastern Association favored a compromise on the Bursum Bill, not its defeat. They formed a "Pueblo Council" consisting largely of non-Indians and some Pueblos Indians with close economic and kinship ties with families that were living on, but did not have title to, Pueblo land. Collier's group informed the Pueblos and urged them to form an "All-Indian Pueblo Council," which they did. The All-Pueblo Council opposed the bogus one as well as the Bursum Bill (Kelly 1983:267-84; 301-334). The Hopis were invited to join and provision was made in the Charter for them to do so, and although they never did, the opposition to the Bursum Bill set the stage for more fundamental and enduring involvement by Partisans in Hopi life.

An End to Ceremonies? Religious Repression

Circular 1665. At the same time as the Bursum Bill came Circular 1665, authorizing agency superintendents to repress dances they thought offensive and in general to discourage Indian dancing they thought harmful to the work ethic. It was the product of lobbying by the reformist Indian Rights Association, strongly pro-assimilationist, led by Lakota Indian Gertrude Bonnin; various missionary groups and Indian agents; and the Board of Indian Commissioners (Kelly 1983:301). The Indian Rights Association and the Superintendent of the Northern Pueblos Agency had collected "affidavits" from Pueblo Indians purporting to show the "depraved character" of clown performances. Supported by the Hopi agent Leo Crane, the ban on dances was just the action that the Indian Rights Association demanded.

Government officials at the Hopi Agency made it "difficult for visitors and the Hopi villagers to meet Hopi other than those who were Christian converts or of proven loyalty to Indian Bureau policies" (James 1974:186-189). Most of these visitors were Liberals, not Reformers. They opposed the Indian Rights Association and the Indian Bureau.[46] Harry James was one of them. James had come out to Hopiland from southern California a few years earlier and returned in response to the "crusade" against repression. Complicating the situation were any number of political crosscurrents masquerading as moral ones. Theodore Roosevelt, who had visited the Hopi in 1913 and had been invited into kivas for ceremonies, had been induced to make a statement, solicited by the Indian Rights Association, characterizing the Snake Dance as barbaric; by 1921 he was dead and could not be asked to explain it. The agency superintendent extended a sanitation campaign aimed at eliminating lice in the animal population to the human population. Children and adults were dragged, kicking and screaming, to sheep-dipping vats and dunked, clothes and all, into solutions of Black Leaf-40.[47] Some Hopis interpreted the delousing dunkings as punishment for opposition to the Government. The delousing was enforced at Hotevilla with seven well armed police and Yukiwma was arrested and jailed once again for defying the Government.

The agency superintendent tried to get Hopis to sign what amounted to a complaint against James, calling it a "pledge of loyalty;" had the chiefs of Oraibi and Moenkopi (Tawakwaptiwa and Siemptiwa) arrested; and deported artist Emry Kopta ("a disrupting element"). But he had some supporters. Charles Fredericks, one of Tawakwaptiwa's brothers and a Christian convert, banded together with five other converted Hopis in a campaign to break down Hopis religious solidarity and even urged the superintendent to throw Tawakwaptiwa in jail (James 1974:189-191). Non-Christian Hopis solicited the help of Liberals in the Santa Fe branch of the Eastern Association on Indian Affairs for help in their efforts against the arbitrary actions of superintendent Leo Crane and his two successors and also went to California, obtaining support from the Indian Welfare League and the National Association to Help the Indian.

It was right in the midst these ideological tugs-of-war that an incident occurred that seemed to bolster the position of the Reformers: the burning of the Bow Clan altar, mentioned in the last chapter. On August 27, 1922, while Hotevilla was holding its Snake Dance, K.T. Johnson, virtually the only member of the Bow Clan, and custodian of the Bow Clan altar, which had been important in Oraibi's men's initiations ceremonies, brought it from his house in Kykotsmovi into the plaza, and burned it. After assembling of the altar and ceremonial paraphernalia and following some Bible readings by him and another convert, he lit a match to everything. Despite Lorenzo Hubbell Jr.'s offers to buy the objects, the flames "greedily licked up the old, old idols and the sacred sticks," wrote a missionary who witnessed it (Means 1960:127-128).

Just prior to the incident, the Indian Office had sent an investigator who took "voluminous testimony under oath" (Kelly 1983:302-303) from the Indian Bureau's field matron, three teachers, a missionary, and seven Hopi converts to support Circular 1665 by ostensibly showing the connection of ceremonialism to lust, adultery, and obscenity. "Men dancers (in Wuwutsim and Maraw)" said one of the testimonials, "carve out of watermelon or pumpkin rinds images representing the women's sexual organs, and present them to the women openly. Likewise women make, out of clay images in the likeness of men's sexual organs and present them to the men. Then they dance in short dresses so that as the women bend over in dancing" the men "see everything." At the Oraibi clown dance, said another, a clown came into the plaza "nude with some cloth or other wrapping around his penis making it longer," and "chased around as if trying to catch up with it." Another document noted a clown with "an artificial penis" protruding from his trousers, "holding the wooden penis in his hand and pointing it in all directions," singing a song "about the penis being the thing that made the women happy" (Duberman, Eggan and Clemmer 1979).[48]

Shocking as the burlesques might have been to outsiders, they relieved a lot of tension and brought a lot of fun into Hopi life; they also taught people how *not* to behave, and often were aimed at a specific person. Clowns are "freed from the usual restraints and it gives them an opportunity to say things that ordinarily wouldn't be said" (Yava 1978:43). School teachers and others who stopped the performances, or did things such as arresting and jailing unmarried women found pregnant (Duberman, Eggan and Clemmer 1979:111) may have precipitated a crisis in Hopi society that would take decades to dissipate (Thompson 1945[?]:89) and may have contributed to what would later be labelled "social breakdown" (Thompson 1950:187).

The divisiveness that such tactics engendered, may well have contributed to the formal ritual separation of Kykotsmovi and Oraibi in 1923 and the abandonment of three important ceremonies in Bacavi between 1917 and the mid-1920s, although Whiteley (1988b:198-200) did not investigate this possibility as an alternate explanation for abandonment of ceremonies. Yukiwma may have "reluctantly" agreed to continue ceremonies at the urging of his villagers in the absence of the strong secular context that Kewanimptewa brought to his leadership. But directed resistance to forced acculturation and religious repression, as well as his prolonged incarceration, may have also played a role in the apparent reversal of his stance.

Reorganization of the Economy:
Cash and Markets

Arts and Crafts: An Early Source of Cash

Amidst the tug-of-wars among missionaries, administrators, Hopi activists and their non-Indian partisans, amidst Hopis' attempts to build a bridge between the reorganizing social fabric and their own personal worlds, a thriving trade in craft items such as pottery and baskets developed. Although it did not bring in much money, sale of craft items became the first dependable source of cash income. Sales were heavily dependent on the tourist trade. The Santa Fe Railroad continued to appropriate the Hopi Snake Dances as its very own tourist attraction, even commissioning a short promotional motion picture of it in 1915 (McLuhan 1985:131-142). At Hotevilla's Snake Dance in 1922, mystery writer Mary Roberts Rinehart (1923:89-90) bought a turquoise and shell bead ("hishi") necklace for $25.00; other necklaces went from $5.00 to $20.00. "Exquisite bracelets" brought from $2.00 to $5.00; rings $.50 and up. But outside of tourist season, pottery, baskets, and woven plaques brought prices from $5.00 down to $.05 a piece with blankets, dresses, belts, dolls, drums, moccasins, and paintings bringing between $2 and $7 (cf. Whiteley 1988a:136-7). The highest price paid for a Hopi craft item was probably for a basket five feet tall and 135 inches in circumference. It brought $300 (Walker and Wyckoff 1983:23, 30).

The School of American Research began promoting Hopi-Tewa pottery in 1919 and when Santa Fe established its Indian Art Market in 1922, hand-made Indian pottery got a big boost. Mary-Russell Colton at the Museum of Northern Arizona encouraged individual potters to sign their pieces, and with establishment of the "Hopi Arts and Crafts Show" as an annual market at the Museum in 1929, Hopi potters and other craftspersons could count on two outlets in addition to the trading posts of Hubbell and Hopi trader Tom Pavatea. Of the two, Pavatea did the better business; three-quarters of the Hopi pottery trade was conducted through his store (Crane 1925:235). Actual prices changed little with the crash of 1929; total value of goods sold at the Museum's Hopi Show in 1934 amounted to only $1,126 for 282 items, an average of $4 an item. The only thing that changed was the volume of tourists, which dropped precipitously, and the number of potential buyers in general.

Tourist volume on the Santa Fe Railroad swelled with the end of World War I, reaching record peaks in 1920 and again in 1922 (Grattan 1980:59). Automobiles, increasingly cheaper to buy and operate, began to replace rail travel; a caravan of cars failed to reach the Snake Dance in 1921 due to flash floods and washouts, but a caravan of cars carried 2,500 people to the Snake Dance in 1925 (Ford 1955 quoted by Laird 1977:213). Harvey cars were taking tourists on one-day trips to Tuba City by the early 1920s (Hegemann 1963:38), and by 1927 16-cylinder packards and cadillacs were bringing tourists to the Snake Dance on the Fred Harvey Company's "Indian Detours" from the railroad stops in Winslow and Holbrook, where they were brought back at night to stay in the comfortable "Harvey House" hotels (Grattan 1980:57) -- a round trip of over one hundred miles.

Grand Canyon. But Hopis had also started going to the tourists, as well as having the tourists come to them. By 1905 Hopis had begun to use the Santa Fe Railroad as a vehicle for pursuing their own economic ends, rather than simply being carried along as cheap hired help on summer repair crews. A Hopi man operated the newsstand at the old Bright Angel Lodge at Grand Canyon, and when the Harvey Company opened its new "El Tovar" Hotel and "Hopi House" craft shop, Hopis began to count on the income from demonstrating and selling crafts. Dressed in Navajo-style velvet shirts, Hopi men greeted every daily train. Every afternoon at 5:00 PM, 8:00 PM in summer, they put on non-religious "Hopi dances" outside Hopi House, and were given one small room on the top floor to use for living and eating (Hegemann 1963:35). The dances were eagle, hoop, and buffalo, aside from the buffalo, rarely performed in Hopi communities. Grand Canyon was made a national park in 1919 and as tourist volume swelled from 44,000 to 100,000 in 1923 and 200,000 in 1929 (Grattan 1980:37), more and more people came to expect Hopis as part of the "Grand Canyon scene." The old "silversmith" connection between certain families at Hotevilla and Second Mesa continued to hold, with many Hotevillans working at Grand Canyon (La Farge 1936a:14).

If First Mesa dominated the pottery trade, it could be said that Second Mesa dominated the painting and entertainment trades. Although the potter Nampeyo from First Mesa had several long tenures there and Tawakwaptiwa from Oraibi occasionally turned up, the core of Hopis at "Hopi House" was a cluster of affinally-related families from Shipaulovi, Mishongnovi, and Shungopavi, including a sister of Second Mesa's only trading family, the Secakukus (Hegemann 1965:35-36). Mary Colter, architect for the

Harvey Company, hired Hopi artist Fred Kabotie and his Hopi assistants to paint murals of free-standing, slightly abstract naturalistic figures and symbols with Snake Dance and Snake legend themes on the interior walls of the "Watchtower" at Grand Canyon in 1932, and the Buffalo Dance and two allegorical myths at the Harvey Company's renovated and expanded Painted Desert Inn in 1947 (Grattan 1980:57). Homer Cooyama from Kykotsmovi independently developed a career as an artist and painted many backdrops and curtains for school auditoriums (La Farge 1936a:46).

The Billingsley Faction. Another cluster of Second Mesa men, virtually all members of the Snake society, got involved in a "Hopi Indian Program" promoted by a "Colonel Billingsley," whom Oliver La Farge (1936a:1) -- who never actually met him -- characterized as an apparent crook but many of whose Hopi followers "sincerely believed in." Billingsley dated his relationship with the Hopis from 1904, when he ran away from his home in the East after hearing about the Hopis as a young teenager.[49] He ostensibly returned in 1908, eventually settling in Apache Junction, outside Mesa, Arizona. Apparently agency superintendent Daniel (1919-1923) offered him a teaching job at Toreva Day School, Second Mesa, and he took it, probably in 1920 or 1921 (Billingsley 1971:36). When missionaries began lobbying to stop the Snake Dance and other dances in response to the Interior Department's infamous Circular 1665, Billingsley, who claimed to have been initiated into the Snake society in 1922,[50] decided to take the Snake society on tour to put on a *Tableau Vivant* for potentates and invited guests at Phoenix' El Zaribah Shrine temple in order to convince the public of the religious and harmless nature of the Snake Dance. Billingsley called it "Legends of the Hopi."

The next step was to take the show on tour to other Shrine Temples. The show included a short segment of the Snake Dance in authentic costume, with real snakes. Billingsley and his Hopis went all the way to Mexico City with their live snakes, eventually ending up in Washington, D.C. where they performed a truncated Snake Dance in front of the steps of the Capitol in November, 1926 (Congressional Record 1926:126; Billingsley 1971:5-6). Some one took a home movie of it and it became the third of only three motion pictures shorts of the Hopi Snake Dance.[51]

Billingsley secured numerous paid public performances and opportunities for sales of handicrafts for Second Mesa's residents; had his hair washed with yucca root suds and was thus adopted into a Hopi clan and family; and brought along Barry Goldwater, then working in his father's trading post at Rainbow Lodge at the foot of Navajo Mountain on the Navajo Reservation, to Second Mesa. Goldwater also had his hair washed and was thus "adopted" into a Hopi clan and family.[52] Billingsley hired Hopis to built him a kiva at his home near Mesa, Arizona,[53] where he arranged meetings between his Shriners and "Billingsley Hopis." He continued periodically to arrange demonstrations, performances, and tours with Hopis in tow; Hopis who toured with Billingsley were said to receive "tremendous fan-mail and endless gifts" (La Farge 1936a:37).[54] Thus, while Billingsley clearly used the Hopis for his own purposes, they also used him.

Hopi Nouveau, Hopi Deco, and the Bases for Public Taste

Even during the Great Depression, the market for pottery held steady and even improved. Hopi-Tewa pottery appealed to Americans for several reasons. A few people collected Indian pottery as novelties, and some individuals in New York and Los Angeles expressed a fondness for Pueblo pottery because of its cultural associations. When they bought a Hopi pot, they thought they were buying a little bit of Hopi culture, a little bit of memory and nostalgia of their visit there. Yet some pieces fit the tastes of the time and were undoubtedly purchased because they were hand-crafted pieces of art signed by the artist. Developed by William Morris' "Arts and Crafts" movement of the 1870s and 1880s in England, the concept of pottery as an art form dated largely from the 1890s, after a group of wealthy Cincinnati women founded the Rockwood Pottery outlet in reaction to the modern, industrialized, mass-produced items associated with "Art Nouveau" (Wyckoff 1990:71). Much of the early appeal of Hopi pottery produced by Nampeyo and her family can probably be attributed to the "Arts and Crafts" movement, as well as to the marketing of train travel as a form of recreation.

Nampeyo, who had sold her "Sikyatki revival" pottery to Thomas Keam and Alexander Stephen in the 1880s and later to Fewkes in 1890-92, demonstrated pottery-making at the Santa Fe Railroad Exhibition in Chicago in 1895 (Nequatewa 1943:42; Walker and Wyckoff 1983:28-29).[55] In 1904-05 at the urging of Lorenzo Hubbell, she went to Grand Canyon to demonstrate pottery making for a year at the Fred Harvey Company's El Tovar Hotel and returned in 1907. In 1910 she was again in Chicago to demonstrate her art. Nampeyo and other Hopi potters, weavers and silversmiths, as well as Tewa potter Marie Montoya Martinez from San Ildefonso Pueblo, demonstrated and sold their crafts at the "American Indian Village" exhibit in San Diego's Panama-Pacific Exhibition of 1915. Thus by the 1920s, much Hopi and Tewa pottery had become collectable as modern art as well as ethnographic artifact.

Marie Martinez, her husband Julian, and other members of her family had become famous for several designs for their "black-on-black" pottery. Among these designs were the stylized *avanyu*, the water serpent, and vertical feathers arranged one next to the other around the circumference of a pot or plate. Nampeyo and her family worked in the polychrome of the "Sikyatki Revival", initially favoring the Katsina face promoted by trader Keam (Wade and McChesney 1983:8-9) but later switching to stylized natural motifs such as birds, clouds, water, rain, sun, feathers, as well as purely geometric shapes.

Many of these designs superficially resemble pre-World War I "Nouveau" styles and the post-war "Deco styles." For example, French potter Emile Lenoble was making stoneware vases around 1925 that were strongly influenced by ancient chinese pottery designs but had ornamenting that coincidentally resembled Marie and Julian's feather design (cf. Klein et al 1986:93). The ziggurat and pyramid forms popular in the "pueblo deco" and "art deco" architectural styles of the 1920s and 1930s also bore superficial resemblances to designs found on Nampeyo's pottery.[56] Even some art historians cannot always tell the difference between Incan, Mayan, Aztec, and Pueblos motifs, attributing the designs of the Tewa potter-designer team of Marie and Julian Martinez to "Aztec and Inca" inspiration! (cf. Klein et al. 1986). Thus in the public's mind, these motifs undoubtedly remained culturally undifferentiated, and perhaps even their appeal within the Nouveau and Deco tastes was largely unconsciously perceived. The influences were undoubtedly mutual to some extent: Overall shapes as well as surface decoration on vases, lamps, and other free-standing decorative objects show the influence of American Indian design on the Arts and Crafts movement in the United States (Klein et al. 1986:159).

Deco art and architecture favored the combination of strong primary colors and sharp contrasts -- red, black, orange or gold, and silver -- and a degree of abstract, geometric stylization of naturalistic forms such as flowers, fruits, sunbursts, and spouting water, combined with the zig-zag, ziggurat, pyramid, oval, arc, lozenge, and octagon motifs (cf. Klein et al. 1986:6-8, 50-53, 65, 70,

93).[57] These matched -- undoubtedly fortuitously -- many of the stylizations found on the "Sikyatki Revival" pottery associated with Nampeyo. Moreover, the fact that the items were hand made and also expressed naturalistic elements associated with the old Art Nouveau[58] style of pre-WW I, must have provided an additional appeal. Hopis adopted or invented tall vases resembling small umbrella stands, the "tulip vases," tiles made by the hundreds, ashtrays, plates, and rectangular lidless boxes, and wedding vases between 1880 and 1930 specifically for the commercial market. Keam introduced tiles or tile molds and even suggested some of the designs (Wyckoff 1990:78-79, 87). No Hopi term exists for the "tulip vase" shape. They are probably "copies of an Art Nouveau form which may have become known to the Hopi through mail order catalogues" (Walker and Wyckoff 1983:71). Huge Nampeyo "umbrella stands" were actually used as such, sitting in corners of entryways to Deco apartments. But most were miniatures and were used as vases. A few were converted to table lamp bases. And the experiential kind of appeal that buying an Indian art object from its maker while stalking the marvels of Grand Canyon or adventuring to the Hopi Snake Dance brought yet another market. Thus there it was a confluence of interests that resulted in the increase of collecting of Hopi art during the 1930s.

Livestock, Stores, and Cash Flow

Livestock were a growing source of cash. In 1915, the Agency began drilling wells, installing Aeromotor windmills, and building stock ponds. It distributed hand plows and encouraged sheep-raising. In 1916 Andrew Hermequaftewa, one of the Shungopavi's silversmithing "Hostiles" from the 1906 split and later a prime mover in the Traditionalist Movement (See Chapter Seven), wrote to the Commissioner of Indian Affairs asking the BIA to construct a reservoir with a windmill west of Burro Springs where he could water his cattle. He said he would also like to build houses there for himself and one of his children, plant a field, and fence it. But two things checked Hopis' expansion onto the range: "There are now Navajo Indians living at that place but they have not got any fields planted just there," wrote Hermequaftewa; "I would try to live peaceable with them" (Stephens 1961:102). But even if Hopis could have developed a sharing of range resources with Navajos, the continent-wide influenza epidemic of 1919-1920 hit Hopis sufficiently hard that the population actually *decreased* from 2,370 in 1918 to 2,236 in 1922. The economy suffered accordingly.

In 1922 Hopis had 20,000 sheep, with the average Hopi band running "from 20 to 100" (BOIC 1922:14-15), down from 50,000 in 1900. The decrease probably reflects hard times; Hopis had to butcher the sheep for food. But some herds ran to 600 sheep, ownership often being shared by a two households, and some individuals' cattle herds were also beginning to grow into the hundreds (Duberman, Eggan and Clemmer 1979:115). By 1937 Hopis had 11,519 sheep and goats and 7,695 cattle (Hack 1942:17); neighboring Navajos with about ten times the population (45,000) had more than 80 times the number of sheep: 944,910 (Aberle 1966:61). Edward Kennard (1965:26) said that between 1932 and 1936, those Hopis who had money used it "carefully and sparingly. There were a number of older men who had worked for a period of years off the reservation, saved their money, and then returned. They used a dollar or two a month for staples (coffee, sugar, flour)." However, there are indications that First Mesa, only eleven miles from the Government Agency at Keams Canyon, continued to garner the advantage in the cash economy.

Leo Crane (1925:235), agent at Keams Canyon from 1911 through 1919, describes Tom Pavatea, "the full-blood Hopi merchant", as "fairly rich in livestock." Pavatea owned a small store at First Mesa, "carrying goods of standard quality." Crane must have accelerated the cash economy when he advanced $10,627 in government loans to Hopis for purchase of wagons, harness, and livestock. "Within four years," says Crane (1925:237-238), "the Hopis had repaid seventy-five per cent of the advance." Few if any Hopis fought in World War I, although several volunteers went with the cavalry to Mexico to fight Pancho Villa in 1911 (Barsh 1991:278), but patriotism was impressed upon them. Selling war bonds on margin, Agent Crane (1925:231) was able to market $11,600 worth to 130 Hopis, loaning them the "balance." Some of the Hopi sheep undoubtedly disappeared in sales to repay Crane's war bond loans.

At Moenkopi, prior to 1915, a dozen or so Indians were employed at freighting, coal mining, carpentry, stone masonry, school housekeeping, laundering, and casual labor at anywhere from $1.00 to $4.00 a day. A "trained" house maid was employed in Flagstaff at $1.50 to $3.00 a week. At least one of these was a Hopi, but the ethnicity of the others is unclear. Whether Indian labor was cheaper by off-reservation standards than non-Indian labor, is uncertain (Nagata 1970:193).

A Hopi from Moenkopi had purchased a couple of trucks by the 1920s and carried the mail under contract from Flagstaff to Tuba City (Hegemann 1963:62). Agent Crane (1925:107, 137) hired Hopi work crews to build a new hospital, and began hiring Hopi-Tewas as police, rather than Navajos. The Agency was still hiring Indian wagoners at the rate of one cent a pound for cartage from Keams Canyon to Holbrook as of 1919 (Crane 1925:109). Crane also devised a plan for Hopis at Walpi to extract money from tourists with cameras by charging them a dollar to photograph the Snake Dance in 1912. But the plan may have backfired. Other Hopis were extremely critical of the idea of putting on ceremonies for show, like a circus, to which admission would be charge. By 1916 there was a universal ban on taking pictures of any ceremonies at all Hopi villages (Harold Colton 1968, personal communication).

By 1926 Joe Secakuku had opened his first store at Canyon Diablo (now "Two Guns," Arizona) along Route 66 (Hegemann 1963:146-147). Joe would later move the store to Holbrook, and with his brother Hale, would open two large stores at Second Mesa, one in Shipaulovi and the other below the Mesa at the junction of Hiway 264 and the Winslow Road. He retired in the 1960s when he acceded to Shipaulovi's Bear Clan chieftaincy, but following Joe's death in 1969, heirs would build the enterprise into the largest Hopi-owned business in the 1980s. Four Hopi men opened stores in Hotevilla in the 1930s and another started a gasoline station; two Hopi-owned stores operated in Bacavi. By 1914 four Hopi-owned stores were operating in Moenkopi and Tuba City. Store-bought Euro-American style clothing replaced the Hopi, Zuni and Navajo styles favoring cotton trousers, ponchos, blankets, and black cotton dresses. Native clothing styles of home-spun and woven cloth became dress-up wear, reserved for dance days, ceremonial occasions, and receiving distinguished visitors such as Oliver La Farge. (See below.) Women favored "Spanish" shawls (actually from Czechoslovakia by way of Mexico), of silk in the summer and flannel in the winter, and often used them as substitutes for cradleboards to carry babies around on their backs.

By 1933, cattle had become an important industry, replacing sheep as the largest source of cash. There is some evidence that at least in some cases Hopis were being paid substantially less for their livestock -- $1.00 a head for sheep as opposed to $4-5.00 each that middlemen were being paid for them at the railhead (Billingsley 1971:7). Clans remained land-holding groups only at First and Second Mesas (Forde 1931:370). Range land was allocated by tradition on a village, rather than a clan basis, and in contradistinction to farmlands, there do not seem to have been any "clan range lands". Livestock were owned and tended by individual men, although several men usually corralled their stock together in one herd for convenience. Often, such a partnership included men of different clans (Titiev 1944:193-195).

   Politics, Economics, Culture, and Land. There was some degree of variance in the economic base among the villages, with the four First Mesa villages having more cash flow. At all villages, the household remained the unit of production as well as consumption, with income being shared among household members (cf. Titiev 1944:181-200), even though what little marketing there was, had been established on a model of individual entrepreneurship. While no one was looking, one of the most important administrative actions to affect the Hopi was quietly implemented in the midst of the flap over Circular 1665, delousing, and "outside agitators." This action was the appointment of a single administrator -- a "Commissioner to the Navajo Indians" -- who had general authority over all five Navajo reservations *plus all areas of the Hopi Reservation occupied by Navajos.* The sole purpose of the appointment was to bypass the Navajo agent in Window Rock and set up a Navajo Tribal Council, composed of twelve elected delegates, favorable to oil companies, who could sanction mineral leasing. The wholesale leasing of mineral leases began in October, 1923 (Bailey and Bailey 1986:120-21), and it would be the various Navajo Tribal Councils that met between 1923 and 1943 that would approve leases on Hopi land that was not immediately adjacent to the villages and in the subsequently-created District Six.[59]

The Indian New Deal and the Indian Reorganization Act

The Reorganization of Politics

   As the source of all fundamental historical developments in Indian affairs in the recent past (Philp 1983:9), the "Indian New Deal" altered the means, but not fundamentally the end, of U.S. Indian policy: acculturation and some degree of assimilation (Cornell 1988:95; Costo 1983:12; cf. also Kelly 1975:298).[60] Its primary political and administrative implement was the Indian Reorganization Act. The Indian Reorganization (IRA) was John Collier's brainchild. After a decade of launching a continuous critique against Indian policy, Collier had gotten himself appointed Commissioner of Indian Affairs in FDR's "New Deal" administration in 1933. Collier vowed to dictate Indian policy after establishing power.[61]

The Indian Reorganization Act intended to "reorganize" Indians on two levels: economically, according to a cooperative and corporate model; and politically, as a government for which the Secretary of the Interior would provide checks and balances. But it also protected indigenous law, culture, religion, language, education, and artistic and symbolic expression by uniformly lifting any and all bans and barriers on these aspects of Indian life. Administratively, the BIA began to encourage perpetuation and revival of Indian arts, crafts, cultures, and religions. Thus, "reorganization" envisioned maintenance of much of Indians' traditions, but also clearly envisioned their adoption of a complex of new traits and behavior patterns in economy and politics.

Implementation: General. Collier did not anticipate bringing the actual law to Indians for their approval; he somehow thought it automatically represented Indians' interests. But Oliver La Farge, head of the Association on Indian Affairs and the man selected by Collier to bring "Reorganization" to the Hopi, was more realistic: "The Indians didn't think this up," he said (La Farge 1936b). It was Congress that finally decided to insert a provision that, in order for the IRA to apply to a specific group, the group must approve the Act by majority vote of adults in a referendum. The Act would take effect only if a majority of tribes approved it. Collier held several congresses in or near Indian country in 1933 to explain the Act; in its original form, called the "Wheeler-Howard Bill" after its congressional sponsors, it ran to over 100 pages. Collier sent copies of the bill to every agency superintendent and to a number of anthropologists, including Franz Boas, and to some Indians. He got a number of varying comments on it. But there were far many more who simply had not had enough time to read and understand it by the time the "Indian congresses" were held.

Access to Political Power. Although the IRA was not approved by a majority of all Indian voters, it was approved by a majority of Tribes, and thus it became law. The IRA granted certain representatives of Indian interests some access to political power. The arena was circumscribed and the amount of power was small, but this access provided tribes with real power because, ironically, it required a certain amount of incorporation into dominant political institutions. Thus most tribal governments became both creations and replicas of those dominant institutions (Cornell 1988:206). In restructuring tribal political forms and processes, the federal government was able to rechannel disputes rooted in Indian-White relations into Indian-Indian relations. This rechanneling of disputes is especially evident in the Hopi-Navajo land dispute. (See Chapter Nine.)

But the IRA did not just grant Tribes access to political power. It also facilitated "some dominant-group control over the pace and direction of change" (Cornell 1988:207). Anthropologist Ralph Linton (1940:505) observed at the time that, in general, "as long as the subject group is allowed to exercise judgment in acceptance a program is not likely to be put over as a whole". As a deliberate attempt to induce certain kinds of changes and to control other changes in Indian societies (Kluckhohn and Hackenberg 1953:29), the IRA was not likely to be put over as a whole.[62]

Implementation at Hopi. The Act's provisions that were directly relevant to the Hopi case were mainly political and economic. But Hopis saw the Act in cultural terms as well as in political and economic terms. The Act's provisions called for purchasing new land for existing reservations; setting up an Indian Revolving Loan Fund of $4 million for economic development and credit unions; establishing tribal governments operating by constitutions and by-laws adopted by tribal referendum; and empowering a tribe to hire a lawyer, negotiate with state and federal government, and prevent the sale, lease, disposition, or encumbrance of tribal lands. But Hopis' political ideology of acceptance/ resistance set up the IRA and its policies as yet another issue on which the Hopi would hone their two modernities in cultural terms. The IRA's promise of economic benefits, especially loans and *the return of land*, initiated Hopis' intense interest in Collier and his programs, no matter what their final dispositions on them might be. But there was much ambivalence. One Hopi man wrote to Collier on March 4, 1934, that "regarding the matter as in forming a self-government, we already have that has been handed down from generation to generation up to this time" (sic) (Wyckoff 1990:56). When the vote was finally held, Collier reported to the Secretary of the Interior that 519 eligible voters had approved the IRA; 299 had voted against it.

Collier visited the Hopi villages shortly after Congress passed the IRA. "Although pleased with this favorable reaction", writes Kenneth Philp, one of Collier's biographers, "Collier knew that the Hopis ... remained suspicious of the bureau." In 1968, referring to one of the "Indian congresses" that Collier held in 1933, a Hopi man told me:

Just before they had that vote, they took all the educated Indians --
mostly Hopi and Navajo, but some Pima, Papago and put them in a
camp up at Cameron. They tried to get me up there, but I didn't go. I
knew something was up. Then they turned them all loose on these
villages with ballot boxes. On the ballots there was a circle and a cross.
No writing. The people didn't know what was going on. They told them,
"If you want to keep your land, choose the cross; if you choose the circle,
you might lose it". Now the circle means continuous life, and the cross
is the four points of life. And on this paper, the two were separate, so
something was wrong. Most of the people didn't vote" (Clemmer
1978a:61; Yamada 1957:58).

In 1955, a Hopi man from a different village gave an almost
identical explanation to a Government investigating team,
concluding that "this Wheeler-Howard Act was without the
consent of the majority of the Hopi people" (Hopi Hearings
1955:235). But was it? The answer lies in a small part of the life and
times of Oliver La Farge.

Oliver La Farge among the Hopi

La Farge had become acquainted with the Kikmongwi of Walpi
and others at First Mesa in 1931, when the Eastern Association on
Indian Affairs (later merged with Collier's Indian Defense
Association to become the American Association on Indian Affairs)
sent him on a horseback trip through Navajo country with Tom
and Pete Dozier, brothers of Edward Dozier, who would later earn
a Ph.D. in Anthropology at University of Chicago. The Doziers
were Tewa Indians from Santa Clara Pueblo, and thus could speak
the Tewa dialect at First Mesa. During that trip, La Farge
strengthened his sympathy with Navajos, but also came to know
and appreciate Hopis, at least those at First Mesa.

La Farge, who had won the Pulitzer prize for his romantic
novel *Laughing Boy* about Navajos in 1931, wrote to Collier in April,
1936 before going out to the Hopi: "I do not wish to assume the task
of pushing the Hopis toward an organization which does not
interest them .... I warn you that my early progress will be quite
slow" (McNickle 1971:107). In a "Running Narrative", a kind of diary
not released as a public document until more than 20 years later,
La Farge gives a candid day-by-day account of his activities,
successes, and frustrations, explaining not only his progress but
also his rationale for drafting the Constitution with unusual
provisions. Among them was an integration of traditional Hopi

political forms with a kind of "committee" form of decision making, a "tribal council" like the "tribal councils" now familiar to virtually all reservation populations.

Boarding at a Hopi woman's house and travelling nearly a hundred miles a day between the Hopi villages in a car with bad shocks, wobbly head lamps, old tires, and a loose steering gear, La Farge held two series of meetings in that summer of 1936. The first series was with leaders at the various villages, and he usually had to hold two or three meetings with each set at each village before he accomplished his goals. The second series was one round of public meetings at the three mesas and at Moenkopi.

Material Conditions. La Farge encountered a growing settlement at the foot of First Mesa that had come to be known as "Polacca" after Tom Pulakaki, who was among the first to settle there. Some of the first houses still had the corrugated iron roofs installed by white workmen as part of a housing project implemented by the Agency in the 1890s. Equally large was Kykotsmovi at the foot of Third Mesa, but unlike Kykotsmovi, Polacca did not have village status. The collection of free-standing houses of dressed stone was merely a residence spot, a kind of suburb of the three First Mesa villages. Nearly all the houses in Polacca were one-storeyed and so were many of those on the mesas as well. But the older villages as well as Bacavi, Hotevilla, and Lower Moenkopi, preserved the ancient architecture of contiguous walls, long streets, and plazas (*Kisonvi*), although by the 1930s stone stairways had been added to outside walls for reaching second stories. Walpi, cobbled together in the 1690s against possible Spanish attack, was a bit crumbly but still had its two- and three-storeyed structure.

Within the houses, La Farge found a variety of material conditions. Most houses had linoleum on the floor of at least one room; a kitchen cabinet with dishes; a wood-burning cookstove, often a white enameled late model from Sears; and a deal table. But most houses still had only one or two chairs and while the primary couple usually had a bed of white enameled iron, children slept on sheepskins on the floor. Burro corrals were found in every village; rabbit meat hung drying on wire stretched across the fronts of many houses; outhouses were hard to find; and no houses had indoor plumbing. Outdoor stone "beehive" ovens, probably borrowed from Zuni in the late Nineteenth Century, had become popular for baking wheat bread and mutton with hot coals.

Reorganization. The fact that two "councils" already existed at First Mesa (the "Rodeo Council") and at Kykotsmovi (the "Hopi

Council") was also a hindrance as well as a help; Otto Lomavitu headed the "Hopi Council" and he helped La Farge get the idea of a Hopi Constitution approved easily at Kykotsmovi. But because Lomavitu had been among those giving testimony on Hopi ceremonies when efforts were being made to stamp them out, many Hopis interpreted his council as "progressive" and "Christian." His enthusiasm for the council La Farge proposed made some Hopis suspicious.

La Farge wanted his Constitution to be acceptable to all the Hopi. In meetings, he found that provisions on ceremonial and religious protection "registered well," since First Mesa, especially, was having trouble with missionaries. He also found that "land, particularly, interested them." Paradoxically, he came to feel that the *old* men understood the point of "organization" but that the younger men, "trying to judge it in the light of a little schooling, don't understand it so well!"

Calculating the minimum number of votes he would need (a plurality of 30% of the voting population), La Farge estimated the voting population at 1,500, with a majority being 751. But he did not need 751; he needed only 30% of the voters, 450, and thus only 251 "yes" votes. He counted Bacavi, First Mesa, and Kykotsmovi "in," and thought he could also "get" Mishongnovi, Shungopavi and Hotevilla. He had written off Oraibi and was dubious about Moenkopi, uncertain of Shipaulovi. La Farge the was torn between his certainty that the Constitution would in fact embody the "General Will" of Hopi society and the pragmatic realization that the mechanics of majority vote could easily be the monkey wrench that jammed it. La Farge wanted to write a constitution "which would be completely in line with the Hopi path and which at the same time would not crystallize unchangebly (sic) a situation which is probably in a state of flux" (La Farge 1937).

Meeting with Dan Kochongva and James Chuhoingva (Pongayawyma) in Dan's "old-fashioned" but spacious house at Hotevilla, he found "these and Chimopavi (Shungopavi), the conservatives, the best to deal with so far ... I wish they were all like these hostiles!" Dan Kochongva was old Yukiwma's son and Chuhoingva was Yukiwma's sister's son, slated to accede to the position of Kikmongwi since Yukiwma's death in 1929. But Kochongva spoke for him as an official of the One-Horn society, installer of Kikmongwis. Kochongva could think of only two criticisms of La Farge's Constitution: the representatives to the Council "would be criticized" for whatever public action they took, and he did not want a "boundary" written into the

Constitution. La Farge, knowing there would have to be a boundary because the territory over which the Council was to have jurisdiction would have to be described, anticipated Hotevilla's opposition for the next 20 years. "Out goes Hotevilla," he concluded. Even though La Farge felt he was getting nowhere at Hotevilla he asked Kochongva what he should do. Go ahead and prepare the Constitution, said Kochongva, and bring it to the chiefs. They would go from there.

Bacavi, a "clean, progressive," but "still Hopi" village had 25 men plus the Kikmongwi, Kewanimptewa, in attendance at their meeting. "They're for it," said La Farge. The final all-village meeting at Kykotsmovi also produced approval; artist Homer Cooyama, "in riding boots and leather made-up bow tie," interpreted.

La Farge almost hit a snag when it came to "tribal membership" in the general meeting at First Mesa. The Tewas, with Albert Yava translating, told him a real Hopi is one who is ceremonially initiated; that is what makes the Tewas Hopi. La Farge knew that such a definition of membership would not wash in D.C.; the criteria would have to be blood quantum. But, he told them, the "blood quantum" requirement could be phrased in terms of future membership through the matrilineal descent rule as long as the Constitution had a provision for adopting half- and quarter-Hopis into the Tribe. Thus the "Hopi Tribe" would start off with only female members capable of producing "new" tribal members "automatically." "The key to the matter," wrote La Farge, "lies in the sentence 'According to the way of doing establishe(d) in that village, the Kikmongwi may accept the applicant for membership, and shall tell the tribal council.' The established way of doing is the initiation ceremony, with final acceptance by the Kikmongwi, but at the same time it is left open for progressive villages to establish a different way." The issue reflected the degree to which the federal government intended to place limits on the "General Will" of any particular community and to control change in Indian societies.

The Constitution

La Farge got around the boundary issue with a provision that not only was unusual but also would assume profound important in the Hopi-Navajo land dispute of following decades: "Article I - Jurisdiction: The Authority of the Tribe under this Constitution shall cover the Hopi villages and *such land as shall be determined by the Hopi Tribal Council in agreement with the United States Government and the Navajo Tribe. The Hopi Tribal Council is hereby authorized to negotiate with the proper officials to reach such agreement, and to accept it by a majority vote"* (emphasis added). Certain broad powers, including the power to prevent sale, disposition, lease or encumbrance of lands, were vested in the Tribal Council, but nowhere in the Constitution was the Council given powers over clan land or other areas of Hopi life that would usurp or replace the powers of the clans or the authorities in the individual villages.

The Constitution required the Agency Superintendent to approve all resolutions and ordinances, and acknowledged the Secretary of the Interior's ultimate power of approval. Thus, any decision made by the Council was subject to review by the local BIA superintendent; the Council could appeal a disapproval only to the Secretary of the Interior. The Constitution also authorized the Council to "exercise such further powers as may in the future be delegated to it by the members of the Tribe or by the Secretary of the Interior, or any other duly authorized official or agency of the State or Federal Government" (Article VI, Section 3). This latter provision was probably the second most important clause, aside from the one granting the Council the power to establish Hopi land boundaries in negotiation with Navajos and with the U. S. Government.

La Farge's Constitution set the total number of representatives to the Tribal Council, divided among twelve villages, at seventeen. La Farge wrote proportional representation, one representative for every 250 persons, by village, into the Constitution, and provided the "Lower District" of Moenkopi, almost completely given over to following Tawakwaptiwa's lead, a separate representative. Representatives could be seated in the Council only if certified by "the Kikmongwi of their respective villages" (Article IV, Section 4). La Farge wanted fundamentally to write a Constitution that would empower the villages, and within the villages, would empower the Kikmongwis. The Council would be an instrument reflecting the wishes of the villages rather than a body governing them.

In giving the Kikmongwis the controlling authority to certify representatives from their villages to the Council, the Constitution also gave them some control over the Council itself. This political authority was something that was not part of the idealized definition of the Kikmongwi's role of religious stewardship. It was a secular kind of authority, authority that they had acquired as a result of the redefinition of the Kikmongwi's role accomplished largely at Oraibi over the previous century. Yet La Farge justified the Kikmongwis' new secular power by referring to their religious status. La Farge called Hopi a "pure theocracy. The controlling group is made up of the so-called chiefs, who are each the head of a particular line of ceremony. At the head stands the Kikmongwi. All the ceremonial lines lead into him, and he has true authority in the villages. Hence the constitution gives the Kikmongwi the controlling authority to certify representatives to the (tribal) council."

Provision was made for "modern," "progressive" villages. Each village was to "decide for itself how it shall be organized." Until a village decided to "organize in another manner," it was to "be considered as being under the traditional Hopi organization, and *the Kikmcngwi of such village shall be recognized as its leader*" (emphasis in original) (Article III, Section 3). "It is vital," noted La Farge (1937:30) "that the significance of Section 4 (of the Constitution) be fully understood. 'Each village shall decide for itself how it shall choose its representatives. There is no mention here of popular election. Where a majority desires to establish such election, it may do so via modernized village organization as provided in Article III." "The decisive general meeting is alien to the Hopi way of doing," La Farge (1937:8-9) stated elsewhere. "It is alien to them to settle matters out of hand by a majority vote. Such a vote leaves a dissatisfied minority, which makes them very uneasy. Their natural way of doing is to discuss among themselves at great length and group by group until public opinion as a whole has settled overwhelmingly in one direction. It is during this process, too, that the Kikmongwi can exert his influence without entering into disputes. In actual practice this system is democratic, but it works differently from ours. Opposition is expressed by abstention. Those who are against something stay away from meetings at which it is to be discussed, and generally refuse to vote on it. In this way they are free later to refuse to abide by the majority decision. Decisions are made after the manner of a political caucus, and if sufficient patience is exercised a relative unanimity can be achieved by the Hopi method. The negative type of opposition is refusing to be bound by the caucus."

La Farge was only trying to model the Hopi Constitution in accordance with the way Hopi society was actually structured. But Section Four of the Constitution would prove vexingly vague in the swings of Hopi politics over the following fifty years and thus also crucially important. If a village did *not* adopt a village constitution (which Kykotsmovi did not), then was it to be considered as still falling under the jurisdiction of the nearest Kikmongwi? If a village did not have a Kikmongwi (which ultimately came to be the case in Hotevilla), then was it to be considered "modern?" If disputes arose about exactly who the Kikmongwi was (as they did in Oraibi and Mishongnovi), then could an election of representatives circumvent the necessity for a Kikmongwi's certification? If a Governor of a "modern" village chose to certify representatives, as a Kikmongwi could, without bothering with an election (as a Governor of Kykotsmovi once did), then could they be legally seated in the Council? Such questions would plague Hopi politics off and on throughout the latter half of the Twentieth century.

La Farge ultimately felt he had failed, and worse, that he had saddled the Hopis with something they did not want. But he could not decide at the end of his stint whether he or the Hopis were more to blame, and if anyone was to blame, what the blame should be for. "The Hopi have been operated on by everyone, official and unofficial from Coronado to Oliver la Farge. In almost every case they have suffered for it. Why they should ever trust <u>any</u> white man is a mystery to me," he wrote. Yet he described the Hopi in terms that indicate his frustration: "These Indians are good business men, penny-squeezing, avaricious, fearful of the future, suspicious. They are magnificently stubborn in their determination to live according to the Hopi path ... cantankerous and tight-minded" (La Farge 1936a:1). Fourteen years later La Farge (1950) admitted that maybe it was himself who had been cantankerous and tight-minded: "The work was done during a time of intense emotional stress," he noted. "The break-up (of) ... my marriage was coming on then."

"Acceptance" of the IRA: Voting Population and Demography

In the end, La Farge got cooperation largely from First Mesa. When the Constitution came up for referendum, the vote was 651 yes, 104, no. First Mesa contributed the heaviest support, although 83 out of 261 voters there said "no." But in Hotevilla, the largest village, only 13 people voted; Kochongva had obviously prevailed. Bacavi had the heaviest turnout, percentage-wise, with 80% of the eligible votes turning out and every single one voting "yes."[63]

A crucial provision of a 1935 amendment to the IRA required that 30% of the eligible voting population participate in any tribal constitutional referendum. In the Hopi IRA vote of 1935, 818 people voted. Collier reported the percentage as a 45% voter participation rate. In the Hopi Constitution vote of 1936, 755 people voted, reported as a 50% participation rate. Washburn (1979) set the number of eligible voters at 1,566 in 1935 on the basis of a census report, figuring all adults over the age of 21 to be eligible to vote. The figure accords well with La Farge's estimate of 1,590 eligible voters in 1936. Washburn (1979) points out that this compares favorably with participation rates in U.S. presidential elections. (The lowest since 1932 was 1952, with a 44% rate; in the 1930s, participation was quite high: 52% in 1932 and 57% in 1936).

But it is quite a stretch to conclude that the Hopi "came together" (Washburn 1975:254) and accepted the IRA as a total program. Some people clearly did not vote in the referendum. Canadian anthropologist George Yamada (1957:59) was told in 1956 that "the ballot slips were gathered up by somebody and maybe somebody cheated and falsified the election." Dan Kochongva denied this, telling Yamada (1957:61-3) that La Farge "said he would not steal my name and put it on that paper without my knowledge ... and he didn't."

It is unlikely that any fraud was committed. But some peculiarities have surfaced and will simply not go away. For one thing, there is neither a voter registration list nor a tribal enrollment list; the estimate of percentage of eligible voters was made from a census report, not a tribal enrollment list. A diligent, four-day search in the National Archives by Hopi Tribal administrative authorities in 1978 failed to turn up the tribal enrollment list of 1936 mentioned in the Constitution as the basis for constituting the "Hopi Tribe" (Johnson 1978). Consulting the U.S. Indian Service's most complete tabulation of votes per tribe and community on the IRA and Tribal Constitutions and Corporate Charters reveals that the Hopi are the only group for which *no figure is given under the column "voting population"* (Haas 1947). La Farge (1936a) has a question mark (?) in his column estimating eligible voters by village.

An even more striking revelation appears when we attempt to reconcile the total population for the Hopi given by government sources over a 20-year period. Tables 6.1 and 6.2 give various population counts from several sources -- but most of them ultimately deriving from the Bureau of Indian Affairs (except for 1980 and 1990, Census Bureau figures, and 1970 #2 and 1986, which are tribal estimates) -- between 1918 and 1990. An influenza epidemic caused many deaths in 1919 and 1920. If the 1920 figure refers to

TABLE 6.1 Population
Estimates, 1918 to 1950[a]

	Estimates		
Year	1	2	3
1918	2370		
1920	2515		
1922	2236		
1925	2619		
1930	2472	2752	2842
1931	2842		
1932	2786		
1933	2980	2920	
1934	3021	2605	2538
1935	2634	2538	
1936	3101	2800	
1937	2800		
1939	3444		
1940	3444	3000	
1942	3558		
1943	4002	3558	
1944	4002		
1945	4069	3600	
1946	4126		
1947	4188		
1948	4250		
1949	4321		
1950	4374	4405	4000

[a]For sources see note #100.

1919, then the 6%-a-year drop between 1920 and 1922 is more than reasonable. But estimates for other years, especially the period 1922-1946, are impossible.

For 1935, two different total population figures for the Hopi in two different government sources vary from each other by 3.5%. The figures are 2,538 and 2,634. Which do we believe? *Between* one year and the next, 3.5% is a respectable growth rate, but a population does not vary so much in numbers *within* one year. The big problem comes along with the 1943 figure of 4,002. In order to get 4,002 people in 1943 we have to assume a growth rate of more than 5% a year. That is impossible, especially when 260 men were away in the armed forces (Thompson 1945[?]:10). The differences in

TABLE 6.2   ªPopulation Estimates 1951 to 1990

			Estimates			
Year	1	2	3	4	5	6
1951	4442					
1952	4498					
1953	4560	4000				
1954	4622					
1960	3354	4123	4834	5876	6000	6476
1963	3259					
1964	4950					
1970	4857	6144				
1980	6601					
1986	10500					
1990	7061					

ªFor sources see note #100.

figures for years between 1935 and 1943 are also impossible: first we get an 18% increase in one year; then a 10% decrease in the next; followed by a 12% increase two years later; followed by no increase; followed by a 2% increase two years later; followed by a 12% increase a year later. Population growth rates of more than

7% in one year are absolutely not sustainable and such apparent fluctuations make no sense.

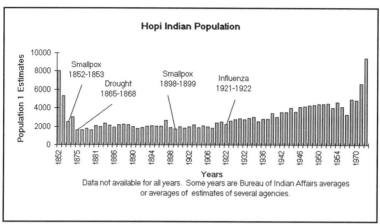

Figure 6.1 Hopi Indian Population. See endnote 100 for sources.

TABLE 6.3	Population Growth and Decline Rates, 1918-1986[a]	
Year	Population	% change from previous year
1918	2370	
1920	2515	3.06%
1922	2236	-5.55%
1925	2619	5.71%
1930	2472	-1.12%
1931	2842	14.97%
1932	2786	-1.97%
1933	2980	6.96%

(continues)

TABLE 6.3   (*continued*)

Year	Population	% change from previous year
1934	3021	1.38%
1935	2634	-12.81%
1936	3101	17.73%
1937	2800	-9.71%
1939	3444	11.50%
1940	3444	0.00%
1942	3558	1.66%
1943	4002	12.48%
1944	4002	0.00%
1945	4069	1.67%
1946	4126	1.40%
1947	4188	1.50%
1948	4250	1.48%
1949	4321	1.67%
1950	4374	1.23%
1951	4442	1.55%
1952	4498	1.26%
1953	4560	1.38%
1954	4622	1.36%
1960	4123	-2.98%
1963	3259	-6.98%
1964	4950	51.89%
1970	6144	8.02%

TABLE 6.3   (*continued*)

Year	Population	% change from previous year
1980	6601	0.74%
1986	10500	9.83%

[a]For sources see note #100.

Could even a 3-4% growth rate have been sustained in the face of an infant mortality rate in the 1930s and 1940s of 180/1,000 (compared to 40/1000 for the general U.S). and a mortality rate of 11.7% of birthing women (compared to 2.7% for the U.S.) (Thompson [1945]?:128, 101-106; Kunitz 1976; Thompson and Joseph 1944:31)? In order to get the figure of 10,500 in 1986, a Tribal estimate and probably the most accurate, we have to postulate a sustained average growth rate of about 4.0% a year from 1936; the Tribe itself estimated a post-World War II growth rate of around 3%, and the Arizona Department of Commerce (n.d.) estimated a 2.3% growth rate between 1982 and 1986.

The huge discrepancies lead me to postulate three possibilities: (1) The BIA did not always enumerate the population of Moenkopi, which represented 23% of the Hopi population, consistently in every census. (2) A fluctuating population of in- and out- migrants resulting from people who happened to be living in the villages when the census was taken in one year but might move to Winslow, Flagstaff, Phoenix, or elsewhere the following year, only to return a couple of years later, could swell one count abnormally while diminishing another count equally abnormally. (3) Because of refusal to cooperate with census takers, populations at Oraibi and Hotevilla may have consistently had themselves under-counted until well into the 1980s. Any one of these possibilities make the figures suspect, especially those of 1934-1942 and 1960-1964. If, however, the population was between 3,600 and 4,000 (cf. Clemmer 1978a:60-61)[64] rather than 3,100 in 1935, all the growth rates straighten out and become more reasonable, starting at about 3.5% a year in 1922 and accelerating to 4.4% in the late 1940s when presumably better medical care was available. This growth rate is high, but is not unknown for some "third-world" populations, and is comparable to the Navajo growth rate.

It is for these reasons that it is difficult to take Collier's figures on the percentage of eligible voters in 1935 and 1936 at face-value (Jorgensen and Clemmer 1978). If, as Washburn's (1979) figures indicate, adults 21 and over and youngsters under 21 existed in a 50-50 ratio with respect to one another, then there were probably between 1,800 and 2,000 adults and thus eligible voters (one of La Farge's early estimates was actually 1,800), in 1935-36. This means that perhaps closer to 42% or even 38% voted in 1936 and between 45% and 41% in 1935, with 29.5%-23% of the eligible voters voting "yes" on the IRA and 36%-32.5% voting "yes" on the Constitution. Hardly an acclamation.

The Fate of Political Reorganization

La Farge did indeed interpret the vote on the Constitution as evidencing a "large abstention" and he "warned Collier that he should interpret this large abstention as a "heavy opposition vote" (Philp 1977:166-167). La Farge understood quite well that non-participation meant a rejection of the whole idea of basing policy and action on a mere vote. "The negative type of opposition is a method of refusing to be bound by the caucus", he noted. "No amount of explaining could convince conservative Hopis that it was right that their failure to vote against the Reorganization Act had not been counted as so many negative votes. This must be borne in mind in judging from the results of referendum the heartiness of tribal support of the measure in question" (La Farge 1937:9). Collier initially interpreted the vote on the Constitution as an acclamation for reorganization (Collier 1936) but eventually admitted that the Hopi Constitution "never worked" (Collier 1963:218). He regarded the BIA as having "muffed the Hopi job" because, although the Constitution conformed to the institutional structure of Hopi culture, it made the "unavoidable assumption" that Hopis would use an "Occidental rationality" in utilizing the Constitution (Philp 1977:167), which apparently they did not.

Redefining the Kikmongwis. Political brokerage, so evident in the upheavals at Oraibi, had become the primary purpose and function of the Kikmongwi's role at every village. Villages that had not been affected by this shift as much as those at Third Mesa now had to confront it. In one village, rivalry for the office of Kikmongwi resulted in a relatively well-educated, gregarious and ambitious man (O'Kane 1953:112) who had actually been groomed for the office by being appointed to the Tribal Council by his uncle, the Kikmongwi, being passed over in favor of a more retiring younger cousin who maintained the office in a traditional manner that is closest to the pre-contact ideal (Clemmer 1978a:29). Although this man was appointed to the Tribal Council, the rivalry resulted in a contrast being made by Hopis between the Kikmongwi's lineage and that of his better-educated cousin's lineage as that of the *"real"* "Black Bear" clan with ceremonies and stewardship responsibilities, as opposed to the "Gray Bear" clan which "is relatively weak, without ceremonies, and of low status" (Eggan 1950:344n., 109).

In another village, a bid for political power was successfully made by a faction who sought and gained influence over the Kikmongwi. At first, this faction made its bid for power by opposing adoption of the proposed Constitution. However, at the villages in question, the Constitution was actually approved. The faction then persuaded the Kikmongwi to appoint its members to the Council. Upon the Kikmongwi's death in 1941, the faction's political rivals were able to install a Kikmongwi who promptly withdrew his rivals' certification as Council representatives. At another village, the Kikmongwi's sudden death left its representatives without certification, and since Oraibi and Hotevilla had not only boycotted the election but also continued to boycott the Council, and since the Lower District of Moenkopi refused to elect a representative, the Council now had only seven of its seventeen members, hence: no quorum. In 1944 the Council disbanded completely (McNickle 1944; Jennings 1944).

Reorganization: The Economic Factor

Following the "yes" vote on the IRA and adoption of the Hopi Constitution, the BIA divided the Hopi and surrounding Navajo reservations into twenty grazing districts in 1936 (Pollock 1984:85) and assigned all but three of them completely to Navajos. Although in theory the "Hopi Reservation" comprised 2.45 million acres, the Hopi jurisdiction was limited to District Six, covering only 624,064 acres (Thompson and Joseph 1944:134). Moenkopi was included in the Navajo District Three.

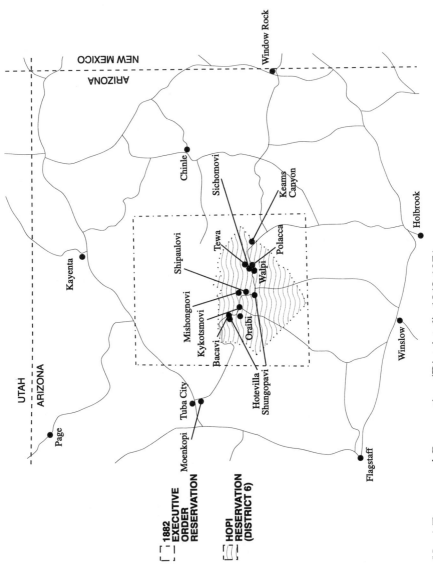

Hopi Towns and Reservation (District 6), 1942-1974

In 1939, four Hopis, all except one members of the Tribal Council, arranged a meeting with Collier in Washington, D.C. The transcript of that meeting reveals the reasons for the IRA's ultimate failure at Hopi. Hopis clearly expected tangible benefits from their cooperation; what they got was just the opposite. The four Hopis made what amounted to demands: (l) that the Boarding School and hospital in Keams Canyon be turned over to Hopis; (2) that the Hopi High School in Oraibi be brought "up to par" (it was not accredited to issue diplomas and Hopis still had to spend their last year at a boarding school if they wanted one); (3) that the Government double the grazing quota assigned to Hopis; (4) that title to at least the 1882 Reservation and at best the Hopi *Techqua* be vested in Hopis; and (5) that the Government rescind the designation of everything outside District Six as Navajo. "We had been led to believe," said delegate Peter Nuvamsa, "that by the acceptance of the Reorganization Act that we could be heard and our claims considered ... but if we cannot get any protection under the Reorganization Act, its seems that the Hopi Tribe will be better off by doing away with it and coming back to his former life" (sic).

Collier replied that the Keams School and hospital would continue to service Navajos as well as Hopis because Navajos were needier; that the Indian Service did not have the money to bring the Hopi High School up to par; that the Navajos had already had to reduce their livestock and "the Hopis may have to" too; and that the Navajos were where they were because Congress, the Secretary of the Interior, and the Attorney General had ruled that they had a right to be there. "We have no power to restore to the Hopis this area" (the portion of the 1882 Executive Order Hopi Reservation outside District 6), said Collier. "I would not have the power and, I think, Congress would not have the power even to put the Navajo off without their consent. The Hopis themselves decided that they did not want to enter into arbitration with the Navajos about this matter" (Collier 1939). Collier advised legal action.

Reorganization: Conclusion

The West's economy boomed and busted on sheep, cattle, silver, railroads, tourism, arts, and crafts, intersecting the vagaries of the Hopi climate and topography that made farming ever more problematical in the buying and selling of commodities and crafts and in the pursuit of careers open to talent: teacher, painter, orator, preacher, cultural broker, culture expert, interpreter. Hopis' apparent indifference or outright opposition to political "Reorganization" has to be explained in an economic, political, and historical context as well as a cultural one. The fact that the IRA failed to bring anticipated tangible improvements must have reinforced some Hopis' convictions that councils and reorganization were not for them.

The Reorganization Era that began in 1906 sent conflicting cultural, political, and social forces crashing against one another. Missionaries placed Christian dogma, doctrine, and values squarely in the paths of aspiring Hopi religious devotees as well as of those who saw many diverse channels for their personal development. Kikmongwis found themselves being criticized by *sukaavungs sinom* -- "ordinary people" -- for speaking out on secular matters and taking positions regarding political issues (La Farge 1936a:32). But the situation was predictable. The 1906 Split had made villages into political statements and had by extension enhanced the political character of village chiefs, several of whom were not ceremonially installed. Politically ambitious men gambled on the probability of constructing new political metaphors for defining power, and arranged alliances along entirely new axes that converged on Washington, D.C., Phoenix, Salt Lake City, or Los Angeles. The Indian New Deal, envisioning a reversal of Indian policy toward an empowerment of the Hopi collectivity and an end to repression, seemed to act as an experiential retort, distilling the chemistry of forty years of history into a pile of ironies: whole villages that boycotted the IRA in the name of Hopi tradition; reduction of land and sheep that followed hard on the heels of promises for more land and an improved economy; the alliances between Hopis and their partisans that seemed to hold more promise than did Hopis' alliances with each other; the guarantee of religious freedom at a time when ceremonialism was ostensibly being deliberately abandoned by some whole villages while becoming a symbol of resistance to forced acculturation at others.

Was it really as John Collier said -- that Hopis simply did not use an "occidental rationality?" Some researchers postulate the necessity of a prototypical "modern person" in order for all modernist innovations -- including democracy and political integration -- to work. This ideal "modern person" would have a certain "state of mind:" an "inner readiness," a "psychological disposition to form or hold opinions over a large number of the problems and issues that arise not only in [the] immediate environment but also outside of it," an "awareness of the diversity of attitude and opinion around them" (Inkeles 1966:141-144 quoted by Haviland 1990:436), an acquiescence to "break away" from "the grip of custom and tradition," a willingness to grant the validity of "merit over birth," to enhance "individualistic competition," to pursue careers "open to talent" and reject the privileges and perquisites of ascribed statuses (Hobsbawm 1969:190). People who did not have the "modern state of mind" would be doomed to the backwaters of traditionalism. But Hopi traditionalism does not quite fit Max Weber's classic conceptualization of it as "attachment to the pietistic relations of fellow members of tribe, clan, and house-community" (quoted by Rushforth and Upham 1992:228). The collapse of the Tribal Council and the failure of the IRA cannot be attributed to Hopis' lack of modernism, cultural conservatism, or traditionalism.

Traditionalism. "Observers of the Hopi," averred Richard Brandt (1954:35) "have been impressed with the extent of internal strife and disharmony among them. Friction and factionalism are the rule in Hopi political life," he continued, "both in intervillage and intravillage affairs. For example, at present various oil companies are interested in leasing Hopi territory, and the finding of oil would clearly improve the Hopi economic position greatly. The grant of a lease, however, legally requires the approval of the tribal political organization. But the village delegates have been unable to make this organization effective, and in the summer of 1948 it was said that the Hopi were further from unified tribal action than in previous years."

But there was more to it than that. Some Hopis did think a tribal council was "*ka-anta*," simply too far from Hopi tradition. But within a few years of the Council's demise, its place would be briefly taken by a kind of "Traditionalist" organization that would push the Council into not only being revived, but also into representing the "Progressivist" metaphor for the next thirty years. Apparently the possibility that Hopis simply did not want to grant oil leases did not occur to Brandt. Yet it was oil leasing as well as the council that would be rejected as "*ka-anta*," and it was not mere cultural conservatism or lack of an "Occidental" rationality that led to that rejection. To find out why, we must focus on the "Traditionalists."

7

The Rise of the Traditionalists: 1946-1977

In 1946 an elderly member of Shungopavi's Bluebird clan, Andrew Hermequaftewa, announced in a kiva meeting that in the early days of his religious training and instruction he was told that when a gourd of ashes fell from the sky, he was to tell certain teachings, traditions, and prophecies that had been previously secret. Andrew had been one of the first Hopi silversmiths, prior to 1900, and had been among the "Second Mesa Hostiles" who moved to Oraibi, and in 1906, to Hotevilla. Leaders of other clans mentioned the same instructions. They agreed that the "gourd of ashes" specified in their oral traditions could be nothing else but the atomic bombs dropped on Hiroshima and Nagasaki in 1945. Other meetings followed this one, in 1947, 1948, and 1949, and the political ideology of a social movement was produced. It was drawn from a combination of prophetic ideology, history, expediency, and an affirmation of tradition, intuition, and revelation over "progress," majority rule, and urbanization. The Movement developed a distinctive political ideology and its leaders issued a series of manifestos, position statements, and petitions beginning in 1949 and continuing into the late 1980s.

The Nature of Political Ideology

Ideology motivates and justifies; it excuses and abjures. It expresses the loftiest sentiments of goals that are larger than life and beyond the individual; at the same time, it propels its proponents and adherents through daily personal hardships. "It is a loss of orientation" says Clifford Geertz (1973:219) "that most directly gives rise to ideological activity. It is when neither a society's most general cultural orientations nor its most down-to-earth 'pragmatic' ones suffice any longer to provide an adequate image of political process that ideologies begin to become crucial as sources of sociopolitical meanings and attitudes."[65] What orientation was being lost in the 1940s, if indeed "loss of orientation" precipitates new ideological activity? It was *not Hopis* who were losing their orientation; rather *it was the Bureau of Indian Affairs*. Because of the Bureau's profound impact on Hopis, this loss of orientation was accompanied by Hopis' development of new sociopolitical meanings and attitudes.

Certainly pragmatism, in the form of cooperation with the Indian New Deal, had gotten Hopis nowhere; the Kikmongwis had not gotten the Council to work, and neither had younger, educated Hopis. Virtually the entire deck of policy cards had been reshuffled between 1910 and 1935, with punishment and repression being replaced with "sweet words of promise." Then, after 1943, the promises had been withdrawn, and a new deck had been dealt. From forced acculturation and assimilation the Bureau had jumped to cultural pluralism and bilateralism; by 1946 it was moving back to assimilation again. The U.S. Government simply did not know what it wanted from, for, or about Indians. The confusion was particularly evident in the economic and political contexts which the U.S. Government deliberately created for Hopis, and in the ways in which degrees of acculturation or resistance to it became the metaphor for interpreting that confusion. Two factors contributed substantially to the BIA's confusion about how to respond to Hopis' needs: stock reduction and the policy on acculturation. Because these two factors are intertwined and because they played important roles in the Traditionalists' development of their political ideology, a short review of stock reduction and of acculturation is necessary.

Consequences of IRA Implementation: Economic Context

In 1943, the Hopi Agency was given exclusive jurisdiction only over District Six, with the Western Navajo Agency in Tuba City having exclusive jurisdiction over District Three, and at first the village of Moenkopi; later Moenkopi was transferred to Hopi Agency jurisdiction. The administrative action effectively diminished the Hopi land base to boundaries that Hopis considered unacceptable. District Six consisted of 624,064 acres of grazing land; created in 1937, this district supposedly reflected the land actually grazed by Hopi-owned livestock. Hopis probably had consistent beneficial use of around 750,000 acres at this time, including 860 acres of farmland and 3,487 grazing units, amounting to about 7% of the 47,288 units in the surrounding District Three. Translated into acreage, this would have given Moenkopi Hopis, in theory, access to about 125,000 acres of the 1,773,397 acres in the Navajo District Three (Nagata 1970:105; 154-155). Hopis saw the remaining 1.8

million acres of the 1882 Executive Order Reservation as having been given to the Navajos.

Creating the grazing districts was part of the IRA's "conservation directive". Although Collier (1963:176) regarded the conservation directive as having "a firmer support than any other of the Act's provisions" from Indians, this aspect of the IRA had resulted in just opposite of one of the IRA's intentions for Hopis. Following their approval of the Act, Hopis had less land, not more, and also fewer livestock. The Soil Conservation Service, later the Soil and Moisture Conservation Service, increased the number of wells with windmills and livestock tanks to twenty-six between 1934-1937, but the BIA simultaneously had tried to implement an unpopular permitting process and some stock reduction (Stephens 1961:168). Drought struck in 1943 and the BIA ordered an "emergency reduction" of 24% of Hopi livestock in 1944, leaving Hopis with 1,000 cattle, 1,200 horses, 1,000 goats, and 12,627 sheep. The need for range improvement and conservation was very real; although the silting up of Lake Mead behind Boulder Dam may have been one factor in the Government's determination to check erosion and runoff (cf. White 1983:212-314), range deterioration was a substantial problem on most of the Acoma, Laguna, Zuni, Hopi, and Navajo reservations. Livestock had reduced protective plant covers in some places and water falling on the land was rapidly carried off in flash floods; in some places six inches to a foot of soil had disappeared (Lockett and Snow 1939). But this 24% reduction hit the three mesas unevenly because Third Mesa was far more heavily dependent on livestock. Owners there collectively sustained a 44% reduction, while Second had 22% and First 20% reductions, respectively (Thompson [1945?]:118). La Farge [1936a:14] had noted weaving as especially important at Hotevilla and Bacavi; men traded and sold weavings to other villages and to New Mexico Pueblos (cf. Whiteley 1988a:136-7). Wool was also an important cash commodity; one sheep yielded ten pounds of wool selling at $.30 per pound, with one out of two ewes producing one lamb a year selling for $8-9 each (Brandt 1954:22). Thus, reductions must have hit some families at Third Mesa particularly hard.

In the area of cooperative economic development, some of the IRA's goals were reached: A "Hopi Agricultural Improvement Association", which had little to do with agriculture, but rather represented cattlemen, was formed. A "Hopi Indian Credit Association" was begun, but not until 1952. The Association made government funds available for private enterprise, home improvements, and the purchase of cattle. The Association never made any sheep loans because sheep were considered too risky (Mason 1966:39-43; 73-76). A "Hopi tribe ram distribution enterprise," organized in 1942 with 274 members owning 20,820 sheep and 100 rams collectively *before* reductions. The Hopi Stockmens' Association, organized in 1940, had twenty-one members with fifteen cooperative bulls and 808 individually-owned cattle in 1945. The Polacca Stockgrowers Association had organized in 1941 with eleven members, eight bulls, and 274 cattle (Thompson (1945[?]:101-106) and a "Hopi tribal livestock breeding enterprise" was listed as being operated by "the tribe" as of 1952 (U.S. House of Representatives 1953:385, 387).

The BIA had opened two coal mines at Keams and Oraibi yielding 4,600 tons per year for its own use (Thompson [1945?]:120). These mines provided regular employment, but no royalties. Farming was still important, with estimates of acres under cultivation in 1943 ranging from 4,510 (U.S. Senate 1948:534) to 7,130 (Thompson [1945]?:101-106), and by far contributed most substantially to Hopi sustenance (U.S. Senate 1948:532). Yield per acre was corn, 5 bushels; melons, 2 & 1/2 tons; beans, 5 bushels. Three-quarters of the farmland was given over to corn. Horse plows had come to supplement hand plows and income was about double what it had been a decade earlier, but still was not high: average family income was $439.82, per capita income $118.22 -- about half that for Navajos (U.S. Senate 1948:532). Of 654 families, 365 had incomes of less than $300 a year. Sources of income were: agriculture (actually livestock sales) - 22%; wages - 36%; sales of arts, crafts, native products - 3%; unearned income - 1% (Thompson [1945]?:101-106). Hopis would readily trade a small Katsina doll for a loaf of Wonder bread.

The human condition was still not good. Nearly 50% of the children were malnourished; infant mortality was still 180/1,000; and maternal mortality took its toll:11.7% of birthing women died in the process as compared to 2.7% for the U.S. in 1943 (Thompson [1945]?:101-106), despite Government expenditures having risen from $71.21 in 1939 to $90.47 per person in 1943 (U.S. Senate 1948:531). By 1949, twenty-seven Hopi families had resettled on acreage at Parker on the Colorado River Indian Reservation; the land had been vacated when the Government closed its Japanese relocation camp there after the War and some irrigation water was available there (Thompson 1950:281).

Applied Anthropology

Laura Thompson's Indian Personality and Administration Project

The Indian New Deal's failure among the Hopi was particularly poignant in view of the lofty ideals professed and in the rigorous, socially scientific principles on which it was to be based. While Collier himself was behind the ideals and the principles, they are best seen in the Hopi case in the activities of Laura Thompson. Just returned from Fiji and Guam, Laura Thompson breezed into the Commissioner's Office and offered her services; she not only had experience as a trained ethnographer, but also some familiarity with colonial administration. Could Commissioner Collier find a spot for her? He certainly could. Within a year she was in the Indian Service; six years later, she was Collier's wife.

Thompson coordinated the Indian Personality and Administration Research Branch of the Office of Indian Affairs and personally headed its Hopi Project. Lasting two years, from 1942 to 1944, the Hopi Project was one of six undertaken.[66] The Project's assumption was that acculturation problems and practical administrative problems were closely related. The applied social scientist's role was *not* one of mediator or trouble-shooter. Rather, the social scientist must be diagnostician and integrative leader, working closely with administrators and community leaders (Thompson 1950:15, 180-181). But what if some community leaders did not want to work closely with administrators? The Project did not address such an eventuality; in fact, some of Thompson's research findings may have been offered as an excuse for *not* working with important community leaders because they were "atypical," or even from whole villages that were "atypical" (Thompson 1950:71-72). Thus she avoided many of the problems that La Farge had encountered six years earlier.

Thompson's framework was acculturation and her methodological assumption rested on applied anthropology; it has been said that Collier's entire Indian New Deal was an exercise in applied anthropology (Washburn 1984).[67] The reservations chosen for "Indian Personality and Administration Research" were also those targeted for stock reduction, and at all except Hopi, the stock reduction had begun long before the research did. World War II intervened in the Office of Indian Affairs' budget in 1942, and therefore, what might have been projected as a long-term administrative policy guided by social scientific research quickly reverted to a top-down kind of administrative planning and implementation, at least at Hopi, following Collier's departure from office in 1945.

The Economic Problem and Applied Anthropology. The study's purpose was unassailably laudable: to suggest how administrators could "help Hopi to understand and cope with their own problems...." Thompson (1945[?]:209) recommended self-determination for the Hopi: "The Indians must do their own thinking and plan for themselves," she admonished. The reason help was needed rested on the Hopis' current crisis. The crisis had four components: (1) settlement of the Hopi-Navajo land dispute to the detriment of the Hopis; (2) a severe drought resulting in the Government's insistence on an immediate 24% reduction of livestock in 1943; (3) departure of one-third of the Tribe for war work and duty in the armed forces; and (4) Hopi leaders' ostensible lack of understanding of the underlying meaning of the emergency (Thompson [1945(?)]:35). Thus, they needed an enlightened Government administration to help them cope.

Why did Hopis not understand the underlying meaning of the emergency? Thompson (1945[?]:34) credited the Hopi with a "planning mentality," an ability to formulate a valid long-range goal in terms of group and individual effort and with knowing "how to deliberately, with an intended effort of the group will, motivate and mold individual personalities and the social whole." Additionally, the "expected" Indian problems apparently did not afflict the Hopi. "Alcoholic beverages are not used," she noted (Thompson 1950:51), "and, in contrast to most Indian reservations, there is no drinking problem...," although a Hopi-Tewa had told Oliver La Farge (1936:27) specifically that they wanted more police protection to put a stop to "drinking and gambling" and Brandt (1954:28, 269) as well as La Farge (1936a) had mentioned drinking.

What, then, was the underlying meaning of the emergency that would hamstring Hopis' ability to cope? It was fundamentally the clash between the old and the new, said Thompson, between the tight fabric of an integrated, perfectly tuned, well-adapted culture and the strains and stresses brought on by contact with Euro-American culture. Thompson (1945[?]:71-72) saw an inevitable, irreconcilable conflict between "the ancient system" and "the new," of which it was the "complete antithesis." The "Hopi system fosters the internalization of the group sanctions within the individual and sets up conditions for the development of a <u>conscience in each individual which is consistent with the social goal</u>" (underlining in original for emphasis). The emergency's underlying meaning boiled down to a "modal personality" issue coupled with acculturative stress, according to Thompson. Acculturative stress definitely formed part of Hopis' socio-cultural situation in the 1940s, but depending on what kind of theoretical framework one uses to analyze it, acculturation may assume a very different form in terms of causal analysis.

The Acculturation Framework

Acculturation can be defined as the process whereby an individual, or a group of individuals -- which may include an entire society -- moves its culture toward that of another group of people, another society, with which it is in direct contact. The acculturation framework has one of two starting points: one, a social-structural starting point, and the other, an individualistic, personal starting point. Traversing the framework from a social-structural starting point eventually yields an overall, grand picture, one that views some whole societies in a structural relationship with certain whole other societies, even though less than 100 percent of the people in both societies -- it might be far less than 100% in one or both -- have contact with each other. Starting with individuals, one builds the framework of collections of persons who are more or less "acculturated," ending up with a continuum of personalities that, on one extreme, are best suited to the "old ways," that is, to the culture as it used to be and can never be again, and on the other extreme, to the "new ways," that is, to an alien culture that bears no resemblance to the culture-as-it-was.

The "Individual Personality" Version. The assumption behind this approach to acculturation is that acculturation is to some extent a matter of choice on the part of individuals. While other factors -- political competition, economic factors, and social history -- might be important, the pivotal issues came down to acculturative orientation. Resistance to acculturative pressures would automatically be found strongest and most fully expressed among individuals in the two "native" categories; while individuals in the "acculturated" and "acculturating" categories could be assumed to be the least resistant to acculturation.

Acculturation, in this model, produces inevitable personality strains. But in Hopi society, the strains may have been there all along. "One is struck," wrote Dorothy Eggan (1943:357) "by the state in which friction predominates in personal relations, and in which the worst is anxiously and habitually anticipated" in Hopi society. "Gossip," she said (Eggan 1956:362), "is rampant throughout the villages; witchcraft is an ever present threat" (Eggan 1943:357). "A slight mistake in a ceremony can ruin it and thus defeat the community prayer for rain," she noted; "so too can a trace of 'badness' in one's heart. Thus their religion teaches that *all* distress -- from illness to crop failure -- is the result of bad hearts, or possibly witchcraft." Brandt (1954:73, 91) too, found Hopi society to be governed by an operative social tension between the individual's concern about public opinion in possibly committing a transgression of norms or a failure to perform duty, and an extreme reluctance to publicly tell others about their transgression or lapses, despite constantly looking for them.

Moreover, noted Dorothy Eggan (1943:359), Hopis' physical milieu subjected them to "an emotional gamut. It is a land of violent moods, of eternal thirst and sudden devastating rains, of searing heat and slow, aching cold. Here the season marched by with scant regard for man's trampled ego." Sandstorms might cut the young plants to ruins and "through long hot summer afternoons" Hopis "scanned the sky where thunderheads piled high in promise and were dispersed by 'bad winds.' When the rain fell, it often came in destructive torrents which gutted the fields and drained away into the arroyos. When the Hopi danced for rains and the rains did not fall, they ... searched among their fellows for 'someone whose heart was not right.'" Hopis probed their own hearts, as well as those of neighbors, to find the cause of a child's death, or the result of a ceremony being wind without rain. Public opinion, about who had spoiled a ceremony of who might be a witch, was "intensely felt and openly expressed," and thus could "be more effective potential punishment than the electric chair." "Gossip is devastating to individual security (but) ... where cooperation was the only hope for survival, it was the *servant* as well as the policeman of the tribe" (Eggan 1956:360-362).

Socially, she found that "inculcation of fear among the Hopi was a gradual but continuous process." There was a "constant parade of horrors" starting with bogey and punisher Katsinas, ending with possible witches, and reinforced by stories that were "recited by the old and listened to with avid interest by the young" (Eggan 1943:370). At First and Second Mesa villages (but not at Third Mesa after 1910) non-human ogres came to eat human children in February or March, being ravenously hungry after hibernating in their special caves near Pinon that connect them to the Hopi world and allow them to "emerge" when the cold winter rouses them from their stupor. Parents arrange for the ogres to threaten children who are bad (*ka-hopi*) but redeeming them at the last minute with mouse meat or other foodstuffs. Children can stay out of the ogres' clutches by being good and especially by helping to clear the fields of mice prior to planting. Thus the ogres are like clowns, "healing social misbehavior on the theory that 'like cures like'" and "like" misbehaving children in being uninitiated and very un-social (Kealiinohomoku 1980:40-41, 58-59).

Therefore, it is unlikely that "personality strains" produced by acculturative pressure were anything new. If "personality strains" were there all along, and it seems they were, then acculturative ones would merely be a variant of what was already an aspect of Hopi society. Nothing in the range of Hopi personality configurations, whether influenced by acculturation or by other factors, can be shown to have contributed to Hopis' "inability" to "cope" with the "emergency." Rather, it was the political economic structure of the acculturation situation that hamstrung them.

The Structural Version. Starting with the structural framework as a concept yields a different set of assumptions regarding acculturation. The structural approach assumes that acculturation is essentially a *political* process that results from *directed contact*. Directed contact interlocks two societies so that one is subordinate, the other dominant. The dominant society selectively applies sanctions to change the behavior of the members of the subordinate society in particular ways (Spicer 1961:520-521). Sanctions were applied to the Hopi in the constant threat of force -- either troops or police -- to enforce unilaterally-implemented laws and regulations such as compulsory education, allotment, and suppression of ceremonies and to maintain the alien political and administrative system headed by the agent or superintendent in Keams Canyon.

In this structural context, acculturation is neither a neutral process nor a simple continuum. The logic of directed acculturation anticipates that the dominant society's laws and regulations will become accepted after a couple of generations; that people will come to think, speak, and behave in ways that are consistent with national culture; that Indians will think of federal, state, and local laws and institutions as their own rather than as alien; and that, in general, the subordinated population will conduct their business economically and politically on the basis of the models that have been provided for them. Most importantly, people in the subordinated society will put aside their narrow, local agendas and loyalties and will channel their energy, time, and strategizing into priorities developed by movers and shakers in the dominant society, such as developing tastes for particular brands of consumer items or plunging into the competitive mainstream to attain ever better jobs, homes in ever better neighborhoods, and ever better credit and investment profiles. Resistance to acculturation on the part of individuals then becomes a political stance, especially if it is directed against specific agendas and goals of the dominant society.

The subordinated society, although it may have innumerable contacts with other societies, maintains an autonomous cultural system which is "self-sustaining -- that is, it does not need to be maintained by a complimentary, reciprocal, subordinate, or other indispensable connection with a second system" (SSRC 1953:974,976). Various boundary-maintaining mechanisms keep the two societies apart; many, if not most, are erected by the dominating society and are usually legal, political, economic and social. However, the subordinated society may also erect boundaries: usually cultural and social ones.

This structural acculturative framework gives many historical events among the Hopi a new interpretation. U.S. authorities saw refusal to accept compulsory education as a refusal to accept the United States' dominant position, and many Hopis intended it that way. On the other hand, U.S. authorities saw acceptance of compulsory education, conversion to Christianity, proficiency in English, and success in business as reflecting acceptance not only of certain aspects of Euro-American culture, but also acceptance of the United States' dominant position in any and all aspects of Hopi life that authorities might choose to control.

Many if not most Hopis who sent their children to school or even converted to Christianity *did not* necessarily intend to accept American political authority in all walks of life. Whether particular individuals "fit" one category or another on the acculturation continuum was less relevant than the degree to which they did or did not contribute to the maintenance and redefinition of Hopi society itself. Obviously at the point where virtually all Hopis replaced Hopi institutions, customs, behavior patterns, language and so forth with Euro-American ones, Hopis would have ceased being a society in contact *with* America and would have become merely "Indians *in* America." However, such replacement did not come close to happening.

Laura Thompson's Analysis and Plan for the Hopi. Laura Thompson ascribed to the "individual personality" version of acculturation. She viewed Hopis as a collection of individuals, some of whom had been pulled farther from their cultural moorings than others. She saw the impact of missionaries as devastating, since it was "generally individuals who have attended mission school and lost their essentially Hopi values" who stepped in and assumed "a political prominence quite out of keeping with their limited influence in the tribe." These "opportunists and misfits" interfered with "effective functioning of traditional leadership in current political affairs" since "the real Hopi leaders have tended to hold back or to work under cover" (Thompson 1945[?]:72-73). She even went so far as to assert that Mennonite missionization was responsible for "a trend toward compulsive neurosis" and was especially "bad" for "the Hopi male personality" (Thompson 1945[?]:89) at Third Mesa, contributing to "social breakdown" (Thompson 1950:187). The "new" system "introduced principles of majority rule and the ballot (both entirely foreign to Hopi ways)," and thus "fosters the emergence of a class of aggressive 'politicians.' The 'politicians' tend to use these alien political devices not as a means of fulfilling their responsibility to the group," she averred, "but as a ladder to raise their personal prestige."

The ironies could not have been more striking! Laura Thompson, applied anthropologist in the Indian New Deal, was criticizing the Constitution of Oliver La Farge, applied anthropologist in the Indian New Deal! Thompson, calling for an application of anthropological knowledge to the Hopi situation, was criticizing the results of the application of anthropological knowledge to the Hopi situation!!

The very nature of the indigenous politico-religious system had provided individuals with "ladders" by which to raise their personal prestige. The key to successfully raising personal prestige, whether in the "old" system or the "new", was to find culturally-legitimated institutions for doing so, and thus avoid criticism. Thus the "new" system was not so much the antithesis of the "old" as it was a graft onto it. Fulfillment of responsibilities had always brought rewards: sometimes tangible ones, such as access to good farm land, and sometimes less tangible ones, such as social prestige. Was it surprising that some Hopis who were totally detached from the politico-religious order would use the Council in the same way?

The Political Context: The "Lousy Plan" of Termination

Laura Thompson had missed the mark entirely. Not only had she confused the ideals of Hopi culture, anticipating life as being predictable, cyclical, harmonious, peaceful, cooperative, and well-modulated with the reality of Hopi life, which was stressful, unpredictable, constantly changing, and held together by pragmatism (cf. Bennett 1946), but also she had mistakenly targeted psychological aspects of acculturation as the culprit in Hopis' problems. The culprit really lay in Hopis' structural position within the framework of acculturation and it had to do with their subordination in the realm of land, economy and politics.

FDR's death and Truman's ascendancy to the presidency forced Collier out of office by the end of 1945 (Parman 1976:289). The real crisis of 1945 lay not merely in the reluctance of "real leaders" to speak out; rather, it lay in the federal government's decision to stop bothering about the "Indian problem" and to stop trying to listen to any Indian leaders at all. The Hoover Commission, chaired by former president Herbert Hoover, proposed steps "to integrate the Indians into the rest of the population as the best solution to 'the Indian problem.'" Assimilation was to be the dominant goal of public policy. The new policy represented a return to the past, an abandonment of bilateralism; thus it proceeded without Indian cooperation. "In an effort to relieve itself once and for all of the financial and moral burden of Indian affairs, the federal government reasserted full control of Indian lives and fortunes and fit them into its plan. It was a lousy plan." (Cornell 1988:122-125). The plan was called "termination" because federal services to Indians, federal trusteeship over Indians and their resources, reservations, and eventually the Tribes themselves would be "terminated."

The Indian Claims Commission. Inferring motivations from what people say or do is always risky. Yet it seems that there was some degree of concordance in the aims of those who wanted termination and the aims of those who established the Indian Claims Commission. Senators Patrick McCarran (Nevada) and Arthur B. Watkins (Utah) were among those who pushed hardest for termination legislation. Watkins phrased the aim in terms of "freeing" the Indians "from the "yoke of federal supervision" (Watkins 1957). Watkins and McCarran also supported establishing the Claims Commission. Congress established the Indian Claims Commission to act as a separate tribunal with special rules that processed claims for monetary compensation pressed by Indian groups and tribes. Remarks in the Congressional Record (1946:5312-5317) reflect some legislators' thinking disbursement of claims monies would aid the termination process by either enabling tribes to finance all their own programs or by providing individuals with sufficient capital and investment funds to make them economically self-sufficient.

The Claims Commission was not a new idea. Commissioner of Indian Affairs Leupp had suggested it as early as 1908, as had Lewis Meriam in 1928 and Collier in 1933. Congressional advocates of the Indian Claims Commission Act argued that (1) the U.S. should pay its "just debts" to the Indians; (2) the U.S. had an obligation to apply "standards of fair and honorable dealings" to tribes; (3) settlement of claims would encourage the "progress of the Indians who desire to be rehabilitated at the white man's level in the white man's economy;" and (4) if the claims were not settled, continuation of this situation would "perpetuate clouds on white men's titles" (U.S. Congressional Record 1946:5312-5317). (What if some Indians started suing individual businesses, city governments, and private parties for squatting on land that Indians had never sold, voluntarily abandoned, or transferred to any other party?) The Act allowed five years after August 13, 1946, for "any Indian tribe, band or other identifiable group" to hire attorneys and file claims petitions. The Commission decided that it did not have the authority to return land, although it could declare that Indian title to particular tracts had never been extinguished. Attorneys would get 10% of the award.

Long Range Planning by the Hopi Agency

The Indian Claims Commission was not of immediate concern to Hopis in the post-Reorganization era. With the Council lacking a quorum since 1942, the Bureau withdrew recognition of it in 1944. Planning was done with an ad-hoc advisory committee. Beginning in 1946, the Agency embarked on a long-range plan, but not one drawn up by Hopis. The plan revolved around range improvement and livestock management.

Hopis were not idle while the Agency was implementing its plan. In fact, men who had not been involved in the Tribal Council started developing policy that ran directly counter to the Agency's plan. They included three Kikmongwis and half a dozen secret society chiefs and the organizer of the short-lived "progressive" Moenkopi Council.[68] Whether or not they were the "real leaders" that Thompson talked about, and whether or not their "concentration on all humanity" (Thompson

[1945]:63) was what she had in mind, are open questions. But they certainly were committed to anything but "voting behavior" and "majority rule," acculturation, and political economic subordination They opposed the Hoover Commission and its suggestions. They were the Traditionalists. They were a social movement.

Social Movements

A social movement is (1) a group of people who (2) look to certain leaders to direct activities and set the pace; (3) profess a distinct ideology; (4) do things together as a group that express the Movement's "groupness"; and (5) share a vision about how the world should and will be and a conviction in the authenticity of that vision . A social movement attempts to mobilize and utilize collective action to advocate or accomplish something. The movement's efforts inevitably place it in a contrasting position to the majority of society at large, and to people who occupy positions of leadership in the society, or at least in some segments of the society. Opposition to the movement arises when either the leadership or the society at large is forced to take a position favoring or opposing the movement. A salient characteristic of all social movements is that they rely to a large extent on the support of a significantly large, but amorphously defined, mass of people. Individuals may "drop into" or "drop out of" a movement, but the movement must be able to count on its ability to mobilize supporters at crucial times, or else face eventual extinction.

Participants assume, and may directly say, that they cannot achieve their goals within society's "normal" social, or political, or religious organizational frameworks, and therefore that some extraordinary effort is required. This effort may be expressed through persuasive rhetoric; or defiance of social and or legal rules; or deliberate isolation from the majority of society; or deliberate establishment of new rules for society; or issuance of broadsides, manifestoes, and petitions; or even violent confrontation; or all of the above. These efforts aim at differentiating the movement from the "run-of-the-mill" society,

A movement usually has a discernible beginning point and sometimes an end point as well, when it either disbands in failure or attains its goals and becomes institutionalized in the society, either socially or ideologically or both. During the movement's most active phase, a communication network links members with each other and with people who may be supportive, but reluctant to profess their support publicly. Such networks consist of local meetings, personal friendships, letters, traveling representatives, common information sources, and sometimes newsletters. Most often, members of a social movement are not related to each other by kinship, but where kinship bonds coincide with movement membership, the movement is more easily able to maintain an active core of people. A movement may have a body of written literature setting forth the goals land behavioral rules, but even if it does not, there is always some "story" connected with the movement that argues for and legitimatizes its existence in the eyes of its adherents. In the early stages of a movement's growth, this "story" may be entirely a matter of oral tradition, and may remain so. But even after being written down the story may be embellished, changed, and reinterpreted by various adherents. A movement's "story" usually stresses the way in which the movement has strived to express or embody values and beliefs that are basic and fundamental, or alternately, values and beliefs in which the movement proposes a new "moral order" that will redeem adherents from the obligations of society's "old" values and beliefs. In some cases, a movement's "story" stresses both.

The Traditionalist Movement

The Hopi Traditionalist Movement was *nativistic* because it attempted to revive or perpetuate certain selected aspects of its culture (Linton 1943) and *millennial* because it sought to bring on a "New Age" promised in mythic ideology by rejecting the ideology of the ruling authority and some of the dominant values and philosophy of that authority -- in this case Euro-American culture -- as well as the authority's economic and political domination (Worsley 1968:xi-xii; 32-44; 243-256 cf. Thrupp 1962). In emphasizing collective resistance, consensual dissent, and political opposition for their own sake, it was *transformative* because it withdrew energy from routines of the larger society -- Hopi as well as U.S. -- so as to bring about an anticipated change in society and because it viewed the process of change as cataclysmic (Aberle 1966:318-20). It was *revitalistic* because it sought to establish a more satisfying culture while espousing specific goals that demanded critical evaluation by other Hopis (Wallace 1956). There are elements of *relative deprivation* in the Movement, since at least one of the manifestos clearly expressed resentment against Americans, who are "very rich," and Hopis who are "still licking the bones and crumbs that fall to us from your tables" and are, relative to the Americans, deprived of land, material comfort, money, and political power.

Who Are the "Traditionalists"?

The "Traditionalists" have been characterized in the writings of objective scholars as the focal points and generators of gossip (Cox 1970); as "deluded fools," "trouble-makers" and "hypocrites" (Geertz 1987b); as a "political party" and a "movement" (Whiteley 1988b:224-236); as a "faction" (Nagata 1968, 1979); and as a "formal cooperative organization" among the "conservative groups" among the Hopi (Spicer 1962:417). They have also been portrayed as an admirable group of men of "stubborn courage, resisting the pressures of the environment so as to uphold 'Hopi way' and to await the return of Pahaana," in the same way that the early Calvinists pursued "worldly signs of *certitudo salutis*, which according to Max Weber, is 'the origin of all psychological drives of a purely religious character' (Gerth and Mills 1958:277-8) (Nagata 1978:81) and as a left-over legacy of the "Hostiles" of 1906 (Titiev 1958). A Hopi word for them is *aiyave*, "non-conformists" (Nagata 1970:93; Cox 1970), but sometimes they referred to themselves as *hopivitsukani*, "living the Hopi way" and contrasted themselves with "progressives" whom they called *"pahanvinaquti,"* "white," or *"pensilhoyam,"* little pencil people (Nagata 1970:93). With no real organization, headquarters, budget, or consistent and systematic campaign within a well-defined political arena, they can hardly be called a party. They were definitely a faction, but that label hardly defines them; the Movement itself is factionated, and there are factions within Hopi society and within particular villages that have little to do with the Traditionalists.

They were very definitely in search of worldly signs of spiritual salvation, and the core of the Movement's founders was indeed from the "second generation" of "Hostiles" who did not plan the split, but took part in it. It might even be said that the pre-1906 "silversmith" connection provided the thread linking Hotevilla with Shungopavi, where the Movement was strongest, since the prominent founders included two of the early silversmiths, and much later, a third. The "Billingsley Faction" also contributed some founding participants; yet another of the early "Hostile" silversmiths had gone with Billingsley on his 1935-36 tour (Wright 1972:16). Until the early 1960s, the Movement was almost exclusively male, although not restricted to males, and until the late 1970s, it constituted and provided the primary forum of political expression for ritual leaders whose villages chose not to send representatives to the Hopi Tribal Council.

While the Movement drew most of its adherents from Hotevilla, Shungopavi, and Mishongnovi, it also has had a smattering of supporters from Upper Moenkopi, Kykotsmovi, and Shipaulovi. Virtually no one from Bacavi had anything to do with it. A handful of individuals from

First Mesa were involved briefly in the early 1970s, and with the death of her father, Tawakwaptiwa, and her successful contest for the Kikmongwi's position over her two brothers, Mina Lanza brought a large contingent of supporters from Oraibi and Lower Moenkopi. Supporters' clan affiliations ranged from Bear, Bluebird, Spider, and Kookop to Corn, Cloud, Katsina, Sun, and Sun's Forehead. The Movement included *pavan sinom* and *sukavungs sinom* and it even included a couple of Christians, including an ordained Presbyterian minister who was pastor of a church in Winslow; and his father who was pastor of the Hopi Independent Christian Church in Kykotsmovi, which most Hopi Christians there joined following a break with the Mennonites in the 1950s.[69]

Thus the Movement was "Traditional" only in an ideological sense. Thomas Banyacya,[70] appointed interpreter in 1948 for the Kikmongwis and secret society chiefs who founded the movement, chose the term "traditional" for the group to indicate its defining character as embracing and validating everything from Hopi culture, history, and daily life that was a product of oral instruction. It had the varying support of some Kikmongwis (See Table 7.1) and of some religious society leaders, but for the most part the Kikmongwis' real involvement was limited to putting their signatures on letters and manifestos. The Movement operated independently of the traditional Hopi politico-religious system, dovetailing with it only on occasions on which the Movement's leaders thought they could count on the religious leaders' support, or when the Movement took up a cause that the religious leaders knew would enhance their secular influence. The movement has tended to rely on clusters of individuals in each village related to each other through lineal and affinal ties, but the Movement also had adherents who were drawn into it by kiva-group ties such as the "Billingsley" people and even economic commonalities such as the silversmithing connection. Many individuals joined with the "Traditionals" on an issue-by-issue basis, and this behavior is what gives them the character of a Movement more than of a political party.

Leaders

Some of the Movement's leaders were "traditional" in the religious sense; they held important politico-religious offices such as membership in the Wuwutsim, One-Horn and Two-Horn societies; Snake Chief; Antelope Chief; Katsina Chief, and so forth. But the Movement's leadership was not an example of "traditional leadership" in the sense that Max Weber meant the term (Mommsen 1974:77). While "belief in the prescriptive order of things" and in "tradition" by "heredity" supported by religious rituals characterized the Movement's ideology, the Movement effectively removed leadership from its traditional bounds by injecting ideological commitment as its defining variable. Many holders of traditional politico-religious offices in the Movement's strong-hold villages had nothing to do with the Movement.

Leaders were not the "charismatic leaders" that one expects to find leading social movements in the sense that Max Weber (1949:329) used the term. The charismatic leader is "set apart from ordinary men and treated as endowed with supernatural, superhuman, or at least specifically exceptional powers or qualities." "By using the words 'charisma' (the gift of grace), Weber emphasizes the inspirational, revelatory nature of this kind of authority. The followers of the charismatic leader show 'complete personal devotion' to him. His authority is based on a 'sign or proof, originally a miracle'" (Worsley 1968:278-81). Having no tradition of charisma or individualistic shamanism, Hopis ideally value just the opposite characteristics in persons, that is, persons who are *pas i unangwaitaqua* -- meek, of pure heart, well behaved, modest. Some one who was "charismatic" would be labelled *ka-hopi*, bad or, *kwiivi*, a snobbish braggart, a know-it-all, or *pas himuniqai naami wuuwantaqa*: one who thinks himself going to be something; conceited, a big shot (Brandt 1954:125-136). The more the Movement's leaders gravitated toward charisma, the more critical Hopis became of them (Geertz 1987b); the more well-known they became *outside* Hopiland, the more they were pushed by Euro-American cultural patterns to assume charismatic roles (cf. Elston 1988:49).

In the Movement's early days, Dan Kochongva, Thomas Banyacya, and Andrew Hermequaftewa took the lead. Dan Kochongva from Hotevilla and Andrew Hermequaftewa from Shungopavi were two of the silversmith-Hostiles from pre-Split Days. Kochongva, of the Sun Clan, member of the Two-Horn Society that has a role in installing Kikmongwis, was Yukiwma's son and "guardian" of James Pongayawyma (Chuhoingva), Yukiwma's sister's son and designated to become Kikmongwi. On one of John Collier's last official visits to Hopiland on September 12, 1944, Kochongva officially installed Pongayawyma by handing over to him the "Fire Clan Tablet" that was the equivalent of Oraibi's "Bear Clan Tablet" (See Chapter 5) in a public meeting in the old day school in Kykotsmovi (Hopi Hearings 1955:285). On some of the Movement's manifestos from the 1940s and '50s, Pongayawyma is listed as "Chief" and Kochongva is listed with the title, "Co-Ruler," or "Regent." In the 1950s, Pongayawyma moved to Albuquerque, according to some, after Kochongva shamed him by seducing his wife. (Courlander 1978:151 quoting *Qua' Toqti*, Sept. 12, 1974). Shortly thereafter, Kochongva for all intents and purposes resumed acting as Hotevilla's Kikmongwi; when

Pongayawyma returned in the mid-1960s, he made an unsuccessful bid to wrest leadership away from Kochongva, but after Kochongva's death in 1972, did not try to re-assume the Kikmongwi's role, even when explicitly asked to do so in 1978. At Hotevilla, David Monongye, who had interpreted for Kochongva now and then since the 1930s, more or less took Kochongva's place in the Movement, although Carolyn Tawangyawma, whose husband Ralph had been yet another of the pre-1906 "Hostile" silversmiths, also took an increasingly prominent role in the 1970s and 1980s.

TABLE 7.1 Kikmongwis' Support for the Traditionalists, 1946-1990

Kikmongwi	Years	Non-support or withdrawal	Explicit support	Tacit support	Total yrs explicit support
First Mesa	(1944)-1971	x			
	1971-75		x		4
	1975-80	x			
	1980-	x			
Shungopavi	(1938)-1952		x		
	1952-88		x		
	1988-		x		44
Mishongnovi	(1937)-50[a]			x	
	1950-74		x		
	1974-87(?)[a]	x			28
Shipaulovi	-1964			x	
	1964-69	x			
	1969-70			x	
	1970-77	x			
	1978-81		x	x	
	1981-86	x			
	1986-			x	4
Oraibi	(1904)-1960			x	
	1960-78	x			
	1978-90			x	18
	1990-	x			

TABLE 7.1 Kikmongwis' Support for the Traditionalists, 1946-1990

Kikmongwi	Years	Non-support or withdrawal	Explicit support	Tacit support	Total yrs explicit support
Hotevilla	(1943)-53(?)		x		
	1954(?)-77		x		25
	1970-72			x	
	1972-77[b]			x	
Bacavi	(1910)-48	x			
	1948-60(?)	x			
	1960(?)-65[c]	x			
Lower Moenkopi	-1962(?)			x	
	1962(?)-78		x		16(?)
	1978-87(?)			x	
	1988(?)-			x	

[a]Position rotated until 1950. In 1987 Village ceremonial leaders declared Mishongnovi to be without a Kikmongwi.
[b]Hotevilla's Kikmongwi #1 took office in 1943, but was pressured out ca. 1953. His successor died in 1972. Kikmongwi #1 returned in 1965 but renounced the office in 1977.
[c]In 1966 Bacavi reorganized as a non-traditional village and thus has had no kikmongwi since 1966.

Herbert Talahaftewa, son of the old Kikmongwi from Shungopavi, as well as Otis Polelonema, a well-known artist (cf. Harvey 1970), and Lewis Tewanima, the aging Olympic Gold medal winner, were early supporters at Shungopavi, as were the remnants of Mishongnovi's "Billingsley Faction." After their deaths, the Movement's leadership shifted to others Shungopavi and at Mishongnovi. Briefly, in the 1970s, Mina Lanza and her husband John and for a while in the 1980s Mina's brother Stanley Bahnimptewa who succeeded her in the Kikmongwi's role at Oraibi,[71] provided leadership.

But the most important linchpin of the founding group was Thomas Banyacya. According to Shuichi Nagata (1978), Thomas came from "a highly acculturated family in Moenkopi." A member of the Coyote Clan, he married into the much more prestigious Bear Clan, and moved into the house of a maternal aunt (actually his clan mother), Sevenka, to assist in caring for her. Sevenka was sister-in-law to Charles Fredericks, brother of Tawakwaptiwa and a Christian convert. Oswald White Bear Fredericks, Thomas' first cousin, actually a "brother" in the Hopi sense, collaborated with Frank Waters on *Book of the Hopi*.

Nagata (1978:77) characterizes Thomas as follows:

> His earlier political career was oriented somewhat against the traditional authority and his initiative in establishing a self-governing organization in separation from the Moenkopi chieftainship in the late 1920s[72]is still regarded by many as a challenge to the traditional order. During the implementation period of the Indian Reorganization Act and the Second World War, he grew disillusioned by the Indian policy and was imprisoned for his campaign against military service. Through these experiences Thomas emerged as a firm right-hand man to Dan (Kochongva) and became the most articulate of the Traditional leaders.

While in prison on three separate occasions between 1940 and 1945 for draft resistance, Thomas studied the art of translating and interpreting from English to Hopi and back again, as well as making at least one important contact in the Conscientious Objector camp run by the Society of Friends (Quakers). Thus he emerged in the late 1940s as a seasoned, experienced, articulate cultural broker who knew the ins and outs of political organizing in the "modern" sense, with some "partisan" contacts on the outside. In 1948 he and Kochongva brought the founding members of the Movement together, and the three Kikmongwis among them, from Shungopavi, Mishongnovi, and Hotevilla, sanctioned Thomas' appointment as "spokesman." In the mid-1960s Kochongva agreed to sponsor him as his ceremonial father and, along with his three sons, pre-teen and teenage, Thomas was initiated into the Katsina Society at Hotevilla.

As the "Traditionalists" became increasingly better known outside of the Hopi villages, some of them came to be increasingly sought as speakers by national and international environmental groups, people interested in alternative medicine, indigenous peoples' rights activists, and college professors. Non-Governmental organizations (cf. Sanders 1991) with consultative status in the United Nations arranged for various individuals to attend or speak before UN-sponsored forums on environmental and human rights issues in Geneva. Thomas was the best-known and thus the most sought-after of these world travelers. His engagements book bulged; he had a telephone installed. By the early

1970s his primary occupation and source of income were the lectures and events arranged for him outside of Hopiland. His address to the United Nations on December 11, 1992, was perhaps the triumph of his Traditionalist career. But as the Movement's founding members died and were replaced by others, new spokespersons and interpreters were found, and according to Catherine Feher-Elston (Elston 1988:49), the majority of Hopis that she asked in interviews between 1983 and 1987 "have explained that Banyacya's duties ended with the death of the last of the religious leaders whom he (in 1948) represented."

Traditionalist Ideology

Letter to the President, 1949

The first public "position paper" issued by the Movement was a four-page letter to "The President, The White House, Washington, D.C.," datelined "Hopi Indian Empire, Oraibi, Arizona, March 28, 1949." It was signed by what looked like a "Who's-Who" of ceremonial leadership: the Shungopavi and Mishongnovi village chiefs; 19 religious leaders from those villages; one from Shipaulovi; and four interpreters. These included the Blue Flute society chief from Shungopavi; the Antelope society chief from Shungopavi; the Snake society chief from Shungopavi; the Kwan society chief from Shungopavi; the Ahl society chief from Hotevilla (Kochongva). Pongayawyma signed as Hotevilla's village chief.

"We, the hereditary Hopi Chieftains of the Hopi Pueblos of Hotevilla, Shungopovy, and Mushongnovi humbly request a word with you," it began. The letter issued a spate of demands and accusations, and directly addressed five specific policy issues: Hopis' land title; mineral leasing; the Navaho-Hopi Rehabilitation Act; the Indian Claims Commission; and the Hoover Commission's recommendations to "turn American Indians into full tax-paying citizens." Rejecting the Hoover Commission's recommendation, the letter also declared, "Neither will we lease any part of our land for oil development at this time. This land is not for leasing or for sale. This is our sacred soil." "The boundaries of our Empire were established permanently and was (sic) written upon Stone Tablets which are still with us," it continued. "We have already laid claim to this whole western hemisphere long before Columbus' great, great grandmother was born." The letter ended with a stinging indictment: "Now we cannot understand why since its establishment, the government of the United States has taken over everything we owned either by force, bribery, trickery, and sometimes by reckless killing, making himself very rich, and after all these years of neglect ... we the Indians are still licking on the bones and crumbs that fall to us from your tables."

When the letter declared that "we, as hereditary Chieftains of the Hopi Tribe, can not and will not file any claims. We will not, ask a white man, who came to us recently, for a piece of land that is already ours," the Kikmongwis were rejecting a major component of U.S. Indian policy: the Claims Commission. In the absence of any other "identifiable group" such as a "Tribal Council" to file a claim, the rejection would have to stand. "We are still a sovereign nation," asserted the letter. "Our flag still flies throughout our land (our ancient ruins). We have never abandoned our sovereignty to any foreign power or nation. We have met all other rich and powerful nations who have come to our shores, from the Early Spanish Conquistadors down to the present government of the United States all of whom have used force in trying to wipe out our existence here in our own home. We want to come to our own destiny in our own way." The letter was a declaration of independence.

The Navaho-Hopi Rehabilitation Act. Kochongva and Banyacya followed up the letter with a personal visit to the Commissioner of Indian Affairs, where they specifically asked that the Navajo-Hopi Act not be implemented. But it was implemented. The Act reflected renewed emphasis on assimilation as the dominant goal of U.S. Indian policy. In response to the deteriorating economic situation brought on by population growth, drought, overgrazing, and stock reduction, "the act authorized money for programs designed to lure industry to the reservations and to relocate Indian families to urban areas. Thus it had two distinct approaches: it returned to an individualist orientation, sending Indians to cities to join U.S. economic and social structures and also "echoed" the IRA's emphasis on community survival but in a new way: the emphasis was now on bringing industry to the reservation, that is, on simply jobs, not on tribal enterprise. Thus "even in reservation development, the individual was again the focus" (Cornell 1988:122-125).

Starting in 1950, the Act authorized $88 million, over a ten-year period, for upgrading roads and infrastructure; renovating hospitals and building new ones; constructing additional boarding schools; improving health care; drilling wells and installing windmills, tanks, stock troughs and water and sewer systems; building flood-control dams and dikes, some of which washed out within a few years; continuing range and livestock improvement; erecting fences (which many Hopis did not particularly want); doing economic feasibility studies; and providing job training, moving expenses, and "household set-up" money for several months for Hopis and Navajos who agreed to relocate to target cities such as San Francisco, Oakland, Los Angeles, Denver, Chicago. Under the appropriation, the BIA built new Day Schools for Polacca, Second Mesa, and Hotevilla-Bacavi; paved the road running east-west through the Hopi Reservation and turned it into State Hiway 264, along with another hiway from Second Mesa to Winslow; built steel and concrete bridges over Wepo, Polacca, Oraibi, Dinnebito, and Dot Klish-Moenkopi washes. It built new agency headquarters with Hopi work crews; completed a tarmac airstrip for light aircraft near Polacca; ran water, sewer, and electricity lines to virtually every house in Kykotsmovi and Polacca; and made sure a tank and spigot system were installed at Sichomovi and Hano-Tewa. Health care was transferred to the U.S. Public Health Service in 1955, and the U.S. Public Health Service built a new hospital at Tuba City. No longer were the Hopi villages isolated or technologically "backwoodsy."

But the Act's most far-reaching impact lay in study of coal mining and marketing feasibility commissioned by the BIA to the University of Arizona (Kiersch 1956). It was to be mineral exploitation that the Traditionalists would most successfully criticize. Oil and gas had been under lease on the Navajo Reservation since 1922; coal reserves had been known as early as 1917 (Gregory 1917). Hopis had mined coal for more than a thousand years, preferring it as a heating and pottery-firing fuel until cast-iron cooking and heating stoves became available in the early 1900s,[73] and the BIA's coal mines fueled boilers at the agency and schools. But distance from railheads, problems of quantity and scale, and the fractionated and competitive nature of the coal industry had discouraged any serious consideration of coal reserves in the Fruitland and Black Mesa Formations on the Navajo and Hopi Reservations. The BIA's feasibility study was intended to change all that.

Traditionalist Ideology During the "Rehabilitation" Decade

After 1950, the Movement added a call for the U.S. Government to protect Hopis from Navajo encroachment; a protest against grazing permits; a successful defiance of the drafting of Hopi youths into the Army;[74] and the position that the .."traditional chiefs" had knowledge of the future, embedded in prophecy, that required them to speak personally with the President of the United States as well as to bring their issues to the United Nations. But the manifestos and the fact that the three Kikmongwis (and possibly a fourth, Shipaulovi's) would block almost anything the Government tried to do in the way of economic development, coupled with the known opposition of Lower Moenkopi's and Oraibi's Kikmongwis to almost everything, almost pushed the BIA into pushing the Tribal Council back into operation. In 1950, the Council finally achieved a legal quorum when First Mesa's Kikmongwi agreed to certify representatives. From that point on, the Traditionalists added opposition to the Council and its actions to its ideology. When the villages that sent delegates to the Council hired a lawyer and filed a claim with the Claims Commission just weeks before the deadline in 1952, the Traditionalists supported a counter claim from Shungopavi that requested return of the entire Hopi *techqua*, rather than money. Filed as Docket 210, it was thrown out of court. When the Council's attorney pushed a piece of legislation through Congress in 1957 that would settle the Hopi-Navajo land question, the Traditionalists

TABLE 7.2 Kikmongwis' Certification of Council Representatives

	1937-1940	1942-1944	1944-1950	1950-1972	1973-1986[a]	1986-
Total Kikmongwis	8-7-6	8	8	8-7[b]	7	7-6[c]
Kikmongwis Certifying	5-3	1	0	2-4	3	3[c]
Representatives Certified	10-12	3	0	5-7	8-2[a]	6-10
Representatives from Non-Traditional Villages	3	3	0	3-5[b]	5-2[a]	5
Total Number of voting Council members	14-16	5	0	10-11	15-6[a]	17
Representatives Necessary for Quorum (simple majority)[d]	9	9	9	10	11	12

[a]1986 saw the temporary withdrawal of representatives from three villages and the decertification of one due to alleged election improprieties.
[b]In 1965 Bacavi became a "non-Traditional" village without a Kikmongwi.
[c]After 1986, Mishongnovi representatives were seated on the Council with contested certification owing to a question concerning the position of the Kikmongwi.
[d]The quorum changed for two reasons. Beginning in 1972, the Chairman and Vice-Chairman were elected at large, increasing the total of Council seats to nineteen and raising the quorum to ten. The Chairman votes only in case of a tie. After 1972, the total number of seats increased to reflect the increase in Hopi population and since representation is proportional by village.

opposed it because it did included a severe compromise of not only the *techqua*'s boundaries, but also those of the 1882 Reservation. Thus, when the Council supported PL 93-531 to relocate Navajos and recover use of half the 1882 reservation, the Traditionalists opposed that too.

Ideology: Summary[75]

The Movement's ideological principles can be summarized as follows: (1) The United States Government has no legal right of authority over Hopis because Hopis never signed a treaty acknowledging the U.S. Government's right of existence. Hopis maintain the same degree of sovereignty that they had following expulsion of the Spaniards. (2) The United States Government has no moral right to pressure Hopis to acculturate or assimilate, nor do missionaries. (3) The Hopi Tribal Council has no authority beyond that granted by the politico-religious leaders and cannot replace them in exercising that authority. (4) The politico-religious leaders, particularly the Kikmongwis but also other *mongwis*, are the only authorities that should be recognized. (5) Public works and other developments or projects that might materially benefit the Hopi people such as mineral leasing can be sanctioned only in accordance with "Prophecy" and with the version of the "Prophecy" predicting the "end" of Hopi life if material benefits are accepted by those who have heretofore rejected them. (6) The "search for Pahaana" is a moral imperative.

The "search for Pahaana" is one of the most important components of the Traditionalist Movement, and roots it firmly to Hopi history and tradition, while at the same time constituting an important characteristic of the Movement's politics. Late in the 19th century, several elderly Hopis prophesied that one day, roads would sweep across the sky, people would communicate through spider webs crisscrossing the land, and Pahaana -- the Hopis' lost white elder brother -- would return to help the Hopis overcome their problems. Pahaana did not return, and a half-century later "Pahaana" had also become the term applied to all "white" people -- Euro-Americans. Despite the fact that none of them seem to have been the fulfillers of the Prophecy, the Traditionalists turned the Prophecy into a "search for Pahaana" which they used to secure allies and partisans among non-Hopis.

Traditionalist Activities

The Traditionalists' first dramatic and immediately effective action came in February, 1955. Dan Kochongva called a meeting with Agency personnel at Hotevilla. The topic was livestock permits. Throughout the meeting, the Traditionalists charged that the Government had developed the permit system to help the Navajo get at Hopi land and resources. Kochongva declared that he would stand on his traditional way of life and graze his livestock accordingly. He walked up to the Agency personnel and handed in his permit. Out of fifty-two men at the meeting, thirty-four turned in their permits, representing 1,096 active sheep units, i.e., 1,096 active sheep. The BIA threatened legal action (Stephens 1961:187-8). But the resistance stuck: by 1962, the permit system had been abandoned (Qua'Toqti 1980).

Dan Kochongva and Thomas Banyacya headed a delegation of Traditionalists to plead the Hopi case directly to Commissioner Glenn L. Emmons in June, 1955. Emmons responded: he and the assistant commissioner along with other BIA officials came out to Hopi country and listened to Hopi views and complaints for two weeks in late July. Out of the meeting came several decisions guaranteed to please at least somebody and not to please everybody: the BIA suspended the permitting process; did nothing about the Navajos or the land situation; and recognized the Hopi Tribal Council as the only legal representative of the Hopi people. It was the last time the BIA would feel obligated to respond to the Traditionalists.

Throughout the 1950s and 1960s, the Traditionalists held meetings at the drop of a press release. Thomas Banyacya could be seen hurrying between mesas and villages in car or pickup, delivering messages of meeting dates and places to key persons. Meetings were most often held in peoples' homes in Shungopavi, Mishongnovi, or Hotevilla. Occasionally they would be held outside or in a kiva. Meetings were always conducted in the Hopi language.

Non-Indian missionaries, traders, school personnel, writers, artists, social activists, anthropologists, and others had placed themselves in the role of partisans since the early 1900s, offering channels through which Hopis have exerted some influence on the outside world. The Traditionalists continued to take advantage of the prophetic tradition of searching for Pahaana that was beginning to become known to the outside world as early as 1925 (cf. Crane 1925: 163-7). Harry Nasewytewa, a silversmith working in a shop in Salt Lake City, arranged for himself and one of the pre-1906 silversmiths, Ralph Tawangyawma, to accompany Kochongva on a visit to the President of the Church of Latter Day Saints, Levi Edgar Young, in 1935. The "Pahaana Prophecy" was published in the Church's "Improvement Era" magazine a year later (Kochongva and Nasewytewa 1936).

In the mid-1950s through the early 1960s Kochongva hosted "meetings of religious people" in Hotevilla which brought a smattering of non-Indian supporters from Los Angeles, Phoenix, New York, and elsewhere. Two men -- one with connections to the Hollywood film industry and a prime mover in the nascent "grass roots self-sufficiency" movement and the other a retired Army general -- aired the Traditionalists' views and their interpretations of them through numerous mimeographed pamphlets printed in Los Angeles during this period (Nagata 1978:77). Starting in 1964, a number of Iroquois and their Native American supporters from other Tribes who traveled the continent annually in a "Unity Caravan" for the following five years joined the Traditionalists in their meetings and provided additional contacts and channels for them. Wallace "Mad Bear" Anderson, a Tuscarora from the Six Nations Confederacy in New York state and Canada, led the Caravan. Thomas Banyacya accompanied the Caravan on at least one such trip.

The Traditionalists followed up their 1949 letter to the President with another to each president in succession: Eisenhower, Kennedy, Johnson, Nixon, Ford, Carter and Reagan, each with the same message: Hopis had special knowledge; it was important that the world share in this knowledge; dangerous times are upon us and greater dangers are foreseen for the future; and the President must come to Hopiland and meet with the real and true leaders of the Hopi people -- the *Kikmongwis* and other *mongwis*. Traditionalists' letter of April 30, 1979, told Jimmy Carter that they had a set of prayer feathers for him "direct from the highest Hopi Kikmongwis," symbolizing the relationship of the Hopi people to the American people. The reference was reminiscent of a pair of prayer feathers sent to President Millard Fillmore through "a delegation of the Pueblos of Tesuque (sic) in August, 1852" representing the "Moqui people" and "the President," respectively, bound with a cotton cord which "is the road which separates them." An offering of cornmeal and honey wrapped in a corn husk, intended to bring rain, accompanied it (Schoolcraft 1853:306-308).

The United Nations. Traditionalists addressed similar letters generally to the United Nations. Meeting in March, 1959 in Hotevilla, they asserted that Prophecy told them that they must "knock four times" for entrance to the "House of Mica" and if refused, dire consequences would follow, generally in the form of natural disasters foreshadowing Purification (See Chapter 8). Requesting the United Nations for redress of grievances was not an unusual move on the part of U.S. minorities; the National Negro Congress petitioned the UN in 1946 to bring "relief from oppression to the US' 13,000,000 Negroes."

In 1971 one Navajo and three Hopis traveled to Stockholm for an environmental conference sponsored by the United Nations. They traveled on passports, bound in buckskin, issued by the "Hopi Independent Nation," thereby testing the international acceptance of their claims to sovereignty. Sweden honored the passports, and the only difficulty they encountered was in from U.S. immigration officials in New York, who at first refused them readmittance. They were released after a few hours, however, after officials realized the absurdity of trying to "deport" American Indians back to their "country of origin"! Subsequently, other Traditionalists made trips to Europe and back on "Hopi passports."

Ostensibly, the Traditionalists' "last" knock on the UN's door took place in 1981 (Buschenreiter 1983:209), but on September 21, 1982, ten very elderly Hopis from Hotevilla sent a message to the UN General Assembly that "now is the most critical period in humanity's existence since the destruction of a previous world," admonishing humankind to "return quickly to a spiritual way of life" and Traditionalists from Hotevilla. In September, 1986, six very elderly Hopis from the "Traditional Community of Hotevilla Village" of the "Sovereign Hopi Independent Nation" went to Geneva and successfully petitioned the Subcommission on the Prevention of Discrimination and Protection of Minorities of the Commission on Human Rights of the Economic and Social Council of the United Nations through EAFORD (Elimination of All Forms of Social Discrimination), a non-governmental organization with consultative status (cf. Sanders 1989; UN Sub-Commission 1989b; Rosen and Weissbrodt 1988) for investigation of grievances. But on December 7, 1987, twenty-six people including the "true Hopi Traditional Religious Priests of Shungopavi, Mishongnovi and Hotevilla" officially withdrew "all requests to address the United Nations and no longer acknowledge its concepts" (Kahtsimkiwa 1987:1). Perhaps, then, Thomas Banyacya's address to the UN General Assembly almost exactly five years later counts less as a Traditionalist triumph than it does as an interesting page of modern Hopi history.

Opposition to the Claims Commission. In May, 1977, several Traditionalists requested legal assistance from the Institute for the Development of Indian Law (later the Indian Law Resource Center) concerning the land claim. Their tactic aimed at a legal opinion concerning the illegality of the Hopi Tribal Council as Hopis' representative body and subsequently reopening or overturning the claims decision and resulting monetary payment on that basis. The Center did generate such a legal opinion (Indian Law Resource Center 1979). Although the Traditionalists could not legally pry open the case again, they did persuade 95% of eligible voters to boycott a referendum on the Claims case in 1977 (See Chapter 9). Much of their persuasive influence rested on the fact that Shungopavi's Kikmongwi, highly respected and not known to have set foot outside the village except on very rare occasions since assuming the office in 1952, appeared at the polling place in Kykotsmovi and urged assembled Hopis not to even enter the polling place, let alone vote.

Opposition to Public Utilities. In 1966 the Traditionalists added another plank to their platform: rejection of public utilities, i.e., telephone, electricity, water, and sewer lines. They insisted that these must be rejected collectively, not on an individual basis, and could not be installed without approval of the Kikmongwi. Eventually, two of the four Kikmongwis (Mishongnovi and Shungopavi) retreated from this position under pressure from their villagers; continuing to live in a backwoodsy, Thoreau-like, 19th century lifestyle did not appeal to many Hopis. But at Hotevilla, a sufficient number of people felt strongly enough about it to join Kochongva in confronting workers who came to install power poles and water lines in 1966 and again in 1968. The anti-power faction won, and the machines and men retreated with their pipes and poles, amidst much publicity; someone whisked Kochongva away on an airplane for his first trip along the "road in the sky" to appear on the Steve Allen television program. Five more confrontations occurred between 1974 and 1992, with the last one ending in defeat for the "Traditionalists" and the possibility that they might go to Tribal court over the matter.

Just exactly why the Traditionalists decided to focus on the water lines and power poles is worth pondering. Certainly the action and the ideology behind it were consistent with the Traditionalists' dissent, opposition, and exceptionalism to routine, conformity, and "things ka-hopi." But they did not oppose automobiles, wage labor, money, machine-made clothes, propane stoves and refrigerators, or even television sets, as long as they ran off car batteries and not from ac sockets. Their rejection of electricity symbolized their vehemence against dependence. Some suggestions for interpreting these actions will be made below, but at this point, it will suffice to say that the Movement was becoming increasingly metaphorical and symbolic as of the 1960s and that in the 1970s much of its ideological platform would be institutionalized in Hopi society and culture generally.

Other actions stand out in the Movement's long history of activities, among them: (1) spearheading a lawsuit and accompanying dissemination of information concerning the Peabody Coal mine in 1971 (See chapter 8); (2) holding meetings between Hopis and U.S. Forest Service officials in 1978 and 1979 to make an ultimately unsuccessful try at stopping additional development of ski slopes on the San Francisco Peaks, sacred territory to Hopis and Navajos and home of the Katsinas that bring rain;

and (3) efforts at getting the Navajo-Hopi Land Settlement Act of 1974 repealed. (See Chapter 9.) With other Hopis, the Traditionalists honored a delegation of Tibetan monks who visited Hopiland in 1980, and sent messages to the Dalai Lama. At Second Mesa, protests delayed a HUD housing subdivision on land which Traditionalists said was sacred from 1967 until 1984, with three die-hards finally burning some plastic water pipes as an ultimate symbolic act (Loftin 1991:109). On February 26, 1986, Traditionalists from Mishongnovi, including the One-Horn, Soyal, Snake, and Maraw secret society chiefs declared the non-existence of Mishongnovi's Kikmongwi, who had joined the Council in 1974, and removed all representatives from the Tribal Council. The Council ignored the declaration. Only a protest against the Council's short-term lease of a gravel pit for road work on Shungopavi's sacred snake-gathering grounds in 1989 has raised general sympathy and support in recent years.

Since the late 1970s, the Movement's adherents have dwindled to handfuls in Oraibi, Shungopavi, Mishongnovi, and Hotevilla. Activities have been limited to public appearances by a few of the world travelers and to manifestos and protests that have become increasingly metaphorical and symbolic. Shungopavi still maintains its Traditionalist-inspired boycott of the Tribal Council, as do Hotevilla, Oraibi, and Lower Moenkopi, whose refusal to send representatives goes back to the time of the Council's founding in 1936.

What Did the Traditionalists Accomplish?

The petition to the UN Subcommission was duly noted and well received in the international movement for the rights of indigenous minorities, although few Hopis knew about it. The effort to stop the ski slope development paralleled an equally strong effort by the Tribal Council, and was an unusual case of Traditionalists and Council not opposing each other. The lawsuit against Peabody initially caused consternation but, although unsuccessful, its effects were far-reaching. It completely bypassed the Tribal Council, arguing its illegality on several grounds including improper certification of a majority of its representatives, and targeted Peabody Coal Company and the Secretary of the Interior directly as defendants. Ironically, the case was thrown out of court on the very grounds on which the Traditionalists filed it: that because the Tribal Council had signed the coal lease, only the Tribal Council had legal standing to sue! Nonetheless the Traditionalists had their finest hour in obtaining support: First Mesa's Kikmongwi, who had consistently remained aloof from the Movement since its inception signed as one of the complainants. Ironically, Kochongva *refused* to sign, arguing that to file a lawsuit in U.S. Court would be to admit a lack of sovereignty. From now on, he declared, Hotevilla would go its own way and would declare its own sovereignty. Traditionalist supporters of the lawsuit from Hotevilla promptly declared that Hotevilla had had no Kikmongwi since Pongayawyma had left the village and the office in the 1950s, and signed in lieu. Pongayawyma, living in Hotevilla since 1965 and favoring utility installation, did not sign. Ultimately, the Tribal Council incorporated environmentalism into its operating policies. (See Chapter Nine.)

But Traditionalists' call for repeal of the settlement act, PL 93-531, initiated widespread confusion. The Act called for relocation of about 10,000 Navajos from 900,000 acres of the 1882 Reservation. In 1956 Traditionalist David Monongye had complained bitterly at one of the "Meetings of Religious People" against the Government's complacency about Navajo encroachment, and in 1958 Thomas Banyacya had told an audience of students in Northridge, California that "the Navajo overrun our land, and the Indian Bureau lets them do this" (Paige 1958). But in 1974 Mina Lanza, David Monongye, Caleb Johnson, and Thomas Banyacya formed the "Hopi-Navajo Unity Committee," declared solidarity with Navajos in the Big Mountain and Mosquito Springs areas, and lobbied for creation of a separate reservation for "traditionalist" Hopis and "traditionalist" Navajos. Twenty-five years later, journalist Catherine Feher-Elston wrote that the Traditionalist Hopis and Navajos in the Unity Committee agreed on only one point: that "the federal government had no business interfering in Hopi and Navajo affairs because the interference violated Native American sovereignty." Mina Lanza, David Monongye, Thomas Banyacya and Caleb Johnson "opposed the Act on principle because the Tribal Council supported it" (Elston 1988:65-66).

One of the points on which Hopis and Navajos in the Unity Committee did not agree concerned ownership of the land itself; Hopis insisted the land was Hopi, even though supporting Navajos' right to live on it with Hopi permission. Navajos, in contrast, saw their living on the land as granting them legal title, especially if they had been born there."Even Thomas Banyacya stressed that all the land in the 1882 area is Hopi land, and that the Navajo requested permission to come onto the land. 'The law is a bad law, and we do not support the law,' Banyacya explained to Catherine Elston (1988:65) 'but the land is Hopi land.'"

Nonetheless the Traditionalists' apparent reversal of their stance was interpreted as a baffling lack of support for an action that would return at least some of the Hopi *techqua*. Continual public appearances by Thomas Banyacya with Navajos speaking against relocation first irritated, then infuriated Hopis. Soon, partisans were drawn into the fray and indignation at the Traditionals' stance pushed more and more non-

Indians to stridently support the Council's position on PL-93-531 (e.g., Eggan 1974a, 1974b, 1974c; Whiteley 1987; Washburn 1989) and even to deny the Traditionalists' very existence (cf. Hieb 1991:151). At hearings before the House Committee on Interior and Insular Affairs in 1987, ten Traditionalists appeared in person to "articulate recognition of who the true leaders in power are in the Hopi Villages and that the Tribal Council is a forced governing body working in collusion with the U.S. Government" (Kahtsimkiwa 1987). Their appearance was countered by the Chairman and Vice-Chairman of the Hopi Tribe, several members of the Council, and Oraibi's Kikmongwi who appeared in person to support the relocation of Navajos. Partisans also submitted testimony, some launching renewed crusades against the Hopi Traditionalists. Yet the Traditionalists were the first to offer conciliation to Navajos in the land dispute and, although not well understood at the time, their conciliatory stance established precedence for later accommodations by the Tribal Council. (See Chapter 9.)

Toward Institutionalization. A.F.C. Wallace (1956) noted that a Movement ceases to be a "Movement" when it either gains such success that it becomes the establishment, or when it suffers so many failures that its participants and leaders became discouraged and disbanded. The Traditionalists are not the Establishment quite yet, but they rooted the tradition of dissent and opposition so firmly in Hopi politics that the "traditionalist-progressivist" debate may well shift to the Tribal Council's chambers and to the halls of Tribal Government in general in the near future.

For example, although the massive lawsuit initiated by the movement to halt the stripmining of Black Mesa was not successful, the Movement's opposition to the strip-mining was very well received by Hopis. "Salt-gathering Trips" to the Grand Canyon, begun again on a regular basis after a lapse of at least 40 years in 1970, were initially accomplished by Traditionalists from Second Mesa. The third and fourth were accomplished by a combination of Traditionalists and some Hopis who had been notably critical of the Movement; and the fifth trip was accomplished by ceremonial leaders from Second and Third Mesas who were publicly opposed to the Movement. The purpose of these trips was to validate and strengthen Hopi claims to shrines in the Grand Canyon, and to affirm the Hopis' spiritual claim to a very large chunk of land whose northwestern boundary is in the Grand Canyon. Pursuit of these claims had always been a Traditionalist strategy, and was consistently ignored by the Council until about 1973.

Another indication may be the heavy involvement of the Council in opposing development of ski facilities in the San Francisco Peaks. The Council sent witnesses to hearings and passed a resolution opposing the development because of the religious importance of the Peaks as the home of the Katsinas. In this opposition, the Council joined many participants of the Movement. Both developments reflect embrace of a strategy which had previously been associated only with the Traditionalists.

The Traditionalist Movement called for sovereignty; embraced Hopi traditions, customs, symbols, and religion; and called for resistance to acculturation at a crucial point in Hopi history, when contradictions and reversals in U.S. policy had created an irrational political economic structure. To some extent, the movement offered a source of dignity and pride to people, especially at Third Mesa, who were already growing old in poverty and had just had an important source of their livelihood -- livestock -- cut by 44% and their land base reduced as well. The Movement praised the Kikmongwis and the *pavan sinom* and for the first few years in the 1950s provided the only collective voice of the Hopi people and their leaders. The Movement also undoubtedly strengthened the secular political power of the Kikmongwis. The Hopi Tribal Constitution reserves ultimate control of the Council to the Kikmongwis. Even though a number of observers have predicted to me that it was just a matter of time before one village after another would abandon the old traditional system, draw up a village constitution, and separate the political system from the religious, this has not happened. The Kikmongwis might well exercise their legal power and either refuse to certify representatives, or reshape the aims and activities of the Council in the image of the Traditionalists' strategy.

In the following decades, and up through the present day, it provided a voice for some entire villages, notably Shungopavi and at times, Hotevilla. At the same time that it has represented the politico-religious leadership of these villages, it has also legitimated a political role for the *sukavungs sinom*, Christians, and in fact, anybody who cared to embrace their ideology or their issues, just as much as the Council has. In 1965 Traditionalists got the Hopi religion declared a "peace religion" and secured conscientious objector and ministerial deferments for young men initiated into ceremonial duties. The deferments were especially important during the Vietnam War. The Traditionalist movement was indeed a legacy of the "Friendly-Hostile" metaphor of the 1906 Split, but it extended the metaphor beyond Third Mesa, opening it to all Hopis, and along with the Council, redirecting the criticism and bitterness of the experience into a new kind of Hopi nationalism. The Movement was as much a Movement toward the secularization, modernization and democratization of Hopi politics as the Council was, and perhaps in some sense even more so, since, in the words of one prominent world-traveler who held no high politico-religious office, "anybody can bring this message out."

The Movement promoted discussion of important issues such as the claims case; strip-mining; and legal strategies with regard to land boundaries, even though not accomplishing resolution in their favor. While the Movement may appear to have been factionating, it actually achieved, for two decades, a rare degree of unity. It tried to subsume the factions that split villages and under two large overarching rubrics and to replace some of the more local issues with more global ones. Thus it provided a vehicle for "political socialization" (Nagata 1979) by seeming to eschew "progress"; maintaining the tradition of freedom of dissent; and legitimating discussion of issues originating outside Hopi society by providing what appeared to be a very "Hopi" and very "non-Euro-American" forum for doing so. Thus it complemented the Tribal Council even while opposing it, and enhanced a kind of political process that was as modernized as that of the Council.

In extending the Hopi "factional field" to include the rest of the world, the Movement created a new political path which is the obverse of the United States Government's intrusion into Hopi life and creation of the Hopi Tribal Council, which extended the *U.S.* political arena irrevocably into Hopi life. The search for Pahaana "directed the attention of the Traditionals in search of external support and thus alleviated their alienation from an otherwise hostile world," defining and legitimating probable sources of the external report (Nagata 1978:81). Traditionalists brought Hopi issues well beyond the parameters of Hopi life and, although they have upset many commentators' image of the "typical Hopi," (James 1974:219); Washburn 1979:96-7; Geertz 1987b), the prime movers have generated much sympathy for themselves in the field of international human rights and, ironically, in the U.S. domestic political arena, for support of the Hopi Tribal Council in its struggle against Navajos.

The Traditionalists in Comparative Framework

The Traditionalists' Vision: New Politics and New Symbols

The Movement's ideology is rooted in a vision of Hopi myth and prophecy that derive from what Eliade (1954:52) has called the "mythico-ritual scenarios of the annual renewal of the World." These scenarios are utilized in a kind of "feedback loop" to constantly generate both new interpretations of the myth and slight variations of the ideology. Thus Traditionalists drew symbols from the well-spring of historic Hopi culture.

But the Traditionalists filled these symbols with meanings that, in themselves, became symbolic and political. They addressed very worldly, concrete issues such as legal representation; relationships with Government bodies such as the Claims Commission and the BIA; the origin and derivation of political authority from the indigenous politico-religious structure as opposed to that locused in Government bureaucrats; and strategies for regaining Hopi land. Opposition to the Council, the Claims case, the Council's attorney, and *any* compromise of Hopis' claim to their *techqua* in turn acquired the status of symbols signifying Hopi sovereignty and tradition.

Any effort to measure Hopi Traditionalism against an ideal category of "Hopi culture" cobbled together from the ethnographic information collected by the 19th- and 20th-century evolutionists and historical particularists working in the naturalist convention, is an exercise in frustration. Resistance to acculturation is neither the opposite of acculturation nor a wholesale autism or rejection of the world. It is nearly always highly selective and usually politically symbolic. Studies have shown that tradition, and thus traditionalism, constitute "less a constraint on activity than" they do resources for "political engineering" (Laitin 1985:300).

The Traditionalist Movement is no exception. The movement affirmed a vision of Hopi traditions, customs, society, culture and religion as superior to those of Anglo-America, but did so in a new and unique way, that is, by attempting to recruit loyalties on the basis of ideological commitment to those traditions and customs rather than on the basis of membership in a particular clan, religious society, or village. The 1906 Split had begun the process and the Traditionalist Movement continued it. The Movement's ideology was not in the least identical or even necessarily concordant with myth and prophecy. Rather, its vision went well beyond it. The Movement was formed during a period in which Hopis' communicative skills, and possibilities for extensive communication, had greatly increased. In the kinds of issues which it addressed and in the ways in which it addressed them, the Movement represents a political sophistication that is parallel to, though opposite of, that of the Hopi Tribal Council.

Parallels with the Iroquois. Gail Landsman's (1988) observations on the Ganienkeh Mohawks are partially applicable to the Hopi Traditionalists. The Ganienkeh Mohawks were younger Indians who invaded and occupied a small area of a public park in New York state, within the boundaries of claimed Mohawk territory. Although the violence and conflict in the situation have no parallel at Hopi, the

Mohawk's ideology does. They contextualized the issues symbolically in a vision of sovereignty; commitment to the traditional political order of the Iroquois League, of which the Mohawks are one of six member nations; and in the refusal of the elective system, U.S. hegemony, and certain kinds of materialism. Like the Hotevilla Traditionalists, they refused electricity. They embraced the vision of the "Two-Row Wampum Belt, signifying a "treaty made with the Dutch in the 1600s. The two parallel rows of purple beads on the wampum belt represent the two nations or ways of life travelling along the same river. One nation or way of life has the canoe and the other a ship or vessel. In the canoe is the Indian with his own land, government, language, and spiritual beliefs and ceremonies. In the other vessel is the white man and his culture. The treaty specified that the Indian in his canoe and the white man in his vessel are to travel side by side in peace and harmony; they are never to legislate over one another nor to impose the other's religion. If an Indian chooses to go into the vessel of the white man, he must give up the way of the canoe and vice versa" (Landsman 1988:63).

The meaning of the symbols is clear, but the meaning itself has become a symbol: "traveling side by side" means a kind of community integrity and cultural equality that, in itself, symbolizes political and economic independence, despite the fact that communities and individuals are so entwined with each other all over the world that true separateness in undoubtedly impossible and undesirable. Landsman (1988:105-106) sees this interpretation of meaning into symbol as a kind of dialectical situation in which there is short-term variation in symbol construction and long-term continuity in symbol use. The Group's values and beliefs, tied as they were to "meanings which are both culturally and historically derived," resulted in Ganienkeh objectifying its culture that amounted to an "invention" of tradition (Landsman 1988:176). Because "traditional" culture is "continually reinvented and negotiated in the present," (Landsman 1988:90-91) Ganienkeh's "traditionalism" operated as a symbol whose content and meaning -- rituals, dress styles, etc. -- constituted yet another symbol, on another level, of the community integrity and cultural equality that, in turn, symbolizes political and economic independence.

In the case of the Hopi Traditionalists, the primary symbols were not a river with a ship and a canoe, but rather, two parallel paths, with punishments and destructions along the way. The symbolic complex was equally as mythic, and the meanings of the symbols as equally newly invented. The meanings were drawn from everyday events in lived experience; the symbolic complex was constructed from Hopi Prophecy and religion. But the Traditionalists had an unexpected pragmatic impact on a very tangible, material issue: the leasing of coal and water to

Peabody Coal Company. Back in 1936, Dan Kochongva had told Oliver La Farge that Hopi minerals could be worked only after Purification -- that is, only after the return of the prophesied Pahaana, and of course, Pahaana never returned. Thus, declared the Traditionalists, minerals should not be worked. Yet mineral leasing became the major source of capital for the Hopi Tribal Council in the decades following the 1960s. It is to the topic of mineral leasing that we now turn.

8

Mineral Leasing, 1961-1989

The Economic Context of Mineral Leasing

The U.S. Context: Economy

After World War II the U.S. experienced a unique combination of demographic and economic factors: continued rural-urban and south-to-north migration; negligible inflation; steady employment; rising wages and salaries; high birth rates; and general social and economic mobility. By 1960, the U.S. was 93% urban. Industrial output soared, service jobs rose in number while production jobs declined, and the leisure class increased. Between 1950 and 1980, more than twelve million people moved from the eastern U.S. into California, Nevada, Arizona, and New Mexico.

A gallon of gasoline that had cost between $ .15 and .25 in 1940 was still cheap, costing between $ .18 and .35 even as late as 1970, depending on brand and octane. Between 1950 and 1975, electricity consumption rose by 65%, but the price remained between three and four cents a kilowatt-hour. Between 1960 and 1970, industry's percentage of electricity use fell from 53.6% of the total to 44.5% while residential use rose from 29% to 33% and commercial use rose from 16.8% to 22.5% Between 1960 and 1970, there was a rapid increase in the air conditioning of homes, office buildings, and store (cf. Cook 1975:314-315). By 1980, probably 99% of American households had electricity, piped water, flush toilets, and telephones, and a majority had television sets. Many had air-conditioners. Heat and cooking fuel were produced or supplied from central locations unknown to most householders using the fuel. Electricity was also produced at central locations unknown to most Americans, and usually from burning oil or coal. Nearly all food was produced through industrial processes on a large scale, not on a household scale. Houses were built by mechanized methods, never hand-built.

These industrial technological developments not only had an impact on the modernization of Hopiland; they were also partially made possible by events there.

Levels of Social, Cultural, and Political Integration

Hopi Economy, Demography, and Material Conditions

Nagata's Study of Modern Transformations at Moenkopi. Few if any of the improved material conditions of America's emerging middle class lifestyle were reflected directly in Hopis' lifestyles of the 1950s and 1960s. Modern transformations of the Hopi social and economic polity were piecemeal, uneven, and marginal.

Shuichi Nagata's study was the first anthropological study of modernization among the Hopi. Working as Julian Steward's research assistant under Steward's "Cross-Cultural Regularities" program at University of Illinois, Nagata did his study of Moenkopi between 1962 and 1966. It clearly shows Steward's influence. The conceptual scheme rested on Steward's (1955) idea of "levels of integration." The "levels" concept views culture *not* primarily as a common denominator of traits shared by individuals in a society. Rather, individuals are integrated with each other on *various* social and cultural levels. A person who has little in common with some one in the same community might find himself or herself having much more in common with someone at the level of a national or regional institution -- for example, the Army or the school. Closely connected with Steward's concept of "multilineal evolution," the "levels of integration" concept assumed culture as a creative process, a resource, rather than a quantifiable, tangible "thing." "Multilineal evolution" refers to social and cultural adaption, to changes through time, that each group of people in a particular physical environment make in order to adjust to material conditions. Social organization is the most crucial determinant of successful adaptation; much of culture may constitute a psychological support for social organization, but may not necessarily be directly adaptive to material conditions. Thus the levels of integration are to some extent determined by the necessity for social and cultural adaptation.

Nagata looked at Moenkopi in its political and economic contexts on several levels: as a colony village of Oraibi, integrated with it politically due to its special history; as a community linked by kin networks and by the necessity to cooperate on certain economic priorities such as allocating irrigation water; as two separate communities divided into two distinct political factions, one with a Constitution (adopted in 1959), village council, and governor, the other with a Kikmongwi, and equally divided ceremonially into Lower Moenkopi with five kivas and Upper Moenkopi with only one "Katsina kiva;" as a Hopi community separated ethnically by surrounding Navajos; as a Hopi community with occasional relationships with the small Southern Paiute settlement at Willow Springs, about five miles away; as a divided polity with varying political ties to the Hopi Tribal Council, the Western Navajo and Hopi Agencies in Tuba City and Keams Canyon respectively and with the BIA's Area Office in Phoenix; as a "bedroom community" partially integrated into the ethnically heterogeneous Agency town of "Greater Tuba" where government services were available; as a rural community that looked to an urban center -- Flagstaff -- as "its town"; and as a general Indian community within the "colonial setting" of the federal Indian reservation system.

Nagata noted Moenkopi residents' participation in national institutions and in wage work, but called its economic integration into the market economy "marginal" due to the Government's control of land capital through the reservation system. While the Government fostered and encouraged the intrusion of consumer products as a means of "civilizing" the Indian, "restricted Indian cash income, difficulty of communication, lack of mobility, structure of the mercantile market, paucity of spending contexts and the conscious control by the government over the trading business on the reservation" isolated Indians as a consumer market (Nagata 1970:213). Nonetheless, partial economic integration had occurred by 1966, and had to some extent overridden culture as an integrating factor: "The rumors and gossip that commanded conformity and cooperation from the people and still do in some villages in Hopiland," noted Nagata (1970:75) "have lost much of their effectiveness in Moenkopi along with the decrease of community solidarity and increasing economic opportunities outside." Only five of 107 household heads were exclusively farmers in 1962, with another seven combining farming with livestock. Even cattle and sheep had diminished in numbers: down from 1,150 and 518 in 1943, respectively, to 392 and 274 in 1962 (Nagata 1970:162-3). Seventy-five percent of the household heads in 1962 depended on some sort of wage work. The subsistence economy had been almost completely displaced, and Moenkopi was a suburb of "Greater Tuba" with the Indians relating it "as proletarian peasants without the right to decide its future" due to Government control (Nagata 1971:157).

The General Hopi Situation. The general trends in the Hopi situation between 1940 and 1992 involve dramatic population increase; a shift from subsistence agriculture to wage labor and cattle husbandry; a huge increase in the amount of unearned income flowing to the Hopi polity along with a radical increase in the proportion of private sector income to public sector income; and further secularization of political institutions. Varying degrees of integration into regional and national economies affected Hopis differently, contributing to the increasing differentiation of Hopi society. Yet lineages and clans persisted in their importance even if they changed in their functions, with clan exogamy still being largely observed, and religion providing a unifying ideology, if not a common experience.

The 1960s. In 1960, nearly all Hopis built their own houses utilizing collective labor recruited from kin, either of wood frame and lath and plaster, or of dressed sandstone blocks cut sometimes with power tools but some times by hand with hammer and chisel. Large beams purchased from lumber yards made larger homes with larger rooms a norm (Titiev 1972:334). One man presaged the recycling movement by filling empty pop cans with water and cementing them into a wall in an addition to his stone house. Hopis grew most of the food they needed. Farmers still used digging sticks, hoes, hand plows, and horse drawn plows. Only a few had invested in tractors and tractor-drawn plows, usually buying them cooperatively and sharing them communally.

Large butane tanks were installed outside nearly all habitations except those in Walpi in the 1950s and 1960s. (The butane trucks could not get there). Butane stoves replaced or supplemented wood-burning ones for cooking, and most households had butane refrigerators. For heating, most households still used one or two wood-burning stoves. Navajos came around in pickups selling pinon and juniper wood, usually from the Hopi Reservation itself or nearby. For transportation, most households had a pickup truck, usually purchased used; half as many sedans were in use. Donkeys and horses were still used extensively until about 1965. For light, Coleman lanterns operating with white gas or kerosene lamps with glass chimneys were more common than electric light, although four communities had electricity. Potters started switching from firing with sheep dung to firing with electric heat in commercial kilns. Corn was still stored in large quantities in interior storage rooms, along with melons and squashes, as well as in corncribs outside. But few women ground corn exclusively with grinding stones; Titiev (1972:330-1) reported that power-driven stone grinding machines and hand-cranked meat choppers with special attachments had nearly replaced the traditional grinding stone. Rabbit meat and pieces of jerked mutton could still be seen drying on wires strung along the fronts of houses. Some households kept chickens and a few had a sow or two as a cash crop. No households had washing machines, dryers, or dish washers, although three coin-op launderettes were heavily patronized. Three settlements had electricity, piped water, flush toilets, sinks, and sewers in 1960, and by 1965 Bacavi had also acquired these conveniences. No homes had telephones until after 1970, when the BIA-operated telephone system was privatized.

Employment. Unemployment was estimated at 40% in 1964 (Rivera 1990:143). Even so, only 15% of the households were on welfare. The "Save the Children" Federation, largely oriented toward communities outside the United States, extended its private support program to individual families at several Hopi villages and some Hopis preferred such private assistance to U.S. Government subsidies. Four primary sources supplied wage jobs: the Indian Health Service; the Bureau of Indian Affairs; the U.S. Forest Service; and private employers. The Forest Service hired 30 to 40 Hopi men for three to four months every summer "on call" as hot-shot fire-fighting crews all over the west. The BIA paved two main roads and provided other jobs for the most part funded with the Hopi-Navajo Rehabilitation Act. Beginning in 1965, other Government agencies such as Head Start, the Community Action Program, the CETA program, and HUD Housing also began providing services, training, and employment. In 1968 and 1969, a small garment factory manufactured bra cups in a building in Bacavi, employing about a dozen women, but closed after operating less than a year. A BVD factory in Winslow met with a similar fate. (See below.)

The Hopi Silvercraft Guild and the Arts. In 1946 the Director of Indian Education arranged together with artists Fred Kabotie and Paul Saufkie, son of Andrew Hermequaftewa who had pioneered silversmithing in the 1890s, for an 18-month silversmithing program for Hopi ex-servicemen on the GI bill. The program trained the men in the overlay technique, which Mary-Russell Colton of the Museum of Northern Arizona had suggested in 1938 as a way for Hopi silversmiths to develop techniques and designs distinctive from those of Navajos. An assistant curator at the Museum created some designs and a half-dozen Hopis had become interested in experimenting with overlay by 1941. One of them had been Paul Saufkie (Wright 1972:38-59). In the 1950s, some women began carving Katsina dolls (Titiev 1972:333).

The program graduated its first class in 1949 and with the help of the Indian Arts and Crafts Board and a $5,000 loan from the BIA, Hopis formed the Hopi Silvercraft Guild, with Fred Kabotie as its head. Eventually, the Guild obtained a Government loan to build a large gallery and began carrying pottery, baskets, paintings, and weavings as well as silver jewelry. Wayne and Emory Sekaquaptewa learned overlay from Harry Sakayesva, in Phoenix, and Emory opened the "Hopicrafts" silversmithing shop in 1961. Although Emory soon left the business to pursue degrees in law and anthropology and later a career in anthropological linguistics, Wayne returned home in 1973 to take over the business, operating it until his death in 1979 (Qua' Toqti 1979). Another silversmithing business opened in Shungopavi in 1978. By 1980, all Hopi silversmiths except for Charles Loloma were working exclusively in overlay. Silversmithing by that date had become such a reliable source of income that some men made their livings exclusively from it.

Between 1964 and 1966 Hopi painting was given a boost when financial support was arranged for five artists, the "*Artists Hopid*", to do nothing but paint for two years. The Museum of the American Indian in New York purchased the paintings at prices above those paid by McGee's Polacca Trading Post and the Silvercraft Guild (Harvey 1970:1-8).

Consumer Patterns. The Babbitt Company, starting with a cattle ranch near Flagstaff, had built a chain of department stores and purchased Hubbell's Trading Post in Kykotsmovi after World War II and expanded it. The McGee family purchased Hubbell's Polacca Trading Post. The Secakuku family expanded their store at the foot of Second Mesa, and one enterprising Hopi opened a laundromat while two more opened restaurants. But seven of the eleven Hopi-owned grocery stores went out of business between 1960 and 1975; an eighth ceased operating after its owner was found the victim of an unsolved murder. Oil shortages of 1974 put three of the seven Hopi-owned gas stations out of business, but not the three non-Hopi ones.

In 1964 family income was estimated at $1,500 (U.S. Department of Commerce 1964) with per capita income close to 1940 levels at probably around $400. Hopis used their cash earnings mostly for buying industrially-made items such as pickup trucks, furniture, stoves, refrigerators, and clothing. But they also used cash to buy some food and kitchen items for distribution to other Hopis, mainly relatives, during Katsina ceremonies in spring and summer and during Lalakon or Maraw in October. For the most part, these distributions are made anonymously. Store-bought oranges and boxes of crackerjacks were distributed as often as piki, baked corn, and home-baked oven bread. Therefore, an individual redistributed a considerable percentage of his or her output to other Hopis in accordance with tradition. Thus Hopi society of the 1960s retained much of the collective, cooperative, and communal character that it had a hundred years previous.

Demography. Thirty-four per cent of the Hopi population (2,300) lived off the reservation in cities in 1960, while approximately 6,000 Navajo Indians lived on the Hopi Reservation in settlements of 200 or less. Between 1965 and 1980, Hopi population increased from about 6,500 to 9,200. Although hospital births became the norm, some women continued to birth at home well into the 1960s. The number living on the Reservation increased from about 5,000 to more than 7,000.

"Great Society" Programs under the Johnson and Nixon Administrations. The Great Society Programs such as Job Corps, Youth Conservation Corps, Head Start, OEO, Community Action Program, CETA, HUD Housing, etc., although not particularly geared to Native Americans, focused attention on the communities and held some people who would otherwise have left as well as causing others to return in a way that the Indian New Deal did not. Funding for them remained consistent for nearly two decades. Indians qualified for nearly all of them because nearly all Indians were below poverty level. They had a measurable impact; by 1970 Hopi per capita had income risen to $1,300, but still low in comparison to $2,283 for the general U.S. population.

In 1968, the Hopi Tribe secured contracts to produce "rag dolls" and electronic components on a piece-work basis. An assembly area was set up in Second Mesa Day School and more than a dozen women began doing the work on a part-time, casual basis. The arrangement worked well and, two decades later, the enterprise was still going.

The Tribe also received a small grant from the Office of Economic Opportunity in 1968 and a larger one of $600,000 from the Economic Development Administration for building a restaurant-motel complex with a museum and craft shops (See Chapter Ten for more details). Opening in 1972, the "Hopi Cultural Center" soon became a rave success in attracting tourists, in generating income, and in providing employment. In 1969, the BIA implemented its "Buy-Indian Contract" policy, a forerunner of "self-determination." The "Buy-Indian Contract" encouraged tribes to submit bids for operating BIA services. The Tribe could charge an overhead for profit and did not have to follow Government wage and salary scales, although the Hopi Tribe opted to take over relatively few programs. Low-cost houses provided by the Department of Housing and Urban Development increased by 20-fold, from fewer than a dozen to more than 400. Throughout the 1960s, '70s and '80s, Hopis used industrially-produced cinderblock and slump block increasingly in preference to native dressed sandstone as well as frame and plaster in house construction; while no other building materials were permitted for HUD homes, virtually all private home-builders preferred to painstakingly save their money to buy materials and build slowly, rather than go through the back-breaking task of quarrying their own stone. By 1970, the first trailer houses were beginning to appear as well.

Cattle Replace Sheep. Numbers of sheep held steady through the 1950s but began to decline after 1960. Between 1965 and 1980, sheep raising ceased to be profitable due to competition from Australia and New Zealand; for example, a sheep herder with 175 sheep made only

$446 on wool in 1965 with wool at $.35 per pound (Mason 1966). The number of Hopis' sheep fell from 6,600 in 1965 to fewer than 1,000 in 1980, while cattle increased from fewer than 1,000 to more than 8,500 (Mason 1966; Qua' Toqti 1980b). By the early 1990s, fewer than ten Hopis would be running herds of more than twenty-five sheep each.

Culture and Society. The traditional religious system stabilized at Second Mesa villages while slowly declining at First and Third Mesas, despite a resurgence of interest in certain aspects of Hopi religion and traditions such as Katsina, Powamuya, and eagle veneration. By the mid-1950s, no major ceremony was any longer being performed in Old Oraibi (Titiev 1972:326,337-9). (See Rushforth and Upham 1992:159 for a slightly different view.) Between 1964 and 1984, two ceremonial religious groups disbanded at one village. Three ceremonial religious groups disbanded at another village. Hotevilla held its last Snake Dance in 1970; Walpi in 1966. The Mennonite missionaries and their followers laboriously rebuilt the grand church in Old Oraibi in the late 1930s, only to have it once again struck by lightning in 1942 (Titiev 1972:333), and thereafter, converts were rare. In 1958 the Hopi Mennonites at Kykotsmovi factioned, the dissenters forming the Hopi Independent Christian Church. They built a little church of dressed stone and selected Fred Johnson, a son of K.T. Johnson who had burned the Bow Clan alter in 1922, for its pastor. The new Hopi Independent Christian Church emphasized the commonalities between the Hopi and Christian religions, and incorporated a heavy component of prophecy into its doctrine. Between 1960 and 1987, English began to displace Hopi as the most commonly used language among persons under thirty at four of the twelve communities (Hopi Health Department 1983:65-68). And by the mid-1950s, rising incidences of drunkenness had made alcoholism a growing problem (Titiev 1972:329). In workshops at the sixth annual Hopi Mental Health Conference in 1987, alcoholism and diabetes were identified as the severest health problems, replacing tuberculosis, dysentery, and respiratory ailments.

The Council's Revival

But perhaps the most far-reaching change of the 1950s and 1960s was revival of the Hopi Tribal Council. The Department of Interior pressured Hopis to revive the Council in 1950 specifically for three purposes (McNickle 1950): (1) to accept the Navajo-Hopi Rehabilitation Act, which it did, although the Act's administration remained 100% in the hands of the Bureau of Indian Affairs; (2) to hire a lawyer to submit a Hopi claim to the Indian Claims Commission, which it did; and (3) to approve mineral leases, which it did not do, at least not for another decade.

The Council began functioning regularly in 1951 with a bare legal quorum of nine representatives from First Mesa, Kykotsmovi, Bacavi, Shipaulovi, and Upper Moenkopi. All of these villages, with the possible exception of Bacavi (cf. Hopi Hearings 1955:219), seemed to be genuinely enthusiastic about the Council; all the villages that did not send representatives to the reconstituted Council seemed to be genuinely against it. Thus the self-identification of the distinct villages with distinct destinies and values that had been affirmed during the 1906 Split was reaffirmed once again in the way in which the Council was revived and set into operation.

For the following five years the Council and the Traditionalist coalition functioned alongside each other as competitive but complementary representatives of the Hopi people. The Council had hired John S. Boyden from Salt Lake City and Boyden proposed that the Council hire him as general counsel as well as Claims attorney. He promised to get back as much of the 1882 Reservation as he could, in addition to getting monetary compensation through the Claims Commission. He proposed mineral leasing as a means by which the Council could pay his salary and legal fees. The Council hired him again as general counsel.

The Quorum Issue

However, the Council was continually threatened by the possibility of lacking a quorum. When Shipaulovi withdrew its representative for a brief period in 1968, only dubious recognition of a representative from Oraibi in the 1960s kept the quorum alive. The recognition was dubious because there were three contenders for the position of Kikmongwi and recognition of one's claim over that of the other two could be considered arbitrary. In 1969, however, an amendment to the Tribal Constitution expanded the Council's membership to include a Chairman and Vice-Chairman elected at large, for four-year terms. The move partially solved the quorum problem, since the Council could still count on a quorum without the representatives from Shipaulovi and Oraibi, if need be. The voter turnout for the amendment referendum was 57% of registered voters. In subsequent elections for the Chairman and Vice-Chairman, voter turnouts hovered at around 55%.

The Hopi Hearings

When the BIA decided to recognize the Hopi Tribal Council as the sole representative of the Hopi people in 1953, the Traditionalists opposed the decision and several letters signed by Kikmongwis appeared in the Commissioner's office protesting the Council as an "illegal" body. In 1955, Commissioner of Indian Affairs Glen Emmons authorized a panel to conduct interviews in each Hopi village in order to determine several things: Hopis' opinions on land issues and economic development; Hopis feelings on stock reduction and range management; and Hopis feelings on whether or not the Tribal Council should be recognized as the exclusive representative of the Hopi people The overwhelming bulk of testimony opposed government policies and expressed no particular enthusiasm for the Tribal Council. Nevertheless, the government chose to recognize the Hopi Tribal Council from then on as the exclusive representative of the Hopi people.

Mineral Leasing and the Hopi-Navajo Land Dispute

Even after the Council was unquestionably certified by the BIA as the only legal representative of the Hopi people, hurdles to mineral leasing still existed. Attorney Boyden had to clear up the confusion about ownership of minerals on the 1882 Reservation. Between 1946 and 1956, the Navajo Tribe dispelled any doubt about the tribal nationality and citizenship of Navajos living in the 1882 Reservation by establishing several chapter houses in the area and ensured their voting rights in Tribal elections by expanding the Navajo Tribal Council to include representatives from the 1882 Reservation's chapters. Thus, Navajos no longer had the legal option of being citizens of a "Hopi-Navajo Tribe," even if they had wanted it.

In 1957, John Boyden for the Hopi Tribe and Norman Littell for the Navajo Tribe hammered out a compromise bill that would grant Congressional recognition of Hopis' exclusive ownership to the minerals and land of District Six, and would submit the issue of ownership of the rest of the 1882 Reservation to adjudication by a special court. The Traditionalists vehemently opposed the bill arguing that Boyden had been illegally hired by an illegal Council; that asking Congress to rule on Hopi land boundaries was a give-away of Hopi sovereignty; and that the result might well be a give-away of Hopi land itself. Congressmen Henry Jackson and Senator Barry Goldwater backed the legislation, however, and Congress passed it. Starting in 1958, the Hopi Tribal Council was free to negotiate mineral leases within District Six, but it was not until 1961 that it did so.

Hopi Mineral Leasing: The Economic Imperative

The period of mineral leasing has been a period of continually increasing economic stability and prosperity for Hopis. It has changed the character of their relationship with the outside world and their relationship, collectively, to money and wealth. Hopi Minerals are not only a natural resource; they are also a capital resource, not only for Hopis but also for the United States.

The Mineral Imperative

"The input of minerals and the output of an industrialized economy are functionally related magnitudes. The critical importance of minerals and the concentration of the world's mineral resources in relatively few, small localities combine with the great physical bulk per unit of the value of the most common minerals to exercise a major influence upon the economic geography of modern nations. Mining production, including the construction of necessary transportation, power, and refining capacities, probably demands more capital for the value of output than any other economic activity (Shimkin 1953:1-2). Although said of the Soviet Union after World War II, this statement could apply equally to the United States. As the U.S. Government expanded its domestic power in the 1930s and its international power in the 1940 and '50s, minerals became increasingly important. Minerals on Indian land therefore also assumed increasing importance.

Minerals on Indian Land

Tribal coal reserves amount to 21% of identified western bituminous and sub-bituminous reserves excluding Alaska and eight percent of all identified U.S. coal resources. The two largest coal mines in the U.S. are the "Navajo mine" operated by Utah International to fuel the WEST consortium's Four Corners Power Plant and Peabody's Black Mesa-Kayenta mine (Pendley and Kolstad 1980:229-230). Much of the coal for the Black Mesa-Kayenta mine comes from Hopi lands. But mineral leasing at Hopi began with dry oil wells.

Mineral Leasing at Hopi

Throughout the 1940s, oil drillers petitioned the Commissioner of Indian Affairs and the Superintendent of the Hopi Agency for advice on how to proceed in obtaining leases. The Indian Mineral Leasing Act of 1938 required Tribal approval for any mineral leases. Thus, oil drillers now needed a lease from the Hopi Tribal Council. But the Hopi Tribal Council had not functioned with a legal quorum since 1942 (McNickle 1944). Leasing jurisdiction transferred to the Commissioner of the Navajo Reservations in 1922 had been returned to Hopi jurisdiction in 1943, and thus pressure from a group of geologists prospecting for Standard Oil prompted the Agency superintendent, Burton Ladd, to query the Commissioner of Indian Affairs in 1944: To whom do drillers go to get a mineral lease? The Superintendent also asked if the Hopi Agency did indeed have jurisdiction over the entire 1882 Reservation.

Acting Interior Department Solicitor Felix Cohen (1946) replied in 1946 that, indeed, prospective lessees would have to go to the Hopi Tribal Council, and of course there was no Hopi Tribal Council. He also ruled that the Navajos living on the 1882 Reservation not only would share in any royalties, but also would have to be brought into the decision-making process. Because the BIA did not know either how to do that or how to get around the issue of the Council's lack of quorum, mineral leasing was tabled.

The Kiersch Report. The BIA, using money from the Navajo-Hopi Rehabilitation Act of 1950, contracted for a feasibility study of developing coal reserves on the Navajo and Hopi reservations. The resulting report identified the location of reserves and discussed methods of exploitation and transportation, concluding that coal could be transported up to "25 to 75 miles from the mine and still compete with natural gas" (Kiersch 1956:53). With the rising economic feasibility of coal development, something had to be done.

The Tribal Council was revived in 1950 in part for the specific purpose of negotiating mineral leases. A bare quorum was achieved. But another obstacle loomed: the Hopi Constitution explicitly authorized the Council to *prevent* leasing. How, then, could it *approve* leases? A constitutional referendum might prove foolhardy: perhaps voters would overwhelmingly endorse the existing phraseology. Or more likely, the requisite 30% of eligible voters would simply fail to show up to vote. Somehow, the awkward provision had to be gotten around.

Oil Leases

The Leasing Memorandum. In 1961, the Acting Secretary of the Interior, on a request from Tribal attorney John Boyden to do so, authorized the Hopi Tribal Council to grant mineral leases (Holum 1961). Even though the Hopi Constitution's Article VI, section 1(c) specifically authorized the Council to "prevent the sale, disposition, lease or encumbrance of tribal lands," Article VI, Section 3 had authorized the Council to "exercise such further powers as may in the future be delegated to it by the members of the Tribe or by the Secretary of the Interior, or any other duly authorized official or agency of the State or Federal Government," and the Secretary had now authorized it to approve leases.

The Council promptly approved a lease in 1961 to Fisher Contracting Company for a coal prospecting permit (Phoenix Gazette 1961). Between 1963 and 1965, the Council let $3 million worth of exploration leases to ten oil companies, one natural gas company, a chemical company, and one independent driller. Peabody Coal Company, which already had an exploration permit on Navajo land, also expressed interest in mining Hopi coal, either in the "Coal Canyon" area near Moenkopi (officially on the Navajo Reservation) or in the Black Mesa area, in 1962. In 1964 the Council signed a lease for exploration on Black Mesa with Peabody, giving it the option of a mining lease if negotiated within two years, which it was.

Illegal Action? On January 27, 1965, Kochongva wrote through Thomas Banyacya to Stewart Udall, Secretary of the Interior, protesting the leases of 1961-64, declaring that "since the Traditional and Religious Leaders and the majority of the Hopi people have never authorized the Council members to lease or sell our homeland they considered this illegal action to be null and void."

Did the leasings constitute "illegal action"? The Mineral Leasing Act of 1938 had effectively taken away from the Secretary of the Interior the authority to lease Tribes' mineral assets and had given it to the Tribes. But the language of the Hopi Constitution's article VI, section 1(c) was drawn word-for-word from Section 16 of the Indian Reorganization Act. Thus a Tribe would be empowered to *prevent* leases, but could only *approve* leases if its own Tribal Constitution empowered it to do so. Since the 1938 Act took away the Secretary's power to lease tribal lands, the Secretary did not have that leasing power to grant in the first place, and without an amendment to the Constitution, the Hopi Tribal Council did not have the power either. Thus, the leases were, in all probably illegal. Kochongva was right. Nonetheless, Kochongva's protest was ignored and the leases went forward.

The Coal Leases

One lease, signed in 1964, gave Peabody the right to strip mine 40,000 acres of the Navajo Reservation on Black Mesa, 820,000 of which had been designated as a "roadless and scenic area" by the Secretary of the Interior in the 1930s (U.S. Senate 1948:119). The other lease, signed in 1966, gave Peabody the right to strip mine another 25,000 acres of Black Mesa in the Joint Use Area of the Hopi reservation, a territory shared by Navajos and Hopis. The lease had two components: a surface lease and a mineral lease. Peabody signed an additional lease for water used in processing the coal and subcontracted Black Mesa Pipeline Company to build a water transport system for the coal. A coal-carrying railroad was planned, and Arizona Public Service company constructed a power plant -- one of two burning Black Mesa coal -- at Lake Powell.

The leases were for a period of ten years, renewable every year for an indeterminate period, until the coal ran out. A new ten-year lease could be negotiated after expiration of the initial one. The leases mandated Peabody to cooperate with the Hopi and Navajo Tribes and with the Secretary of the Interior in reseeding mined areas at the company's expense. Peabody further pledged to "commit no waste on said land" and to "surrender and return promptly to the premises (sic) upon the termination of this lease, in as good condition as received, except for the ordinary wear, tear and depletion incident to mining operations" (Clemmer 1978b:20-21).

Mining Coal on Black Mesa

In early September, 1969, more than sixty men from Hotevilla assembled with picks and shovels, in pickup trucks and wagons, to repair the road down to the local village coal mine and to load up coal for the beginning of winter. It would be for the last time. A year later, Hopis would being picking up their coal, for free, already mined, at Peabody Coal Company's installation on Black Mesa.[76]

Peabody uses one of the world's biggest scoop shovels and originally projected a thirty-five year life for the mine, but in 198 revised the estimate to 65 years. The coal goes in two directions: to the northwest, by railroad, to a 2,310-megawatt Salt River Project power plant at Page, on the shores of Lake Powell; and to the west, through a 283-mile pipeline, to a 1,580-megawatt Southern California Edison power plant at Bullhead City, Arizona. Water for cooling the enormous generators is drawn at the Page plant from Lake Powell and at the Bullhead City plant from Lake

Mohave; both lakes tap the Colorado River. The mine has become the largest open-pit coal mine in the United States. A total of 200 million tons were originally estimated as theoretically minable, but that estimate has been upped to at least 370 million tons.

The Pipeline

For many years the only coal slurry line in the United States, the pipeline is an ingenious method for shipping coal: it avoids the expense of a railroad and the untidy prospect of locating too many power plants in one area. The pipeline is filled with a mixture of coal and water at a .5 -.5 ratio disgorged from a slurry preparation plant at the mine site. When the pipeline runs at full capacity, pumps move the slurry, containing 43,000 tons of coal chunks and dust floating in water, at two to three miles per hour 283 miles to Bullhead City, where the slurry is fed into the power plant. The pipeline moves between 6.6 and 10 tons of coal per minute; it takes a piece of coal 2.8 days to make the journey. Water for the slurry is drawn from six deep wells tapping a fossil aquifer, embedded deep in the earth for millions of years.

The Consortium

The power plants at Page and Bullhead City are two of six linked to an energy consortium of twenty-three power companies and municipal utilities known as WEST Associates. The consortium's plants eventually added 36,000 megawatts to the electricity it supplies to five states, and particularly to the cities of Phoenix, Tucson, Albuquerque, Las Vegas, Los Angeles, and San Diego (Josephy 1971:54). Peabody negotiated ten-year contracts with the operators of both plants to sell the coal for $2.00 a ton.

Planning. In the words of historian Alvin M. Josephy, Jr., "all the planning, testing, negotiations, and lease and contract signings associated with the different elements of the huge power complex were carried out so quietly that they provide a classroom example of ... government agencies working hand-in-glove with industry in the United States today." The operators persuaded the Navajo Tribe to give up its claim to 34,100 acre-feet of water annually for operation of the Page plant; thus they got that water free (Levy 1980:5). For the water to run the pumps, Peabody paid the Navajo Tribe $5.00 an acre-foot and the Hopi Tribe $1.67 an acre-foot. No one -- Hopis and Navajos included outside the Tribal Councils -- could protest the leases at the time because the parties to them kept them so quiet. But people *did* find out about them.

Reactions

The first protests came from Hopi Traditionalists, but they were the culmination of a series of protests begun in 1964.

1964: The Oil Lawsuits. In November, 1964, five Traditionalists, including one Kikmongwi, filed a complaint against the eleven oil and gas operators and the Tribal Council asking for "injunction from any further exploration or extraction of minerals or petroleum products from lands located within the confines of the reservation of the Hopi Tribe of Arizona" in U.S. District Court in Phoenix on behalf of the villages of Mishongnovi, Shipaulovi, Oraibi, Shungopavi, and Hotevilla. John Boyden, in a blatant conflict of interest, represented not only the Hopi Tribal Council but also Aztec Oil and Gas Company as defendants. An attorney representing both the Tribe and an oil company, entities that were on different sides of the same commodity (Lessor, Lessee) was an odd arrangement to say the least. But a federal circuit judge ruled in favor of the Council and the oil companies, denying an injunction, and dismissed the case in December, ruling that the "Hopi Traditionalists cannot interfere with the action of the Hopi Tribal Council" (U.S. District Court 1965). The ruling was both a foreboding and a prediction of what was to come.

1971-75: The Traditionalists' Coal and Water Lawsuits. In May, 1971, Pawnee attorney John Echohawk of the Native American Rights Fund filed a complaint on behalf of Traditionalists and five Kikmongwis, listing altogether sixty-two Hopi plaintiffs, naming Peabody Coal Company and Secretary of Interior Rogers Morton as defendants. The Hopi plaintiffs included First Mesa's Kikmongwi and the Kikmongwis of Mishongnovi, Shungopavi, and Lower Moenkopi. Mina Lanza signed the complaint as Kikmongwi of Oraibi. Only Bacavi, Kykotsmovi, and Upper Moenkopi's leadership stayed completely away from the lawsuit.[77] The suit alleged that the Secretary of the Interior's approval of the lease was unlawful because it "was in excess of the Secretary's statutory jurisdiction and authority and without the observance of procedures required by law." It also alleged that the mining "violates the most sacred elements of traditional Hopi religion, culture and way of life. The land is sacred," said the plaintiffs, "and if the land is abused, the sacredness of Hopi life will disappear and all other life as well" (Lomayaktewa et al. 1971).[78]

Beyond the religious and jurisdictional issues the suit alleged that the Hopi Tribal Council did not have the power or authority to approve the lease because the Hopi Constitution authorized the council only to "*prevent* the lease of Hopi lands." The suit further held that, at the time the lease was signed in 1966, only eleven of eighteen[79] seats on the

Council were filled, and of those eleven, "five members were not certified in accordance with the procedures mandated by the Hopi Constitution." One of those contested seats was the one from Oraibi, filled by Don Talayesva, the Sun Chief (Talayesva 1942), who had been certified by Mina's brother, whom the Council and the BIA had chosen to recognize as Kikmongwi rather than Mina. Two seats from Kykotsmovi were contested on a technicality: Kykotsmovi had never had a Kikmongwi, nor did it have a village constitution specifying how representatives were supposed to be chosen and certified. The village, in accordance with the Constitution, simply had decided for itself how it would be organized, and had opted for having neither a Kikmongwi nor a constitution. The seven unfilled seats were from villages whose Kikmongwis were committed to the Traditionalists: Hotevilla, Lower Moenkopi, Shungopavi, and Mishongnovi (Clemmer 1978b:29-31).

Partisans surfaced once again, supporting and assisting Hopi opponents of the strip-mining.[80] Environmental activists formed Black Mesa Defense Fund and the Central Clearing House, in Santa Fe, to lobby against the consortium's plans for additional power plants fired by strip-mined coal that would foul the air and create a "brown cloud" for much of the Southwest. At the same time, five other environmental lawsuits were filed on behalf of Navajos, Chemehuevis, and the Sierra Club.

The Fate of the Traditionalists' Lawsuit. In 1973, however, Mishongnovi's Kikmongwi decided to decamp from the Traditionalists. He took his name off the lawsuit and from then on, certified representatives to the Council, one of whom was often himself. The Ninth Circuit Court of Appeals threw the lawsuit out in 1975 on a technicality known as "indispensable parties." The Hopi Tribal Council, said the court, was an indispensable party to the suit because it had signed the lease. The Council had to be either plaintiff of defendant. The Council was not a defendant because, under federal law, an Indian Tribal Council cannot be sued unless both the Council and Congress give permission.

Significance. According to analyst Marjane Ambler (1988:59), "federal policies toward Indian energy development might not have changed significantly if it had not been for Black Mesa. Through the critics' efforts Black Mesa became the most notorious mine in the country within a few years after mining began there, a symbol of the exploitation of Indian tribes for energy resources. Later, interviews with the ... tribal council members revealed that they did not know the value of their coal, the potential impacts of mining, or the alternatives to coal development. They believed the ludicrous assertion that nuclear power would soon make coal obsolete. The Interior Department, under the direction of Stewart Udall, worked with industry and the tribal attorney to convince the council to act immediately." Thus the impetus for coal development came initially from Peabody to the Navajos, and through the Navajos, to the Hopis. "Both the Navajo and Hopi governments lacked a process for accommodating different points of view in their decision - making process," says Ambler (1990:59). "Thus they relied upon secrecy -- just as the federal government and industry did -- to mask decisions that directly affected the lives of their members. The Black Mesa coal leases resulted from this flawed process. Outside of the Hopi Tribal Council, the Hopi people knew almost nothing about the contracts until a non-Indian anthropologist and a Pawnee attorney provided them with information in 1970."

The Traditionalists had gotten the political leaders of five villages to file the lawsuit. But Kochongva refused to be a party to the lawsuit but he issued his own statement in the form of a letter to the Tribal Council and the BIA, through a new interpreter who had taken the place of Thomas Banyacya and David Monongye. The letter read, in part (Clemmer 1978b:28:)

> ...Without sufficient fact weighing you have blundered most dangerous positions, our land is in jeopardy and the generations to come...
>
> Your organization are being unjust and unfair to those who you suppose to serve, including all the people in effected areas, for the very small dead end wager of very small value, comparason (sic) of values of the Mother Earth, her resources, the air, water, people and wild life.

Had the Council "blundered?" Royalties were divided equally between the Hopi and Navajo Tribes: each getting a royalty of 6.67% of "gross realization" but no less than twenty-five cents per ton for all coal going into the slurry line, and 5.33%, twenty cents per ton, for all coal burned in the Page plant. With over 300,000 tons a year being mined, the Hopi Tribe could expect annual royalties of about $ 400,000. Peabody also agreed to set up an escrow fund and to pay one-half of all annual royalties and rents into it for the first seven years of the lease or until the Hopi-Navajo land dispute was settled,[81] in case either Tribe should obtain 100% legal ownership of the minerals in the Joint Use Area. Peabody also agreed to give Navajos and Hopis employment preference.

But the mine was too far from the Hopi villages to be a source of regular employment, and few Hopis were partial to mining in the first place. Between its opening and 1987, Hopi employment fluctuated between none and a dozen.

The Moratorium. An Act of Congress in 1970 may have had the unintentional consequence of granting to the Council the leasing powers that the Hopi Constitution had withheld. (See below.) But aside from re-affirming the 1964/1966 lease and renegotiating it in 1987, the Council would grant no more leases after exploration leases granted to Peabody in 1969 and Dresser Minerals in 1975. In 1975, the presidents, chairmen, chiefs, and governors of twenty-one Indian Tribes formed CERT, the Council of Energy Resource Tribes, to broker better deals for Indians in the development of their resources. Hopis were among the chartering members (Ambler 1990:91-117).

In 1972 a constitutional referendum took effect that made the Hopi chairman and vice-chairman elected at large rather from the body of the Council itself. At the same time, some Council members who had been with it since its revival retired, leaving room for younger candidates. These younger Council people often had more sympathy with the resistance and nationalism of the Traditionalists than with the "me-too" passivity of the old Council. Attitudes of the new Council favoring greater self-determination were reflected in a remark made by one of the younger councilmen in 1977: "From now on, that Tribal lawyer is not going to tell us what to do. *I'm* going to tell *him* what to do" (Clemmer, Field Notes, 1977).

In 1977 the Council placed a moratorium on leasing and in 1979 enacted a permanent ban on mineral leasing and exploration. In 1982 it affirmed its intention to renegotiate the Peabody leases for more favorable terms. In 1991 it explicitly refused a request Peabody had made in 1989 to expand the lease onto the "Big Mountain" area, newly re-acquired by Hopis as a result of the 1974 Navajo-Hopi Land Settlement Act, to mine additional coal for the Japanese market and to pump additional water for another slurry line (Parlowe 1989; Indian Law Resource Center 1989).

Relocations. Other protests came from Navajos living on the lease site, about 300 of whom would eventually have to move either their homes or their sheep or both from the 65,000 acre lease between 1964 and 2005. Starting in 1972, various families and individuals successfully began filing complaints against Peabody demanding damages and relocation expenses. But the legal actions with the most important long-range implications for Hopis as well as for Peabody Coal Company concerned taxes, royalties, and honesty in reportage.

Audits, the Severance Tax, and the New Royalty Rates. Peabody's contracts to sell coal to the WEST consortium at $2.00 per ton expired in 1976. But by the mid-1970s coal prices had skyrocketed to over $20 per ton (Ambler 1990:78). Additionally, inaccurate computation resulted in Peabody underpaying its royalties between 1976 and 1979. By 1984, annual royalties had climbed to over $2 million (U.S. Department of the Interior 1978a, 1978b, 1980, 1989:III-45). In 1982 the Hopi Tribal Council drafted a severance tax ordinance that would have required Peabody to pay additional revenues for selling coal off the reservation. But Court rulings with regard to severance taxes enacted by other tribes mandate that tribal severance taxes cannot be collected without agreement of the state, since states collect taxes on coal, even from Indian lands, and without a specific "power to tax" clause in the Tribe's constitution. Ironically, tribes that rejected the Indian Reorganization Act, and thus that have no Constitution, are free to levy such a tax simply by enacting a taxing ordinance. The Navajo Tribe was one of those tribes. In 1974 the Black Mesa Coal Mine yielded $22.9 million in state property taxes, more than the Hopi *or* Navajo Tribes realized from royalty and lease payments from all the coal, natural gas, and petroleum production ($17.8 million (cf. Levy 1980:7) and more than 25 times the amount paid to the Hopi in royalties. The Navajo Tribe enacted their tax, but due to constitutional complications, the Secretary of the Interior did not approve the Hopi Tribe's ordinance. Nonetheless, the Navajo Tribe's success in having it severance tax approved was to have enormous implications for the Hopi-Navajo land dispute, to be covered in the next chapter.

In 1987 the Hopi Tribe tacitly admitted that, indeed, the earlier Council had blundered. It had settled for a"very small dead end wager of very small value," accepting far too little in terms of the dollar-amounts of royalties; in letting a most precious and sacred Hopi resource -- water -- slip away in gargantuan proportions with negligible compensation; and in giving no attention to the damage that Peabody's mining could inevitably inflict on the environment. But finally, the Tribe was able to hire better legal counsel and finalized a renegotiated lease that was acceptable to the Navajo Tribe, Peabody, and the Interior Department. Hiring its own geologists, the Tribe was able to show that the going rate for coal and the amount under lease justified a new rate. The lease upped the water price from $1.67 per acre-foot to $150.00 an acre-foot and included a sliding scale tied to future consumer rate increases; the price was still about half the going price for "municipal quality" water. The new lease established an educational fund to which Peabody would contribute $150,000 a year and required various "up-front" bonus payments. Various other components of the lease increased the Hopis share of revenues. According to the Tribe's Chairman, the new lease escalated the Tribe's income from Peabody to over $10 million in 1988 (Parlowe 1989). Peabody was also authorized to mine an additional 170 million tons from the lease area after hitting its initial limit of 200 million tons in 2005. But environmental concerns that had surfaced in the 1970s still nagged many Hopis in the Tribal administration.

Environmental Concerns

A large part of the reason for the Council' moratorium stemmed from environmental concerns targeted initially by Traditionalists but shared by most Hopis. In 1974, the National Academy of Sciences (1974:18-20, 92-93) (NAS) warned that "restoration of a landscape disturbed by surface mining, in the sense of recreating the former conditions, is not possible" in most parts of the arid West. "Reclamation," continued the report, "creates conditions ... so that the site is habitable to organisms that were originally present or others that approximate the original inhabitants." True reclamation on Black Mesa would require reforestation with pinion and juniper and revegetation with native grasses suitable for grazing sheep and not requiring perennial management. "Rehabilitation," noted the NAS report, "is the most feasible alternative in the West" and it "implies that the land will be returned to a form and productivity in conformity with a prior land use plan including a stable ecological state that does not contribute substantially to environmental deterioration and is consistent with aesthetic values." The problem was that the area's "prior use plan" was grazing that in itself contributed to environmental deterioration, even though sheep, pinons, junipers, and a minimal ground cover were aesthetically pleasing to just about everyone except environmentalists.

After abysmal reclamation results, Peabody was presented with a "water-harvesting and fish culture" rehabilitation project by a range management team from the University of Arizona in 1973. Seventeen acres of minespoil were reshaped to form an asphalt-lined cachement basin to catch snowmelt and rain runoff. Topsoil was trucked in by virtually digging up the bottom of a whole valley elsewhere . Navajo students tended the gardens. In 1975 warm-water fish were stocked in Peabody's "Black Mesa Pond." The fish increased 30-fold in weight in 78 days when fed nutrients. But the pond became too hot in summer to support native cold-water fish such as trout. The pond idea was abandoned (Clemmer 1985:86-87).

Neither the Hopi Tribal Council's Chairman nor the Tribe's Resources committee was pleased with the situation. Hopis drew up their own plan and submitted it in June, 1981 to the Bureau of Land Management's Office of Surface Mining Reclamation and Enforcement for supervision and enforcement under the Surface Mining Control and Reclamation Act of 1977 (Clemmer 1985:88). Yet some environmental problems appeared insurmountable. One was water depletion.

Water. The wells on Black Mesa operate twenty-four hours a day, except for maintenance shutdowns, and pump water at a rate of 2,700 gallons per minute. At the rate of 4,400 acre-feet per year, over thirty-five years, about 154,000 acre-feet were projected for depletion. This amount would be the equivalent of a one-acre pond nearly thirty miles deep, if such a thing were conceivable. Drilled to a depth of 3,650 feet, the wells are cased with concrete to a depth of 2,000 feet. The casings would prevent inadvertent depletion of high water tables, assured Peabody (1970). The lease required Peabody to "provide the Indians with water" if the Secretary of the Interior "finds the local supply endangered" due to its pumping.

The water is of "municipal" quality: that is, it is not only potable, but good-tasting and free of noxious bacterial or mineral contamination, right as it comes from the tap. Black Mesa water from Peabody's wells was the highest quality water found in test of eighteen water sources by Museum of Northern Arizona (Reno 1981:59). Peabody installed faucets from which local Navajos obtain water free of charge and haul it to their homes in stainless steel garbage cans.

The United States Geological Survey (USGS) established monitoring wells and as early as 1973, a USGS report concluded that "the rate of groundwater movement is too slow for recharge to balance the withdrawal in the artesian part of the aquifer. Although present withdrawals (including Peabody's pumping) seem small compared to the extent of the aquifer, and artesian aquifer is a pressure system and any significant withdrawal will reduce the artesian pressure over a wide area. The water levels have not declined in any of the observation wells during the year of monitoring. It should be stressed, however, that development of the water supply will result in interference between wells" (McGavock and Levins 1973). By 1980 USGS had 22 monitoring wells in the area and in accordance with the lease, Peabody had added 37 monitoring stations to measure the effects of its pumping. But the damage had already started: The Hopi Tribal Council received a hydrological report that, along with normal light commercial and domestic use, Peabody's pumping had lowered the water table by nearly ten feet (Clemmer 1985:89).

Hopis Take the Situation in Hand

The EIS. Realizing the developing dilemma, the Council commissioned an independent study of the water situation. The study confirmed fears: the water table tapped by most of the Hopi wells, well above the 2,000-foot level, was dropping from ten to thirty feet. The Council hit upon a strategy to bring in the Federal Government to force Peabody to address Hopi concerns.

Peabody requested a right-of-way for a road across part of the lease to another area that it wished to mine. All such requests had been routinely granted by the Navajo and Hopi Tribes as well as the BIA and Office of Surface Mining (OSMRE). But things had changed: as a result of the 1974 Navajo and Hopi Indian Land Settlement Act, part of the southern part of the lease was under Hopis' exclusive surface control. Hopis denied the request for a right-of-way.

Since a new lease had been negotiated providing for mining of nearly as much coal again as the initial lease had permitted and the project life of the mine had been extended through 2023, the Hopi Tribe proposed that a completely new permit be issued for the 100 million-plus tons that Peabody still had to mine under the 1964/1966 lease *and* the additional tonnage under the new lease. This total tonnage amounted to 292 million tons. The new permit would not be tied to the time period of the leases, but rather, would be a "life-of-mine" permit granting Peabody authorization to mine "forever" without further environmental assessment. Thus also projections would be made for an "extended mining scenario" that would simulate environmental consequences if the mine operated through 2057, which was not unlikely given the probable reserves of coal within the current lease and nearby. Issuing a new permit, rather than simply amending the two previous permits to include additional mine infrastructure such as roads, etc., would require a new environmental assessment. The original environmental assessment had been perfunctory to say the least. The National Environmental Policy Act had just been enacted (1970) and technically, Peabody's operations were not covered by it since they had begun in 1966 and 1968. But issuance of a new permit *would* require Peabody and the OSMRE to do a full environmental impact assessment (EIS). That was exactly what the Hopis wanted.

Once the EIS was completed, most of its conclusions surprised no one: Mining was changing the landscape and ecosystems irrevocably; rehabilitation of the mined area would cost Peabody about $20,000 an acre for a total of more than $5 million; the mine was an unmitigated visual eyesore; overall impacts to sacred and ceremonial sites would be major and would require detailed investigation; and not only the 750 employees of the mine, railroad, and pipeline plus their families, but also the Hopi Tribe could not live without it. Contributing 65% of the Tribe's revenues, Peabody's royalties were absolutely crucial to the Tribe's administrative operations and its employees.

"Sacredness of the Earth": Continued physical disruption of land resources at the mine site would also "contribute to the alienation between Hopi traditionalists and those who are seen as 'progressives'" noted the report, ... "because most traditionalists view mining and other

land-disruption activities as violating Hopi values." However, continued the report, interviews determined this "to be a minority viewpoint" (U.S. Department of the Interior 1989:IV-75), even though a comprehensive study of Hopi religion determined it to be dominant among more than 80% of the Hopi population and asserted that "the Hopi perceive the earth as their mother" and "revere the earth as their mother in a manner that cannot be reduced to economic concerns" (Loftin 1991:9, 10).

But one conclusion was not expected: "The simulations show that at no time would the total withdrawal from mine and non-mine pumping under this scenario damage the structural integrity of the aquifer. OSMRE concludes that impacts of Alternative 1 on the N-aquifer would be minor in the short-term and negligible in the long-term" (U.S. Department of the Interior 1989:IV-25). Hopis were stunned. They could not believe the conclusion. Water levels in stock wells and in some springs had already fluctuated and gone down. A private individual did his own computer simulation showing that at current rates of mine and non-mine pumping, *all wells in the area drawing on the "N" (Navajo sandstone) aquifer would go completely dry by 2060*. The Kikmongwis of Oraibi and Lower Moenkopi wrote to OSMRE saying, "We do not approve the activity of mining the coal at all, but we feel that the waste of precious drinkable water simply to transport coal to the power plant is irresponsible." The Hopi Tribal Chairman called a press conference to contest the EIS findings. Labelling OSMRE's and Peabody's contention that its water use did not harm the tribe's domestic water supply tragically wrong and the EIS' water data unreliable, he insisted that Peabody abandon the slurry and find a new method to transport the coal. But the water, like the coal, had become a commodity and a source of capital not only for Peabody, but also for the Hopi and Navajo Tribes, and reversal of the situation seemed unlikely.

Mineral Leasing: Source of Capital

Capital in General

A commodity has three values: its intrinsic value; its use value; and its exchange value, that is, its commodity value. For Hopis, coal had only use value until 1964. Its use value is the value in terms of how, and the extent to which, it could be used. But a commodity is not valued for its use; it is valued for its potential role in producing wealth and capital. Thus, it can become a kind of capital by acquiring an exchange value. Exchange-value masks a commodity's intrinsic value as well as its use value, because exchange-value can only be measured in terms of how much money it can/ will produce in exchange. The commodity is a repository of value whether it is used or not (Levine 1978:75, 83). Hopis' water had use value as well as intrinsic value because water is not only necessary for life, but also is culturally/ symbolically/ ideologically defined and valued. Water has intrinsic value in Hopi thought as a gift from the ancestors (Katsinas) or a god (Balolokong, the Water Serpent). With mineral leasing, Hopis entered the capitalist market place in a new, different, and much larger way than ever before, not as individual producers of labor, crafts, etc. and consumers of others' products, but as a collectivity exchanging two things -- coal and water -- as commodities for money that could either be used to purchase more goods and services or could be invested as wealth to make more money. Once initiated, there was little possibility of retreat.

Tribal Income: Entry into the Capitalist Market

The Lawyer Gets a Gift. Entry into the capitalist market began after the Council garnered $3 million from the oil leases of 1963-65. The Council chose not to distribute the income in per capita payments. It built its own Council Hall in Kykotsmovi and no longer had to meet at the BIA Agency in Keams Canyon. It maintained some money to begin compensating Council representatives with modest *per diem* payments on meeting days and to hire a full-time secretary. Seven-hundred-eighty thousand dollars paid the salary and expenses of John Boyden, who had worked for the Council for nearly 14 years without remuneration. In 1964 the Council voted to award Boyden an additional $220,000 as a gift of appreciation for "taking the (claims) case when no one else would" (Phoenix Gazette 1964), making Boyden a "millionaire." In 1970, Boyden's salary was $9,000 annually (Hopi Action News 1970).

Investing Mineral Capital: The BVD Fiasco

The remaining money was invested in constructing an undergarment factory for Western Superior Corporation, maker of BVDs. Before the Hopi Tribal Council took on the BVD project in 1967, the BIA's economic development branch had already been negotiating with Western Superior Corporation for a BVD factory that would employ Indian labor, would be financed in part by an Indian tribe, and would be located on or near Indian land in the Southwest but also near a railhead. Winslow, whose economy had been in decline ever since the Santa Fe had moved its diesel repair shop to Barstow, California and tourists had started coming increasingly by car rather than train, was chosen as the most desirable location. From the BIA's standpoint, Indian industry in Winslow would ease reservation unemployment and draw the Indian Tribes into the national economy to a greater extent.

Negotiations between Western Superior and the BIA brought tentative agreement. Western Superior would locate at Winslow if a Tribe could be found to build the plant according to Western Superior's specifications, provide reliable labor, and furnish a tax-free building site. The industrial package was first offered to the Navajo Tribe. The Navajo Tribal Council insisted that the BVD factory be located on their Reservation, not in Winslow. Their insistence forced the BIA to take its industrial package elsewhere. The BIA took it to Tribal attorney John Boyden.

Boyden presented the package to the Hopi Tribal Council and the Council accepted the idea. The City of Winslow and a local businessman offered to donate 240 acres for an industrial site. But there were legal snags: to construct the building on the site, the Council would have to use nearly every penny of its lease income, since it was not a corporation and could not borrow money. It also might possibly get stuck with something it did not want, without being able to get rid of it, and unless the site were deeded over as trust land, it would have to pay state property tax. Furthermore, the little problem of the Council's authority to lease still nagged.

Leasing Powers at Last. Boyden contacted Arizona congressman Sam Steiger and together they drew up H.R. 4869. Enacted in 1970, it had the United States acquire the donated acreage in trust for the Hopi Indians as the "Hopi Industrial Park and provided the Council with the powers of a corporation: to mortgage, sell, or exchange lands within the Park; to use any tribal funds from any source "to secure the indebtedness of the Hopi Tribe"; to "enter into any business venture as a share-holder of a corporation"; and "to lease lands within the Hopi Industrial Park, any other tribal lands, and the improvements thereon, in accordance with the provisions of Federal laws." Finally, the Council acquired from the U.S. Government the powers withheld from it by the Hopi Constitution.

The Tribal Council and Western Superior Corporation signed a contract providing that the Council would build the factory according to Western Superior's specifications. In return, Western Superior would pay rent amounting to not less than 5-1/2% of the Council's initial $1.6 million investment, $88,000, annually for a ten years; provide on-the-job training; and give employment preference to Hopis, Navajos, and other Indians in that order.

Work Begins. Hopi stone masons began building the plant in February, 1968 and in July, 1968, Western Superior began a training program in the Winslow National Guard Armory. By October the factory was completed and although the legal kinks still needed working out, BVD "came with its suitcases and moved right in," as a critical Councilman put it. In June, 1969, Forty-five Hopi women began commuting daily back and forth on a school bus provided by the BIA from Second Mesa and Hotevilla to their jobs at the BVD factory 70 miles distant (Winslow Mail 1969). By 1970 the number of Hopis employed had doubled but the nearly exclusively female work force worried attorney Boyden and he noted that the plant's employment of only 70 or 80 men from a potential work force of 200 was disappointing. "We must see that there are jobs for the men," he said, "so that the family can live in Winslow together" (Gallup Independent 1971).

But few Hopis wanted to live in Winslow. They found discrimination in housing and were not happy with their employment situation. The work was boring, they suffered injuries, the cafeteria food was lousy, and the wages were too low. With no union, workers were powerless to fight the $1.60 hourly wage and the "piece work system" that sometimes netted them even less (Clemmer 1977). Commuters complained of the bumpy 140-mile round-trip ride on the BIA bus and people who had been refused employment pointed out that the requirement for a high school diploma as a condition of employment was ridiculous. Western Superior in turn complained of high employee turnover; slow work; and lack of success with the training program. The bottom line was: Western Superior was not making the kind of money it had hoped. In 1974, it closed the factory, although it paid the entire stipulated rent of $880,000. The Tribe continued to spend $90,000 a year to maintain the factory, but it lay idle until 1986 when the Young An Hat Company, a Korean firm, leased it from the Tribe, producing 500 dozen baseball caps and 130 dozen straw hats a day. Once again women from Second Mesa and Hotevilla started commuting to Winslow, but on a much smaller scale; in 1989 the plant employed fifty-six people, only seventeen of them Hopi (Hopi Tribe 1989).

Other Strategies. After the BVD debacle, the "new" Council chose to invest mineral income not needed for operational expenses in stocks, bonds, mutual funds, and securities. High interest rates of the 1970s, coupled with steadily improving royalty amounts, made the strategy has pay off. For example, by 1977 annual income from the Peabody leases had risen to more than one million dollars and by 1986 to nearly seven million dollars, permitting the Council to fund more than 15% of its expenditures from interest on funds as well as adding more than one million dollars annually to its invested principle (U.S. Department of the Interior 1989:III-45). Combined with other sources of income such as rent from the Cultural Center and transfer payments from the Federal Government, the Council created a Tribal administration with nearly 500 employees, accounting for more than a third of the Reservation's jobs (Robinson 1986). Per capita income rose to $2,632 in 1980. But the Council's greatest investment of time, energy and funds went into pursuing and advantageous settlement of the Hopi-Navajo land dispute, and although Congress ultimately provided the enabling legislation, there is much more to the story than mere passage of a law.

Summary and Conclusion: Bringing the State Back In

Beginning in the 1880s, all Hopi communities became increasingly constrained within the "colonial setting" of the federal Indian reservation system. Participation in national institutions such as the armed forces and in wage work created by Government agencies is only one reflection of this context. Another is the degree of repressive control that Government personnel were able to exercise over Hopi life and religion. Yet another, however, is the marginal character of Hopis' integration into the market economy due to the Government's control of land capital through the reservation system. While the Government fostered and encouraged the intrusion of consumer products as a means of civilizing the Indian, lack of cash, the structure of the mercantile market, and the government's deliberate "protective" control over the trading business on the reservation created an artificial and unrealistic business climate.

Thus, even when Government policy ostensibly shifted radically to "bilateral relationships" in the Indian New Deal, Hopis experienced little actual sovereign decision-making. The Tribal Council was, in a sense, pre-adapted to rubber stamp various economic development schemes from leases to underwear.

Hopis themselves forced a more self-determining, modern approach. The Traditionalists pressed for discussion of the most crucial points of integration between Hopis and the nation-state: the Claims Commission case, mineral leasing, and the Hopi-Navajo land dispute. While they may not have always had the most practical solution to all these problems, tackling the problems resulted in the Council joining CERT and eventually developing strategies for using the nation-state, which I will simply call "the state" from now on, to its own advantage, rather than having the state use Hopis to its advantage. While mineral development still serves a national purpose, the situation is a far cry from the "leased and lost" days of the 1960s.

In the U.S., state autonomy is fragmented due to the separation of powers and the dispersion of authority through the federal system, that is, the various branches of government, Congressional committees, etc. Clearly, the U.S. affects Hopis' political culture by encouraging some kinds of group formation, such as the Tribal Council, and not others, and by making possible the raising of some political issues but not others (Skocpol 1985:12, 20-21). Because authority is dispersed through the federal system, and because the Hopi Tribe is a "finger" of the U.S. Government, Hopis have been able to use U.S. political culture to their advantage in recent years by bringing the state back into Hopi politics on Hopi terms for more equitable leasing conditions as well as for other goals. Thus, while the U.S. nation-state has always had a role in trying to direct Hopi life and culture, it could be seen until recently from purely an instrumentalist perspective, that is, as an instrument of particular interests in U.S. society: first missionary and trading interests, then mineral interests. But a large part of a state's pursuit of goals may accrue no particular advantage to anyone except those in the administrative, legal, and bureaucratic systems (Skocpol 1985:9). In other words, the state does some things simply to keep itself useful. And it is this aspect of the state that Hopis were able to use to their advantage in pressing for an advantageous solution to the Hopi-Navajo land problem, achieving the status of an effective interest group itself and pressing the state to use its authority and power for Hopi goals and to place the responsibility for doing so solely on the state itself.

9

The Hopi-Navajo Land Dispute: 1958-1993

A Range War?

In June, 1972, a Navajo man said to be ninety-eight years of age filed a damage suit claiming his civil rights had been violated by the Hopi Tribal Council's non-Indian range rider. The range rider had impounded his stock, arrested him for trespass, and allegedly dragged him off his horse and roughed him up. A few weeks later, nine Hopis complained that, while rounding up a few hundred trespassing Navajo sheep, they had been attacked by a gang of Navajos wielding tire irons and monkey wrenches. Each Tribal Government -- Hopi and Navajo -- blamed the other for escalating range conflicts. Navajo Chairman Peter MacDonald insisted his people were using land assigned to them by local grazing committees sanctioned by the Bureau of Indian Affairs, and they could not help it if stock occasionally wandered over into Hopi territory. He threatened to complete a fence around District Six. Abbott Sekaquaptewa, Chairman of the Hopi Negotiating Committee and Director of Hopi Community Action Program (and later Tribal Chairman), called such an action the establishment of a "concentration camp of Hopis" and argued that the Bureau never should have assigned that land to Navajos in the first place. The media suddenly started paying attention and headlined stories of a "tribal range war" (Donovan 1971; Gallup Independent 1972).

No Range War

But really, there was no range war (Whitson 1985:383), even though there were continuing and long-standing conflicts and disputes. In the 100 years following Navajos' release from Bosque Redondo, Hopis renewed their custom of trading agricultural products for Navajos' mutton. In the 1960s, some Hopi families regularly loaded pickups with

232

cans of water and ears of corn for trips to Navajo trading partners, returning with one or two live sheep for butchering for a special ceremonial feast day. Ceremonial dances -- especially the Summer Niman and Snake Dances -- brought several dozen wagon full of Navajos who ate, traded, and bantered with Hopis in their houses and in the plaza. Marriages also linked some Navajo and Hopi households. At the same time, Hopis continually came into conflict with their Navajo neighbors when, setting out to graze stock at a known pasture or watering hole, they would encounter Navajos who had already staked out the area, and told them to leave. As well as countering the political power of the Navajo Tribe, Hopis also looked increasingly to moral pressure lodged in the tradition of the "Navajo *tiponi.*"

The *Tiponi*

A *tiponi,* meaning "object containing sources of spiritual power which authorizes action and protects like a guardian spirit," is a special object fashioned and used by ritual specialists of Navajo, Hopi, and other Southwest Indian cultures. Its use is always ceremonial. The *tiponi* functions as a charter, permitting the keeper to commemorate in ceremony what the *tiponi* commemorates in form. In permitting, it also obligates. The keeper must store in his or her memory all the details of history, ritual, and cultural significance that give the *tiponi* its chartering power.

This *tiponi* consists of a bundle of objects wrapped with rawhide and capped by a crown of feathers extending from the bundle. Also called an "emblem" or "wand" by Hopis and "fetish" or "medicine bundle" by anthropologists, its importance lies in memorializing the boundary within that Shrine which marks the westernmost point beyond which Hopis say Hopis and Navajos agreed Navajos would not encroach. Its keeper was Duke Pahona, First Mesa's Crier Chief, until his death in 1977.

In 1955 during the Hopi Hearings which the Interior Department held in the Hopi villages, John Lomavaya, of First Mesa, said that, sometime after Navajos' ambush of a small party of six Hopi men -- probably in the early 1860s -- and after Navajos signed the Treaty of Fort Sumner and returned to part of their southwestern homeland in 1868, Navajos came to Walpi and asked the Hopis to accept their offer of a permanent peace between Hopis and Navajos, and offer the *tiponi* "in order to convince the Hopis. Hopis accepted the emblem and recognized it as a truce, but stipulated that if they ever repeat what the had done, the Hopi would remind Navajo of their promises and in that case Navajo would forfeit all rights and Hopi would demand that they be taken off of this land."

Thomas Banyacya also referred to this *tiponi* at a Meeting of Religious People in Hotevilla in 1956 (Bentley 1957).

It was decided not to show the *tiponi* to the Interior Department committee at that time, but two years later, in 1957, Duke Pahona shipped it to Washington and did show it to a Senate committee during hearings on legislation to partition the 1882 Reservation. He testified that when they were released from Fort Sumner, "the Navahos came to the Snake Clan at Walpi with peace offers. The Navahos brought with them a symbol of peace, a sacred emblem called a Tee-po-ni. The Hopi did not make a peace offering, the Navaho himself did saying, "I bring you this peace symbol to signify that should I ever again recall my ways and return to be depredations upon you, that this, my symbol of peace, my own making, will turn on me and pass sentence on me.' The Navaho has now reverted to his former ways, and his own word must now be carried out." He quoted anthropologist Gordon MacGregor who had written to Commissioner John Collier on August 6, 1938, that "'the First Mesa or Walpi people made an agreement with the Navaho some time about 1850 establishing a boundary line. The Navaho were to cross it only on condition of good behavior. As a sign of good faith the Navajos are said to have presented a feather shrine or symbol, which First Mesa still preserves. A pile of rocks some distance west of Ganado and on the old road once marked this line.[82] First Mesa, of course, would like to see this line form the east limit of the reservation'" (sic) (Pahona 1972:175-6).[83]

Fifteen years later, in 1972, Hopi-Tewa Logan Koopee submitted a written document to the House Committee on Interior and Insular Affairs, which mentioned the *tiponi* and its presentation at Walpi by seven Navajo leaders. One morning in 1977 Duke Pahona made his last statement on the matter: "The Navajos made an agreement with us," he said, "that if they ever bothered us again like they had in the past, we should remind them. It's our right to do anything to them, if they disobeyed that. That's what this *tiponi* says. That's what it means." But the explanation could not continue. A victim of black lung, Duke Pahona had to be assisted with oxygen tanks and could not get up from his bed. Whether from physical debility or emotional strain, the thread of the narrative was lost. Pahona began to unwrap the *tiponi*, tied up in a clean piece of linen, but his wife had objections. "Maybe you can come back this afternoon," his wife suggested. "I don't want him to open that in the house. I'm afraid of it..." (Clemmer 1978a:12-13). That afternoon, Duke's nephew unwrapped it outside in front of his house and Dan Budnik (1979:44) photographed it.

Thus in Hopi thinking, Hopi-Navajo relations are governed as much by the *tiponi* as by the various actions and acts of the U.S. Government. Where some Hopis part company with others is on the appropriate role of the U.S. Government in enforcing Hopi-Navajo relations with respect to the *tiponi*. Some review of the historical context of the Hopi-Navajo land dispute puts the apparent internal disagreements among the Hopi into perspective.

The Land Dispute: Historical and Demographic Context

President Chester A. Arthur's Executive Order of 1882 establishing the "Moqui Indian Reservation" encompassing 2,427,166 acres for "the use and occupancy of the Moqui (Hopi), and such other Indians as the Secretary of the Interior may see fit to settle thereon," disregarded the settlement patterns and symbolic attributions of both tribes respecting their sacred lands: the Hopi settlement of Moenkopi was well outside the reservation's boundaries, and the existence of an estimated 300 Navajo settlers inside the 1882 boundaries went unacknowledged. The Government made virtually no attempt to expel Navajos from the area or to prevent them from further settling it (Clemmer et al. 1989:748).

Presidential executive orders of 1884 and 1900 extended the Navajo Reservation to the north and east so that the Navajo Reservation then bordered the 1882 Reservation on two sides and established the Western Navajo Reservation for the Navajos and "such other Indians as the Secretary of the Interior shall settle thereon." Besides Navajos, Paiutes were already living on the reservation at Willow Springs and Hopis were living on it at Moenkopi. Between 1901 and 1930, a series of presidential executive orders, actions by the Secretary of the Interior, and Congressional Acts culminating in 1934 expanded the boundaries of this reservation so that by 1934 it surrounded the Hopi Reservation completely on all four sides. Thus, by congressional statute, the Navajos acquired contemporaneous rights in the Hopi Reservation, but Hopis also acquired contemporaneous rights in the 1900 Executive Order reservation along with Navajos and Paiutes.

Hopis and Navajos Within the 1882 Reservation

Another boundary marked by stones dates from 1891 and is far closer to the Hopi villages than the one on the "Ganado Road" mentioned by MacGregor. Military officials under General McCook called a joint Navajo-Hopi council on January 8, 1891 and established a boundary line separating Navajos from Hopis. The line traced a perimeter in a sixteen mile radius from Mishongnovi, barely taking in Jeddito but corresponding remarkably to the later-established District Six. The boundary came to be known as the "sixteen-mile limit." Navajos ostensibly agreed to remove their herds from within this boundary but within a year there were reports of Navajo trespass (Stephens 1961:90-93). The situation worsened in 1910. Hopis from First Mesa spotted a group of Navajos twelve miles away, "trying to sneak up on our mesa and kill and steal our food and our children," according to Hopi elder Ethel Mahle. Hopi "warriors went out and fought and killed them all" (Elston 1988:27). In 1911 agent Crane suggested partitioning the 1882 Reservation, and in 1920 the House of Representatives requested an investigation of Hopi-Navajo relations. In 1925 special investigator Dorrington reported that, indeed, Navajos were moving into the area circumscribed by the "sixteen mile limit." Recovering from the influenza epidemic of 1919-21, Hopis again began establishing ranches away from the mesas. But Navajos who had migrated to Leupp from the Sunset Crater/ Wupatki area were once again on the move, coming into conflict with Hopis in the Oraibi Valley (Stephens 1961:110-119, 158).

In 1930 and again in 1933 Shungopavi village requested more land, presenting the BIA with maps of the aboriginal Hopi *techqua* in support. Area commissioner Hagerman, who had been given oversight responsibility for Navajos and Hopis in 1922, also launched an investigation that resulted in a conference of eleven Navajos, five from the Hopi Reservation, and thirteen Hopis including three from Moenkopi to try to resolve the conflicts. The Hopi delegates refused to commit themselves on specific boundaries and ended up requesting a separate Hopi Agency (Stephens 1961:122-127). Out of the conference came the "Hopi Council" established by Otto Lomavitu and Wilson Tawakwaptiwa at Kykotsmovi in 1931. In 1940 the BIA decided to remove Navajos from District Six and in 1943 declared District Six exclusively Hopi.

In 1954, the Hopi Tribal Council finally got the Hopi Agency detached from the oil-industry inspired Navajo Area Commissioner established in 1922 and placed under the newly-created Phoenix Area Office (Stephens 1961:168). In 1945 the U.S. House Committee on Indian Affairs held hearings on the "Condition of the Hopi Tribe," especially focusing on the Hopi-Navajo land issue, but nothing came of them.

Between 1946 and 1970, but especially after 1954, the Navajo Tribe established one chapter for each 1,000 Navajos on the 1882 Reservation. By 1962 there were a dozen Navajo chapters either on the 1882 Reservation or overlapping its borders. In 1965 the Secretary of the Interior took 20,000 acres from one of the exclusive Navajo grazing districts around Moenkopi and added the acreage to District Six. Even though not contiguous, this acreage now came under the jurisdiction of the Hopi Tribe and the Hopi Indian Agency in Keams Canyon. In 1930, 3,300 Navajos lived on the 1882; by 1958, 8,800, nearly twice the number of Hopis, and by 1970, closer to 12,000. In 1970 the land-to-person ratio for Hopis was about ninety-three acres per person; for Navajos, ninety-eight. Hopis' per capita income was $1,300; Navajos', $900; Americans', $4,200. Hopis had about 2 head of livestock for each person; Navajos had 10 head per person.

The Indian Claims Commission

But partitioning the Reservation, settling the mineral estate, and recognizing land titles were inextricably tied up with the Indian Claims Commission established by Congress in 1946. Congress can recognize a tribe's title to land at any time. The ICC was a mechanism for doing this; in some cases, such as that of the Hopi, recognition was retroactive and title was extinguished simultaneously with title recognition. The Commission entered a decision on June 29, 1970, declaring Hopis' aboriginal claim to the 2.5 million acres of the 1882 Reservation plus another 1.9 million acres surrounding it -- 4.4 million acres altogether. The Commission decided that creation of the 1882 Reservation had "effectively terminated and put to rest all Hopi aboriginal title claims beyond the limits of the 1882 Hopi Executive order Reservation." Inaccurately, the Commission also decided the Hopi had always been a small tribe, "probably never exceeding 2500 Indians prior to 1882, and that by nature the Hopis were inoffensive and somewhat timid Indians whose pueblo oriented culture and environment confined them to permanent village sites" (Indian Claims Commission 1970).

Aboriginal Title

The decision included a determination of the boundaries of the land to which the Hopi Tribe had aboriginal title in 1832, and the dates when the Hopi aboriginal title was extinguished in various portions of it. The concept of "aboriginal title" had been established by Chief Justice John Marshall of the U.S. Supreme Court in a case decided in 1832. The court ruled that Indian tribes hold title to their lands by virtue of having occupied and used them "from time immemorial." Until and unless Congress takes away the land of any particular tribe by treaty, purchase, or some other way, that tribe continues to hold title to their land and the minerals beneath it (Churchill 1992). The Commission refused to acknowledge Hopis' aboriginal title to their entire *techqua* marked by the shrines because they said the Hopi had abandoned many of the shrine areas and they had been used by other tribes. Because Congress had already declared its recognition of Hopi title to the 631,000 acres in District Six and to half of the JUA, the Claims Commission declared these lands still held by Hopis continuously since 1832. But the Commission ruled that because the BIA had restricted Hopis to District Six on April 24, 1943, Hopis had lost the rest of the 1882 Reservation in addition to 1.9 million acres outside the 1882 Reservation. "Hopi non-use of a large part of the 1882 Reservation can be attributed to Hopi superstition and fear of the more warlike and aggressive Navajos and not to Hopi abandonment of the land," concluded the Commission (Indian Claims Commission 1970). The Navajos, it decided, had been "settled thereon" in 1937 when the Secretary of the Interior issued grazing permits to them.

The Traditionalists, supporting the kikmongwis of Mishongnovi, Shungopavi, and Oraibi, rejected the ruling and the Hopi Tribe appealed it to the U.S. Court of Claims. The Court of Claims denied its requests for a rehearing, and issuing final findings of fact on December 2, 1976. Attorney Boyden suggested a compromise settlement of the Hopi claim for $5 million. The award was made but Hopis did not accept it. The Kikmongwis of First Mesa, Shungopavi and Oraibi successfully urged a boycott of the award referendum, mandated by law. Only 250 people, less than 10% of the eligible voters, voted in the referendum, with 221 favoring acceptance of the money and 21 against. The Council, too, ultimately voted to table acceptance of the award, leaving it untouched in an Albuquerque bank account.

The final compromise settlement acknowledged Hopis' continuing claim to an area corresponding to the boundaries of their *techqua* but modified by the westerly boundary line of the Navajo country as fixed by the "Merriwether Treaty" between Navajos and the U.S. Government of 1855. As all such settlements did, the Claim Commission's compromise settlement disposed of all rights, claims, or demands of Hopis against the U.S. Government, but stipulated that the settlement would not affect the outcome of any legal action the Hopi Tribe had the right to bring under the Navajo-Hopi Settlement Act of 1974. Thus the settlement was one of the few that extinguished title to land, but did not specify the boundaries of that land. Instead, the Act extinguished title only to land that was not included in reservations established for the use and occupancy of Indians that included Hopis. This meant that most of the Hopi *techqua* was lost and gone forever from the Government's viewpoint, but that the Western Navajo Reservation was still up for grabs.

Act of Congress, 1958: Settling the Mineral Estate

Joint Hopi-Navajo ownership of the 1882 Reservation's mineral estate had first been suggested in 1933. Otto Lomavitu, a prime mover in the Flagstaff Conference of 1930 and in Kykotsmovi's "Hopi Council" of 1931, wrote Agency Superintendent Miller on February 13, 1933: "Now should oil or other mineral resources ... ever be ... developed on either the Hopi or Navajo occupied area of the Hopi Reservation, how would fees or royalties be handled?..." Miller queried the Commissioner of Indian Affairs and received this answer: "Such Navajos as are permanently residing on the reservation would probably be entitled to share with the Hopis in any income from future mineral production" (Stephens 1961:178-179). Acting Solicitor Cohen (1946) had issued a formal legal determination in 1946, in response to a similar query in 1944, finding that leases could not be negotiated unless Navajos living on the 1882 Reservation were brought into the decision-making process and shared the royalties. Thus one of John Boyden's first moves as the Tribal Council's attorney was to petition the Department of the Interior in December, 1952[84] for reconsideration of the 1946 decision. Interior did reconsider, but did not produce the answer Boyden sought. In 1955 he requested reconsideration of the reconsideration, setting out a more detailed argument that title to the mineral estate should be vested exclusively in the Hopis. The Navajo Tribal attorney petitioned against exclusive Hopi ownership.

But by 1957 the two Tribal attorneys agreed to lobby a bill through Congress that would let a court determine ownership. "There was a confluence of interests in having the issue of land ownership decided. The Tribes had had to live too long in ambiguity; energy firms needed to clarify title; Tribal attorneys wished to settle the issue; and so, apparently, did the BIA. In 1957 the Tribal councils agreed with their attorneys in seeking federal permission to sue each other, and the BIA drafted legislation" (Aberle 1993:160).

Healing v. Jones

Traditionalists opposed the bill because it looked to them like a giveaway to the Navajos. They mounted an impressive campaign to stop its passage, submitting a petition signed by 373 people from eight villages, declaring, "we do not consider the Navajo Tribe of ever having a claim to our traditional Hopi lands ...." But the Tribal Council favored the bill and in 1958 Congress passed it, setting up a special three-judge panel of the U.S. District Court in Arizona and granting permission for the two tribes to sue each other to determine who owned what land. The legislation cleared title to part of the 1882 Reservation and the lawsuit cleared the remainder. The suit was filed by the two tribal chairmen, Dewey Healing for the Hopi and Paul Jones for the Navajo. The court decided the *Healing v. Jones* case in 1961, issuing its final decision as an appeal court in 1962.

The JUA. Both Tribes consider themselves to have lost the case. The court decided that by implication the Secretary of the interior had seen "fit to settle" both Tribes "thereon" because nothing had ever been done to expel the Navajos or prevent them from settling there, and thus the Navajos qualified as "such other Indians." Taking into account the Collier administration's designation of grazing District Six as exclusively Hopi and the removal of Navajos from that district, the court assigned the surface and mineral rights of District Six exclusively to the Hopi. It judged the remaining 1,822,000 acres belonged to the two Tribes, which had joint and equal rights in its surface and subsurface (minerals). It ruled that each Tribe had "joint, equal, and undivided" possession to the surface as well as the subsurface (the minerals) property of the 1882 Reservation outside District Six. This area subsequently became known as the Joint Use Area, or JUA. The phrase, "joint, equal, and undivided" in the ruling was to have enormous implications in the years to come.

The court did not feel it had authorization from Congress to divide the 1,822,000 acres into exclusively Hopi and exclusively Navajo areas and so it did not. But some members of Congress had expected it to do so. Congressman Wayne Aspinall introduced a partition bill in 1964. Hopi Traditionalists opposed it. The bill died. Between 1963 and 1969, Hopi efforts at attaining a negotiated sharing of the JUA failed. Navajos would not give up residence and use of land that they already had. Many had been given to understand that they could settle there legally if outside the "sixteen miles limit" after 1891, and still others had settled there legally after 1944. Many represented third and fourth generations living in the JUA.

Traditional Navajos

The Bennett Freeze. But the Government seemed to regard partition as constantly imminent, and everyone knew that further court cases might also re-arrange the boundaries of the Western Navajo Reservation. Commissioner of Indian Affairs Robert Bennett imposed a freeze on construction of structures and on changes to any and all surface and subsurface leases and rights of way in 1966 on parts of the JUA and on 1.5 million acres of the "1934 Western Navajo Reservation," knowing that

Hopis would also claim right to this reservation under the "see fit to settle thereon" clause because Moenkopi was located on this reservation. The freeze effectively banned any "improvements," from remodeling of houses to paving of roads. He defined the area by extending the northern and southern boundaries of the 1882 Executive Order Area to the western boundary of the Navajo reservation. At some point, the freeze was clarified as also banning constructions, repairs, etc. on all *new* leases and rights of way, unless both Tribes concurred on a particular request. Only concurrence of both Tribes on a particular request could circumvent the restrictions and only the Secretary of the Interior could over-ride a Tribal veto (Colby et al. 1992). Since 1966, the entire area has come to be known almost as a separate reservation and is called the "Bennett Freeze" area.

The result was a large area of more than two million that included the Bennett Freeze area and contiguous portions of the JUA where roads remained unpaved and unimproved; where the norm for homes continued to be hand-made hogans built in the 1950s or earlier; where there were no mines, industries, housing subdivisions, convenience stores, gas stations, or trailer parks; and where virtually no one had running water, electricity, or telephones. The only exception was Peabody's mining lease. Trading posts and missions established in the 1920s, '30s and '40s continued to be the centers of trade, communication, and contact with the outside world in the JUA and Freeze areas. Navajo women continued to make most of their own clothing, bright-colored pleated skirts and velveteen blouses, and to weave saddle blankets from their own coarse, home-grown wool. Navajos continued to raise much of their own food, growing corn and herding sheep, butchering them for meat and selling the wool. Diets heavy in corn, lard, mutton, flour, sugar, salt, and coffee were the rule, supplemented with pine nuts gathered from upland slopes and cans of peaches and tomatoes purchased from the trading post, and cooking and heating continued to be done with pinon and juniper wood in cast-iron stoves. Many residents assembled earth bundles from elements of the land where they lived to invoke the spirits' protection of themselves, their animals, and their homes, and mothers continued to follow traditional customs such as burying their babies' umbilical cords in the earth near the house.

Settlement clusters of matrilineally-related kin and affines remained isolated, especially in winter; most people spoke only Navajo and did not read or write; and many children grew up never attending school because it was too far to go, and if they did, they often settled elsewhere. Few residents had any contacts with Navajo Tribal Government, or cared to. The Bennett Freeze and the parts of the JUA contiguous with it became a stronghold for Navajos practicing traditions and living a way of life that resembled that of 1870 more than 1970. Many probably thought it would continue to go on that way and some undoubtedly hoped it would.

Prospects of Evictions and Federal Marshals

But changes began to come in 1969, even though few Navajos who would be affected knew about them. The prospect of dependable funding from the Peabody Coal lease royalties coincided with the development of a two-pronged strategy by the Hopi Tribal Council's attorney, John Boyden, that pushed two very tender legal and legislative buttons, pressure points deriving from the principle of "tribal rights." First, in 1970 he petitioned the U.S. District Court in Phoenix for a "writ of assistance" allowing the Hopi to enforce their rights to the JUA. Enforcement would have permitted confiscation of livestock in pursuit of the mandate for livestock reduction; the JUA was badly overgrazed. The District Court declined, but on appeal, the Ninth Circuit Court of Appeals in San Francisco ordered the District Court to do so. The judge agreed to issue a writ of assistance and order of compliance directing reduction of Navajo livestock in the JUA by 85%, from 120,000 sheep units to 8,139 (a "sheep unit" is the same as one sheep and one-quarter of a steer, i.e., one steer or cow = 1 animal unit; one horse = 1.25 animal unit; one sheep = .25 animal unit) and prohibiting any new construction in the JUA without permits from both Tribes (Whitson 1985:378-379). Thus the "freeze" now encompassed more than three million acres. The Court ordered that thenceforth, no Navajos could initiate new construction of buildings on the JUA without the Hopi Tribe's written permission, and no Hopis could initiate new construction without the Navajo Tribe's written permission. The Council hired a father-and-son team of cowboys to patrol the range and pick up Navajo stock that had trespassed onto District Six.

Then, Boyden sought Arizona Congressman Sam Steiger's help in pushing a settlement bill through Congress. Steiger introduced his partition bill in 1970 and Congress held hearings on it in 1972. The Kikmongwis of First Mesa, Mishongnovi, Shungopavi, and Oraibi objected to the proposed bill, declaring, "The Hopi Chiefs have never consented to boundaries established by the U.S. Government and expressing their desire for a negotiated settlement." The Traditionalists initiated negotiations of their own with Navajos living in parts of the JUA.

The congressional hearings revealed that Navajos had continued to exercise exclusive control of the JUA for all practical purposes, including surface leasing and granting of rights of way without consulting the Hopi Tribe. Navajos had beneficial use not of 50% of the JUA, but rather, 98%

Tribe. Navajos had beneficial use not of 50% of the JUA, but rather, 98% of it. Hopis testified that harassments such as Hopi corrals and fences being torn down and stock water being diverted had discouraged and prevented them from trying to use the other 48% to which they had rights.

The "Steiger bill" would have provided no special relocation benefits. It passed the House with a voice vote. Immediately following the House's voice-vote approval, Navajo Chairman Peter MacDonald announced the opening of a full-time lobby office, calling Steiger's testimony in support of the bill "completely a big lie ... It can, will take away millon of acres of Indian land ... We will continue to fight it..." (Indian Legal Information Service 1972:32).

PL 93-531: An Act to Provide for Final Settlement...

The Steiger bill stalled and died in the Senate. But the right buttons had indeed been pushed and a response was forthcoming. The U.S. District Court's Order of Compliance of October 14, 1972, was accompanied by a Writ of Assistance requiring the United States Marshal to evict Navajo families living on the JUA, by force if necessary (Congressional Record 1986: H3432-3). The specter of federal marshals dragging Indians out of their dirt-floor hogans in response to eviction orders made Government officials and legislators wince. Legislators offered a kinder, gentler alternative. In 1973 Senators Fannin and Goldwater introduced the bill that eventually became PL-93-531, known as the "Settlement Act" of 1974. At hearings held pursuant to the Act in 1973 and 1974, even some prominent Traditionalists, usually opposed to involvement with any Government- or Council-sponsored project, broke ranks and came forth with statements affirming Navajo trespass. According to Congressman Morris Udall, PL-93-531 was enacted in order to prevent "the potential disaster stemming from the court-ordered eviction of Navajo families" (Congressional Record 1986: H3433). The number of relocatees was anticipated in 1974 as 775 Navajo families and two Hopi families.

The Act included provision for sixty "life estates" for those Navajo families who wished to remain; they could not, however, pass the land onto their heirs. At the holder's death, a life estate would revert to full Hopi Tribal ownership. The Navajos began calling them "death estates." Only one person applied for one.

Management of Relocation was turned over to a Navajo-Hopi Indian Relocation Commission (NHIRC) of three members appointed by the President but responsible to the Secretary of the Interior, with was stock reduction, which diminished Navajos' herds by 85%. The second step was fencing the perimeter of the new "Hopi Reservation." The BIA undertook both the stock reductions and the fencing. The Act allocated sufficient money for the Government to purchase sheep at more than market value. Stock reduction began in 1977. By 1982 it had been largely accomplished though some individuals continued to run stock in excess of permitted numbers. The Act provided for a negotiated settlement at any time, but authorized the U.S. District Court in Phoenix to take over the case after 180 days and to ask a federal mediator to draw a partition line. Sections 4 and 25 of the Act authorized the Government to make allocations for an unspecified number of lawsuits that could be initiated by one tribe against the other for damages and "further original, ancillary, or supplementary actions against the other tribe as may be necessary or desirable to insure the quiet and peaceful enjoyment of the reservation ...." The Hopi Tribe's allocation was $250,000 a year (Sidney 1989).

In 1975, after actually a nine-month period of more than a dozen meetings between representatives appointed by the two Tribal administrations failed to produce a negotiated settlement, the Court accepted a mediator's partition line on February 10, 1977. After two years of unsuccessful appeals, surveying of the area to begin in April, 1979. The Hopi area -- 905,000 acres -- would become known as Hopi Partitioned Lands, or HPL; the 922,000 Navajo acres as NPL, Navajo Partitioned Lands. The mediator created a "Navajo island" near Jeddito. Navajos within this "island" would be permitted to continue to live there, under the jurisdiction of the Navajo Tribe. About forty Hopis had homes in this Jeddito island and would have to move.

The line drawn by the mediator followed a suggested line drawn in 1972 by Albert Purchase, a former Soil Conservationist transferred to the BIA in 1942, and in charge of land operations at the Hopi Agency ever since. "Many Hopis can't stand this work," he had said at the time. "They don't believe land can be divided. A lot of Hopis think that way. Others know that this dispute is going to be settled the white man's way by the white man's law. They know they'd better take their half while they can. It won't be done in the Hopi way" (Bingham et al 1984:198). At that time, the figure for Navajos that would have to be relocated was 680 families consisting of 3,500; for Hopis, 2 extended families consisting of 40 people. Relocation could not begin, however, until a Report and Plan were submitted to Congress. Preparation of the Report and Plan took two years. In the meantime, the Tribes tried more than a dozen additional fruitless negotiations before the NHIRC completed its plan in July, 1981.

245

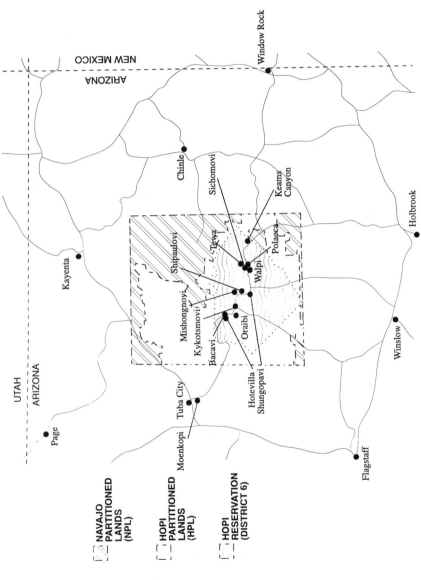

Hopi Partitioned Lands (HPL), Navajo Partitioned Lands (NPL), District 6, and Former Joint Use Area (JUA): 1978

The Relocation Plan

The law specified that Navajos and Hopis on "wrong" sides of the lines had five years to move voluntarily from the date of the plan's completion. It was another lousy government plan. For Navajos, there was virtually no place to move.

By 1981, the estimate of potential relocatees was 1,520 Navajo and 20 Hopi households. Hopis almost immediately secured home sites on the newly-acquired "Hopi 'Partitioned' Lands" (HPL). Many Navajos had already moved off HPL, crowding in with relatives, while awaiting the opening of new lands to which to relocate. A 1980 amendment raised the maximum compensation to $55,000-$66,000 per household, depending on size, for new housing, although the first relocatees had been eligible for only $17,000-25,000. A $5,000 bonus was offered for moving in 1981 decreasing to $1,000 in 1985. The 1980 amendment also broadened eligibility criteria; extended the deadline for application to July 7, 1985; and increased the number of potentially available life estates from sixty to one-hundred-twenty, providing for up to ninety acres for each with limited grazing rights. Still, no one applied for one.

These liberalizations enhanced the Plan's implementation. But the Plan was deficient on any number of counts. First, there was still no place for the relocatees to go once they moved, except to the already overcrowded Navajo reservation or into a border city -- Flagstaff, Winslow, Gallup. The process for obtaining home sites in other Navajo communities was long and tedious, requiring many hearings and approvals. The NHIRC's efforts to set up local committees in potential host chapters to plan for the relocatees had had little success (Aberle 1993:165). And more than a million acres adjacent to the JUA -- the Bennett Freeze -- were off-limits due to the ban on new construction. The freeze was removed from two administrative areas, Tuba City and Moenkopi, but the 1980 Amendment removed the provision for a Secretarial over-ride of Tribal refusal of consent and made concurrence from *both* Tribes required for home construction or improvement. The Hopi Tribe enacted a housing moratorium in 1982, effectively refusing consent for housing development outside Moenkopi and Tuba City, but because Moenkopi and Tuba City had become exempt from the freeze, Hopis could and did construct several large subdivisions of HUD housing.

The NHIRC Relocation Plan provided no effective planning for economic or community development or relocatee livelihood and had no provision for moving functioning groups of relatives (Aberle 1993:165). These problems were not remedied until well into the late 1980s, and although they affected Navajos directly, they also affected Hopis. Navajos stalled in relocating and thus delayed the point at which Hopis could begin to use their new lands. By 1993, 43% of on-reservation Navajo relocations finished up on NPL (Aberle 1993:181), increasing its population significantly, thereby creating the same kinds of crowding problems that had pushed Navajos into the 1882 Reservation in the first place, and thereby heightening some individuals' temptation to sneak their stock hugger-mugger back over into HPL, now recovering its forage potential after decades of overgrazing.

The Relocation Process

Land-to-person ratios after division and addition of Navajos' new lands were 167 acres per person for Hopis, and about 80 acres per person for Navajos, as of 1990.[85] In the early years the vast majority of Navajo relocations were urban (Aberle 1993:172). By 1984, 40% of the 2,169 persons relocated to off-reservation communities no longer owned their homes (Whitson 1985:389), having lost them to loan sharks or simply due to unfamiliarity with the urban milieu. By 1985, relocation had cost $339 million and in 1989 a knowledgeable commentator mentioned the possibility of an ultimate figure of $500 million. By March, 1993, 2,930 households consisting of about 11,250 individuals for Navajos, and 26 Hopi households of 90 individuals had been declared eligible for relocation. Number of households actually relocated was 2,216 for Navajos and 23 for Hopis. Although the relocation program began badly, it was gradually improved by a crucial series of steps taken by Congress at NHIRC's behest (Aberle 1993:165).

Impacts. Perhaps the most frequently cited study of Navajo relocatees and the impacts on them is the study by Scudder et al. (1979). This study documented abnormal rates of death, misfortune, illness, and psychological trauma among Navajos relocated from District Six in 1972. The impacts are undeniable. But the analogy, or concordance often drawn between these relocatees and Navajos relocated under PL-93-531 is somewhat misleading. None of the District Six relocatees were provided with any but the most minimal assistance. No law provided them with benefits, compensations, or counseling. In contrast, PL-93-531 did provide for these kinds of assistance. The 51 families relocated from District Six filed a lawsuit and were, albeit belatedly, finally included under PL-93-531 and its amendments and were given until July 6, 1986 to apply for benefits.

But relocation under the best of circumstances is a situation of "multidimensional" stress (Aberle 1993:189-90). The threat of relocation has had a definitely negative impact on Navajos' mental health. "Among self-referred patients to Indian Public Health facilities in four service areas of the Reservation," says David Aberle (1993:190), "those living on HPL and thus facing relocation showed a higher rate of self-referral than those living on NPL or those living outside the JUA. They were more likely to be clinically diagnosed as depressed, and to attribute their negative feelings to such impacts as moving, the freeze on housing, and livestock reduction." Relocations from the period 1977-1987, prior to the availability of the new lands, were especially stressful and unsuccessful, and stock reductions often recalled bitter memories of those of 1933-34.

Resistance to the Settlement Act

Even before the law was passed, Navajos and even some Hopis expressed opposition to it. Calls went out for its repeal. Relocation was not acceptable to many HPL Navajos. Resistance started at Big Mountain in 1977 when some Navajo ladies chased off a Navajo fencing crew hired by the BIA. That incident was followed by a stream of others. Major confrontations between fencing crews and individual Navajos resulted in arrests in 1979, 1980, and 1987. Receiving support to "stand up for their rights" from Hopi Traditionalists such as Thomas Banyacya (Simross 1981), the resisters made the fence into a symbol of their determination. They successfully blocked completion of a six-mile segment of it for sixteen years.

The resulting publicity brought support from thousands of sympathizers. Big Mountain partisans came from Los Angeles and San Francisco to help out Navajo elders at Big Mountain: they renovate structures, tended cornfields, herded sheep, provided transportation, and ran errands. In 1978 the American Indian Movement held its first "survival meeting" at Big Mountain and established an "AIM Survival Camp." In 1979 AIM held its Annual International Indian Treaty Council meeting there and in 1980 carried the Big Mountain case to the Fourth Russell Tribunal in Rotterdam, charging violation of human rights. Big Mountain support groups formed in Berkeley, Los Angeles, Boulder, Brooklyn, and elsewhere, initiating monthly newsletters, charging the U.S. Government with genocide and conspiracy with energy companies, and funneling aid to HPL residents. Annual gatherings of Big Mountain supporters started in 1981 with over 300 people, and in 1982 Lakota spiritual leaders began holding an annual Sun Dance -- later two of them -- at Big Mountain. Slogans appeared in bright colors painted on a new water tank installed by the Hopi Tribe: "Economic Development is Cultural Genocide. BIA YOU are still native people. YOU are responsible

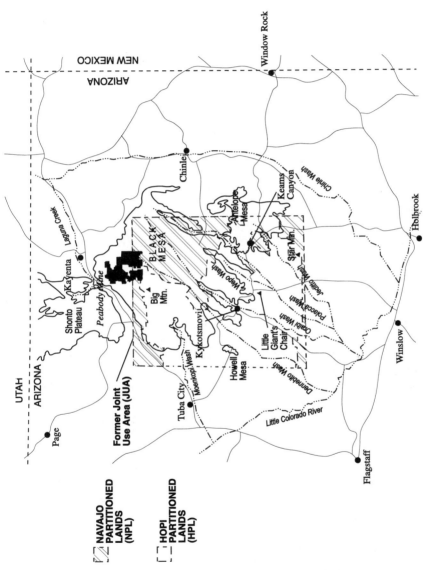

Peabody Mine in Relation to Hopi Reservation and NPL

for the destruction of a culture. Big Mountain Elders Protect YOUR Future."

Between 1979 and 1986 hearings were held on various amendments, some initiated from the Hopi position and some from the Navajo, proposing various land exchanges and cash settlements to avoid relocating the Big Mountain people. All were defeated. In 1982 Boston attorney Lew Gurwitz founded the Big Mountain Legal Defense/Offense Committee (BMLDOC) in Flagstaff with support from the Los Angeles chapter of the Big Mountain Support Group, which sent the BMLDOC substantial funding on a monthly basis, collected mostly from grass-roots contributions of sympathetic urbanites, from 1982 through 1986. BMLDOC searched for legal ways of stopping Navajo relocation and also encouraged a negotiated settlement, sponsoring several meetings between Hopi and Navajo elders at Big Mountain in the mid-1980s. It also started its own lobbying campaign, opening an office in Washington, D.C. in 1986. In response to BMLDOC's lobbying, the European Parliament added the Navajo-Hopi relocation to its list of human-rights concerns along with those in South Africa, the Soviet Union, and Nicaragua in 1986. The June 6th Resolution called for repeal of PL-93-531 (Brinkley-Rogers 1986).

Dragnets? Because PL 93-531 specified that Navajos on the "Hopi" side of the line had five years to move voluntarily from the date of completion of the survey permanently fixing the line and because the survey was completed in July, 1981, Big Mountain Support Groups and BMLDOC interpreted July 6, 1986 -- the last day on which to apply for relocation benefits -- as also the deadline for relocation to be completed, and began expressing fear that tac squads would swoop down on remaining Navajos. As July 6, 1986 approached, things had really heated up. Many observers expected federal marshals and troops to surround Navajo families with dragnets and began packing them into removal vans. Support for Navajo resisters on HPL intensified. But support for Hopis also intensified, and appeared from some surprising quarters. In April, 1986, American Indian Movement activist Russell Means went to Hopiland and apologized to the Hopis, saying he had been misled in his earlier support for resisters and that he now supported Hopi elders who want to reclaim their land. "It is Hopi land, and the old Navajos know it," he declared. "They are afraid that if they go to the Hopis, in light of all the past history of trouble, the Hopis will not let them stay" (Elston 1988:73-4). Tribal Chairman Ivan Sidney, a Hopi-Tewa from First Mesa, declared the beginning of a public-relations drive, presenting the Hopi position to various public forums.

A Normal Day. But the BIA declared July 6 a "normal day," saying the deadline was meaningless and that there would be no action to evict anyone. Ivan Sidney also declared there were no plans to evict the remaining Navajos. In June, 1986, a scuffle broke out between Navajos in the Seba Dalkai area of HPL with two Hopi-BIA police officers and a Hopi tribal ranger. It turned into a confrontation with about 100 Navajos eventually surrounding the three policemen; one had his revolver taken away. The crowd held them for nearly six hours before tensions eased and everyone departed. On July 7, 1986, the Hopi Tribal Council passed a resolution officially claiming HPL and the first non-relocated Hopi placed a claim on HPL, just across the line from the District Six boundary, and Navajos, estimated at 200 to 500 marched and demonstrated at a portion of the fence dividing HPL from NPL at Big Mountain, cutting the fence, and thereby symbolically defying the relocation mandate. Many of the demonstrators anticipated Huey-helicopter-loads of assault teams to swoop down upon them. But nothing happened.

Traditionalist Actions. In April, 1987, a delegation of ten Hopi Traditionalists from four villages, including Lower Moenkopi's Kikmongwi, spent a week in Washington, D.C. Organized by the San Francisco based Network for Hopi/Navajo Land Rights and Big Mountain Defense/ Offense Committee's Washington, D.C. office, a series of meetings was arranged with various senators and representatives. The Traditionalists "went to convey the Hopi position on their own self-governance. The intentions of the leaders were to articulate recognition of who the true leaders in power are in the Hopi Villages and that the Tribal Council is a forced governing body working in collusion with the U.S. Government" (Hopi Epicentre 1987). They met with Senator Inouye, Chairman of the Senate Select Committee on Indian Affairs as well as Congressman Udall and Senators MCain and DeConcini from Arizona. Several attended appropriations hearings for the Navajo-Hopi Relocation Commission.

Inouye promised to take time within the following nine months to personally visit with the people in Hopiland. He did, expecting to meet with the village leaders; they decided not to meet with him. Instead, he met with Tribal Chairman Ivan Sidney and other members of the Tribal Council and administration. Shortly afterwards, the BMLDOC's lobbyist resigned, and its Washington lobby office was closed.

MacDonald's Defiance. In 1988, Peter MacDonald, then Navajo Tribal Chairman, deliberately defied the administrative Bennett Freeze, the Hopi Tribal moratorium, and the freeze imposed by PL 93-531 by having Navajo Tribal work crews repair a number of Navajo houses in the Freeze area and on HPL, and by constructing half a dozen new houses on HPL under what he called "Project Hope." Not surprisingly, the Hopi Tribe sought to stop construction with a preliminary injunction. The

Federal District Court in Phoenix admonished MacDonald (Colby et al. 1992). After September, 1988, an appeal process was implemented to allow the Navajo Tribe ten days to appeal the Hopi Tribe's denial of consent for improvements.

But resistance continued. In February, 1989, three Navajos and seven non-Indians were arrested at Big Mountain while trying to stop a BIA bulldozer from deepening an old cachement basin. Charges were dropped and the range improvement halted. In August, 1989, Hopi Tribal officials again expressed no intention of forcing Navajos to move, because using force would be contrary to Hopi tradition. Hopis said the matter had already been decided by the *tiponi* given to Hopis by Navajos. Hence, Navajos would come to an accommodation with circumstances either by requesting to stay under certain Hopi-mandated conditions or by eventually moving. In June, 1989, a Veterans Peace Convoy arrived at Big Mountain, sponsored by the Veterans Peace Action Teams that formed in 1986 to send humanitarian aid to Nicaragua oppose U.S. policy. They delivered some food, clothing, and tools, stayed a few days, and left. A second convoy delivered food to Big Mountain at Thanksgiving. Another one went at Thanksgiving, 1990, and again in summer, 1991. By summer, 1993, the convoys had become regular events.

Navajo-Hopi Unity Committee

The Hopi Traditionalists' position called for repeal of PL 93-531; abolition of all fences and boundaries; abolition of all reservations including the 1882 and 1934; acknowledgement of the boundaries of the Hopi aboriginal claim and Hopis ownership to all land within it; federal recognition of Hopi politico-religious leaders and the sovereignty of Hopi villages; and non-interference from the U.S. Government. Many Hopis -- perhaps most -- agreed with that position in principle. But most thought it impractical.

Mina Lanza, acting as Kikmongwi of Oraibi and a leader of the Traditionalists, formed the Navajo-Hopi Unity Committee. Under her guidance, Navajos from the former Joint Use Area met with Hopi Traditionalists on how to change the relocation law. Mina and the Traditionalists opposed the Tribal Council on principle, and also believed the Council was being used by the energy companies and the government to remove Navajos from coal-rich lands. Indeed, coal *does* underlie the Big Mountain area of HPL and NPL. Perhaps Mina did not embrace her father Tawakwaptiwa's prophecy of doom and demise for Oraibi and wanted to re-establish Oraibi's former pre-eminence in the region. But according to her spokesman, Reverend Caleb Johnson, Mina was also motivated by a concern for "'the well-being of all people because as chief, all the people were her children'" (Elston 1988:65), including Navajos. Her proposal for a joint Navajo-Hopi reservation under Traditionalist governance was not greeted seriously and although the Unity Committee continued to meet after her death in 1978, its participants consisted largely of Navajos.

The UN Subcommission

In 1987, the United Nations Subcommission on Prevention of Discrimination and Protection of Minorities authorized investigations of Hopi-Navajo relocation after several Hopi Traditionalists and Navajos made statements and submitted petitions in 1986. Statements on behalf of some Hopis in Hotevilla charged racial discrimination due to the U.S. Government's unilateral power to extinguish title to Indian lands and conflict of interest in the Government's power to exercise veto power over a tribe's choice of attorney while at the same time setting the terms under which tribes could sue each other. The statements requested assistance from the UN's programme on advisory services and expressed sympathy for Navajos facing relocation. Statements on behalf of Navajos at Big Mountain requested advisory services and a halt to relocation.

In 1988 UN investigators Erica-Irene A. Daes, a Greek, and John Carey, an American, carried out separate investigations on HPL, NPL, the Bennett Freeze area, the Hopi villages, and Tribal offices in 1989 and submitted separate reports. Carey's Report stated in part, "certain Navajos object to relocation on grounds that their religious beliefs require them to reside on particular land, just as certain Hopis object to alleged interference by Navajos with their visiting religiously significant areas which are now under Navajo control." Overall, Carey recommended close attention to the religious freedom issue (UN Sub-Commission 1989a).

Daes recommended among other things that an eighteen-month moratorium be placed on relocation and that "the United Nations Programme of Advisory Services" be made available "to the Traditional Hopi people."[86] In the relocation process, she averred, "the rights to freedom of religion and property, and, in many cases, the principles of equality and non-discrimination were disregarded and certain United Nations human Rights standards were not observed" (UN Sub-Commission 1989b).

In 1990 the Subcommission's Working Group on Indigenous Populations heard testimony from Navajo elders protesting relocation and from Hopi elders including Oraibi's Kikmongwi (Mina's younger brother who had taken over at her death), who reversed his earlier position and announced that now he wanted Navajos to move because he believed that they were making false land claims (Elston 1988:72; 1990). This body also heard testimony from representatives of the two Tribal administrations and voted to maintain the land dispute as a concern. It rejected a proposal for UN-sponsored mediation services for the dispute, but eventually supported mediation mandated by the U.S. Ninth Circuit Court of Appeals that would "result in a settlement that respects the rights and dignity of the families directly affected" (UN Sub-Commission 1992).

Land Exchange Proposals

Basing itself on its own household count in June of 1991, the Navajo Tribe asserted that about 300 families lived full-time on HPL, and another 360 or more who were living there part-time. Another 10 had received relocation benefits but had moved right back onto HPL. The Navajo Tribe would not provide its list or its criteria for full-time residence to investigators (Colby et al. 1992), asserting that some resisters did not wish to make themselves known, but did provide it the Relocation Commission. The Relocation Commission independently estimated somewhere between fifty and one hundred resisting households.

Continued resistance at Big Mountain, Mosquito Springs, Starr Mountain, Tees Toh, and a few other communities compelled the Navajo Tribe to continue to seek a negotiated settlement that would reduce or end relocations. The Relocation Act authorizes the two Tribes to exchange lands which are already part of their respective reservations. Aware that Big Mountain presented the most vocal resistance, Senator Barry Goldwater urged the Hopi Tribal administration to initiate "a series of meetings with Big Mountain residents at their request to discuss possible land exchanges that would reduce the numbers of potential relocatees" (Hopi Tribe 1986a:6). Under the aegis of the Relocation Commission, the Hopi Tribe offered a chunk of acreage at Big Mountain[87] in exchange for sixteen separate smaller parcels in NPL in 1981. In 1982, the Navajo Tribe said "no," countering with three land exchange proposals.

The Senate Select Committee on Indian Affairs held hearings at Barry Goldwater's behest in July, 1982 on legislation that would have effected a land exchange; Goldwater wanted the "'traditional' Navajo people of Big Mountain" to be able remain living where they were (Qua Toqti 1982). The legislation was not passed and the Hopi Tribe said "no" to the Navajo Tribe's land exchange proposals in March, 1984, proposing instead an exchange of approximately 48,000 acres in the "Big Mountain" area for 48,000 acres of NPL on the Peabody lease. The Navajo Tribe said "no," countering with yet another proposal of its own. In June, 1984, the Hopi Tribe gave its answer: "no."

At this point, the Federal Government stepped in directly. President Ronald Reagan appointed former Interior Secretary William Clark as special negotiator to initiate "a speedy and final resolution of the issues." As one observer put it, "The specter of Navajo grandmothers shooting it out with federal marshals, and having it report on the evening news would not be palatable" (Sills 1986:67). Clark personally delivered a letter to Tribal Chairmen Zah and Sidney in a meeting at Keams Canyon urging a negotiated settlement in February, 1985. He left his assistant Richard Morris in place to carry out investigations. Morris visited Navajo people in the former JUA February through May, 1985, and also met extensively with Tribal officials and Hopi villagers. He found the Moenkopi representatives resigned from the Council; certification of Kykotsmovi's and First Mesa's representatives in question; and no representatives at all, of course, from Oraibi, Hotevilla, and Shungopavi. A Tribal Council without a quorum and the usual dissensions from Traditionalists gave Morris (1985) the impression that the Hopi were "a deeply divided people"; Clark brought the two chairmen to the White House for a meeting in August, 1985 but got nowhere. Relocation, he concluded, was inevitable even for resisters.

A Better Relocation Plan for Navajos?

The Navajo New Lands

In line with a provision of the 1974 Settlement Act, the Navajo Tribe selected 250,000 BLM acres for purchase near the Vermillion Cliffs just north and west of Grand Canyon and of the Navajo Reservation in 1974. But opponents to the purchase, including such diverse groups as the Kaibab Paiute Tribe; Congressman Sam Steiger; the National Wildlife Federation; Navajo-Hopi Unity Committee; the Arizona Cattlemen's and Varmint Callers Associations; and the owners of forty-four uranium claims in the area forced the effort to be abandoned.

The 1980 Relocation Amendments Act increased the acreage authorized for Navajo expansion to 400,000 acres which could come from private as well as Government holdings. It specified that the U.S. Bureau of Land Management would supply 250,000 acres at no cost to the Tribe but barred all land north and west of the Colorado River from selection in response to public pressure. The Navajo Tribe's first selection was the "Paragon Resources Ranch" and contiguous BLM land near Chaco Canyon. It anticipated leasing most of it for coal and uranium mining.

Public Service Company of New Mexico drew up plans for a large coal-fired power plant there.

The Tribe also selected 200,000 acres of privately owned land near Winslow and Holbrook, but again ran up against local objections. Finally, the Tribe selected 379,000 acres consisting of eight ranches, two of them already owned by the Navajo Tribe and leased to independent operators, one of which was Navajo, and some BLM and state-owned land near Chambers, abutting the Zuni reservation to the east and contiguous to the Navajo Reservation on the north. The two ranches already owned by the Tribe would be in lieu of the purchase of 150,000 acres. In mid-1987, relocations to the new lands began. Additionally, the Commission implemented "group moves," permitting extended families and households linked by marriage to relocate together, and obtained funds for economic development on the New Lands.

If this discussion of the Navajo situation has seemed inordinately complicated, it is because the situation itself is byzantinely complex. In contrast, the Hopi relocation situation has always been conditioned by one relatively simply issue: clearing HPL land of Navajos so that Hopis can use them.

Hopi Relocations onto HPL

The earliest relocatees all relocated from the Jeddito area either to the southeast of the Navajos' Jeddito "Island" or to the Tees Toh area. These relocations proceeded more or less without a hitch. Electricity was supplied by active solar panels for the first few years until the Navajo Tribal Utility Authority agreed to provide electricity at two dollars a month. Aside from problems of poor house construction by the Relocation Commission's contractor, the first experiences of Hopis on their newly won land were satisfying.

But other Hopis' use of HPL came much more slowly. Applications from non-relocated Hopis for grazing permits on HPL doubled between August, 1989, and August, 1991, from 102 to 209, of which 143 were approved, and there were 184 applications for agricultural assignments on HPL, of which 50 had been approved. These figures represented a sizable Hopi interest in moving out of District Six -- more than a 400% increase from August, 1989. In 1991, there were 216 applications pending for home sites. The Council planned to turn a dirt road into a paved highway called the "Turquoise Trail" and at its junction with the Dinnebito Road, the Council planned a police station a housing subdivision primarily for Tribal employees, and various Tribal facilities. The Tribe allocated $2.9 million for the new community and planned to build the houses out of recycled material much cheaper than cut stone, cinder block, or slump block: polystyrene insulation and pressboard made from sawmill wood chips that otherwise would be burned (Wicoff 1993). The Hotevilla Board of Directors also planned a separate community that would include 50-odd house sites, a trailer park, and a cooperatively-owned store. The plan would get those who wanted modern conveniences out from under the village's stubborn cadre of anti-power-pole Traditionalist elders.

But almost no Hopis were living on HPL as of the mid-1990s. Although Hopi cattle owners were eager to move as much of their stock as possible into HPL, few Hopis were anxious to move from the villages; most anticipated not so satisfying experiences. The reasons had to do with jurisdiction. HPL was initially divided into 38 range units, in which the Council's Tribal civil and criminal law applied. But fear of harassments, such as the knocking down of fences, deliberate dumping of trash on HPL, vandalism of vehicles and stock ponds, verbal abuse of Hopi range monitors, menacing use of vehicles, shots fired at Hopis gathering ceremonial eagles, and prevention of access to shrines on NPL, contributed to Hopis' reluctance. Most of the harassment was surreptitious in nature; there was little direct evidence to connect the vandalism with specific persons. Hopi Tribal and BIA personnel would find fences cut, knocked down, or in some cases actually realigned, apparently, so that livestock could meander from NPL onto HPL. The 6.5-mile gap near Big Mountain -- the symbol of resistance -- also let livestock to stray into HPL.

A long history of overgrazing compounded the problem. All of the JUA was badly overgrazed, even in the 1930s. Range management held the line on erosion, but effected little improvement. Lack of Hopi access to HPL until 1989, and to the "Joint Use" area for 50 years prior to that, resulted in some parts of District Six also being badly overgrazed

"Original, Ancillary, Supplementary Actions"

More than two dozen lawsuits were filed between 1974 and 1990, most of them either by the Hopi Tribe[88] against the Navajo Tribe or by Navajo individuals against the Relocation Commission (Whitson 1985). Under PL 93-531, the Government pays some portion of the legal fees.

The Accounting, Owelty, Damage, Use Rental, and New Construction Lawsuits

The accounting case resulted from the 1962 *Healing v Jones* decision and was intended to settle proceeds from businesses on the JUA that were never divided. A settlement was reached in 1993 and the Navajo Tribe started paying the awarded amount according to a payment schedule.

Owelty refers to the division of jointly owned property and to the fact that the jointly owned property, in this case HPL and NPL, did not have the same value on the date of partition. The argument was that HPL is not as valuable as NPL; NPL has more water holes. The use rental lawsuit referred to the fact that Navajos continued to use HPL after partition without paying rent. The damage suit successfully argued that overgrazing by Navajo livestock had severely damaged HPL and should be compensated. The New Construction lawsuit requested contempt citations and monetary damages to be awarded to the Hopi Tribe for Navajos' deliberate construction of a large hogan on HPL in violation of the construction freeze and in violation of the permitting process. These lawsuits were tried in July and August, 1992. The Court awarded $21 million to the Hopi Tribe for the New Construction, Use and Owelty cases, and $1.5 in damages.

The Mineral Tax Case

The Mineral Tax case requires the Navajos to share the proceeds of their mineral tax with Hopis. This would ultimately result in huge amounts going to the Hopi -- figures in the double-digit millions. The Navajos will be squeezed by this judgment because they have levied the tax, then forgiven large amounts of it as a concession upon Peabody's agreement to fund Navajo Community College, set up a scholarship fund, etc. But the court ruled that Navajos must pay half the taxes *assessed*, whether they were collected or not, because the according to the ruling in *Healing v Jones*, that each Tribe enjoys "joint, equal, and undivided" possession to the surface as well as the subsurface of the 1882 Reservation outside District Six, minerals are jointly owned in equal amounts, no matter how the surface might be divided. The exact amounts had not been decided as of August, 1993. Despite the fact, then, that the Hopi Tribe was not able to get its own severance tax ordinance approved, it may reap as much or more in revenues from the Navajo Nation's severance tax.

The "Fiduciary Trust" Trespass Suit

The trespass suit, with fines amounting to $1 a day per animal on HPL since 1974, is against the U.S. Government in the U.S. Court of Claims. This lawsuit requests $270 in fines without interest. It is against the US because, under the 1974 law, the US should have been collecting the fines from Navajos whose livestock has trespassed on HPL in order to fulfill its obligation as fiduciary trustee for land owned by an Indian Tribe but administered by the BIA on its behalf. The BIA has not done so consistently. Hopi complaints about trespassing livestock are supported by BIA statistics. At one time, as many as 2000 trespassing sheep were identified in one Hopi range unit. Between January 15 and July 31, 1991, BIA personnel noted close to 200 head of trespassing stock in various HPL range units in 11 different monitoring trips, but succeeded in capturing fewer than 70 (Colby et al. 1992). Thus, the number of trespassing livestock documented was far more than the number actually impounded against which fines were levied.

The 1934 Navajo Reservation Boundary Case

The Hopi Tribe filed a lawsuit against the Navajo Tribe claiming an interest in the 4.4 million-acre Western Navajo Reservation on the basis of being the "other Indians" in the language appearing in the 1934 legislation defining the Western Navajo Reservation's boundaries. PL-93-531 sent that case to the same Federal District Court as one of the "ancillary and supplementary" legal actions (Whitson 1985:381). Hopis' attorneys argued that Hopis should have half the Reservation, just as Navajos had gotten half the Hopi Reservation. In 1990 the San Juan Southern Paiutes, living in two small communities at Gap and Willow Springs, gained recognition as a Tribe and intervened in the lawsuit, claiming an interest in the same area. Their interest was supported by the Hopi Tribe, contested by the Navajo Tribe. The Court ultimately denied any land to the Paiutes since they were mentioned in the 1974 Settlement Act, but had not been an authorized by the Act to be a party to the lawsuit. The Court noted that their claims did not overlap those of the Hopis.

On September 25, 1992, the Court issued its final decision. It ruled that, indeed, Hopis living in Moenkopi were "such other Indians." It distinguished three areas of the 1934 reservation: an area that was exclusively Navajo; an area that was exclusively Hopi amounting to 22,000 acres; and an area that was jointly used by Hopis and Navajos. Modifying the boundaries administratively granted to Moenkopi Hopis in 1972, the Court reset the boundary for Moenkopi's lands based on 1934 aerial photographs, partitioning 22,675 acres to the Hopi Tribe, an amount slightly larger than acreage encompassed by the administrative boundaries. It also granted the Hopi Tribe an easement to maintain irrigation ditches running across Navajo farms, long a point of contention. Allotments made to Hopis and Navajos between 1897 and 1903 were not affected.

The jointly used lands (JUL) amounted to 152,843 acres. The court awarded 25% of those lands -approximately 38,000 acres -- exclusively to the Hopis. Total exclusive Hopi acreage amounted to 60,518 acres. Judge Carroll drew the boundaries separating Hopi and Navajo areas in a way that avoided relocations, rather than acceding to the Hopi argument that religious shrines should be the basis for determining which lands should be Hopi. The Court based this division on contemporary use, relying on testimony from individual Hopis and Navajos.[89]

The ruling exempted 1.5 million acres -- about 90% -- of the Bennett Freeze area from the building and construction freeze and moratorium, but maintained the freeze on the 120,00 acres of the JUL awarded to the Navajos following Hopis' appeal of the decision. Because the 1974 Settlement Act authorized partition of the surface *and* subsurface rights in the 1934 Reservation, the Hopi Tribe also gained exclusive ownership of the minerals underlying the 60,518 acres. Hopi Tribal Chairman Vernon Masayesva called the acreage "inadequate" (Associated Press 1992). The Tribe appealed the ruling in 1993.

Manybeads and Mediation

But the most far-reaching lawsuit was a class-action by forty-seven Navajos on HPL against the US Government. Filed by BMLDOC (Jenny Manybeads et al v United States of America et al CIV 88-410 PCTEHC), it attempted to halt relocation on grounds that it interfered with Navajos' freedom of religion by removing them from the lands where they perform their rituals. The District Court in Phoenix issued a ruling on October 18, 1989. The judge based his decision on a precedent set in *Lyng v. Northwest Indian Cemetery Protective Ass'n* (1988) regarding a claim by the Karok, Yurok, and Hoopa Tribes in California -- the so-called Gasket-Orleans (G-O) Road case -- about road building on public lands sacred to these Tribes, and quoted it: "The fact that a person's ability to practice their religion will be virtually destroyed by a governmental program does not allow them to impose a religious servitude on the property of the government [much less property which the government holds in trust for another sovereign Indian tribe.] The nature of the religious rights claimed cannot create a de facto beneficial ownership of public (or private) property, in order to practice ones religion" (U.S. District Court 1989). Noting that PL 93-531 guarantees Navajo access to religious shrines on HPL (as well as Hopi access to shrines on NPL) the judge decided that relocation did not violate guarantees of the Constitution or the American Indian Religious Freedom Act, even if relocation impaired a specific Navajo's ability to practice religion in specific ways.

BMLDOC appealed the decision. The Ninth Circuit Court of Appeals in San Francisco heard the case but was puzzled by it. "You make it sound," said one of the judges to BMLDOC's lawyer, "as though the government passed this statute for the purpose of interfering (with) religious beliefs." No, BMLDOC was not arguing that; they were arguing only that an ancillary effect of the Act was to deny Navajos access to certain shrines: hogans. Hogans, argued BMLDOC, are shrines because "that's where ceremonies take place." Navajos would need in essence then occupancy of the areas.

The court questioned the Government's attorney, telling him, "You're wiping out the religion of these people, that's what the complaint says. You're destroying it. The most fundamental Western religion we know is Judaism. And it has the same view of the land as sacred. If you said 'oh, that's irrelevant, that doesn't apply to Orthodox Judaism" you would be destroying that religion." "I understand your point," countered the Government's attorney, "but the Hopi as well as the Navajo have land based religion. They can't have a land-based religion on the very land the Navajos are on. If they go to claim that these are religious shrines of the Hopi we have a very curious problem. That could take us to Jerusalem."

It did, figuratively speaking. "Welcome to Jerusalem," opened the Hopi Tribal attorney. " "The Hopi go out to these areas and collect herbs, and they have a number of shrines ... that they go out to and try to use. We have a very serious problem where both religions are coming up against one another."

"If there was a settlement conference between the government and the Navajo would you boycott it? Take sort of a middle-eastern position?" "What if we were to provide you with a settlement process for you to discuss with an expert person experienced (in) achieving unbelievable success? Would you be willing to participate?" (U.S. Ninth Circuit Court 1991).

Mediation

Attorneys representing the Hopi Tribe, the Manybeads plaintiffs, and the U.S. Government affirmed that they would. The Circuit Court determined that "with the assistance of an experienced settlement mediator, there is a reasonable possibility that a settlement, satisfactory to the parties, can be achieved." The mediation was also to include issues appealed to the Ninth Circuit in the "New Construction" case involving alleged illegal construction by Navajo people of a hogan on HPL without Hopi written permission.

The Ninth Circuit ordered mediation on May 10, 1991. The Court selected magistrate Harry R. McCue from San Diego, California as mediator and brought in Government negotiators from the Departments of Justice and the Interior as well as the *Manybeads* plaintiffs' attorney. The Navajo Nation appointed its Navajo-Hopi Land Commission as its task team. McCue's success was indeed unbelievable: he did not achieve it.

Hopis' Objections to Mediation

The Hopi Tribe refused mediation at first, on the ground that, "every time someone tries to resolve the issue, the Hopi Tribe ends up losing more of its land and its resource base" (Hopi Tribe, 1993:2). Then, two things happened: First, in the summer of 1991, Magistrate McCue began obtaining written pledges on 3x5 notecards from a number of Navajo residents of HPL that they acknowledged HPL as being Hopi land. By early January, 1992, the magistrate could affirm that 116 HPL residents had committed themselves in writing to acknowledging that HPL is Hopi land. Second, Peterson Zah, President of the Navajo Nation, appeared personally before the Hopi Tribal Council and affirmed that the Navajo Nation acknowledged HPL as Hopi land. This was a turning point; it was the first time the Navajos had officially admitted this was not Navajo land.

Hopis' Ten Preconditions for Participating in Mediation

The Hopi Tribal Administration then finally agreed to mediation, even though from the very beginning, Hopis had no confidence that mediation would work. The Tribal administration responded to Navajos' unprecedented gesture of good faith and appointed a mediation task team from the Council. Each village appointed a representative from its Council delegation to the Task Team. Mishongnovi had no one involved in the Mediation Team, out of choice, and Shipaulovi did not have a certified representative at the time, and thus did not either. Thus the representatives s from First Mesa, Bacavi, Kykotsmovi, and Moenkopi, plus the Chairman, constituted the Team.

Before participating in mediation, however, the Hopi team stipulated that ten preconditions had to be met:

1. *The fencing gap at Big Mountain must be completed.* It was, without incident.

2. *The wall around Kiisivu -- Cliff Springs -- a Hopi religious shrine on the Navajo Reservation, constructed by the U.S. Public Health Service in the 1960s, must be removed and access must be guaranteed to Hopi religious shrines and eagle nests. The U.S. Government and the Navajo Tribe must agree to bar development near eagle nesting areas.* The wall was removed in 1992, but not without incident. Hopi religious leaders placed *pahos*, prayer feathers, at the shrine but were confronted by local Navajos who had not been informed about the agreement and regarded the Hopis as trespassers, confronted them and removed the *pahos*. The Navajo Nation issued an official apology regretting the incident. At one point the Navajo team proposed five-day notices for visiting shrines. The Hopi Tribe opposed this proposal on the grounds that it denied religious freedom. The Navajo Tribe and the U.S. Government eventually agreed to all points of precondition number two.

3. *The Coal Mine Mesa chapter compound must be removed.* As of 1993, the Navajo Nation had not yet removed the buildings on the compound, which included a day school and a communications facility as well as a chapter house, but had pledged to do so.

4. *The Big Mountain Survival Camp meeting hogan must be dismantled.* It was.

5. *No land exchanges will be contemplated, suggested, or discussed.* "The Hopi Tribe has lost over 90% of its aboriginal land base," asserted the Tribal administration, "entirely at the hands of the United States and the Navajo nation. At every step the Navajo have been rewarded for their aggression and the Hopi have been penalized for complying with the law. They refused to let the Hopi use the land when it was a joint use area, and they have refused to vacate the land partitioned to the Hopi even though the Hopi dutifully abandoned the land that was partitioned to the Navajo .. This is why the Tribe will never support a land exchange" (Hopi Tribe 1993:6).

6. *The Navajo Nation and Navajo residents of HPL must give their commitments in writing to acknowledging HPL as Hopi land.* By January, 1993, these commitments had been made.

7. *The Navajo Nation must enact a grazing ordinance applicable to NPL and must agree to prevent trespass by complying with notices giving owners five days to remove trespassing stock or have them impounded.* The Navajo Tribe did enact its grazing ordinance in 1992.

8. *Mae Tso's large hogan must be dismantled.* It was.

9. *Jurisdiction over grazing on HPL must be turned over to the Hopi Tribe.* The Interior Department agreed to do so in principle, but the Bureau of Indian Affairs took the position that enforcement, permitting, and impoundments are not contractible to the Hopi Tribe, citing statutory regulations.

10. *The Navajo Tribe agrees to pay rent for residents' use of HPL.* The Navajo Tribe started paying rent in installments in 1992.

The "Agreement in Principle"

By November, 1992, fifteen months of steady negotiations had produced a tentative settlement. The Hopi Tribal Council, the Navajo Nation, and the negotiators from the Departments of Justice and the Interior ratified the Agreement in Principle (AIP) on December 23 and 25, 1992. The attorney for the Manybeads Plaintiffs agreed to support the AIP fully and signed it, but his signature did not constitute ratification of the AIP by Manybeads plaintiffs. In fact, the *Manybeads* plaintiffs eventually refused to ratify the Agreement and thus it was never actually implemented. But the Agreement's provisions are worth close review since the Agreement represented the point closest to actual solution to the land dispute to which the two Tribal governments had come to in nearly 60 years of negotiations.

The Agreement (known as the "Agreement in Principle" and referred to hereafter as the "AIP") would have provided for the Hopi Tribe to accommodate Navajos on HPL with about 200,000 acres, consisting of 113 homesite leases of three acres each; up to ten acres of farmland; and a total of 2,800 sheep units,[90] nearly 1,200 more than the Government permitted them under PL 93-531, with four sheep units being equalled by each head of cattle. New structures would be permitted. The leases would run for 75 years and could be extended. Thus, they would be better than life estates. The Navajo Nation would pay the rent. The Hopi task team emphasized that 75 years was a minimum guarantee; if the lessees and their descendants proved to be good neighbors, arrangements might be extended beyond 75 years. Some Hopis even made an analogy with the Tano-Tewas, who were now, after nearly 300 years, the Hopi-Tewas. Judge McCue ordered meetings to be held throughout the HPL in which Hopi Tribal officials explained the lease and answered questions.

The AIP specified that the Hopi Tribe would have received 300,000 acres of state and private land; 200,000 acres of federal land; and $15 million from the U.S.Government. The Navajo Tribe would purchase private ranch land for the Hopi Tribe and provide the Hopi with a corridor from the new lands to the 1882 Reservation.

The U.S. Government pledged to purchase another ranch for the Hopis, and Hopis also would have received additional state acreage contiguous to the two ranches and to the federal lands to fill in gaps. The attorney for the Manybeads plaintiffs agreed to withdraw the appeal and accept the lower District Court's dismissal of it.

The Hopis agreed to cancel the Accounting, Owelty, Damage, Use Rental, and New Construction Lawsuits, thereby saving the Navajo Tribe close to $23 million, and the Trespassing lawsuit in the Court of Claims, thereby saving the U.S. Government possibly $270 million. The Hopi Tribe also pledged to ask the Court to drop the contempt citations against the Navajo Tribe for Navajos' construction in deliberate violation of the Court-imposed ban.

Reactions

The regional forester, a Government official having no connection with the negotiations, the Tribes, or the Court, leaked the terms of the settlement to the press the day before Thanksgiving Day, 1992. Reaction were swift. Although the Hopi Tribe affirmed that the moratorium on mining would be extended to these new lands but that existing permits, rights, privileges in the new lands would be honored for a five-to-six-year transition period; fees for camping, hunting, and livestock grazing would not be raised; the Forest Service's Multiple use concept now in force would be accommodated in terms of public use; and transfer of land from Forest Service ownership to Hopi trust status would not affect the applicability of environmental laws and the necessity for environmental assessment of any changes in land use, reaction from non-Indians was intense in its opposition, echoing opposition to the Navajo Tribe's efforts at purchasing land near the Vermillion Cliffs just north and west of Grand Canyon and of the Navajo Reservation in 1974. Arizona Senator De Concini even held congressional hearings in Flagstaff as a way of facilitating local non-Indians to organize against the AIP and start lobbying (Arnold and Porter 1993).

HPL residents held a diversity of opinions, and while some residents welcomed the opportunity to cooperate with Hopi jurisdiction, some were dead-set against the AIP. On April 1-4, 1993, a gathering of residents of Big Mountain rejected the proposed settlement because it did not allow them enough livestock or acreage and because they did not like the "concept of living under the jurisdiction of Hopi Courts and law, which are foreign to our traditions." Additionally, many HPL Navajos felt a good deal of anxiety about not being absolutely certain of passing on their assignment to future generations in perpetuity, or even of being barred from doing so.

Despite these sentiments the Hopi Tribe implemented "Phase Two" of the AIP in June, 1993: identifying HPL residents who wanted leases and would ratify the AIP. The Hopi Tribal administration made presentations on the AIP not only to Navajos on HPL but also to the Hopi villages.

Failure of the Agreement in Principle

Despite rejection of the AIP by Big Mountain residents in April, Hopi Tribal outreach began in May, 1993, and extended into June. The ratification deadline was extended from June 15 to August 5, 1993, when the *Manybeads* Plaintiffs met to vote on the AIP. Two-hundred-eight families attended the ratification meeting; two-hundred-seven rejected the AIP entirely (Henry and Sills 1994: 10). Reasons given were the lease provisions prohibiting the burial of human remains anywhere on HPL and placing the burden of relocation on a generation of HPL residents seventy-five years in the future. Hopi Tribal officials immediately suspended the outreach meetings with Navajo HPL residents.

Because efforts to get the AIP implemented ultimately failed, the Ninth Circuit may have to eventually rule on *Manybeads*. If dismissed, the constitutional grounds of freedom of religion on which it was presented might well be in jeopardy. But if affirmed, the argument would amount to a precedent that the U.S. could not accommodate. This precedent is one that says that access to land on a religious basis must be accommodated through occupation of that land. This precedent could be used as a basis for reopening the 1934 case and Hopis' making the same religious arguments with regard to shrines on 1934 as a basis for occupancy, and could lead to innumerable land claims by countless groups of indigenous peoples throughout the U.S., since virtually all indigenous religions are land-based.

Land Dispute Explanations I: Conspiracy Theory

The Mineral Imperative

The Agreement in Principle seemed to counter a long-standing argument by some Indians and non-Indians that Relocation had been brought about by a Mineral Conspiracy. Throughout the Land Dispute's recent thirty-year-long legal and legislative history, certain individuals "enigmatically seem to have appeared at every turn" (Sills 1986:61). Harrison Loesch, energy and natural resources consultant, was Assistant Secretary of the Interior for land Management when the Peabody leases were signed in 1964 and 1968 and when Steiger's partition bill was under consideration in 1972. In 1974, he lobbied for the Settlement Act as minority counsel for the Senate Interior Committee before becoming a Vice-President for Public Relations for Peabody Coal Company. By 1982 he had left that post and had become a lobbyist for the Relocation Commission in Washington. John Boyden, the Hopi Tribe's attorney, had negotiated the Peabody leases and also worked on the partition and relocation legislation during periods when his law firm represented Peabody Coal Company in unrelated legal dealings. Morris Udall, Chairman of the House Committee on Interior and Insular Affairs, was heavily involved in all the partition and relocation hearings and legislation of the 1970s and 1980s. Brother Stewart Udall, former Secretary of the Interior, had been heavily involved in the leasing of Navajo and Hopi coal and water to Peabody in the 1960s. The Udalls' great-grandfather was no one less than Jacob Hamblin, and their uncles were attorneys who represented, at various times, the Salt River Project and Tucson Gas and Electric Company, purchasers of electric power generated by Hopi and Navajo coal; and two of the Hopi mineral leaseholders: Sun Oil and Peabody Coal (Sills 1986).

Do these connections and coincidences mean anything? "There are some 23 billion tons of coal under Black Mesa. The Big Mountain community lies at the approximate center of the deposit. If the underground resources were ever to be exploited," note Sills et al. (1990:13), "the inhabitants of the surface would surely be in the way. The relocation program is a product of clear conflicts of interest on the part of the US itself, serving its own ends simultaneously as prosecutor, judge, jury, executioner, estate trustee, and fortuitous inheritor of a stolen patrimony." But Sills et al. stop short of charging conspiracy; they note a "vast confluence of interests" (Sills 1986:60; 1991:20).

Conspiracy theorists conclude, from the confluence of interests, that "the United States acted on behalf of large multinational corporations to clear up legal title to the former Joint Use Area. Big business and big government would then be able to exploit coal resources from the Hopi Tribe" (Gilmore and Schrichte 1991:15).

In fact, in response to one publication (Whitson and Roberge 1986), Peabody adamantly insisted that "Peabody Coal is not involved in any way in the Federal government's relocation of Navajo and Hopi Tribal members residing in the joint use area referred to as Big Mountain. Our

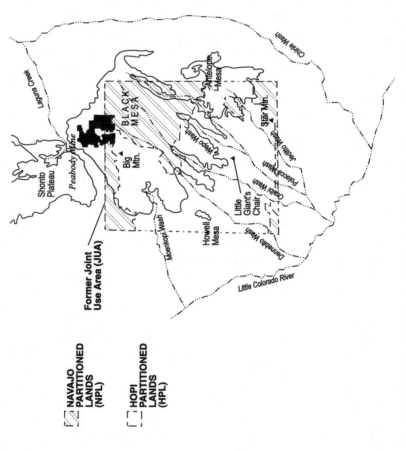

Big Mountain In Relation to Peabody Mine, Hopi Reservation, NPL

company never lobbied nor hired any one to lobby on our behalf for the passage of the Federal law which established the relocation program in 1974. Harrison Loesch had no involvement with the Navajo or Hopi Tribes nor Peabody's Arizona operations while employed by Peabody from 1976-81." Peabody also denied an intention of mining coal in the Big Mountain area (Greenfield 1986).

Smoking Memos? In place of a "smoking gun," only one "smoking memo" seems to have surfaced to support the conspiracy theory: a memorandum linking a legal claim by the Hopi Tribe to Peabody's intentions to use more water for two additional slurry lines for coal under Big Mountain. But Peabody did not get the lease for mining coal under Big Mountain and cannot get it unless the Hopi Tribal Council lifts its ban on mining and reverses itself on denial of Peabody's request for one. And even though the Hopi Tribe has exclusive control of the surface of HPL, relocation makes no changes in mining arrangements. Mineral interests on the FJUA (Former Joint Use Area, i.e., HPL and NPL) are still held jointly and equally by Hopi and Navajo, completely independent of surface rights. Neither tribe (sic) can engage in new mineral development without the consent of the other. While the Navajo Tribe has not banned mining and its position on Peabody's expansion of the lease onto Big Mountain is unknown, it can do no mineral leasing on HPL or NPL while the Hopi Tribe maintains its ban. Thus, "those who charge 'conspiracy' have yet to come up with evidence as to how the energy companies and government benefit from this arrangement" (Gilmore and Schrichte 1991:15).

Explanations II: "Determinisms": The Helpless Giant

Yet the fact that not only the relocation but also the coal leases were facilitated by the U.S. Government at every step cannot be denied. How *is* the role of the U.S. Government in a dispute between two Indian tribes to be accounted for? One view is that the U.S. Government has become trapped into becoming a reluctant arbitrator in a dispute "with no apparent comfortable resolution", "vulnerable to attacks by proponents of every persuasion" (Elston 1988:viii, xxii, xxv), a helpless giant caught in the grip of history. In this view, materialistic and historical processes make certain things nearly inevitable (cf. Harris 1979). Westward movement and population explosion of Americans pushed Navajos onto the most inhospitable lands. Tribes such as the Paiutes, Hopis, and Zunis just happened to be living there in little oases. A happenstance of history resulted in the U.S. Government neglecting to recognize Hopi land title either through treaty or other means, but assuming the "trust obligation" for each Tribe. Minerals were useless or irrelevant until the industrial age and until technological sophistication made their exploitation feasible and profitable. Conflicts between herders and farmers happen all the time (Elston 1988:xxv) (but of course, Hopis as well as Navajos are farmers and herders, simply with different settlement patterns). The U.S. Government found it had no choice but to intervene in the land dispute in order to settle the question of ownership of the mineral estate so the mineral estate could be exploited, and once having intervened to settle ownership questions, it had to assume the trust obligation for the individuals affected by the implementation of ownership rights, which eventually required partition and consequent relocation.

The historical materialist explanation accounts for why there did not have to be conspiracy and why there is a confluence of interests in the relocation situation. After all, the U.S. Government first heard complaints about Navajos from Hopis in 1849, and had complaints of its own through the 1860s. Following release from Bosque Redondo in 1868, however, Navajos constituted no threat to the U.S. Government or its citizens and Hopi complaints were ignored or handled haphazardly. Only when the drillers for Standard Oil's subsidiary, Midwest Petroleum, asked, "Who do we go to for a lease?" did the Government become interested in settling the question of what Indians owned which lands. But the Government could have simply left the minerals in joint ownership and let the Tribes and the mineral companies deal with any relocations. Why, then, spend more than a third-of-a-billion dollars and risk attraction of international attention on human rights issues?

Conclusion: Levels of Integration and Modernization

Explanation III: Tribes, Ethnicity, and Internal Colonialism

The Hopi-Navajo land dispute and its outcome involved more than just the interests of Hopis and Navajos. The dispute resulted from non-Indian jurisdiction, the history of bureaucratic control over Indians, and the transformation of land and resources into capital assets as well as political ones, as well as from conflicting interests of Hopis and Navajos. The dispute did not result from some primordial conflict between all Hopis and all Navajos, but it was also not a conspiratorial fabrication. The dispute and its attempted resolutions strengthened the ties through which Hopis are integrated into the national U.S. political system, while at the same time strengthening the distinction of Hopis as a"Tribe" on the local level with interests that are opposed to those of the Navajos as a "Tribe" on the local level.

Ethnicity. Since the Indian Reorganization Act, Indian tribes have had increasingly greater political voices as interest groups. Tribes are interest groups on the basis of being ethnic groups. Tribes are much more than mere ethnic groups, of course; they have a distinct legal status in U.S. law. They are semi-sovereign nations, on the one hand, and constitute "fingers" (not full arms) of the U.S. Government on the other. But the entire Hopi-Navajo land dispute and its legislative, legal, and bureaucratic resolution is *based on the assumption of ethnicity as the basis for the allocation and possession of material resources.* Despite more than 2,000 mixed Hopi-Navajo marriages (Elston 1988:114) and a probable 4,000 - 6,000 children of mixed Hopi and Navajo heritage, division of property rights and relocations have been implemented on the assumption that Hopis and Navajos are fundamentally separate from and at odds with one another, and furthermore, that it is easy to tell the difference between the two. Rather than a melting pot of pan-Indianism, the Hopi and Navajo reservations have been contexts in which ethnicity and tribalism have become reinforced and entrenched. The situation confirms political scientist Cynthia Enloe's (1972) assertion that modernization does not create melting pots but rather, promotes tribalism and ethnic groups as interest groups. With non-Indian voices also joining the dispute surrounding land use issues, in opposition to what some called the "Hopi land grab," ethnic competition became a three-way struggle.

Internal Colonialism. Internal colonialism refers to a process of national integration and centralization in which the products of one region (wool, arts and crafts, coal, uranium, oil, gas, electricity, water) are consumed in another, and in which the centers of decision-making are removed farther and farther (to Phoenix, Washington D.C., Los Angeles) from the local people (in Hotevilla, Shungopavi, Kykotsmovi, Tuba City, Window Rock). As peripheries of cores and satellites that are tied to metropolitan loci of power and wealth, the Hopi and Navajo Tribes experienced increasingly greater loss of autonomy and relative impoverishment, to the extent that Navajoland was characterized as a "third world scenario" as late as 1988 (Elston 1988). But Hopis and Navajos have experienced some reversal of that situation and increasingly greater degrees of local control since implementation of the "Buy Indian" contracts of the 1970s and the subsequent "Self-Determination" Act of 1975. This increase in local control corresponded to a pattern of administrative decentralization in American politics generally, and even in other parts of the world. Decision-making remained centralized, but implementation of decisions was tailored increasingly to regional, state, and local interests in the last three decades of the Twentieth Century.

In the case of Indian Tribes, local implementation depends on strong identification with local interests defined, in turn, by tribalism. Tribal governments are, on the one hand, fiercely nationalistic in defending the perceived interests of their people and, on the other, are inherently attached to U.S. dominant political institutions (Cornell 1988:206). In order to make local implementation work, Hopis had to maintain and even strengthen their distinctiveness from Navajos on the basis of having not only different interests in the same things (land, minerals, water) but also on the basis of being ethnically different from Navajos, which of course they are. McGuire (1992:816) even suggests that "'tribalization' replicated the political process of nation-state formation ... Tribes then assert their legitimacy in struggles against the state (and in this case against each other) by claiming to be nations, entitled to the same privilege as the nation-state they are in." Nationalism is the political principle holding that the political and ethnic unit should be congruent, requiring that a culture must have "its own political roof" (Gellner 1983:1-2, 43), that is, that the political boundaries of a territory that is nationally (or tribally) defined cannot include members of another nation; it must either expel or assimilate all non-nationals.

To the extent that these efforts have been successful, expansion and competition between ethnically based interest groups -- in this case the Hopi and Navajo Tribes -- can be expected to be maintained and even increase, but only, as one commentator has put it, "as far as the American government allows it to go" (Elston 1988:44-45). This rise in tribal ethnic nationalism is especially likely if rising expectations are confirmed following a long period of concerns based on relative deprivation. The Traditionalists' letter to the President of 1949 outlined those concerns.

When previously disadvantaged groups such as the Hopi begin to experience improved conditions and success in achieving goals, their sense of injustice will generally increase, rather than decrease, especially if comparisons are drawn between a previous "golden age" and "now." The analogy cannot be pushed too far, but the situation is not unlike that of Wales and Scotland with respect to England and perhaps also the linguistically and culturally different regions of France (Elsass, Occitan, Provence, Brittany, Flanders, etc). to the "Isle de France" and those of Catalan and Euskadi to Spain (Hechter 1975). Being Hopi, toughening it out, so to speak, was beginning to pay off by 1970. Hopi nationalism developed a hard edge and increasingly resisted outside interference in the areas of culture, religion, and tourism beginning in the early 1970s.

10

Repatriation: The Present, the Future, and Beyond

Repatriation refers to the return of an object belonging to one person or institution by a different person or institution. Repatriation of certain objects to Native American tribes and groups has been mandated by law since November, 1990, but repatriation in a broader sense refers to the return, or reassignment of control over, cultural materials from one group of people to the group from which those materials originated, and implies not only physical return of objects but also return of control over their interpretation.

In this case, of course, the term refers specifically to the return of control over Hopi cultural property to Hopi people. Repatriation assumes a commitment to what Cornell (1988:153) refers to as "segregative goals." Segregative goals "advocate a separation of Indian communities from the institutions of the larger society and the values they represent and the preservation or adoption of distinct institutional patterns specifically tailored to distinctive Indian needs, concerns, and historical experience. Segregative goals are fundamentally anti-assimilationist and anti-acculturational." Ironically, pursuing segregative goals often depends upon promoting integrative institutions, that is, those that increase the ties between Indian and non-Indian economic and political institutions, for example, between the federal government and Tribal Council governments, which "have a stake in the institutions of the larger society ... in which they are embedded, but also want to increase their autonomy" (Cornell 1988:155).

Hopis have been struggling with issues of control over Hopi culture for a century. The issues are played out in Hopis' relationships with the contemporary primitive art market, the museum collections made in the early part of the Twentieth Century when unilineal evolutionary anthropology held sway, in the general commodification of Hopi culture, and in tourism.

Tourism

For nearly seventy years, the scenario was the same: several days prior to Snake Dance the slow steady infiltration of tourists would have begun. In some of the villages the occasional meanderings of an early-arrived consumer of culture might raise cries of "Pahaana! Pahaana!" from children with residents hurrying to secure their private lives against potential intrusion. Eyes had to be sharp to make sure one of the tourists did not slip away down the mesa slope to surreptitiously pocket potsherds or prayer feathers. Villagers responded to their exciting and distressing presence with offers of Katsina doll carvings, basketry plaques, or pottery. Tolerated but resented, appreciated but deprecated, tourists were (and still are) sometimes burlesqued by clowns between summer Katsina dances in hilariously funny skits. Often they were portrayed by masked mudheads, *koyemsi*, the knobby-headed "mudheads" said to be the products of incestuous unions between members of the same clan from the previous world. Sometimes even real tourists were brought into the clowns' shenanigans for some good-natured ribbing.

Tourism is part of the relationship that metropolitan "core" areas have established with "peripheral" areas, and in the Hopi case, tourism has become an important economic sustainer. Metropolitan centers are concentrations of wealth and control over tourism. High levels of productivity in industrial society lead to more leisure activities, and to the commodification of culture. Generating the motivation of touristic impulses as well as the wealth to finance them occurs in the metropolitan centers. Tourist areas then serve their needs (Nash 1977) but also serve the periphery's needs by bringing into it some of the metropolis' wealth. The challenge to peripheral communities is then one of controlling the tourists and the tourist industry.

The U.S. Department of Commerce's Area Redevelopment Administration (ARA) surveyed tourism potential and the adequacy of water supply in the Hopi area in the 1960s. It recommended development, citing prehistoric ruins; arts and crafts; ceremonies; and the "Indian way of life" as resources. The Report (U.S. Department of Commerce 1964) did, however, note potential opposition by "traditional members of the tribe" (Rivera 1990:143-44). A large influx of tourists could prove problematic, warned the Report.

Tourists in Hopiland had always had to be prepared to rough it. For more than thirty years, only "Mrs. White" -- Polingaysi Qoyawayma (1964) -- offered rooms for rent, but following the death of her grand-nephew's wife in 1969, she assumed full-time care of her three very small great-grand nephews and niece that put an end to her taking-in of paying guests. The BIA constructed five small guest rooms in the 1950s which tourists could rent if they were vacant (Rivera 1990:145), and the McGee family built a small, ten-room motel next to their trading post-restaurant-laundromat-gas station in Keams Canyon in 1965. But most tourists came prepared to camp, either in the Tribally-run camp ground next to the trailer park at Keams, or at picnic areas next to the Arts and Crafts Guild at Second Mesa or at Tribal facilities near Oraibi Wash and Prophecy Rock. Tourist traffic picked up considerably after completion of paved roads in 1959 and 1960, and according to Armin Geertz (1987b), publication of Frank Waters' *Book of the Hopi* sent hordes of people out to the Hopi Mesas seeking the exotic. Tourists eventually came to resemble pilgrims pursuing a prophetic destiny: the witnessing of a spiritual, non-materialist Hopi antidote to the commercial secularization of modern daily life in the American metropolis.

The Cultural Center. The outcome of the ARA's study was the Hopi Cultural Center. The Hopi Cultural Center was planned by Hopi advisors and was a joint project of the Economic Development Administration, which contributed $582,000 for its construction, and the Hopi Tribe, which supplied $144,700. Opening in June, 1971, the Center would prove by far to be the best investment the Council ever could have made in improving the cash flow and multiplier effects of dollars coming into the Reservation economy.

The ARA Report of 1964 did indeed prove prophetic: organized tourism became increasingly problematic. In 1966 and 1967, large numbers of "hippies" descended upon the Hopi villages (cf. Courlander 1982:137-41). Before long, insensitivity and bad manners caused them to wear out their welcome; Hotevilla's villagers would not allow Agency police into the village to evict the "hippies," but withdrew their hospitality. By the end of 1968, the "hippies" had left, finding more karmic magnets elsewhere.[91]

But the "hippies" were a much less enduring problem than ordinary tourists. By 1973, Mishongnovi had decided to ban all non-Indians from its August Snake Dance. Contravening the Winslow and Flagstaff Chambers' of Commerce advertisements, Mishongnovi's Kikmongwi announced the dance would be closed. But it was too late. The announcement did not hit the press and radio waves until the day before Antelope Dance, which precedes Snake Dance by twenty-four hours. The tourists had already arrived, filling the picnic areas and the Cultural Center's motel. At the last minute, Mishongnovi's Snake Chief contravened the Kikmongwi's announcement and opened the dance to non-Indians.

Why did some Hopis want to close the dances to tourists? Tourists continued to violate Hopi law and failed to observe common courtesy:

some tried to sneak photographs; others wandered about, poking their heads into private homes and tramping down the slopes of the mesas where there were shrines off-limits to the uninitiated. Prayer feathers and potsherds disappeared into pockets and purses. And then there was the sheer crush and clutter that two or three thousand people, all arriving in cars and buses, brought to village residents. They parked anywhere and everywhere; crowded into the plaza; and overloaded the flat tops of the houses and jarring loose the dried-mud roofing materials and sending dirt and sand cascading through ceilings and over residents, onto tables and into stew pots below. The real question is why Hopis tolerated and even encouraged tourists for so long, and why they appear to have reversed their stand on outside visitors rather abruptly. The answer to the question lies in politics, economics, culture, and society.

Politics, Economics and Society: The 1970s and 1980s

By the 1980s, the Hopi Tribal Government was providing over 450 jobs -- about 45% of the jobs available. (Robinson 1986). Per capita incomes had risen to $2,232 in 1986 (Robinson 1988) and to $4,865 as reported by the U.S. Census Bureau in 1990. Cattle almost completely replaced sheep in terms of livestock; approximately 8,400 "animal units"[92] were being grazed on Hopi land in 1978 (Qua Toqti 1980b), with cattle probably representing 90% of those units, that is, about 7,500 head. The U.S. Census Bureau reported that the number of families owning livestock had risen from 544 in 1942 to 667 in 1989 (Colby et al. 1990). Unemployment went down steadily, from 37% in 1986 (Robinson 1988) to 28.7% in 1990 (compared to 55% for all Native Americans). Median household income, $7,470 in 1980 rose to $13,750 in 1990. The number of families below poverty level was reduced from 50.5% in 1980 to 45% in 1990. And as of 1986, 80% of Hopis lived on-reservation (Robinson 1988). Hopi-owned shops supplanted the trading posts as arts and crafts outlets, and according to the Census Bureau, some Hopi artisans and artists were earning up to $50,000 a year from sales of arts and crafts by 1979 (Wyckoff 1990:72). Hopi-owned small businesses proliferated generally; clan land near the hiway became important for its commercial value. One of the most successful Hopi businessmen, a large cattle owner and member of a long-time trading family, was appointed the first Hopi to be Superintendent of the BIA's Hopi Indian Agency. Another successful businessman, owner of the Hopicrafts silver enterprize and of a construction company, Pueblo Builders, began publishing an excellent weekly newspaper (*Qua' Toqti*). Utilizing wage labor, animal husbandry, farming and craft production, most households were self-sustaining.

By the 1990s, all but about 400 households had electric power lines running to them and every household had at least one late-model sedan, with usually a pickup in addition. Donkeys were virtually non-existent. Hardly a single Hopi was without a television set and sometimes two and a VCR, while continuing to make do without running water or even outhouse. At least 20% of the households had telephones. The Traditionalist leaders of Old Oraibi and Hotevilla, however, concerned about preserving the autonomy and sovereignty of village entities, still resisted electricity, not wanting people to become "hooked" on public utility power. A private foundation offered a compromise: solar electric systems. Between 1987 and 1991 it executed design and installations of solar electric systems to more than fifty Hopi homes (Lomasumi' nangwtukwsiwmani 1991:6-7). Thus the Traditionalists, resisters of a kind of technological modernization that had become commonplace in America by 1950, were in the vanguard of embracing a kind of technological modernization symbolic of the new deep ecological consciousness of the Twenty-first Century.

These improving material conditions were not mere accidents of history or due solely to U.S. Government intervention. They resulted at least in part from the rational pursuit of goals that were carefully calculated by the Hopi Tribal Council. By the 1980s, the Tribe had constructed two additional buildings to accommodate its administrative offices and had established the Office of Hopi Lands to deal with the Hopi Partitioned Lands (HPL) resulting from the 1974 legislation which the Tribe had lobbied through Congress. Through partial incorporation into U.S. political and administrative structures, the Hopi Tribal Government was getting about $800,000 annually in transfer payments for its citizens, based on eligibility criteria of people serviced through U.S. Government contracts and programs. Most tribes are heavily dependent on such transfer payments. But more than 60% of the Hopi Tribal Government's revenues come from private sources. Upwards of seven million dollars annually come into Tribal coffers from mineral leases. Elected "Village Boards", established in the 1970s to administer revenue-sharing monies allocated by the Tribal Council, began to also administer village budgets provided from Peabody coal revenues in the 1980s.

The Economic Benefit of Tourism Recedes. To put it bluntly, by the 1980s, Hopis no longer needed tourists in the same way that they once did. The tourist industry continues to be an economic asset, but it no longer means the difference between surviving comfortably and merely surviving, as it once did, even as late as the 1970s. Religion and cultural traditions were cited as more important than tourism and tourism was cited as potentially to them. As one Hopi woman put it, "'People sell food and concessions to tourists who are permitted to watch the dances. It's a sacrilege, because we're really depending on rain now, not money'" (Barnett 1990:140). But as economic problems have receded into the past, cultural and social ones loom ever larger.

Society in the 1980s

Accusations of witchcraft continued to be common in the 1980s (Wyckoff 1990:25) and conflict in general persisted and even escalated, with fights, murders and suicides on the increase. The BIA built a new courtroom - jail complex near Keams Canyon. The Council planned an ambulatory care facility for the 1990s to replace the U.S. Public Health Service's policy of sending Hopis to Phoenix for such long-term treatment. It built and staffed dental and health clinics at Second Mesa and, under contract from the Indian Health Service, it initiated community health services in 1969 including patient transportation, an elders program, dialysis support, and a program for the developmentally disabled. A registered nurse was hired to make the rounds of the BIA day, contract, and public schools, and Tribal Social and Mental Health Services provided educational, guidance, child abuse, marriage, and alcoholism counseling. In 1978 the Tribe opened an alcoholism rehabilitation center and half-way house in the old school building at Toreva, below Second Mesa. "All Hopis see the violence and death that has come from alcohol abuse," noted a workshop flyer in 1987, "... within the family, the village, the work place and sadly within the kiva." The possibilities of dealing with survival issues through craft sales, political alliances, and cash income that tourists once had provided, had been replaced by the necessities of dealing with problems for which tourists could not possibly offer any help.

Culture in the 1980s and 1990s

In the 1980s the Tribal Council completed construction of a "Civic Center." Partially funded from a Department of Commerce grant, on a site between Kykotsmovi and Shungopavi off highway 264, it was outfitted like a combination auditorium - gymnasium with a stage and a springy, polished oak floor. Unsuccessfully contested by an elderly Oraibi man who claimed it was being built on his clan land without permission, its completion provided a locus for functions so necessary to modern life in the West: conferences, basketball games, rock concerts, western dances. Tribal health, mental health, and planning conferences during the week alternated with Rodeo dances and rap groups on weekends. In a move to revive the long-standing tradition of running associated with ceremonies such as the Snake Dance, the Tribe instituted the annual "Lewis Tewanima Memorial" footrace in honor of the famous Hopi olympic gold medal winner, and a private non-profit foundation also began sponsoring annual races. Reggae bands came to the Civic Center all the way from Jamaica and fans streamed in from Phoenix, Albuquerque, and Salt Lake. During *Powamuya*, a Santa Claus Katsina could be seen distributing gifts (Loftin 1991:109), and almost overnight, young Katsina doll carvers changed their styles from realistic to representational.

At First Mesa and Moenkopi, the Baptist church experienced a steady growth in attendance, while at Third Mesa the Mennonites turned their church and buildings over to the village of Bacavi and, reduced to a handful of stalwart Hopi converts, held services only at the aging white clapboard church in Kykotsmovi. Nonetheless the Mennonite Mission school continued to offer an alternative to the BIA day schools through the eighth grade. At Second Mesa, Hopis continued to patronize the Sunlight Baptist Mission while vigorously participating in traditional Hopi ceremonies. In fact, the number of children initiated into Powamayu and Katsina societies mushroomed at all villages.

In general, some traditions were well on their way to being institutionalized at the same time that innovations were being made. The ritual gathering and ceremonial sacrifice of eagles and hawks at the time of Niman had become something in which many Hopis participated whether they took part in other ceremonies or not, and interest in crafts increased as federal grants became available for elders to teach the craft of making yucca and willow-splint sifter and peach baskets and piki trays, as well as embroidery and twilling. At Hotevilla, corn planting in spring continued to be a group communal activity for some clans. Clan exogamy still largely regulated marriage, although some marriages and liaisons were known among people of the same clan or clan group but of different matrilineages, and marriages between people of different villages as well as between Hopis and other Indians -- mainly Navajos -- were on the increase. Clan and secret society "chiefs" still exercised their prerogatives in determining ceremonial performances and withholding certain ceremonies by withholding *wuyas*. Villages remained the basic sociopolitical units.

Yet technological modernization accelerated apace. Satellite dishes installed along the mesas brought television programs from Chicago and Denver, and the Secakuku family built a new, pueblo-style (but not pueblo-deco) supermarket near its old trading post. The Navajo Tribe developed a bus system with service to the Hopi villages twice a day, and HUD homes and trailers dotted the landscape along Highway 264.

The Hopi Tribe installed computers and word processors in its administration buildings, and the parking lot outside the complex at Kykotsmovi was often so crowded 9-5 Mondays through Fridays (deserted on weekends) that parking was impossible.

The Tribe embarked on an aggressive enrollment campaign, trying to account for every Hopi individual and put them all on the Tribal rolls, following approval of a constitutional amendment by referendum that permitted children of Hopi fathers and non-Hopi mothers to become enrolled if not already enrolled in some other tribe. As 1991 gave way to 1992, Tribal politics continued as usual, with the Council once again, as in the past, facing gridlock due to lack of a quorum. From December, 1991 through April, 1992, Hotevilla, Shungopavi, and Lower Moenkopi had once again been joined by other villages in their boycott. Under threat of losing BIA contracts, however, the Council eventually achieved its quorum.

Education became a major priority. Northland Pioneer College, a state community college based in Flagstaff, began offering college classes in Hopi communities. The Council persuaded the BIA to built a Hopi High School on the Reservation. And Hopis began experimenting with an innovative curriculum at Hotevilla School.

Hotevilla-Bacavi School. Under the "Buy Indian Contract" policy, the BIA had set up advisory school boards of Hopi parents for all the Hopi day schools in 1969. In response to long-standing complaints about Hotevilla Day School, the retiring non-Indian principle was replaced in 1970 by Vernon Masayesva, a Hotevilla-born Hopi with a B.S. in education from University of Arizona and a former assistant director of the Hopi Action Program. Acting in conjunction with the Advisory Board, Masayesva began making changes that would reflect priorities developed by Hopis rather than by the BIA. An emphasis on "things Hopi" replaced deference to "things Euro-American." But when the school purchased kilns and began pottery instruction in 1971, potters from First Mesa announced their opposition on the grounds that pottery-making was the right of certain clans in certain villages and none of those clans were in Hotevilla. The ladies smashed the school's kilns to make their point (Wyckoff 1990:81).

Other innovations were better received, at least for a time. Changing its name to Hotevilla Bacavi Community School in 1974, the school instituted evening and recreational activities for adults and students as well as a GED program and various classes for college credit through Northern Arizona University. A grant from the National Endowment for the Humanities brought consultants from the two villages into classrooms to assist with instruction in weaving, sports, construction, auto mechanics, "environmental literacy," "Ethnic Heritage studies," and Hopi language.

In 1976 the Tribal Council sought a direct contract from the BIA under the Indian Self-Determination Act and the 1978-79 school year began with the school being entirely administered under a subcontract by the Hotevilla Bacavi Community School Board of Education. The school's statement of philosophy, developed by the school board and administration, reflected the kind of experiential, individually-tailored, multicultural approach advocated by John Dewey and pioneered by John Collier: levels of learning that progressed from the concrete to the abstract; a curriculum structured "according to the levels of development of the children;" and adjustment of the curriculum to the child rather than the child being adjusted to the curriculum. "Evaluation should include assessment of the learning process as well as subject matter knowledge," averred the statement (Rhodes 1985). The little school became a symbol of Hopi cultural resurgence and control over the affective aspects of modernization.

In 1978 the consultant positions were converted to full-paid assistant teacher positions filled by Hopis, and 1980 and 1981 seventh and eighth grades were added. At the same time, actual grades were abolished and replaced by "developmental levels defined by the Swiss educational psychologist, Jean Piaget" (Rhodes 1985). An optional year-round school was begun in 1980, and truly bilingual, bicultural education was implemented. Funding levels, largely subsidized by a total of fourteen separate grants supplementing the BIA contract of $2,000 per pupil, went from $150,000 in 1970 to a high of over $900,000 in 1981, but had dropped back to levels of the late 1970s by 1984. With a tripling of Hopi employees from nine out of fourteen in 1970 to twenty-eight of forty-two in 1980, the school became a substantial economic contributor. Emphasizing spontaneity, creative and plastic arts, personalized curriculum, and minimal instruction, the school promoted self-motivation, development of strong, positive self-images, and fulfillment of each child's unique requirements. Older youngsters were encouraged to teach younger ones, in the traditional Hopi way of enculturation, and the teacher's role was changed to that of facilitator rather than instructor and disciplinarian. Traditional arts, hands-on learning-by-doing, and emphasis on life skills and community involvement made the school more of a Hopi institution than any other school, before or since, on the reservation. But in 1984 the Council and the BIA -- and even some of the parents -- put the brakes on accelerated innovation. The school returned to a "BIA educational philosophy" and Masayesva resigned (Rhodes 1985), later acquiring the post of Tribal Vice-Chairman and being elected Tribal Chairman in 1989.

The Nature of Cultural Property

But while the Hotevilla-Bacavi School was using modern methods to encourage Hopi customs, traditions and language, Hopi cultural property was slipping away and being usurped in an alarming fashion. In traditional Hopi life, people are exhorted to remember their heritage by living it through constantly and oft repeated rituals. In the security of such rituals, the doors and windows of intuitive memory are opened, letting fears and anguish fall away for a time. But without the proper ceremonial equipment, those ceremonies cannot be performed. And even for Hopis who are not involved in ceremonialism, cultural property is heritage, a source of collective memory that preserves identity.

Cultural property is any collectively-held heritage, material or non-material, not created for sale or for purposeful dissemination, that can be traced to a specific cultural and historical origin. Religious items are one obvious category. Other categories are national prehistoric treasures of nation-states and the cultural-historical items of indigenous peoples such as Inca weavings and Iroquois wampum belts (Gillette 1970; American Indian Historical Society 1970a, 1970b; Akwesasne Notes 1971).[93]

The Tourism Debates

The 1970s and 1980s brought increasing controversy over tourists. Walpi, Oraibi, and Moenkopi erected new signs advising appropriate behavior. The Council authorized the "Walpi Restoration Project," funded by federal grants, which included an archaeological component headed by Arizona State Museum archaeologist E. Charles Adams (1982; 1989:79,84). Walpi's religious leaders supervised the project carefully; it was one of the earliest cases of successful collaboration between archaeologists and Native Americans (cf. McGuire 1992:829). The project yielded a collection of artifacts that went on tour to museums, coordinated by the Museum of Northern Arizona. Following reconstruction and stabilization of the buildings, the Council tried to systematically control tourism by offering guided visits of reconstructed Walpi, now inhabited by fewer than thirty people, to groups of tourists that happened to show up. It also issued a four-page handout on newsprint including a list of guidelines for tourists, a short history of the Hopi people, and a summary of Hopi religion.

At the entrance to Oraibi, the Council erected a sign reading: "Visitors are welcome in Old Oraibi. Please obey the following regulations: 1) No picture taking 2) No fees for entering 3) Crafts may be purchased from individual Hopis." A few yards closer to the village another sign advised visitors, "No pictures. Ask permission to enter here. (Arrow) Park here." The arrow pointed to the home of John and Mina Lanza, where Mina, "strongwilled and fiercely traditional," warned visitors not to take photographs or pick up anything, and to stay in the village and avoid religious shrines (Clemmer 1978a:35; Rivera 1990:154). But the problems continued. Finally, in 1976, Mina erected a sign closing the village to all "white visitors." The closure was uniformly enforced, even for patrons of the Hopi-operated Hopiland Tours. Although briefly opened again in 1979 by Kikmongwi Stanley Bahnimptewa, who charged tourists a dollar, it was closed again in 1982 and remained so until 1987.

Tourists at religious dances also continued to spark debate. Once again in 1975, an announcement was sent out closing Mishongnovi's Snake Dance. A counter-announcement came from the Snake Chief that the Dance would *not* be closed. "When you turn people away, it is the same as chasing the rainclouds away," he said. The announcement alleged that a "dissident faction," composed of some Snake Society members but also of some political activists from other villages had sent out the closure notices. These were, of course, the proponents of the Traditionalist Movement. But the Snake Priest also "charged that those attempting to bar the *Pahaanas* were the same persons who had spent much time travelling throughout the United States and abroad 'exposing and exploiting the sacred rituals of the Hopi.'" Thus did the traditionalist-progressivist arguments become embedded in arguments over tourism (Rivera 1990:161).

But commitment to Hopi values and to a traditionally historical interpretation continued to clash with economic concerns. The publisher of *Qua' Toqti*, a convert to Mormonism and a partner in operating the Cultural Center under lease as well as owner of Pueblo Builders, a contracting firm, the Hopicrafts silversmithing shop and retail outlet, and "Hopiland Tours", opposed banning tourists. "I know several little old ladies on First Mesa," he wrote in an editorial, "who kept warm and fed themselves all winter long with dignity and without welfare, all because some *Pahaanas* kept knocking on their doors and took their pottery away" (Rivera 1990:159).

In 1977 Mishongnovi finally closed its Snake Dance to non-Hopis forever. The following year, Niman and Flute Ceremony were closed, and by 1982 Bean Dance and So'yoko/Natacka were also closed. By 1989 all three Second Mesa villages had closed all ceremonies, and in 1991 Walpi followed suit. Only the Third Mesa villages kept Katsina dances and Bean Dance open, with Hotevilla having the only open Niman ceremony.

The Council tried to maintain tourism while respecting the Traditionalists' insistence on not sacrificing religion and peace of mind to commodification of culture and to economic cash flow. Cultural preservation and visitor control program ordinances that would have set up organized tourism with fees and guides were proposed to the Council but never enacted. In 1986, permits to conduct bus tours were canceled for the Fred Harvey, Ray Manley, and Nava-Hopi companies, although later the Council issued a special temporary permit to allow the Harveycars to continue their "elder hostel" tours. The Council continued to offer tours of Walpi. But proposals for an Office of Tourism were put on hold and the Council tabled plans for a second "Cultural Center" motel complex at Moenkopi when Lower Moenkopi's Kikmongwi and villagers objected. In August, 1990, in conjunction with the Arizona Tourism Bureau, the Council sponsored a tourist survey that revealed tourism as the source of millions of dollars in income and cash flow, and there was once again talk of some sort of organized, managed tourism, perhaps including the ruins of Awat'ovi (Rivera 1990:167-177).

Intellectual Cultural Property

Yet the dilemma of balancing tourism's economic benefits against the commodification of culture rasies a crucial question of just how far economic and political integration can proceed without forcing a certain degree of cultural and social integration and unanticipated acculturation, as well as how much control Tribes should have outside of their territorial boundaries.

For examples, in 1990 a linguist's proposed book on the Hopi Salt Journey, detailing the ritual route to the Salt Shrine in Grand Canyon in Hopi and English texts, was opposed by the Tribal Council as "revealing what should remain closely guarded knowledge transmitted only to a few privileged religious initiates" (Raymond 1990). Above all, Hopis feared that thousands of people would flock to the sacred trial and desecrate the shrines located along it. Representatives met with the author to request that he not proceed with plans to publish the book, which he had co-authored with a recently deceased Hopi Tribal member. When the author refused to withdraw the book from publication, the Council passed a motion declaring him *persona non grata*, stopping just short of excluding him from the Hopi reservation (Hopi Tribe 1990). Eventually, however, Tribal and scholarly pressure prevailed; the author voluntarily agreed not to have it published.

Hard on the heals of this modest victory, however, came the publication of a comic book in early 1991 featuring a story about

"Traditionalist" and "Progressive" factions of a southwestern Tribe suspiciously like the Hopi, with the "Traditionalists" retreating to a long-abandoned prehistoric cliff-dwelling and the "Progressives" being duped by non-Indian gangsters into signing leases for gambling casinos. When a couple of young Tribal sleuths catch onto the shenanigans, the gangsters don facsimiles of masks used in Hopi religious ceremonies and attack them with machines guns and chain saws.

When Hopi youngsters re-appeared at their parents' cars during trips to town toting the comic book, Hopis' outrage was universal and unremitting. Religious leaders and Tribal administrative officials called for the comic book to be withdrawn from circulation. It was, but not before thousands of readers -- Indian and non-Indian alike -- had been exposed to the sacrilege. Disgusted religious leaders at the First and Second Mesa villages closed the last of the ceremonies open to non-Indians.

Hopi Repatriation: A Short History

But the complex and myriad issues surrounding the possession of cultural property of a religious nature may prove far more challenging than those surrounding the closing or non-closing of the ceremonies themselves to non-Indians. In 1936, while working at the Museum of New Mexico in Santa Fe, Hopi artist Fred "Nakayoma" Kabotie discovered two large "Corn maiden" masks stored in the basement. Each had an elaborate "tablita" headdress and Kabotie concluded they "could only have been the legendary Hopi *Shalako Mana*." He portrayed the masks in paintings, showing them worn by the ten-foot-high Hopi Shalako figures, in their ceremonial context. He brought the paintings home to show to his grandfather and to his uncle, Andrew Hermequaftewa. His grandfather "explained that the ceremony hadn't been performed for at least seventy-five years," since the series of droughts, famines, and smallpox epidemics between 1852 and 1868 that had so greatly reduced the Hopi population. Andrew Hermequaftewa felt that the Hopi Shalako should be revived. Kabotie's grandfather, although a youth at the time, had participated in the ceremony and remembered some of the songs and details. Other masks necessary for the ceremony were taken from their secret hiding places and in July, 1937, the Shalako ceremony was performed once again at Shungopavi after a lapse of 75 or 80 years (Kabotie 1977:65-66). It has been performed every five to ten years ever since.

The ceremony could not have been revived if the masks had not been repatriated. It turned out that they belonged not to the Museum, but rather, to Frank and Betty Applegate, two of the pioneer "Santa Fe artists" who had been among those who joined the All-Indian Pueblo Council, John Collier, Mabel Dodge, Witter Bynner and others in fighting Circular 1665 and the Bursum Bill a decade earlier. They had purchased the masks from a Hopi policeman, Pat Tawawani, but realizing that they should not own the two masks, they returned them, purportedly to the same Pat Tawawani (Wright 1982), who presumably turned them over to Andrew Hermequaftewa, sponsor of the 1937 Shalako. The incident not only demonstrates the religious importance of repatriating ceremonial objects, but also emphasizes the points that items which are placed in storage are not necessarily discarded forever, and that, prophecy or no prophecy, ceremonies are revived and re-instituted after long and what may seem to be irrevocable lapses precipitated by material, demographic, and social conditions.

Museums

"Looted artifacts form the backbone of major museum collections throughout the world," noted Winifred Creamer of the Field Museum in 1990, "and the kinds of objects acquired from looting vs. research are sharply different. Looting provides whole objects, paragons of the civilization they represent. Research sample may include equivalent works of art, but surrounded by the detritus of life, often substantially less glamorous than a singular objet d'art." Nonetheless, looted objects turn out to be important in many museums' collections. Laws passed in 1906, the 1930s, 1960s, and 1970s still impose penalties for looting but these laws defined Indian sites as archaeological resources, not as cultural patrimony, thus maintaining, effectively, the blurring of differences between objects acquired for research and those acquired from looting. To correct this situation and in response to more than twenty years of protests and lobbying by Native Americans, Congress enacted the Native American Graves Protection and Repatriation Act (PL 101-601). As of November, 1990, museums must return objects no matter how they were acquired if the appropriate Native American individual or Tribe makes a request.

The Act provides for the return of "sacred objects," specific ceremonial objects which are needed for the practice of traditional Native American religions by their present day adherents, and of "cultural patrimony," objects "having ongoing historical, traditional, or cultural importance to the Native American group or culture and cannot be alienated." The Act (known as NAGPRA) covers all federal agencies and all museums receiving federal funds and all collections in colleges and universities receiving federal funds, regardless of whether they are public or private. Requests for return of objects can be made by individuals who can demonstrate that they are lineal descendants of an individual who owned the object; or by a tribe or organization that can show that the object was owned or controlled by the tribe or organization.

The Act's framers anticipated conflicting claims, for obvious reasons. The NAGPRA specifically conceptualized "individual ownership" of objects, but denied their status as disposable property. This provision moved Congress farther toward empowering tribalism than any Act since the Indian Reorganization Act. But in the return of an object, whose claim would take precedence? The lineal descendent of a known owner? Or the Tribe? And among lineal descendants, which one? Competing claims that could not be resolved would result in the disputed item being held in custody indefinitely by the agency or museum until the claimants themselves could come to agreement.

Within weeks of the Act's passage, the Hopi Tribal Chairman notified the Heard museum in Phoenix that Hopis would eventually like twenty-five Katsina masks in the Heard's collection to be returned. The masks were part of a collection, never displayed, acquired from the Fred Harvey Company in the 1960s and had probably been "collected" by H.R. Voth in 1912, following the Oraibi split. The Museum agreed to keep the masks off display, but made no immediate plans to return them.

In 1992 the Heard did return a shield to religious leaders of the Soyal secret society from Oraibi after they had been tipped off that the Heard had it. The shield, also never displayed, had been stolen sometimes in the mid-to-late 1970s and sold to an Arizona dealer, ostensibly for $50 (Barnett 1990:147). It changed hands several times but eventually ended up in the hands of a "reputable dealer" from whom the Museum acquired it in 1978. The purchase price was paid by one of the Museum's regular donors. The Hopi Tribal Chairman wrote to the Museum asking that it be returned, and the Heard agreed (Sackler et al. 1992). But because Oraibi's Soyal society had split into three separate societies at Hotevilla, Bacavi, and Oraibi between 1897 and 1910, there were several possible claimants. The shield's return came after what one journalist described as "weeks of delicate secret negotiations among Oraibi, the museum, and the Hopi tribal government, which has been at odds with the traditional leaders" (Brinkley-Rogers 1992).[94]

Collecting? or Looting?

Finer lines than one would suspect separate craft products made for commercial markets such as tourists; products made for museums; craft items collected for museums; items collected for private collections and the commercial "primitive art" market; and items falling into the category of "found objects" that enhance the prestige of the finder by affirming his or her "bold taste" or "glorious adventuring." J. W. Powell, founder of the Bureau of American Ethnology, had collected ceremonial and technological items in Oraibi in 1870.

Ethnographer Frank Cushing initiated the museum market for Hopi material culture in 1882 by making collections of "more than twelve hundred specimens" for the Smithsonian Institution. Alexander Stephen paid potters to make replicas of ancient forms and designs. Along with Thomas Keam, Stephen had already been collecting Hopi pottery for some time, paying Nampeyo and other potters to make reproductions of ancient forms and designs. Keam virtually invented the painted pottery tile as an art form, making tile molds for Hopi artisans to use. They did the art work, but it was Keam who had invented the art form and perhaps the market for it as well. Thus it was Thomas Keam, a trader, and Alexander Stephen, an ethnographer, who increased the commercial market for Hopi material culture.

But it was J.W. Fewkes' purchase of Thomas Keam's collection for the second Hemenway Expedition that intertwined the commercial market thoroughly with the museum market; artists such as Nampeyo who got their starts making pottery for sale to these museum collectors went on to become successful commercial potters for private collecting. A Dr. Joshua Miller of the Arizona Antiquarian Association, who was "interested in museum business" wanted to excavate Hopi cemeteries in 1901 (Seaman/Nequatewa 1993:122). It was the private collecting of pottery, blankets, baskets and silver by Santa Fe's artists and writers that formed the inspiration for building the Laboratory of Anthropology Museum (Laughlin 1982; Weigle and Fiore 1982:19-21).

The Chicago exhibitions had not only touched off a collecting craze for Hopi religious and artistic artists, but also resulted in some commissioned replicas being made. Missionary-ethnographer Heinrich Voth not only collected items, but also manufactured Hopi altars and collected ceremonial paraphernalia for the Harvey Company's "Indian room" at Albuquerque's Alvarado Hotel; for Chicago's Field Museum; for the Santa Fe Railroad Exposition of 1895; for the Harvey Company's "Hopi House" at Grand Canyon; and for the Heye Foundation's Museum of the American Indian.

Exhibiting

It was Nampeyo's sale of her pottery to Thomas Keam and Alexander Stephen in the 1880s and later to Fewkes in 1890-92 that resulted in her demonstrating pottery-making at the Santa Fe Railroad Exhibition at the Columbian Fair in Chicago in 1895 (Nequatewa 1943:42; Walker and Wyckoff 1983:28-29); at Grand Canyon along with other Hopi artisans in 1904-05 and 1907; in 1910 again in Chicago; and at the "American Indian Village" San Diego's Panama-Pacific Exhibition of 1915. Thus, beginning as artisans-for-museums, Hopis became artisans-for-the-market and finally cultural specimens organized and labelled for display.

World fairs and commemorative exhibitions are examples of the surge in labelling items (and people and cultures) for display (Mitchell 1989:212) that began in the Victorian era and persisted until 1940. The "Victorian ecumeme," which encompassed the United States as well as Great Britain and Europe, developed the concept of the "cultural other" (Breckenridge 1989:197) and the concept of "savage" ethnographic items and intellectual creations that they thought were in danger of fading away with their creators and becoming relics of the past (Rose 1992:402-409). It was this conviction that "primitives" were "fading away" that compelled much of the ethnography, collecting, exhibiting, and displaying of cultural artefacts in the last Nineteenth and early Twentieth centuries. "Hopi aboriginal life is fast fading into the past," averred Fewkes, "and the time for gathering ethnological data is limited" (Fewkes 1902a:510).

Collecting objects therefore was regarded as saving them from oblivion. It was only a short step from displaying the art work to displaying the artist; this is why Nampeyo was in demand for the Columbian Exhibition, the Santa Fe Railroad Fair, Grand Canyon, and the Panama-Pacific Exhibition. By 1889 context had assumed major importance at expositions and world fairs because people wanted a simulated experience (Mitchell 1989:219), the authenticity of "being there" without all the inconveniences, transported as if by enchantment. Thus the Panama-Pacific Exhibition featured an "Indian Village" with ersatz pueblo houses.

And from the exhibition, it was not a terribly big step to the experience itself, in which one stood and stared not at the objects or at simulations, but at life. This phenomenon has been called "the world as picture" and "the world as exhibition, the world conceived and grasped as though it were an exhibition." The desire for the immediacy of the real became a desire for direct and physical contact with the exotic and the bizarre, despite its inconveniences (Mitchell 1989:219-220, 231). Thus, following its Chicago exhibition in 1895, the Santa Fe Railroad specifically began advertising its routes using specifically Indian themes in 1897, commissioning ethnographer Walter Hough to write his pamphlet on the "Moqui Snake Dance," with explicit directions on how to get to the Hopi mesas for the famed Snake Dance. The Harvey Company arranged with one of the Volz Brothers to provide transportation from the rail stop at Canyon Diablo to the Hopi villages for Snake Dances in 1900, and was still taking tourists to the Hopi villages in the 1980s.

The "Primitive Art" Market and the Looted Collectables

Not everyone can or wants to have the exotic experience. For some individuals, finding an ethnographic object in a gallery or catalogue -- an object that was once actually used in real life -- is as good or better than "being there." If the object represents a way of life that the collector thinks is extinct, or was used in an esoteric ritual that happens only one a year or once every few years in only one place, so much the better. The "world-as-exhibition" can be brought right into the den, the living room, the private gallery. And NAGPRA does *not* cover *private* galleries, collections, or museums. Thus the huge commercial business of supplying items to "primitive art" collectors remains on its honor, and sometimes honor takes a back seat to the effort of avoiding the knowledge that a certain object might in fact be stolen.

The development of the "primitive art" market has turned what used to be "collectable curios" into high-priced antiques and rare "found objects," in what one museum curator has called "an assault on native American cultures by the collectors of Indian art" that is "merciless in stripping the Pueblo people of ceremonial objects" (Wright 1982: 11). The whole idea of "primitive art" excludes creators' intentions from an understanding of their works; the visual surface of the work becomes equivalent to its content (cf. McEllivey 1991:46-48). To formalist "primitive art" collectors, it does not matter that Hopis intended certain objects as sacred, rather than secular. Thus the Hopi, storing objects in isolated caves and crevices in cliffs and in old house repositories, have been looted by the native suppliers in answer" to the demand for "primitive" art which began to accelerate in the early 1960s and shows no signs of slowing down.

To get back stolen objects owned by individuals, a Tribe must first report the items stolen; if the items are not reported stolen within the statute-of-limitations time period established by the state in which the alleged thief resides, the owner might successfully claim "adverse possession," i.e., right of possession by virtue of having had the object long enough without the possession being contested.

Where Sacred Things Are. In the mid-1960s one could see displayed prominently on the wall of a curio shop on old Route 66 near Joseph City, Arizona, an old Hopi Katsina mask that the owner proudly claimed had been a "gift." Was it a gift? Unlikely. In the late 1960s Hopis from

Shungopavi traced a different Katsina mask to the Heard Museum that a Hopi man had sold to pay for an expensive operation that the Indian Health Service had not been able to do immediately; the Heard returned the mask discretely. Hopis asked the FBI to investigate the theft of three masks stolen in December, 1973. Two were returned in time for a ceremony in February, 1977, but the third, a "Black Ogre" mask, had been sold to a collector in Bonn, Germany, and its return in mid-April, 1978 required international negotiations. In the meantime, the suspected thief had "'suffered an accidental death on the reservation'" according to an article in the *Arizona Sun* (Frisbie 1987:355).

How They Disappear. In 1980, Mishongnovi's Katsina Chief returned home to find that his house had been broken into and numerous items taken, including two pairs of eagle dancer wings and three butterfly headdresses. It turned out that the items had been stolen as part of an on-going relationship between a Hopi man and an Anglo dealer, who had previously purchased a pot, two figurines, and other items at less than a tenth of their estimated value on the primitive art market. "One way non-Indians make contact with Hopis," said the Anglo, when confronted, "is to go to Winslow near the bars and talking with intoxicated individuals. A deal is made and the non-Indian will bring the person or persons back to the reservation where a purchase is made," the Hopi individual selling a "priceless item" for $200 or $300. Investigation by Hopi police in this case revealed that "two ogre beings and other sacred and secret items were located in a chicken coop northeast of the village," apparently ready for sale. The Hopi was arrested and convicted in Tribal court, but prosecution of the Anglo proved far more difficult (Qua' Toqti 1980a).[95]

In 1991, three sacred masks -- one Navajo and two Hopi -- were advertised on consignment in Sotheby-Park Bernet May 21 catalogue of its annual auction of "Fine American Indian Arts." The two Hopi masks were an *Aholi* Katsina and *koyemsi* mask listed at $12,000-18,000 and $2,000-3,000 respectively. The Hopi and Navajo tribal administrations asked Sotheby's to remove the three sacred objects from sale. But privately owned objects are not covered by NAGPRA unless the owning individual acquired an item from a Museum after November 16, 1990, and so, "not bound by law, Sotheby's chose to ignore the request" (Sackler et al. 1992).

It was not the first time that the prestigious New York auction house had run afoul of religious ethics not covered by law. In its auction of October 26, 1978, a private California collector had offered a Zuni War God for sale, suggesting a price of $1,000. The Zunis notified the Justice Department and the U.S. Attorney for the southern district of New York issued a search warrant. The FBI seized the statue as being held in violation of a statute prohibiting the theft or embezzlement of tribal property. Sotheby's has not handled any Zuni War Gods since these events transpired (Childs 1980:7), but it continues to handle other Native American sacred objects (Sackler et al. 1992).[96]

The Mask Bandit

On a rainy Thursday in October, 1989, First Mesa' Katsina society chief, Herman Lewis, walked into the high-end Sanford I. Smith Fall Antiques Show at New York's Pier Exhibition gallery with two other Hopis, three FBI men and a photographer. Pointing to a mask hanging on a wall, he identified it as *Wupomo*, a Katsina mask that, he said, must have been stolen from Hopis. It turned out that the mask, probably 140-150 years old (Baer 1989: Plate 10), indeed had been stolen from its resting place in Oraibi. Dan Budnik, a Tucson photographer with Hopi associations going back twenty years, spotted the mask at a Santa Fe gallery opening in July, 1989. He notified Hopi religious leaders and police and tracked the mask's journey to the Antiques Show in New York.

Held by the U.S. attorney in Phoenix for two years, the mask was purified, fed corn meal and reclaimed by Oraibi's religious leaders in a ceremony in the Badger Clan kiva on December 2, 1991 (Brinkley-Rogers 1991). When it was at last brought back, 87-year-old Mike Gashwarza identified it more specifically as *Wuyaktaka*, old ancestor, and said he had last seen it in a religious ceremony in 1927 at an initiation into the Katsina and Powamuyu Societies for Oraibi's youngsters during Bean Dance (Blair 1989; Barnett 1990:142). Because the man who had stewardship of the mask died and his logical successor had not been initiated, the mask was "retired" and put in a secret place; later it was moved to the house of the deceased village chief, Tawakwaptiwa, along with other ceremonial objects that were no longer used. Described by Hopis as a "spirit friend," *Wuyaktaka* and other masks were fed with cornmeal daily while they rested in the old chief's house because they "'are alive and their spirits are still there'" (Barnett 1990:140). But sometime after the death of Tawakwaptiwa's daughter, Mina, in 1978, the mask disappeared.

Because the mask was privately owned and shown in private galleries, it did not fall under NAGPRA. But it does fall under the Archaeological Resources Protection Act of 1979. Under this law, conviction of a theft of a religious artifact like the mask carries a federal penalty of up to $5,000 in fines and five years in prison (Childs 1980). Yet no one was ever charged. The two Hopis believed responsible for selling *Wupomo* had died; the gallery owner had a bill of sale certifying that the mask was not contraband; and the trail of sales and purchases through which *Wupomo* had been put, was hard to trace.

It turned out that the mask had been bought and sold several times over by a gallery owner in Santa Fe, New Mexico, who said a private dealer from California had bought it "from Tribal elders" in 1980. (Others thought the date when the mask disappeared was closer to 1987, however [Brinkley-Rogers 1991.]) According to the gallery owner, the California dealer had bought a number of artifacts from the same cache of about 60 sacred objects in the old chief's house in Oraibi from which the Heard Museum's shield had also come, ostensibly discovered behind a "false wall" by "a Hopi man who was enlarging his living room." The California dealer then sold the mask to an Arizona collector, who sold it to the Santa Fe gallery owner, who sold it to a couple in Connecticut, who placed it on loan for display at an exhibition curated by the Santa Fe gallery owner in the New York Antiques show at the invitation of the Museum of American Folk Art, a private museum located in New York. But another story says that by the time Stanley Bahnimptewa, who became Kikmongwi at Mina Lanza's death in 1978, began renovating his father's house in 1980, most of the ceremonial objects had already disappeared and that the mask never went to California at all. Rather, the Santa Fe gallery owner bought it directly from a door-to-door Arizona dealer (Barnett 1990:147) for $34,000, then sold it to an investor for $40,000, then sold it on consignment for the investor for $60,000, then bought it back for $70,000 (Blair 1989; Page 1990), then sold it to the Connecticut couple for $75,000 (Solis-Cohen and Pennington 1989).

Because the American Indian art market is what has been described by one Santa Fe dealer as "an 'old-boy's network,' in which everyone knows everyone else's business" (Barnett 1990:104), perhaps the trail will never be traced. But evidently, each time *Wupomo* changed hands, sizable sums went into everyone's pockets. The gallery owner who was at the center of the latest series of sales and purchases cynically described what he called a ""scam" in which a tribal member sells an object and then reports it stolen several months later,'" only to sell it once again. "'The dirty little secret of this whole affair ... is that Hopis want it both ways: they want to be able to sell things and get them back.'"[97] But Dan Budnik, the Tucson photographer who had tipped off Hopis and the FBI about *Wupomo*, had a far less devious and much more painful scenario. "Nothing is safe," he maintained. "Hopis will risk stealing old items because the prices are right. If this was happening to Christian, Jewish, or Muslim religion or to anyone with political clout, we wouldn't allow it. But that is the way it is with Native Americans" (Brinkley-Rogers

1991). He described a "primitive art" dealer as "'the devil himself,'" showing up in the Hopi villages "'with a fistful of dollars in every hand ... To a Hopi who's an alcoholic and thirsty, a fistful of dollars looks pretty good'" (Barnett 1990:109). Placing ads in a local newspaper for "old Katsina dolls, broken or unbroken old Hopi made pottery" and "anything that is old Indian made," the dealer also goes door-to-door in the Hopi villages ... 'He'd look around," said one of Old Oraibi's residents, and ask, "'You have any old Katsina dolls? *Anything* old?'"' (Barnett 1990:140).

Katsina dolls, made for instructional purposes, have long been sanctioned as legitimate items for sale. But masks, figures, and anything falling into the category of *wuya* or *tiponi* are contraband. The *wuya*, both ancestor and object, may be an effigy, a bundle, or a mask. The *wuya* has a connection with the spiritual aspect of some object in nature. The owning clan -- actually an extended matrilineage within the clan -- keeps the *wuya* in a "clan house" and the women of the house feed the masks and *wuya* every day; thus the clan's ceremonial paraphernalia are really in the custody of the eldest woman of the clan who headed the female membership of her lineage. The *wuya* may temporarily be in the custody of the head of a secret society performing the ceremony owned by the clan; possession of the *wuya* or *tiponi* is the tangible sign of chieftainship (Titiev 1944:82 n. 117).[98]

Other ceremonial objects that do not quite fall into the category of *wuya* or *tiponi* may be made and owned by individuals, but a person cannot dispose of any sacred object any way he or she likes. Nobody stopped K.T. Johnson from burning his Bow Clan altar in 1922; but this kind of permissiveness is part of Hopi culture's inherent fatalism and ascription of punishment to the supernatural. For example, when asked what she would do if she knew some one was selling sacred objects, an Oraibi woman replied, "'I wouldn't say anything. Something will happen to him. it's his own fault'" (Barnett 1990:147). At Third Mesa, disposing of ceremonial property would seem to fit right in with the prophecy that Oraibi's ceremonial life was supposed to end (Whiteley 1988a; 1988b). But as we have seen, prophecy not only is self-fulfilling and self-justifying, but also varies in content, detail, and purpose from person to person, from prophet to prophet. Most Hopis would deny that ceremonies were prophesied to die out; as Rushforth and Upham (1992:141) suggest, the insistence on the demise of ceremonies having been prophesied is probably a "dissimulation."

Because the right to make and use ceremonial objects derives from collective sanction, clan, secret society or village, no Hopi individual has the right to dispose of anything ceremonial without permission of the collectivity. As the Tribe's director of cultural preservation told a reporter, "these particular items are held collectively by the clan or society responsible for the ceremony." Thus, "any ceremonial object in a museum or private collection has to have been illegally removed" (Barnett 1990:104).

But four crucially important Hopi ceremonial objects remain missing. Stolen in 1979 from their resting place in cave shrine, the objects are described as four *Talatumsi* (father, mother, corn maiden, and a baby) used by Shungopavi's men's secret societies in their kiva initiation ceremonies. Without them, the initiations cannot proceed, and there have been none for nearly two decades. Hopis "have been willing to go public and even allowed photographs of the items (or similar ones) to be circulated" (Frisbie 1987:258). The figures might actually be the deity *Maasaw*, who features prominently in some of the initiation rights, along with his female counterpart, *Tuwapongwuuti* ("Sand-Altar Woman") and *Talautumsi*, goddess of childbirth, who is regarded as the mother of the initiates, who are likened to helpless little birds, and are symbolically "reborn" through the ceremony. *Tuwapongwuuti* is sister to Muyingwa, another god of seeds and germination along with Maasaw, and the mother of Hahaiwuuti who is mother of the Katsinas, and wife of Maasaw (Parsons 1939:203; Titiev 1944:131). Once an item enters the art market, it not only escalates in value, but also acquires a legitimate history that makes proof of its theft all that much more difficult. The case of Oraibi's stolen *Wupomo* mask serves as an example.

Conclusion: Hopi Resistance to Commodification of Culture

The problem of religious objects being stolen and sold for profit is part of the general problem of the commodification of Hopi culture, which extends in many Hopis' eyes to information *about* their religion as well. Information can be regarded as being "produced" in the same way that a physical items is produced (Raymond Williams summarized by Ulin 1984:160-166). This idea would seem far-fetched if it were not for the fact that people pay for information and communication all the time: books, magazines, newspapers, cable-tv. Songs, tunes, records, photographs, sketches, and design motifs *are* copyrighted. What happens, then, when photographs, sketches, and paintings of religious ceremonies, daily life, and personal clothing and decoration are sold for money? They become commodities. What happens when the ceremonies and daily life itself become experiences for which people will pay? They also become commodities. Hopis thought they had stopped the process when they banned auditory and visual reproductions of ceremonies around 1916 and prohibited photography of villages without permission and appropriate payment. Tourists surmounted these barriers, not so much by violating the rules -- although some did -- as by treating Hopi life and ceremonies as leisure-time entertainment. Even sincerely valuing them as important multicultural experiences does not correspond to how Hopis intend them: as prayers for rain, health, and good life.

Banning visitors, or at least strictly controlling them, constitutes an effort to repatriate Hopi culture itself, to bring it back home as a strictly Hopi resource. The Hopi are not alone in this effort; Zunis banned all non-Zunis from all ceremonies in 1990, and have only selectively relaxed the rules. The Rio Grande Pueblos have banned non-Puebloans from most ceremonies for centuries. And repatriation of cultural property has accompanied most nationalist movements of the post-colonial era. Yet the entire cultural repatriation effort depends heavily on economic stability on the individual as well as on the social level, and paradoxically, to some extent on the degree to which culture can be used as a resource to cure some of the social ills that result in illegal and clandestine dealings in contraband in the first place. To the extent that culture becomes an economic commodity, it also becomes a "thing" that can be used to revitalize society and build political solidarity; "ownership" of culture will then become as contested as ownership of land, water, and other resources.

11

Conclusion:
Hopi Society, the World System,
and Modernization

Answers to Questions

Hopis in the Modern World System

The concept of a "world system" and the ideas of modernization and cultural pluralism provided the framework for this study. At its beginning, I posed several questions about six events, or more accurately, six situations, from Hopi history. The answers are now self-evident.

The Split of 1906

Cultural and social responses to economic and political pressures and processes resulted in a fragmentation of one village into five and eventually six at Third Mesa and also a fragmentation of Hopi cultural ideology that had been embedded in religion.

The factionalist schism of 1906 was not a product of purely Hopi internal dynamics. It was indeed a self-induced reshuffling of political relationship within an indigenous nation, but an indigenous nation already partially incorporated into a world system. Imposition of U.S. rule did not bring about total social disintegration, but in tandem with deteriorated material conditions, it did change the nature and functioning of various parts of the pre-existing Hopi social system.

Demographic and economic pressures and Anglo-American, Mormon, and Navajo intrusions exacerbated nascent political rivalries on Second and Third Mesas. Dilemmas concerning how to incorporate economic, cultural, and political changes emanating from the Anglo-American metropolis provided the backdrop against which these political rivalries played themselves out. Unlike some Pueblos such as Taos, Zuni, or Santo Domingo, where threats of punishment such as public floggings,[99] ostracisms (Lasswell 1935), or denials of land and house assignments (Fenton 1957), enforce cultural norms such as dress and hair codes, religious participation, and village endogamy, Hopis appear to have had only minimal enforcement mechanism. The warrior societies seem to have enforced norms, but if Awat'ovi is an example, the enforcement seems to have been an all-or-nothing matter: given sufficient time to mend one's ways and come back into line, continued defiance of propriety results in swift and irremediable punishment. It seems that only in economic matters involving communal clearing and working of land for chiefly families did the warriors take physical action, and once climatic conditions had taken land around Oraibi to such a deteriorated state that no amount of work could bring it back, the assembling of work gangs lost its point.

At the beginning of the Twentieth Century, Hopis were still nearly entirely economically self-sufficient, but plagued by the fourth or fifth smallpox epidemic in less than fifty years as well as by alternating drought and torrential rains and heavy snowpack. Hopis had previously handled deteriorated material conditions by calling in social debts and moving in with Puebloans to the east -- Zunis, Santo Domingos, Isletas. But those alternatives were made much more difficult not only by Americans' and Mormons' geopolitical penetration, but also by a combination of pressure from non-Indian homesteaders along the San Juan River; population increase; and a pastoral lifestyle that encouraged Navajos to move into areas temporarily vacated by Hopis decimated by disease and famine and to eventually surround them. A booming wool market between 1860 and 1919 encouraged Navajos and Hopis alike to increase their sheep herds, but traders found Navajos to be a much better source of larger amounts of wool and thus concentrated their efforts among them, rather than among Hopis.

Economic alternatives in the form of wage labor for the BIA and the Santa Fe Railroad; craft production for museums and a nascent tourist trade; freighting and postal contracts; and entertainment of tourists with Indian dances at Grand Canyon were supplementing subsistence farming and wool sales by 1910. Villages, clans and secret societies divided Hopis into groups with conflicting and cross-cutting loyalties, but a universal ideology strongly rooted in ritual and religion united Hopis at all villages culturally. Under Euro-American intrusion religion and ritual continued to function with relative autonomy, but with the development of tourism, they began to function in some sense as subsystems of the world system. Tourism and museum collecting changed the Hopi, but Hopi tourism and museum collecting also changed the world system to some extent because closer inclusion of the Hopi specific cultural system brought new social patterns to it as well as to the Hopi, including the commodification of culture. American missionaries and government officials imposed their own culture, values, and religion; traders exchanged cash and goods for crafts and wool; anthropologists collected crafts and information, sometimes offering cash in exchange and sometimes not.

Reorganization

Various zealots, aided by the U.S. Government, tried to impose a kind of cultural and religious homogeneity beginning in 1887 when agents imposed school attendance. In 1900 the "haircutting order" added to this effort, and from 1915 through 1925, missionaries and Indian agents collaborated on various occasions to impose cultural and religious hegemony for assimilative purposes in a last-ditch effort to draw Hopis into an arbitrary and ethnocentric version of U.S. national culture.

Coincident with these impositions, several major ceremonies were abandoned at Oraibi and Bacavi, but Hopis began to gain allies in the form of partisans committed to the preservation of autochthonous cultures and religions. The Pueblos formed the All-Indian Pueblo Council, which Hopis did not join, but at the same time, Hopi artisans and artists received a boost in the growing popularity of their arts and crafts. These artistic expressions in painting, pottery, silversmithing, and basketry, achieved innovation and traditionalism at the same time, continuing the naturalistic motifs of the Hopi and Pueblo world view but also sometimes stylizing Hopi scenes or symbols straight out of Hopi history, religion, and traditions, vaguely along the lines of Euro-American tastes stemming from Nouveau, Arts-and-Crafts, Deco, or Abstract styles. Perhaps Charles Loloma and his nieces, producing jewelry in the 1960s, 1970s, and 1980s were the only true iconoclasts in terms of art, not working necessarily with any easily categorized style or motifs.

The 1930s and '40s saw a reorganization of Hopi culture and society on many levels. The Indian Reorganization Act did indeed implement a "prevailing system of colonial governance" (Robbins 1992:97) but largely because Collier's and La Farge's efforts to assist Hopis through providing access to credit with the Indian Revolving Loan Fund and improvements in range forage and water sources failed to offset the effects of stock reduction; reassignment of Hopi land to Navajos; and the ineffectiveness of the early Council. The Act did grant Hopis a relief from domination but more importantly, provided an issue -- the Tribal Council -- which some Hopis worked into an ideology of resistance.

The Traditionalists

The Traditionalists started a social movement deliberately confronting the U.S. Government and Hopis as well on a number of political and economic issues, basing their stance in the tradition of resistance to acculturation established and pursued most forcefully at Oraibi between 1880 and 1906, and later at Hotevilla. Insisting on a position of indigenous sovereignty in 1949 that would not become current among most spokespersons for other indigenous peoples for another twenty years, the Traditionalists relied on an intuitive, revelatory, apocalyptic, and mystical interpretation of Hopi geopolitics in order to achieve cultural interpretations of pragmatic, hard-headed, legalistic issues. The Traditionalists did indeed help to maintain Hopi cultural and political autonomy. They obstructed things just enough to raise questions and sufficiently effectively to have some influence and impact, even if inconsistently.

The ideological opposition of traditionalist and progressive ideological rubrics placed the brakes on rapid and wholesale acculturation and on any kind of wide-eyed idealism on Hopis' part about "good times ahead" or "prosperity around the corner." Traditionalists' constant pessimism and nay-saying warned that White people might indeed come bearing gifts, but they might also crowd Hopis out of their own land; be wooed by persuasive Navajos; or take away more than they would give. Yet to completely resist the Americans could spell disaster and would not be in Hopis' best interests; Traditionalism thus became almost a fail-safe mechanism, predicting disaster if Americanism did not work.

The Energy Leases

Ironically, the Indian Reorganization Act increased the Kikmongwis' secular political powers as well as bringing previously unempowered Hopis into the political system. But new sources of political influence also arose. Mounting pressures from energy companies not only indirectly caused the revival of the Hopi Tribal Council in 1950 but also resulted in mineral leases, first oil and then coal. Oil and coal leases granted Hopis little immediate economic control and like nearly all Indian leases prior to the mid-1970s, were mere giveaways to multinational corporations. But by 1987, the Hopi Tribal Council had not only negotiated agreements that were 500-600% more favorable, but also had begun enforcing environmental responsibility well in excess of administrative regulations and had frustrated efforts to expand the coal lease area. In combination with the U.S. Government's efforts to quiet aboriginal Indian land titles through the Indian Claims Commission, a series of complicated legal and administrative maneuvering lasting more than two decades resulted in Hopiland joining Navajoland in becoming an economically important periphery, supplying electricity and coal to the American metropolis.

Ethnic Competition: The Hopi-Navajo Land Dispute

The lease revenues paid legal fees for pursuing the re-acquisition of land through U.S. courts, and legislation brought relocation to 10,000 Navajos and a re-empowerment of Hopis as an ethnic group with concordant political and territorial boundaries. Hopis did indeed achieve a victory in a long-standing, on-going contest with Navajos, and although that victory may ultimately be attributed to the avarice of outside interests wanting to drill for oil back in the 1940s, it appears that Hopis used outside interests and engaged in political maneuvering to a greater extent than the outside interests were able to use or maneuver them. The situation confirms Enloe's (1972) assertion that modernization does not create melting pots but rather, promotes tribalism and ethnic groups as interest groups. The ethnic competition between Hopis and Navajos may ultimately prove to have been a bad idea in terms of regional political power balances and may ultimately give way to a Hopi-Navajo alliance on some issues. Altogether, as of 1993, far less physical conflict had resulted from the situation in twenty years than an average American city of 20,000 sees in a week.

Repatriating Culture

In the area of culture, Hopis have successfully asserted their own cultural rules, norms, attitudes, values, and institutions as the basis for collective decision-making, problem-solving, and interaction with other indigenous nations (Navajos) as well as with the nation-state and with international bodies. While the Tribal Council is embedded in U.S. political forms and processes, it continues to operate little like an Anglo-American political body; what other American legislature has at least a quarter and sometime half of its representatives in a state of continual boycott? And village Kikmongwis are, if anything, more vocal and heard oftener now than they were in the 1930s, sometimes at the expense of an elected Tribal Chairman.

The return and repatriation of ceremonial objects was not initiated by the 1990 NAGPRA. Hopis began seeking the return of illegally obtained ceremonial items as early as 1936. Art objects and even information to some extent constitute "renewable" resources that can be turned into capital. While museums and many collectors have slowly turned hostility at the idea of giving up some of this "capital" into sympathy with Native Americans' efforts to repatriate their religions and cultures, little impact has been made on the general public or on much of the dealers in primitive art. The Hopi Tribal government now joins religious leaders in pressing for the return of ceremonial objects that have gotten into the hands of "primitive art" dealers or ended up in museums. Ironically, as specific Hopi artists producing secular art become increasingly commercially acknowledged and appreciated, objects created for strictly religious purposes became the increasing target of collectors and thieves. Tourists, seeking to consume Hopi culture in the same way that collectors consumed Hopi art, crowded the mesas in ever-larger numbers to look at religious ceremonies having no counterpart in contemporary Euro-American culture. Increasing integration into the world system has provided economic dependence, on the one hand, but has also provided a kind of stability that moots the necessity to pander to the tourist trade so carefully nurtured over the decades. Thus, in efforts to take back their culture from the maw of commodification, Hopis began closing more and more religious ceremonies to outsiders and even trying to restrict or at least discourage publication of certain bodies of research.

Political and Economic Modernization

Hopis' legal and economic victory required some degree of incorporation into the political structure of the U.S. Bureau of Indian Affairs. Congress' passage of the Indian Reorganization Act in 1934 accomplished that incorporation (Cornell 1988:89-96; 205-208) and brought increased integration of Hopi politics as a subsystem of Euro-American politics, even alongside major dissent from many Hopis. Local implementation of decision-making powers depended on strong identification with local interests defined, in turn, by tribalism, and the land dispute issue seems to indicate that, under the rubric of tribalism, a good deal of flexibility can be added to the system, sometimes benefitting participants in the subsystems as much, or more, than it does the power brokers who ultimately control the larger system.

Against some measures of autonomy, and within the context of the world system, then, the Hopi have increased some of their autonomy as an indigenous nation on the one hand, but have lost some on the other. They have clearly expanded their territorial base, but only after losing more than they gained back. They were finally able to bend the nation-state's political apparatus to their own political objectives, but only after putting up with the nation-state's political whims for nearly a century. This empowerment also fits the federal government's agenda; by increasing the powers of tribal governments and responding to their demands, the federal government has created buffers against "more hostile political actors and constituencies" (Cornell 1988:206) whose goals might diverge more sharply from those of the dominant society, such as the American Indian Movement. Dealing with Indian demands on a group-by-group basis deflects conflict from the intergroup to the intragroup arena and rechannels disputes rooted in Indian-White relations into Indian-Indian relations (Cornell 1988:207).

Against other measures of autonomy, largely economic ones, Hopis are no more independent than any other community north of Mexico. The transfer of property rights in some forms of capital such as natural resources such as coal, oil, and water, completed the economic aspects of modernization begun by Euro-American intrusion. As peripheries of cores and satellites that are tied to metropolitan loci of power and wealth, the Hopi and Navajo Tribes experienced an internalized colonial situation through the increasingly greater loss of autonomy and relative impoverishment. But Hopis experienced some reversal of that situation and increasingly greater degrees of local control after implementation of the "Buy Indian" contracts of the 1970s and the subsequent "Self-Determination" Act of 1975. Economic disparities between Hopis and the larger U.S. society and even to some extent between some Hopis and others have given way to a modicum of uniform economic stability, if not outright prosperity. By the 1980s the Hopi Tribal Council had superseded the BIA as Hopis' major source of employment and economic stability, with coal royalty revenues supplying more than 60% of Tribal revenues. The Tribal administration embarked upon a series of social programs for coping with stress, substance abuse, and social pathologies. But all of these social and political indicators of autonomy were funded through economic dependency. Hopis have lost determining control over the products extracted from Hopi land - primarily coal and water - but have asserted control over distribution of goods through improved cash flow and varying degrees of control over services contracted from the federal government and over cultural patrimony.

A Homogenized World Culture?

Finally, I posed the question of whether or not the standardized, driving motivations of producing and selling things are pushing the world toward a single, homogenized cultural system, and whether or not the case of Hopi history and culture in the Twentieth Century could be used to demonstrate that process. A kind of structural-functionalist materialism predicts, on the one hand, that systematic interdependencies link work organization, administrative structures, education, beliefs in causes and consequences, norms of achievement, the structure of kin and family, and so forth. Therefore, goes such reasoning, a change in one will necessarily result in a change in the other (Moore 1979:27, 28). But Native American theorist Duane Champagne's (1989:7) observation that "incorporation into markets or world-system relations is largely beyond the will and control of the members of indigenous societies (while) cultural-normative penetration differs from market incorporation and geopolitical relations," applies as much to specific Hopi situations as it does to those of many Native Americans.

The Hopi case does not demonstrate homogenization. Although Hopi culture today is as much a product of the last 150 years of history as it is the product of something "aboriginally Hopi," Hopi culture remains distinctly Hopi. The Hopi offer a case of resisting various aspects of modernization, whether rightly or wrongly, and for a diversity of reasons, while strongly embracing others. The economic needs of the metropolis have generated cultural changes in the Hopi polity. But a change might fundamentally reorganize the cultural or institutional order, or it might be considered sufficiently secondary and therefore acceptable (Champagne 1989:9) so that the cultural definitions of the society can be "stretched," so to speak, in order to accommodate it. Hopis have "stretched" various cultural traditions to accommodate modernity to tradition and pragmatics to prophecy.

The Modernity of Tradition

The Hopi offer a case of incorporation of tradition with modernity that has actually prevented Hopi society from becoming prey to intransigently opposed political factions or parties that must thoroughly defeat the other in order to maintain viability, or from being torn apart by religious schisms that tore apart European communities for two hundred years in the Middle Ages. Hopis incorporated traditionalism as a defining characteristic of modern Hopi life, suffusing traditionalism with widespread social, cultural, artistic, religious, and political significance that retained the essential dualism of modernization: improvement of material conditions, increased cash flow, secularization of life experiences, and standardization of routines and procedures such as "tribal enrollments" and "environmental protection," along with opposition to foreign influences and skepticism about institutions such as "Tribe" and "Tribal Council."

Traditionalism is a thoroughly modern phenomenon among the Hopi, revealing itself in political factionalism, prophetic mythology, craft-production and social relationships with non-Hopis. Traditionalism's message, rooted as it is in the past, ostensibly opposes the kind of modernism deriving from technological and economic liberalism associated with progress, as well as the kind of calculated formulaic radicalism that would strip away historical encrustations and philosophical elaborations in favor of bare essentials. Paradoxically, Hopi Traditionalism requires intimate familiarity with non-traditional law, economy, politics, industrial technology, and progress in order to better oppose them and fit them into a traditionalist interpretation. Thus traditionalism should not be expected to "give way" to "progressivism," or the other way around.

While impetus for change has come from outside Hopi life in some periods, in others, Hopis have generated the impetus themselves. Hopis have created their own versions of the "two modernities," "progressivism" and its denial, by combining technical, secular, factual knowledge and goal-orientation with an ideology stressing fate, tradition, myth, prophecy, interpretation and the wise teachings of founding ancestors and ancestresses. Tradition constitutes part of this "second" modernity: the modernity of challenge, criticism, dissent, exceptionalism, resting on apparently impossible goal attainment. As one Hopi woman who was raised a strict Mennonite once told me, "We are all traditionalists out here."

While so many Hopis lived in grinding poverty, the Traditionalist Movement provided an alternative interpretation of life for those Hopis who had no economic alternatives. Embracing ceremonialism, even if not participating in it fully, and rejecting materialist ideology, provided a degree of dignity to those in poverty that could not be acquired through material possessions. Now that virtually all Hopis can aspire to a modicum of material comforts and now that the Hopi economy is irrevocably integrated into the core/periphery relationships defined by the American metropolis, Traditionalism has become increasingly focused on the expressive, symbolic, intellectual, and personal aspects of Hopi life. The ideological leeway that economic security has permitted, can be seen in architecture, settlement patterns, and land tenure.

Construction with native stone has returned in some contexts; residences on the Mesas continue to be maintained; women continue to own many of the houses; some men still farm clan land and turn the produce over to the household's eldest female. The Second Mesa villages maintain the full round of ceremonies, with nearly the full round still being maintained at First Mesa. Progressivism -- in construction of frame or cinder block houses; purchase or rental of houses rather than inheritance or self-construction of them; use of land for grazing rather than farming; salaried labor rather than self-sufficiency; and supply of 80% or more food from grocery stores rather than from field and pasture -- counterposes Traditionalism but does not replace or supersede it. Independent villages continue to provide important -- perhaps paramount -- arenas for discussion and debate of social and political issues, just as they did in 1540, even though most of them are defined by Tribal, state, or federal governments. Between a quarter and a third of the Hopi population remain officially unrepresented on the Tribal Council, by choice, even though their critical distance from it does not by any means indicate an isolation from or denial of the importance of events and issues on the Tribal level.

A Final Word on Analyses of Indigenous Societies

A trend toward a kind of idealist symbolic structuralism has crept back into scholarly works that assumes that "primitive" societies have a kind of seamless ideology that does not admit internal dissent. Furthermore, it is assumed that this seamless ideology grants them an autonomy from economic, political, and material conditions brought about by processes not of the peoples' own making, and even further, that peoples' ideological spinnings can make those economic, political, and material conditions irrelevant in a causal sense. This trend is an unfortunate one, and it is even more unfortunate that it is also often coupled to an oddly romantic, post-modern resurrection of the Eighteenth-Century version of idealist symbolic structuralism that asserts that because ethnographies are constructed of words, symbols, and ideas, then the cultures and societies -- the people -- that they describe must also be mere thought forms, disembodied from their historical and material contexts, represented only by the ideas in their heads. Nothing could be farther from the truth.

For example, Laura Thompson's (Thompson and Joseph 1944; Thompson [1945?]; Thompson 1950) perception of the Hopi as an autonomous, self-regulating society took no account of the climatic vagaries that could upset Hopis' most carefully laid plans and result in demographic upheavals severely compromising ceremonial, kin, and clan activities and categories. Hopi society has always been socially and economically in flux.

Since the 1880s, explanations for change and continuity lie as much in U.S. institutions and history as in the Hopi communities. Rather than remaining as peculiar administrative units preserving quaint customs and odd traditions, Indian reservations became important satellite areas for national U.S. metropolises. The fact that Hopis may have incorporated Mormon, Navajo, Zuni, and later Euro-American and even "New Age" cultural elements into their own on the other, underscores the point that societies are never bounded systems set off from other bounded systems. They are always in flux.

Through structures created by Washington that were preadapted for metropolis-satellite political economic relationships, Hopis' allocations of time, energy, and resources were turned from farming to stock raising and then to wage labor, industrial activities, and the creation of political bureaucracies modeled on U.S. examples. Acknowledging this point does not eliminate the possibilities of Hopis pursuing their own goals. Modernization includes the process of pursuing goals, directly or indirectly, through rational methods. Hopis have leant a new twist to this process because they have pursued goals obliquely as well as directly, with a sophistication and a degree of success rarely matched by any other minority within a pluralistic society.

Notes

1. Rushforth and Upham (1992:15, 48-52, 74-5, 94-5, 109) suggest that smallpox was brought by the Spaniards but preceded them by 20-25 years, spreading through air, water, and human contacts to the Hopi villages by the 1520s. They propose massive depopulation as a result, setting pre-contact Hopi population at 29,305 and setting the date of contact -with disease rather than people - at 1520. They set Hopi population at between 12,000 and 14,359 by 1581-2, on the eve of Espejo's expedition to the Hopi in 1583. They propose a drop of another 2-4,000 in the following century, relying on Spanish records and statistical extrapolations from archaeological data. The estimates for 1520 and 1581-2 are 100%-400% higher than estimates generally accepted by other scholars.

2. I use "modernization," "modernism," and "modernity" interchangeably, although "modernization" implies more of a process and "modernism" denotes more of a principle or doctrine.

3. Later, Hopis named the Kawaiiokuh, "place of the horse," from the Spanish "caballo," meaning horse, plus Hopi "-kuh" or "-ki," meaning "stone buildings."

4. It is also possible that the Spaniards had interrupted Flute or Snake ceremonies, and that Hopis were trying to tell them to stay outside the village for ritual reason.

5. Gutierrez' general overview of Pueblo culture and society is flawed in a number of ways. See Clemmer 1993 and Native American Studies Center, University of New Mexico 1993 for details and extended critiques.

6. Bailey and Bailey (1986:313) report an Acoma Indian stealing two horses from a Navajo man in 1870.

7. Estimates by Americans within the first decade after U.S. conquest range from 200,000 to 500,000 (Bailey and Bailey 1986:19-21). Charles Bent, short-lived Acting U.S. military Governor of New Mexico, estimated Navajo herds at 500,000 sheep; 10,000 horses and mules; and 3,000 cattle in 1846, with some individuals having 5-10,000 sheep and 4-500 head of other livestock each. His estimates for Navajo people show an equally wide range, somewhere between 7,000 and 14,000 (Abel 1915:6-7), but perhaps 10,000 is a reasonable figure. In 1980, a scholar estimated an

average of 240 sheep per Navajo household as necessary for subsistence during this period, and in the 1940s, various sources estimated 400-500 as a bare subsistence minimum for a "large Navajo family" (Bailey and Bailey 1986:19-21). But such figures may mean little without knowledge of average household size and the exact role of sheep in the economy of a century ago. Certainly there is no reason to assume that all sheep were consumed, rather than sold or traded. Navajos stole an estimated 400,000-500,000 sheep between 1847 and 1851 alone. If they already had 500,000 in 1846, some Navajos must have made tidy profits on the turnover. A growing class of Navajo "ricos" who had much more wealth than others stratified the Navajos by wealth at this time (Aberle 1966:25).

8. For fifteen years after the U.S. takeover of Mexico's northern territories in the Mexican-American War of 1846-1848, the trading-and-raiding network linking Navajos and neighboring tribes and Spanish-American communities continued to flourish and persisted to some extent into the 1870s (Bailey and Bailey 1986:56-57). Navajos captured by Utes, Apaches, Mexicans, and Comanches and sold to Spanish-Americans were still turning up as household servants in Abiquiu, Taos, Arroyo Hondo, and Albuquerque as late as the 1860s (Aberle 1966:25; Correll 1979 II:348; Correll 1979 III:198, 216-217, 246).

9. Navajo people increased from 14,800 to 42,000; Navajos' sheep from 4,190 to 1,200,000 (Bailey and Bailey 1986:38; Aberle 1966:30; Johnston 1966:362). In contrast, Government statistics reported Hopi population at only 2,980 in 1933 (ARDOI,IA 1933:149; See Table II) and Hopi livestock at 10,641 in 1881 (RCIA 1881:272, 292-3) and at 17,500 sheep and goats; 5,085 horses and burros; and 7,695 cattle in the late 1930s (Hack 1942:17; Mason 1965:15). The Navajo ratio of sheep to people increased from .27:1 to 28:1; the Hopi ratio of sheep to people increased from 5:1 to only 8:1.

10. Patriarch Young would "call" specific individuals to found new settlements and the church would supply them with capital: cattle and stored surplus food (Leone 1979:20).

11. Bailey based his account on Hamblin's diary. But his account is garbled: he has the missionaries being taken to all the other Hopi villages, listing Polacca and Hotevilla, which would not be built until 40-50 years later!

12. Indian agent Mateer reported that ten Hopi families raised wheat "at the Mormon settlements upon the Little Colorado River" (ARCIA 1878:9).

13. The scheme developed by the Scots enlightenment thinker Adam Ferguson in the 1770s was the most widely used. Civil society had two sub-stages: ancient and modern. Savagery was characterized by a

hunting, gathering, and fishing subsistence system; communal property; a stone-and-bone, hand-made, hand-held technological system; lack of a commitment to monogamy; and a tendency toward what was called "Mutterrecht" ("Mother-right"): descent traced in the female line, ownership of house and food products by women, and matrilocality -- the custom of men relocating to their wife's mother's home upon marriage. Horticulture might have developed in this stage, but was rudimentary.

Barbarism was marked by the domestication of animals. This domestication resulted in people developing a sense of private property because each animal could be individually owned. Surpluses developed and thus trade, because surplus meat, whether on-the-hoof or butchered, could not be kept. A surplus of animal products stimulated agricultural production and economic specialization: some people herded while others tilled, now with the aid of oxen. Privatization of property became more pronounced because fields had to be fenced for protection against livestock. Technological innovation -- first in bronze and then in iron -- was stimulated by the desire for economic improvements, but also depended on superior intellect, which, the evolutionists pointed out slyly, had not been evenly distributed throughout humankind, because if it had, all peoples would have "progressed" through the bronze and iron ages just like Europeans had! Population expanded and society became stratified into haves and have-nots. Trade expanded too, but so did warfare.

Only some of the European societies had reached the stage of civil society: England, Scotland, the Scandinavian countries, France, the Netherlands. They were staunchly patrilineal and patriarchal, with political control, ownership of land, houses and industrial production, and rule of the family roost firmly in the hands of men, not women.

In America, unilineal evolutionism is most closely associated with Lewis Henry Morgan, whose scheme was also adopted by Soviet anthropology and remained in vogue in the United States until the ascendancy of the Boasians and A.L. Kroeber in the mid-1920s. Morgan believed that all Indian tribes had to be led gently through a "pastoral" stage, where they could get used to owning wealth-producing private property - livestock - before being brought into "civil society." He conceded, however, that the Hopi and other "village Indians" might be as high as the "Middle Stage" of "Barbarism" (Hinsley 1989). John Wesley Powell, founder of the Bureau of American Ethnology, was heavily influenced by Lewis Henry Morgan (Green 1990:355).

14. Nampeyo died in 1942. Her husband, Lesou, who decorated many of her pots and drew many of her designs, died in 1932. Her descendents continue to produce fine pottery.

15. The men retaliated by tossing water at the women, or by peeing at them and smearing them with mud and dung (Voth 1912:29-32).

16. Peter Whiteley (1988b:49) voices confusion about the relationship of clan and lineage, asking, "Which is the primary unit? Clan or lineage?" This confusion may stem from a failure to understand a fundamental point about Hopi social organization which Parsons and Lowie discovered during their research in 1915 and in the 1920s and which was later elaborated by Titiev and Eggan in the 1930s and 1940s: that clan and lineage are *not isomorphic* with regard to one another. Neither was ever the primary unit, nor is there any reason either should have been. Hopi social organization is flexible, not rigid, and started to undergo modification at just about the time under review: around 1900 (Forde 1931: 377-393.) However, Levy (1992: 47-8) attributes Whiteley's confusion to Titiev's ambiguity in using the term "household" to refer to the people living in a house dominated by a nuclear family as well as to a matrilineage -- a woman, her daughters, and granddaughters -- who have inheritance rights to the house.

17. Whiteley (1985: 360) attributes an "evolutionist bent" to Titiev merely because Titiev's first summer among the Hopi was spent with Leslie White in 1932. But White's genealogical work there seems to be totally outside the evolutionist paradigm and he did not publish anything within the evolutionist tradition until he announced his "reworked," universalist version of evolutionism based on energy capture in 1943. Nothing in Titiev's work is remotely evolutionist. The attribution seems entirely spurious.

18. Peter Whiteley (1988b: 170-171) has credited himself with this discovery. But it is quite clear that Titiev originated the perception.

19. Whiteley (1988b: 170-171; 244-247) inexplicably refuses to credit Titiev with the view that households constituted the basic sociological unit in Oraibi. Instead, he tries to credit himself with Titiev's discovery, falsely attributing to Titiev the "orthodox view" that clans were cohesive, unassailably coherent units, using his misrepresentation of Titiev to characterize Titiev's analysis as "flawed."

20. Titiev greatly elucidated the real nature of Hopi social organization by modifying what might be called the "orthodox" view. This view, largely expressed by Fewkes, conceptualized clans as isomorphic units, migrating to the Hopi villages as distinct entities; bringing along their

ceremonies; and constituting the changing building blocks of Hopi society. While the clans might well have brought their ceremonies to the Hopi villages, and probably did straggle in one by one as Hopi oral histories pictured them doing, Titiev showed conclusively that matrilineages and households were far more important than the clans, which tended to be amorphous and conceptual.

21. This point has been misunderstood more than once. Laura Thompson (1950: 71n13) misunderstood it. She stated: "Both Titiev and Eggan apparently confuse the concept of *centralization* with *integration,* concluding that since they have strong clans which are not highly centralized politically, the Hopi pueblos are not and cannot be loosely knit and highly integrated sociologically." This was not what Titiev or Eggan said. They *did* regard the Hopi villages as *remarkably* well integrated, and said so. They noted the *weakness* of clans, not their strength, and asked, "How do these villages hold together in the face of no political centralization on the part of clans?" Their answer was: ceremonialism. Thompson incorrectly characterized Titiev as "inferring" (sic) that the clan system was the underlying principle in Hopi society; if anything, Titiev implied just the opposite--that it could not be the clan system alone. "Titiev's conclusion," asserted Thompson (1950: 71) "seems to be based on an investigation into the organization of atypical villages only, where a breakdown in traditional social and ceremonial structure has apparently obscured the traditional unifying principle and dynamics of the system." Apparently, Thompson regarded fully half the Hopi population - those inhabiting the Third Mesa villages - as "atypical."

22. Eggan dedicated the book to Radcliffe-Brown.

23. Whiteley (1985:360) makes the assertion that Eggan and Titiev supplanted the "prevailing theories" of Kroeber and Parsons, but this assertion is not true. They utilized and built upon Kroeber's, Lowie's, and Parsons' theories. They disputed them only in details--i.e., Kroeber on the "polarity" or duality of related clans and on his insistence that kin terms were solely psychological, that is, without sociological veracity (Eggan 1950: 295.) Eggan countered Parsons only very gently on her insistence that Hopi kivas were associated primarily with clans. Eggan (1950: 97) noted that kiva *membership* is *not* principally by clan. Whiteley (1986: 71-73) also tries to insinuate a distinction between Eggan's approach to Hopi clans and lineages and that of Titiev. But the distinction is spurious. Both researchers note Hopis' identification of the basis of *wuya.* Only Whiteley's selective quoting makes them appear different.

24. Whiteley (1985, 1986) has insisted that African clans and lineage systems provided the model for Eggan's and Titiev's conceptualizations of Hopi clans. But the evidence points to just the *opposite* conclusion. Whiteley based his confused and confusing "challenge" to Eggan's and Titiev's theory of Hopi society on the assertion that Eggan and Titiev had based their analysis on an "African" model but that the Hopi, exerting their will against such models, had refused to remain frozen in the ethnographic present of 1932-34, when Titiev did his field work. And because the Hopi had changed, and were not in 1979-81 as they had been in 1932-34, the year 1980 thus constituted the most appropriate basis for understanding Hopi clans of 1906. Titiev, of course, was attempting to reconstruct a picture of Hopi society has it had probably been in 1906 or even earlier, not to describe Hopi society as it was in 1932-34. Whiteley aimed at duplicating Titiev's efforts, and coming out with different results. To this end he made it seem as if he had originated the idea that descent groups were weak, rather than strong, and that Titiev and Eggan had asserted Hopi descent groups as strong, when in actuality, they never did. It was Eggan and Titiev who first pointed to the weakness of Hopi clans, thereby "unpacking" Hopi clans from the prevailing African model proposed by Murdock.

Eggan actually set out to show that Hopi clans were *not* the same as African clans. He specifically rejected the "African model" proposed by G. P. Murdock. Murdock (1949:68) had advocated a definition of clan as a corporate descent group with a unilineal descent rule; residential unity; "actual social integration;" and capacity to virtually redefine the lineage affiliations of in-marrying spouses as members of the corporate group in an economic and reproductive sense. The in-marrying spouses not only produced offspring and labor for their in-laws, but also became "an integral part of the membership." This definition is based squarely on the "African model" of a clan as a residential homestead. Hilda Kuper's (1986:20, 27-28) summary of the Swazi homestead illustrates Murdock's definition: "In control of the homestead is the patriarchal headman. A homestead may include the headman, his wives, his unmarried brothers and sisters, married sons with their wives and children, and unmarried sons and daughters, as well as more distant relatives. The term 'father' is extended from one's own father to his brothers, half brothers, and sons of his father's brothers. 'Mother' embraces his mother, his sisters, her co-wives, and wives of his father's brothers. The word for father's sister is literally 'female father,' and the mother's brother is 'male mother.'"

The Swazi obviously emphasize genealogical relations according to a rigid descent line. A Swazi behaves toward mother's brother very much as he behaves toward his mother, and treats his father's sister much like he does father, with dignity and respect. All wives of all homestead members become part of the homestead's work force, contributing offspring, labor, and products to it. This is obviously not the model Eggan tried to construct for the Hopi. The Hopi situation could not be more different. A "father" is almost a stranger in his own household. His children call his sister, *ikya'a*, "our aunt," and their mother's brother *itaha*, "our uncle." A male child may call him *!BaBa (ivava)*, "older brother," in which case uncle calls nephew *itupko*, "younger brother." It is older brothers and mother's brothers who are treated with deference and respect, not father's sisters. Boys especially have a joking, teasing, flirting relationship with *ikya'a*. Hopis are monogamous and there are no "co-wives" or co-husbands." The "married-ins" do *not* become part of their wives' clans, although they do produce offspring, labor, and products for the wife. A man may farm his wife's clan's lands and may be asked to contribute produce to her parents or sisters, but he also contributes to his own parents and to his own father's sister(s).

Eggan followed Forde (1947) in clearly distinguishing Hopi clans and lineages from those of the "African model." In his comparative sections, Eggan cited a theoretical overview by Daryll Forde, who had done the earliest research on Hopi ecology and farming. Forde noted the strong contrast between Hopi unilineal groups and those of African societies such as the Nuer. Forde (1947; cf. Forde 1949:4, 8-9) saw the Hopi and many African peoples as polar opposites where unilineal descent groups are concerned. The Hopi matrilineal groups are small, with each small lineal segment having a specific set of rights and responsibilities - *wuya* - differentiating it from others. In contrast, the Nuer patrilineages and patriclans are large and their segments are like nested boxes. Nuer patrilineages and patriclans are *not* socially *different* from each other; rather, they are smaller units of larger units. *Unlike* small Hopi matrilineages, the large Nuer patrilineal segments *do* have *the same* mutual obligations, rights and responsibilities with regard to one another, based on *common* descent. *Unlike* the large Nuer patrilineages, the small Hopi matrilineages and clans *differentiate* themselves from one another on the basis of *different* rights and responsibilities. "The Hopi have emphasized *social recognition*," Eggan (1950:16) stated emphatically "at the expense of *genealogical relations*." "With reference to the father's lineage the treatment of the lineage as a unit becomes clearer," Eggan (1950:25) went on. In father's matrilineage, "all women are either "grandmothers" or "father's sisters" and all the men are "fathers," regardless of generation." Eggan made it clear that neither "lineage" nor "clan" could be the "primary unit" of Hopi social organization because neither clan and lineage is a residential corporate group. Clan and lineage each denotes a degree of inclusion or exclusion. Neither is a neatly-defined, well-bounded, socially integrated group. Thus it is the *residential household* headed by a woman that is the primary *minimal* unit and the village that is the primary *maximal* unit. Eggan made it clear that only the rule of exogamy binds all members of all lineages and clans in a clan-cluster (phratry) *behaviorally* together in that the people they *cannot* marry constitute exactly the same individuals no matter which clan or lineage a particular member belongs to.

25. Not really millet, but actually a wild grass, Oryzopsis, "Indian ricegrass."

26. Rushforth and Upham (1992:43, 98-9, 117-120) have recently proposed a major re-interpretation of Hopi history and social organization. While provocative, their re-interpretation is fraught with errors. They propose that the ethnographic picture of Hopi social organization reconstructed by Eggan, Titiev, Parsons, and Lowie, dates only from the 1850s. They suggest that, in the half-century following the depopulation resulting from the smallpox epidemic of 1852-3, many ceremony-owning clans *created* the ceremonial secret societies because they did not have enough men for the clans to continue performing the ceremonies themselves. Although such a sudden change is a possibility, no Hopi ever mentioned anything about such a shift to Alexander Stephen, who interviewed numerous people in the early 1890s whose experiences and memories stretched far back before 1850. Rushforth and Upham make their suggestion with virtually no support from a comparative analysis of social organization of Zuni, Acoma, and Laguna - the other Western Pueblos - or the Eastern Pueblos. Eggan (1950:303-21) *did* do such a comparative analysis and concluded that in the Eastern Pueblos, clans and kinship ties were much less important than secret societies and other associational institutions. The growth in the importance of these associational institutions, said Eggan, probably resulted from a general tendency toward centralization brought on by efforts to regulate use of water for irrigation. But Hopis, having no permanent streams, emphasized prayers for rain rather than control of water. The emphasis on rain ceremonies would have promoted integration of virtually all members of a Hopi village, regardless of clan affiliation, into secret societies.

In contrast, Rushforth and Upham propose that prior to the epidemic, each Hopi village was composed of discrete units, clans, whose members had nothing to do with one another except in superficial social interactions and in marriage. No ceremonial secret societies cross-cut the clan system to integrate members of different clans with each other or to promote "associational" ties over kinship ties. While this suggestion is logical, its historical reality is doubtful. Besides the lack of ethnohistorical evidence for such a shift, several other facts argue against it. First, the striking parallels between the "roll-call" type of oratory in meetings witness by Escalante in the kiva in 1776 and that witnessed and documented by Stephen in the 1890s argue for corresponding parallels between the social roles associated with the "roll call" of the 1890s and that of the late 1770s. Secondly, if such a social organizational shift of ceremonial organization from clans to secret societies really did result from massive and sudden depopulation, why would it not have occurred after the smallpox epidemics postulated by Rushforth and Upham for the 1520s and 1580s? Or after the drought-induced depopulation of 1778-80? Or after the epidemic of 1681 (Spicer 1962:196)? Rushforth and Upham do not mention the epidemic of 1681, arguing that Hopis avoided epidemics from 1664 to 1851 by avoiding contacts with other groups. But Hopis were *not* isolated during this period, as has been shown in Chapter 3.

Thirdly, Rushforth and Upham (1992:118-9) are confused about Elsie Clews Parsons' (1922:297) documentation of men from "other clans" being brought in to fill the ceremonial role of Agave (Kwan, or One-Horn) Society Chief around 1905 at Shungopavi when only three male members of the Katsina-Parrot clan, which owned the right and obligation to fill that role, as well as the role of Singers (Tao) Society chief, were left. The Katsina-Parrot Clan kept the Singers Chief role, rotating it among the three men at four-year intervals, but gave up the One-Horn Chief's role to other clans. By 1922, that office had been filled four times by four different men of different clans, chosen by the Society's members. Rushforth and Upham confuse this situation with the asserted possibility of only Katsina-Parrot clan men being members of Tao and Kwan! Their assertion is ridiculous given the fact that all men were initiated into one of the four societies; if society membership was really so clan restricted, then there could have been only three clan groups in Shungopavi! Clearly, such could not have been the case.

Finally, Rushforth and Upham seem to be laboring under a misunderstanding of Hopi physical environment and Hopis' adaptations to it. They call Hopi farming techniques, as described by Hack (19420 "enormously successful" (Rushforth and Upham 1992:30-31). In reality, nothing could have been farther from the truth. The success of Hopi farming is unpredictable, with low rainfall, floods, pests, and a lack of permanent streams all intervening to frustrate even the best-calculated and most labor-intensive farming. Droughts and other environmental disasters probably kept Hopi society in constant danger of social and demographic upheaval. Spicer (1963:189) cited "the failing water supply which had been making life difficult in the Jeddito Valley for many years before the Spaniards' arrival" as causing abandonment of Sikyatki and other Hopi villages in the 1500s. If true, this increasing desiccation would have initiated increased efforts on Hopis' part to intensify ceremonies for rain in the absence of any permanent water supplies except springs. If clans shifted from performing ceremonies with their own members to creating secret societies composed of people from many clans to do the clan-owned ceremonies, they would have done so during this initial period of depopulation and contraction in the 1500s, not in the 1850s. Therefore we can be reasonably confident that the ethnographic reconstruction of the early 1900s describes the *structure* of Hopi social and ceremonial organization, allowing for much variation in its *content*, as it had been for at least 400 years.

27. Peter Whiteley (1986:73) tries to make it seem as if Hopis' distinctions of lineages and households as *de facto* groupings contrast with Eggan's embrace of what Whiteley calls (1985:363; 1986:72) "classic descent theory": the theory that unilineal descent groups are corporate, are structurally and functionally isomorphic, provide the structure of political action based on segmentary opposition, possess productive property, and thus may be compared within the same theoretical framework. But neither Eggan nor Titiev ever used, embraced, or advocated what Whiteley identifies as "classic descent theory." In reality, Eggan saw Hopi social organization as greatly modifying "corporate descent theory" and Titiev especially showed that Hopi descent groups were not isomorphic with regard to one another and that the structure of political action *defied* and largely cross-cut the clan system in the 1906 split. Titiev and Eggan certainly did think the clans possessed productive property and Titiev showed why: some clans had choice, fertile land on the banks of the Oraibi Wash, where it could be easily irrigated, while other clans had none. Eggan did not value a theoretical framework solely for the sake of comparison; it could also be used to *contrast very different kinds of "unilineal" descent groups*, and although Eggan did not do this, Forde (1947) did.

28. Peter Whiteley mentions a "diligent search" in the National Archives turning up no mention of a trip to Washington by Hopis in 1880. I do not know whether this "diligent search" is his or mine. I searched the National Archives in 1970 (Clemmer 1978: 30,n.5) If Whiteley also searched and found no record, it is hard to believe that both of us could have overlooked documentation of it. One Hopi man did go to Washington in March, 1882, but with Cushing, not with Keam. That was Nanahe, Cushing's interpreter, who accompanied him and Metcalf to Oraibi in November, 1882. Nanahe was apparently half-Navajo, half-Hopi, and had lived at Zuni, where Cushing met him. He was married to a Zuni woman and may have moved to Zuni during the 1864-68 drought, or may have even been born there. He was an adopted member

of the Zuni "Little Fire Order," but moved back to his home at First Mesa along with other "Zuni-Hopis" in the 1880s (Hinsley 171; cf. Cushing 1881 in Green 1990: 167.)

29. The ideology that framed this program justified it in the following terms: The experience of handling private property would promote knowledge of how to handle it; encourage entrepreneurship; promote the ethical values of nascent capitalism and wage labor; and shift the concept of responsibility from tribe and community to the individual, thereby heightening awareness of the obligations of individualized citizenship. Isolating children in boarding schools away from the "barbaric" influences of parents and community and result in the quick breakup of Indian societies. Suppressing Indian religion would ease missionaries' efforts to replace Indian beliefs and moral codes with Christian ones. The ideology rested on the false assumptions that Indians would naturally want to be like Anglo-Americans; that tribal ties, conducive to lack of competitiveness for upward social mobility, were doomed; and that Indians could not succeed economically without shedding most of their culture.

30. Mateer seems to have learned as much as he could about the Hopi and to have cultivated their interest; he was the first to advocate changing the Agency name from "Moki" or "Moqui" to "Hopi."He pointed out that, in Hopi language, "moki" meant "dead" (actually mo'moki = to have died), whereas "hopi" means "peaceful," and "right-living," and they much preferred to be called that. But the name "Moki" hung on officially until 1922.

31. Keam died in England, his home, in 1904.

32. Hubbell gave this trading post to his son, Lorenzo Hubbell, Jr., to operate. Hubbell, Jr. tried to expand the business by opening an outlet in Laguna Beach, California, in 1922 that marketed Hopi and Navajo arts and crafts, but it was unsuccessful and closed after six months. After Hubbell Sr.'s death in 1930 and Hubbell Jr.'s death in the 1940s, Roman Hubbell operated the post. Following his death, Roman's widow sold the post to Babbitt Brothers in 1958 or '59.

33. Too much moisture has caused similar problems in recent times. Rains and snowlmelt in February and March, 1978, were so heavy that disaster aid was provided to the Hopi area.

34. Ben and Nancy Priest, who raise churros in Parker, Colorado, inform me that churros are not as hard on the environment as other sheep because they move constantly, browsing. By 1977, however, fewer than

500 purebred churros were still alive because the strain had been bred almost to extinction with larger, more productive breeds.

35. The figure may be suspect. Since a permit system was not implemented until the 1940s, the Government Agency's sheep dipping records provide the only accurate counts. Government sheep dipping for sheep tick did not begin until around 1910. Navajos' sheep were trespassing on Hopi land as early as 1890. Thus, Navajos' sheep may have been included in some Hopi sheep counts since agents would not necessarily know how to tell the difference.

36. Even as late as 1971 commercial interests thought that publishing ethnographic information on the Hopi Snake Dance would lure travelers to the Four Corners area (cf. look 1971).

37. "In 1958, company officials allowed return of five Voth specimens for use in Second Mesa ceremonies," including "two masks believed to be the property of the Shungopavi Kachina and Cloud Clans, a stone fox, and a gourd ceremonial vessel" (Harvey 1963: 39-40.)

38. Scott Rushforth (Rushforth and Upham 1992) has proposed the split as the result of a revitalization movement, with the "Hostiles" generating the movement's leadership and ideology. He interprets the material conditions and acculturative pressures summarized here and by Clemmer (1978a) as relative deprivation establishing an important condition for the movement. The idea is intriguing but assumes that all of the "Hostiles" were of one mind. There is good evidence that they were not. Also, the ideology of resistance became much more highly developed and associated with prophecy *after* the split. See Chapter Seven.

39. The phrase is surely misapplied to the Hopi case. Joseph Stalin, called his take-over of power in the Soviet Union in the 1920s a "revolution from above." Skocpol (1985: 10), citing Ellen kay Timberger's *Revolution from Above*, notes that there must be a state and a bureaucratic elite that is "free of ties or alliances with dominant classes" to accomplish the revolution. Classic examples are the Meiji Restoration; Ataturk's overnight secularization of Turkey; Nasser's coup in Egypt; Peru's coup of 1968. The toppling of Kaiser Wilhelm II by Germany's Junkers also fits the definition.

40. Whiteley (1988a, 1988b) follows Nequatewa (1936: 125) in suggesting three rankings for Hopi society: *Mongcinum*: leaders of the kivas and high priests; *Pavan-cinum*, who hold no offices but belong to societies and take part in ceremonies; and low - *sukavung-cinum*, who do not belong to any societies and take part in no ceremonies. A tripartite ranking scheme is consistent with other Puebloan ideologies (cf. Ortiz 1969: 17-18.) But it

is doubtful that there were any Hopis who did not take part in ceremonies prior to the arrival of missionaries. Levy (1992) infers only two ranks: those who hold specific ritual offices and those who do not, regardless of ceremonial participation.

41. On an African model, for example.

42. Thus what seemed like the demise of ceremonies was actually the demise of the people who owned them. A parallel situation may have existed at Shipaulovi and Mishongnovi. Edmund Nequatewa in his autobiography mentions an observation by his father that, "You will find that clans that support different ceremonies will be vanishing. If this was the true way, the clans that have carried these ceremonies should be the only ones to prosper, and the poor people who never had any ceremonies would have vanished long ago because they would have no god" (Seaman/Nequatewa 1993:113.) But even though some clans did die out, their ceremonies did not die out in the Second Mesa villages because of the dynamics of Hopi clanship reviewed in Chapter Four.

43. The idea of being "free from all ceremonies" is mentioned by Edmund Nequatewa in his autobiography (Seaman/Nequatewa 1993:169.)

44. Whiteley's (1988b: 277) statement that Hotevilla's Wuwutsim society ceased public performances in the mid-1950s is puzzling, since their performances are never public and they were still doing them in the late 1960s.

45. One need only recall that in the 1920s D.W. Griffith made the film, "America" with the support of the DAR; Attorney General Palmer and his young assistant, J. Edgar Hoover, rounded up "subversive immigrants" in dragnet raids and deported them under the bogus Alien and Sedition Act; the trials of Sacco and Vanzetti and the Scotsboro Boys drew international attention as symbols of oppression and the rise of xenophobia in America; the Ku Klux Klan had a resurgence; and Africa-Americans were murdered publicly by lynchings.

46. Perhaps the most effective was Mabel Dodge Luhan, old friend of radical John Reed and wife of Taos Indian Tony Luhan and she started a crusade against first the Bursum Bill, then Circular 1655, enlisting writers Mary Austin, Mary Roberts Rinehart and D.H. Lawrence, who made his first and brief trip to New Mexico in September, 1922. She also enlisted the support of John Collier, later to become Commissioner of Indian Affairs, whom she had known from New York in the years 1913-1916, and who arrived at the same time. Mabel Dodge finally got Lawrence to the Hopi Snake Dance until 1924, when she persuaded her husband Tony to drive her and the Lawrences to Hotevilla one Sunday

in August. Lawrence hated the experience (too much sand, wind, heat) but he managed to write two sympathetic articles lending weight to the argument for religious freedom (Lawrence 1924, 1925, 1927). Collier, a crusader for social reform and better treatment of immigrants (Kunitz 1971), began crusading for better treatment of Indians in the then-muckraking sensationalist magazine *Sunset*. He even enlisted the General Federation of Women's Clubs in the cause (Kelly 1983:126-129; 272-3).

47. Sheep dippings in Black Leaf-40 were for sheep tick. But most sheep "dippings" were in a mixture of lime and sulphur against scabies. Indians and non-Indians alike dipped their sheep against scabies.

48. Historian Duberman's interest lay more in what the depositions and affidavits about public sexual burlesques and fertility rituals may have revealed about Hopis' private sex lives. But of interest here is the possible connection between the repression of public ritual expression and the subsequent factionalism and problems that La Farge encountered a decade later.

49. Billingsley's (1971) autobiography is so full of inaccuracies that it is hard to know how much to believe without confirmation from other sources.

50. He may have been. But photographer Charles Curtis claimed to have been the only white man initiated into the very same Snake Society at Mishongnovi, either in 1912 or sometime prior to 1907 (Graybill and Boesen 1976:78.)

51. The film was incorporated into the Hollywood-style documentary, *Broken Rainbow* (Clemmer 1987).

52. As junior senator from Arizona, Goldwater would co-sponsor the first Hopi land settlement legislation in 1957 and as senior senator, would shepherd the Navajo-Hopi Land Settlement Act of 1974 through the Senate.

53. Albert Yava, a Hopi-Tewa from First Mesa, described the kiva as "authentic." Yava was not part of the "Billingsley faction" and condemned his commercialization of Hopi ceremonies, as did nearly all other Hopis who knew about them. Yava was either under the impression that Billingsley was Hopi or considered him as such because Billingsley had been initiated into an important secret society: the Snake Society.

54. The last of these major tours seems to have been in 1934-35, but Billingsley continued to trek to Mishongnovi with his Shriners and was still able to commandeer a kiva for their meetings as late as 1969.

Notes

55. James (1956:157) places this exhibition in 1898. There may have been more than one.

56. The best examples are Albuquerque's Kimo Theater; Denver's Mayan Theater; the Federal Building in Albuquerque; and the Clovis and Shaffer Hotels in Clovis and Mountainair, New Mexico, respectively. The Harvey Company's Indian Room in the Alvarado Hotel; its El Navajo and La Posada Hotels in Gallup and Winslow; its El Tovar, Hopi House, and La Fonda as well as other hotels and the Santa Fe Railroad's Union Station in Los Angeles, all designed by Mary Colter (Grattan 1980), expressed the popularity of this style, and although edifices such as London's Hoover Building and Frank Lloyd Wright's Barnsdell House, built in 1917, were also ostensibly based on Mayan architecture (Klein et al. 1986:162).

57. Most Deco art was mass-produced. Deco art achieved a break with Art Nouveau and owed much to cubist painting (Klein et al. 1986; 110). Cubist painting in turn is said to have been inspired by African and Oceanic art to be found in the chaotic collections and dingy halls of the old Trocadero Museum, "where superb ethnographic collections lay neglected by all but a handful of artists and specialists" (Ades and Neff 1986:456). Cubist painting also contributed to the dada and surrealism movements in art literature following World War II (Ades and Neff 1986:29, 31).

58. Art Nouveau was a modernist "outgrowth of a desire to return to allegedly 'pure,' pre-industrial 'folk' forms of art" (Cantor 1988:11). The impetus for the pre-WW I Arts and Crafts Movement, the reaction against the out-of-the-same-mold products of the machine and the desire for the one-of-a-kind-and-I-have-it unique piece, was transferred to the collecting of Deco art (Klein et al. 1986:165-166).

59. Most notable were uranium leases in the Hopi Buttes in the early 1940s.

60. Its context had been established by a devastatingly frank report by the Brookings Institution, commissioned in 1927 by the Secretary of the Interior to investigate and report the administration of Indians. The Report targeted the failure of administrative decrees and policies to successfully guide the quasi-colonized wards of the Government into the American melting pot. It made one thing very clear: the assimilation policy had not only failed to work, but had also plunged Indians into the depths of poverty, illness, short life expectancy, and psychological malaise *because of* the very commitment to enforcing conformity (Meriam 1928).

61. Collier thought that once the Act was in place, however, Indian Tribes would automatically create their own autonomy. Collier's inspiration was the method of "indirect rule" pioneered by Lord Lugard in India and used by British colonial officials in Africa, particularly Nigeria (Philp 1977:74-5). Collier based his "Indian New Deal" on the proposition that Indians would rationally and logically plot the destiny of their culture and construct, or reconstruct, everything they needed in order to prosper as communities in the modern world, from ethics to economies. In this assumption, he was quite right. The irony in the policy lay in Collier's assumption that what constituted "Indian culture" would be immediately clear, and not open to debate, among Indians themselves. In this assumption he could not have been more wrong.

62. Opposition was most pronounced among "Traditional" Indians. According to Deloria and Lytle (1984:169), "Traditional" Indians understood what Collier was doing, but "Traditionals" frequently aligned themselves with "chronic critics" when they wished to criticize the tribal governments that Collier had helped establish (cf. Biolsi 1985). Traditional Indians by and large boycotted the IRA referenda. "Following most of the social and religious customs of their indigenous group, they also maintained nearly monolingual proficiency in the native language and relied upon oral tradition, rather than written records for an understanding of the bilateral relationship between the U.S. and the indigenous nation." When the IRA elections came along, "many traditional people did not vote because they felt they already had a government of chiefs; allowing any other government on the reservations would prove injurious to their rights" (Deloria and Lytle 1984:232). Thus, opposition to the IRA was, to some extent, linked to protecting indigenous autonomy. The Hopi were no exception.

63. Wyckoff (1990: 570) attributes Mishongnovi's vote "overwhelmingly in favor of the Constitution" to the influence of converts made by the nearby Baptist mission. But there is neither evidence connecting the vote to the mission's influence nor substantiation of many converts. Today, Mishongnovi remains one of only two villages with a complete Hopi religious ceremonial cycle.

64. In 1978, I thought 4,000 was closer to the mark and it probably is.

65. One might add that ideology can result in certain activities being undertaken, and at the same time justify those activities with reference to a set of fundamental beliefs that are either neutral in a larger context or reflect the underlying basis of the entire society. A viable political ideology will generate strategies in particular situations that can be successfully changed or reversed in new circumstances without

compromising the fundamental beliefs to which the ideology refers. Political ideologists often refrain from telling people exactly what their goals are for fear of being caught with some inconsistencies or contradictions somewhere down the line. A successful ideology allows individuals to slide back and forth between activity and inactivity; between commitment and indifference.

66. Most of the staff worked on all six projects and the list of participants in the Hopi Project reads like a who's who in social science: W. Lloyd Warner, Robert Havighurst, Erik Erikson, Clyde Kluckhohn, Alexander Leighton, Margaret Mead, Felix Cohen, Conrad Arensberg, Fred Eggan, Ruth Benedict, D'Arcy McNickle, Ruth Underhill, Edward Spicer, and many more. However, only two Hopis were included on the Project as actual researchers.

67. Collier created an entire unit of "applied anthropology" staffed with a half-dozen anthropologists. Half of them resigned after the first year (cf. Kelly 1980; Makeel 1944; Collier 1944; Steward 1969) because of profound philosophical differences about what could, should, or would be done on behalf of Indians, based on anthropological knowledge.

68. Thomas Banyacya

69. His grandfather was the Bow Clan man who had publicly burned his ceremonial altar in 1922. His father was never really a part of the Traditionalist Movement but did have close ties to Traditionalists in Oraibi. The grandfather, however, remained a staunch Mennonite, sponsoring prayer meetings outside his home two or three times a year; in the late 1960s he amplified them and thus "broadcast" them all over the village.

70. Personal communication, 1987

71. For details on the succession see Titiev 1972:344-5; James 1974:144-5; and Clemmer 1978a:33-35) for three slightly different accounts.

72. Nagata calls him "Kenneth Loma" in *Modern Transformations of Moenkopi Pueblo* (1970.) He has him born in 1902 but this is a misprint; Thomas was born in 1912.

73. Coal fires are too hot for nearly all wood-burning stoves and will cause the iron to warp and crack.

74. The Movement attained "peace religion" status for Hopi religion in 1965, resulting in the near-automatic ministerial and conscientious - objector status for Hopi boys who requested it. This proved important, of course, during the Vietnam War.

75. Lydia Wyckoff (1990:5, 6) also detects an expression of traditionalist ideology in pottery designs. She found "the differences between Traditionalists and Progressives" to be "not mere social preference, party politics or economic policies but ... so fundamental that each group conceived of the world around them differently. Different styles of decoration used by Progressive and Traditionalist potters are a material expression of their world view." The different ways in which Traditionalist and Progressive "potters present objects in space parallel their differing views of the world" (Wyckoff 1990:92). The depth of division between Progressivists and Traditionalists was revealed to her in one potter's statement: "We are two different people now" (Wyckoff 1990:6).

Wyckoff studied five Progressive and five Traditionalist potters from Third Mesa. It is not clear whether or not this sample was the entire universe of Third Mesa potters. One of the Third Mesa Progressive potters was Elizabeth White (Polingaysi Qoyawayma). (Wyckoff [1985: 86] has Polingaysi's birth date as 1892 but it was probably closer to 1886 or '87. She was running off to the mission school by 1893 or '94.) Two of the Progressivist potters are married to First Mesa men, and a third is the daughter of one. Thus, they all have ties to First Mesa, and although Wyckoff does not mention it, Elizabeth White's pottery-making was sanctioned by First Mesa potters because her clan, the Water Coyote Clan, was thought to have originally come from Sikyatki. They are all Christian. In contrast, the Traditionalist potters are all Corn Clan; married to Traditionalist men; learned pottery making either from mother, grandmother, or matrilateral aunt; and have no kin or affines on First Mesa.

The differences revolve around two distinct styles, one called "Polacca Polychrome," the other "Sikyatki Revival." Polacca Polychrome had been used by potters at all villages beginning around 1780. Oraibi potters developed a glazed variant known as "Oraibi crackled ware." But potters had ceased making the crackled ware by 1860. Additions of the "rain bird" motif and Moroccan-Spanish motifs such as dotted and solid crescents, rosettes, and petal flowers were made between 1860 and 1870 under Zuni influence, following Hopis' return from Zuni after the smallpox epidemics. Voth collected Polacca Polychrome pieces from Oraibi in 1909 that went into the Heye Collection in 1918 (Wyckoff 1990:76-77). Polacca Polychrome continued to be common Hopi pottery up to 1900.

But Sikyatki Revival almost entirely supplanted it as commercial pottery, probably because of its "deco" appeal discussed in the previous chapter. All the Progressivists except Elizabeth White work in the Sikyatki revival style, favoring many thin, fine lines, a mass of motifs and elements, a design structure in which design elements frequently abut or interlock, thus drawing the eye along a horizontal line, and more stylized and representational forms. They frequently use the feather, lightning, and raincloud motifs. In contrast, the Traditionalist potters working in the older Polacca Polychrome favor more naturalistic forms, and use a design structure of a single, free-standing motif surrounded by unpainted space that draws the eye to the center of a surface rather than along a horizontal line. Their motifs include free-standing Kachina faces; the hump - backed flute player; rainbird; sun; Four Corners/ Hopi land; bear paw; and corn - fertility symbols.

"Third Mesa Traditionalist pottery was not manufactured for the tourist market nor recognized as art pottery" by the Museum of Northern Arizona, according to Wyckoff (1990:83). Traditionalist potters preferred to barter their pottery to other Hopis or Puebloans rather than sell it, and kept their pottery out of the cash economy because of attitudes. Pottery, to them, was not considered an element in the cash economy (Wyckoff 1990:118-119). In contrast, the "Progressive potters, with their desire for Anglo- American goods and services, sell their pottery for money," making it specifically for the cash market. However, whether the concordance between differences in outlook toward money, use of different design structures, and religious participation is a variable of orientation toward or away from Traditionalist ideology and activities; or is a variable of economic and social factors, is not clear. That the Traditionalists were simply working in a long-established family tradition of Polacca Polychrome and in long-enduring bartering relationships, as opposed to the Progressivists who simply put their products into usual cash markets for Sikyatki Revival pottery to which they had access through their First Mesa in-laws, seems an equally plausible possibility.

Wyckoff also sees differences in use of space; furniture placement; and types of furniture between the Progressive potters as a group and the Traditionalist potters as a group. She sees coffee tables as especially diagnostic of Progressives.

76. At first, Peabody barred "unauthorized" removal of coal but then made it a policy to allow one pickup-load per household after a story appeared in a national news magazine exposing Peabody's ban on Indians helping themselves to the coal that they owned.

77. Since Shipaulovi's Kikmongwi, Joe Secakuku had just died, and since Shipaulovi was ceremonially affiliated with Shungopavi as its "daughter village", Shungopavi's Kikmongwi decided to represent Shipaulovi for purposes of the lawsuit. Representation for Bacavi and Kykotsmovi was claimed by the signatories from Hotevilla and by Mina Lanza.

78. Exhibit "A" was a statement to this effect drawn up by four Kikmongwis, David Monongye, and his brother Jack Pongayesva, Hotevilla's Snake Chief, together with the Traditionalists' interpreter, Thomas Banyacya, and Carlotta Shattuck, secretary-recorder from Walpi.

79. Upper Moenkopi had acquired an additional representative through population growth, in accordance with the Constitution's provision for one representative for every 250 people.

80. James (1974: 219) garbles this situation badly, confusing the Black Mesa Defense Fund with the Traditional Indian Unity Caravan and even with the "hippies" who briefly invaded Hopiland in 1966-68! While a couple of Hopi Traditionalists prominent in opposing strip-mining also participated in the Unity Caravan, the Caravan was organized by Iroquois from New York state. (See Chapter 7.) It predated the strip-mining issue by five years or more and was 100% Indian. In contrast, Black Mesa Defense was organized by non-Indians from Santa Fe. It had nothing to do with the Unity Caravan. James disparages all three categories of individuals as "divisive." The Black Mesa Defense and Unity Caravan people were probably no more "divisive," however, than James had been fifty years earlier in taking the side of Hopi religious traditionalists against Hopi Christians and missionaries.

81. Passage of the Navajo-Hopi Settlement Act of 1974 released the escrow funds and increased production upped the royalty revenues. By 1977 annual revenues to the Hopi Tribe were approaching $1 million.

82. Marking boundaries with piles of stones was not uncommon at the time since Alexander Stephen was told in 1888 that about forty years previous, before the smallpox epidemic (1853), men had marked the boundaries of clan farm lands with piles of stones.

83. According to Pahona (1972:175-6), this line was "in the same ... vicinity as the line drawn by Gov. David Merriwether in 1855 to mark the boundary line between the Navaho and the Hopi people".

84. Whitson (1985: 393 n.166) erroneously gives 1944 as the date of Boyden's appointment as Hopi Tribal attorney and the Secretary of the Interior as *making* the appointment. Boyden was contracted as claims attorney by the four consolidated villages of First Mesa and three other Hopi villages and by the Tribal Council in 1951 and as General Counsel by the Tribal Council in 1952. The Secretary of the Interior *approved* the contract.

85. Based on the Navajo Tribal estimate of 178,124 for the reservation population; the Census Bureau's figure was 136,698 on the reservation for 1990 (Navajo Times 1990.)

86. In a footnote to his report, Carey explicitly excepted himself from the recommendation, raising an objection to such services being intended for "only a selected few individuals."

87. Hopi Tribe 1986a: 6 gave the figure as 34,000 acres but Hopi Tribe 1986b: 5 gives it as 39,000 acres.

88. John Boyden initiated six of them before his death in 1980. His law practice was taken over by relatives and in-laws who had been his partners. In June, 1986, unhappy with the firm's representation of an energy firm in a lawsuit with regard to a different Tribe's sovereignty in tax matters and with the contract offered by the firm for pursuing the 1934 Reservation case, the Hopi Tribe severed its ties with the firm and hired different lawyers.

89. The Court also relied heavily on expert witness testimony from Scott Russell, on the Navajo Tribe. Peter Whiteley provided expert witness testimony on the Hopi side.

90. A "sheep unit" is the same as one sheep and one-quarter of a steer, i.e., one steer or cow = 1 animal unit; one horse = 1.25 animal unit; one sheep = .25 animal unit.

91. James (1974: 219) confuses the "hippie invasion" of 1966-68 with involvement of environmental activists from the Black Mesa Defense Fund and the Sierra Club in the opposition to strip-mining and pollution from power plants in the Four Corners area between 1970 and 1972.

92. One steer or cow = 1 animal unit; one horse = 1.25 animal unit; one sheep = .25 animal units. In terms of overall grazing, Hopis were grazing more livestock in 1978 than they had since 1900.

93. But does it also include traditional songs, oral histories and legends, recorded by ethnomusicologists and ethnographers (Seeger 1991)? Does it include styles, motifs, images, forms and cultural customs such as Katsinas or curing with crystals? Some Native Americans would say that it does (Durham 1992) and have called for equal treatment of all Native American and Euro-derived literature, whether fiction and poetry created by individuals for sale and dissemination or traditional oral-historical literature, as "literary" as well as "ethnographic" (Rose 1992:409). For example, the Hopi Tribal Council tried unsuccessfully to copyright "Katsina" in the 1960s not only to protect Hopi Katsina doll carvers from suffering inroads into their market from Navajo, non-Indian, and other Indian carvers, but also to stop the debasement of the concept trough commercialization: Katsina motel, Katsina gallery, Katsina dry cleaners. Another case concerns the "Smokis." For years various Hopi religious leaders and Traditionalists protested the "Smoki" Snake Dance, put on by

a group of Anglo businessmen from Prescott, Arizona calling themselves "Smokis" who started performing Native American dances just when they were most under assault, in 1921. The first protests from Hopi Tribal administration were lodged in 1980 and in 1990 the Tribal Council not only registered its official protest but also organized a demonstration in Prescott led by the Tribal Chairman and Vice-Chairman. Billed as the performance of a "Pueblo dance which has not been performed in the Pueblos of new Mexico for several decades," a Smoki performance in 1989 attracted eleven spectators from Zuni Pueblo. Surprised to find a bunch of painted and costumed non-Indians dancing with bull snakes in their mouths in a clumsy aping of the Hopi (not the Puebloan) Snake Dance, the Zunis notified the All-Indian Pueblo Council which prepared a request for the Smokis to stop. The Smokis' response was to carry on. "You are only minorities protesting here today," said a spokesman from Prescott, adding that the Smokis were preserving a dying Hopi ritual. Nonsense, replied a Hopi, this "important Hopi ritual is being preserved not by white people for money, but by the Snake and Antelope Societies of Mishongnovi and Shungopavi villages." "They have not gone through the phases of initiation," objected religious leader Herman Lewis. The Smoki dances "are an affront to the Hopi people and we ask that these gross misrepresentations of our sacred ceremonials be immediately stopped," declared Tribal Chairman Vernon Masayesva (Qua' Toqti 1980c; Hopi Tribe 1990:1,4).

94. It was reported that this was the first time any museum and the Heard especially had returned anything to a religious society rather than to a tribal government, but this was not quite true. Both the Heard and the Denver Art museums had returned ceremonial items to heads of Hopi religious societies in the 1970s and 1960s (cf. Childs 1980: 19.)

95. Arrests of Hopis were made in two more cases in 1983. Frisbie (1987:258) reports that "in one a Hopi individual was fined and sentenced to six months in jail for stealing and selling three sacred ancestral figures. Hopi police and the FBI were still trying to recover the sacred items" as of the mid-1980s. "In the other, a Flagstaff individual was arrested for trying to sell two Hopi masks reportedly stolen earlier by a man from Hotevilla." Several Hopi items were identified for sale in various southwestern Indian arts and crafts stores and galleries between 1980 and 1985: Hopi Snake Dance rattles going for $75 to $100; a Mudhead (*koyemsi*) mask for $750; various Hopi dance masks for $1,400-1,500 (Frisbie (1987:359). In 1985 the FBI seized three stolen masks donated to the Chicago Art Institute and returned them to the Hopis (Barnett 1990:142).

96. What NAGPRA does not cover, a private philanthropic association hopes to. Elizabeth Sackler just happened to see the catalogue; went to the auction; bid on the masks until she got them, paying $24,200 for *Aholi* and $1,650 for *Koyemsi* (Reif 1991), and returned them to Herman Lewis, First Mesa's Katsina chief on July 4, 1991. Sackler then founded the American Indian Ritual Object Repatriation Foundation with Heard Museum Director Martin Sullivan and several Native Americans, including Tuscarora attorney Richard Hill, as co-trustees. AIRORF solicits gifts of sacred objects from donors for return to their Native American stewards (Sackler et al. 1992).

97. Another scenario erroneously attributes the loss of ceremonial objects to political changes: "A liberal Hopi regime in the early '80s voted to sell material," wrote Amy Page (1990) in *Art and Auction.* "That regime has been replaced by conservative elders who are actively interested in recovering ceremonial artifacts sold legally or illegally in past years." The scenario is entirely wrong and completely in error; no Hopi "regime" ever "voted to sell" artifacts.

98. Titiev (1944: 82 n. 117) says that "once an individual has taken office he is regarded as the owner of it, and may dispose of it as he likes." But arbitrarily "disposing" of a sacred object puts the individual at considerable risk of peril.

99. Childs (1980) reports the date of the last public flogging at Zuni as 1917, but in fact, a Zuni man's illegal sale of a ceremonial mask, which was recovered, resulted in his being publicly flogged in 1989.

100. All population figures are drawn from the following sources: 1846-1954, U.S. BIA estimates, except 1853, drawn from Donaldson 1894:177 and 1890, from the U.S. Census Bureau. In Table 6.1, 1940 #2, is from Thompson 1945[?]; 1953 #2 is from U.S. House of Representatives 1953. The 1960 estimates are as follows: #1 - *Southwest Indians* (1969, Albuquerque: New Mexico State Tourist Information Agency); #2 - U.S. Census Bureau; #3 - Sam Stanley, Smithsonian Institution, figures compiled for the fourth edition of map, *The North American Indians* (Chicago: University of Chicago); #4 - U.S. Economic Development Administration, *Federal and State Indian Reservations* (1971, Washington, DC); #5 -U.S. Bureau of Indian Affairs, *Hopi Indian Reservation* (1970, Keams Canyon) (This figure is for total population; the BIA estimated 4,400 on-reservation); #6 - Henry Hough, 1967, *Development of Indian Resources* (1967: Denver: World Press) The 1963, 1964, and 1970 estimates are from the BIA. Table 6.2: the 1970 #2 and 1986 estimates are from Hopi Tribe in U.S. Department of the Interior 1989: III-39. The 1980 and 1990 figures from the U.S. Census.

References

Abel, Annie Heloise, ed. 1915. The Official Correspondence of James S. Calhoun, While Indian Agent at Santa Fe and Superintendent of Indian Affairs in New Mexico. Washington, D.C.: U.S. Government Printing Office.

Aberle, David F. 1966. The Peyote Religion Among the Navaho. Viking Fund Publications in Anthropology 42. New York: Wenner-Gren Foundation for Anthropological Research.

_____ . 1974. Statement of David F. Aberle before the Committee on Interior and Insular Affairs, United States Senate, *and* Statement for submission to the Senate Committee on Interior and Insular Affairs, July 24, 1974. Pp. 3ll- 388 in U.S. Senate Committee on Interior and Insular Affairs, 93rd Congress, Second Session. Hearing on Navajo-Hopi Land Dispute, July 24, 1974. Washington, D.C.: U.S. Government printing Office.

_____ . 1993. The Navajo-Hopi Land Dispute and Navajo Relocation. Pp. 153-200 in Michael M. Cernea and Scott Guggenheim, eds. Anthropological Approaches to Resettlement: Policy, Practice, and Theory. Boulder: Westview Press.

Adams, E. Charles 1982. Walpi Archaeological Project: Synthesis and interpretation. Flagstaff: Museum of Northern Arizona.

_____ . 1989. Passive Resistance: Hopi Responses to Spanish Contact and Conquest. Pp. 77-91 in David Hurst Thomas, ed. Columbian Consequences. Volume 1: Archaeological and Historical Perspectives on the Spanish Borderlands West. Washington, D.C.: Smithsonian Institution Press.

Adams, William Y. 1963. Shonto: A Study of the Role of the Trader in a Modern Navaho Community. Bureau of American Ethnology Bulletin 188. Washington, D.C.: Smithsonian Institution.

Ades, Dawn and Terry Ann R. Neff 1986. In the Mind's Eye: dada and surrealism. Prepared on the occasion of the exhibition "Dada and Surrealism in Chicago Collections," Museum of Contemporary Art, Chicago, December 1, 1984-January 27, 1985. Chicago: Museum of Contemporary Art.

Akwesasne Notes 1971. Return of Wampum Belts, Treaty Concern Indians; Iroquois Sculptor Says Indian "Can No Longer Wait for Help"; Tired...; Reply...; "Like we Locked Up Your Bible and Crosses..."; Belts Belong to Iroquois; An Open Letter to A Museum Director; 100 Indians Protest; 12 Indians Jailed Over Protest at Museum. Akwesasne Notes 3(1): 11; 3(2): 38,40; 3(3): 9.

Albuquerque Journal 1985. Hopis Present Case at Inter-American Congress. November 1.

Albert, Roy and David Leedom Shaul, comp. 1985. A Concise Hopi and English Lexicon. N.P.: John Benjamins.

Ambler, Marjane 1990. Breaking the Iron Bonds: Indian Control of Energy Development. Lawrence: University Press of Kansas.

American Indian Historical Society 1970a. Issue of the Iroquois Wampum. Indian Historian 3(4): 63.

_____. 1970b. The Iroquois Wampum Controversy ...; Belts ...; Law...; Constitution ...; Religiosity ...; Rebuttal to 5 Anthropologists. Indian Historian 3(2): 4-18.

Anaya, S. James 1990. The Capacity of International Law to Advance Ethnic or Nationality Rights Claims. Iowa Law Review 75(4): 837-844.

ARCIA=Annual Reports of the Commissioner of Indian Affairs 1877-1908. Washington, D.C.: U.S. Government Printing Office.

ARDOI,IA=Annual Reports of the Department of the Interior on Indian Affairs 1901-22. Annual Reports of the Secretary of the Interior, Indian Affairs. Washington, D.C.: U.S. Government Printing Office.

Arizona Department of Commerce n.d. Hopi Reservation Community Profile. Phoenix: State of Arizona.

Arnold and Porter, Attorneys at Law 1993. Communication to Hopi Tribe. February 16. Denver.

Associated Press 1992. Hopis deride land award as meager, vow to appeal. The Arizona Republic. September 17: B3.

Baars, Donald L. 1972. Red Rock Country: The Geologic History of the Colorado Plateau. Garden City: Doubleday.

Baer, Joshua 1989. Twelve Classics. Santa Fe: Joshua Baer.

Bailey, Garrick and Roberta Bailey 1986. A History of the Navajos: Reservation Years. Santa Fe: School of American Research.

Bailey, Paul 1948. Jacob Hamblin, Buckskin Apostle. Los Angeles: Westernlore Press.

Bandelier, Adolph. 1892. Final Report of Investigations Among the Indians of the Southwestern United States, Carried on Mainly in the Years From 1880 To 1885. Part II. Cambridge: Wilson and Son, University Press.

Barnett, Catherine 1990. Of Masks and Marauders. Art and Antiques. October: 98-109, 141-148.

Barsh, Russell Lawrence 1991. American Indians in the Great War. American Indian Culture and Research Journal 38: 276-303.

Bartlett, Katherine 1936. Hopi History, No. 2, The Navajo Wars -- 1823-1870. Museum of Northern Arizona Notes 8(7): 33-37.

Bennett, John W. 1946. The Interpretation of Pueblo Culture: A Question of Values. Southwestern Journal of Anthropology 2: 361-374.

Bentley, Wilder, ed. 1957. Hopi Meeting of Religious People. Hotevilla, Arizona. August 4,5, 1956. N.P.: Wilder Bentley

Berkhofer, Robert F., Jr. 1978. The White Man's Indian. New York: Alfred A. Knopf.

Billingsley, M. W. 1971. Behind the Scenes in Hopi Land. [Mesa, AZ?]: M.W. Billingsley.

Bingham, Sam and Janet; Hank Willie; Wayne Charlie; Rudy Begay; Rex Lee Jim; and Judy Apachee 1984. Between Sacred Mountains. Tucson: Sun Tracks and the University of Arizona Press.

Biolsi, Robert 1985. The IRA and the Politics of Acculturation: The Sioux Case. American Anthropologist 87: 656-659

Black, C.E. 1966. The Dynamics of Modernization. New York: Harper and Row.

Blair, William G. 1989. Hopi Priest Claims Mask at Pier Show Was Stolen. New York Times Oct. 21: 27,30.

Bodley, John 1989. Victims of Progress. Third Edition. Menlo Park: Cummings.

BOIC=Board of Indian Commissioners 1922. Fifty-Third Annual Report of the Board of Indian Commissioners to the Secretary of the Interior for Fiscal Year Ended June 30. Washington, D.C.: U.S. Government Printing office.

Bourke, John G. 1884. Snake-Dance of the Moquis. New York: Scribners.

Bradfield, Richard Maitland. 1971. The Changing Pattern of Hopi Agriculture. Royal Anthropological Institute Occasional Paper 30.

Brandt, Richard B. 1954. Hopi Ethics. Chicago: University of Chicago Press.

Braudel, Fernand 1981. Structures of Everyday Life: The Limits of the Possible. New York: Harper and Row.

_____ . 1982. Wheels of Commerce. New York: Harper and Row.

_____ . 1984. Perspective of the World. New York: Harper and Row.

Breckenridge, Carol A. 1989. The Aesthetics and Politics of Colonial Collecting: India at World Fairs. Comparative Studies in Society and History 31: 195-215.

Brew, John Otis 1949. The History of Awatovi; Excavations of Franciscan Awatovi. Pp. 1-43, 47-99 in Ross Gordon Montgomery; Watson Smith; and John Otis. Franciscan Awatovi. Papers of the Peabody Museum of American Archaeology and Ethnology, Harvard University. Volume 36. Cambridge.

Brinkley-Rogers, Paul 1986. Hopi-Navajo relocation hurts rights, Europe says. Arizona Republic. July 5.

_____ . 1991. Prosecution is unlikely in theft of Hopi mask. Arizona Republic. December 5: B5.

_____ . 1992. Museum gives ancient relic back to Hopis. Arizona Republic. April 15.

Brugge, David M. 1983. Navajo Prehistory and History to 1850. Pp. 489-501 in Alfonso Ortiz, ed. Handbook of North American Indians, Vol. 10, Southwest. Washington, D.C.: Smithsonian Institution.

Budnik, Dan 1979. A Hopi Portfolio. Rocky Mountain July/August: 44-48.

Buschenreiter, Alexander 1983. Unser Ende ist Euer Untergang: Die Botschaft der Hopi und anderer US-Indianer an die Welt. Dusseldorf: Goldmann/Econ Verlag.

_____ . 1988. Mahnung zur Umkehr. Pp. 114-21 in Albert Kunze, ed. Hopi und Kachina: indianische Kultur im Wandel. Munchen: Trickster Verlag.

Calinescu, Matei 1977. Faces of Modernity. Bloomington: Indiana University Press.

Cantor, Norman F. 1988. Twentieth-century Culture. New York: Peter Lang.

Carrington, Dorothy 1971. Granite Island: A Portrait of Corsica. London: Longmans.

Castaneda, Pedro de 1940[1596] Castaneda's History of the Expedition: Narrative of the Expedition to Cibola, Undertaken in 1540, in Which Are Described All Those Settlements, Ceremonies, and Customs. Pp. 191-238 in George P. Hammond and Agapito Rey, eds. Coronado Cuarto Centennial Publications, 1540-1940, Volume 2. Narratives of the Coronado Expedition 1540-1542,. Albuquerque: University of New Mexico Press.

Champagne, Duane 1989. American Indian Societies: Strategies and Conditions of Political Survival. Cambridge: Cultural Survival.

Childs, Elizabeth 1980. Museums and the American Indian: Legal Aspects of Repatriation. Council for Museum Anthropology Newsletter 4(4): 4-27.

Churchill, Ward 1992. The Earth is Our mother: Struggles for American Indian Land and Liberation in the Contemporary United States. Pp. 139-88 in M. Annette Jaimes, ed. The State of Native America: Genocide, Colonization and Resistance. Boston: South End Press.

Clemmer, Richard O. 1968-87. Field Notes. Ms.

_____ . 1969. The Fed-up Hopi. Journal of the Steward Anthropological Society 1: 18-40.

_____ . 1972. Truth, Duty, and the Revitalization of Anthropologists. Pp. 213-247 in Dell H. Hymes, ed. Reinventing Anthropology. New York: Random House.

_____ . 1973. Culture Change and the Hopi Nation: The Impact of Federal Jurisdiction. Binghamton: Department of Anthropology, State University of New York (processed ms.).

_____ . 1977. Hopi Political Economy: Industrialization and Alienation. Southwest Economy and Society 2: 9-33.

_____ . 1978a. Continuities of Hopi Culture Change. Ramona: Acoma Books.

_____ . 1978b. Black Mesa and The Hopi. pp. 17-34 in Joseph G. Jorgensen, ed. Native Americans and Energy Development. Cambridge: Anthropology Resource Center.

_____ . 1982. Nationales Opfergebiet: Die Energieentwicklung auf dem Colorado Plateau und ihre wirtschaftlichen, okologischen und kulturellen Folgen fur die indianische Bevolkerung. Pp. 66-112 in Stefan Dompke, ed. Tod unter Dem kurzen Regenbogen: Das Colorado Plateau als heiliges Land -- Indianische Traditionen, Energieentwicklung und Neue Physik. Munchen: Trikont-Dianus.

_____ . 1985. Effects of the Energy Economy on Pueblo Peoples. Pp. 79-115 in Joseph Jorgensen, ed. Native Americans and Energy Development II. Boston and Forestville: Anthropology Resource Center and The Seventh Generation Fund.

_____ . 1986. Hopis, Western Shoshones, and Southern Utes: Three Different Responses to the Indian Reorganization Act of 1934. American Indian Culture and Research Journal 10:15-40.

_____ . 1987. Review of "Broken Rainbow," a film by Maria Florio and Victoria Mudd. American Anthropologist 89(4):1014-1015.

_____ . 1988. Politische Macht bei den Hopi. Pp. 44-60 in Albert Kunze, ed. Hopi und Kachina: Indianische Kultur im Wandel. Munchen: Trickster Verlag.

_____ . 1993. Review of When Jesus Came, The Corn Mothers Went Away: Marriage, Sexuality, and Power in New Mexico, 1500-1846, by Ramon A. Gutierrez. The Journal of Peasant Studies 20:538-41.

Clemmer, Richard O.; David F. Aberle; Joseph G. Jorgensen; and Thayer Scudder 1989. Anthropology, Anthropologists, and the Navajo-Hopi Land Dispute. American Anthropologist 91: 743-753.

Clifford, James 1988. The Predicament of Culture. Cambridge: Harvard University Press.

Cohen, Felix 1946. Ownership of the Mineral Estate in the Hopi Executive Order Reservation. Opinion of June 11. P. 1396 in Opinions of the Solicitor, Indian Affairs. Washington, D.C.: Government Printing Office.

Colby, Benjamin N., David F. Aberle and Richard O. Clemmer 1992. Hopi-Navajo Land Dispute: Report for 1991. Washington, D.C.: American Anthropological Association.

Collier, John 1936. Letter to Secretary of the Interior, September 11. Copy in Healing v. Jones files, Museum of Northern Arizona, Flagstaff.

_____ . 1939. Minutes of Meeting among John Collier, Oliver La Farge, Peter Nuvamsa, and other Hopis. Mimeo. Copy in author's possession.

_____ . 1944. Collier Replies to Makeel. American Anthropologist 46: 422-426.

_____ . 1963. From Every Zenith. Denver: Sage Books.

Colton, Harold S. 1934. A Brief Survey of Hopi Common Law. Museum of Northern Arizona Notes 7(6): 21-24.

Colton, Mary-Russell F. 1936. Notes. Pp. 125-135 in Edmund Nequatewa, Truth of a Hopi. Flagstaff: Museum of Northern Arizona Press.

Congressional Record 1926. Congressional Record-Senate. Sixty-Ninth Congress, First Session. Congressional Record 67.

_____ . 1946. Indian Claims Commission. Proceedings and Debates of the 79th Congress, Second Session. Congressional Record 92(4).

_____ . 1986. Navajo-Hopi Land Dispute. June 5. Pp. H3431-H3434.

Connelly, John C.

_____ . 1979. Hopi Social Organization. Pp. 539-553 in Alfonso Ortiz, ed. Handbook of North American Indians, Vol. 9, Southwest. Washington, D.C.: Smithsonian Institution.

Cook, Earl 1975. Man, Energy, Society. San Francisco: W.H. Freeman.

Cornell, Stephen I. 1988. The Return of the Native. New York: Oxford University Press.

Correll, J. Lee 1979. Through White Men's Eyes, A Contribution to Navajo History. Six Volumes. Window Rock: Navajo Heritage Center.

Costo, Rupert 1983. The Indian New Deal 1928-1945. Pp. 10-14 in Kenneth Philp, ed. Indian Self-Rule: Fifty Years under the Indian Reorganization Act. Sun Valley: Institute of the American West.

Courlander, Harold 1971. The Fourth World of the Hopis. New York: Crown.

———. 1978. Notes. Pp. 150-156 in Albert Yava, Big Falling Snow. New York: Crown.

———. 1982. Hopi Voices. Albuquerque: University of New Mexico Press.

Cox, Bruce. 1970. What is Hopi Gossip About? Information Management and Hopi Factions. Man 5: 88-98.

Crane, Leo 1925. Indians of the Enchanted Desert. Boston: Little, Brown.

Creamer, Winifred 1990. Archaeologists' Ethical Dilemmas: Collecting, Collectors, Collections. Anthropology Newsletter. May, 1990: 43.

Cushing, Frank Hamilton 1883. Origin Myth from Oraibi. Unpublished Ms. Copy in author's possession.

———. 1923. Origin Myth from Oraibi. Elsie Clews Parsons, ed. Journal of American Folklore 36: 163-70.

Deloria, Vine Jr. 1974. Behind the Trail of Broken Treaties. New York: Delta.

———. 1992. Trouble in High Places: Erosion of American Indian Rights to Religious Freedom in the United States. Pp. 267-290 in M. Annette Jaimes, ed. The State of Native America: Genocide, Colonization and Resistance. Boston: South End Press.

Deloria, Vine Jr. and Clifford Lytle 1984. The Nations Within: The Past and Future of American Indian Sovereignty. New York: Pantheon.

Dockstader, Frederick J. 1979. Hopi History, 1859-1940. Pp. 524-532 in Alfonso Ortiz, ed. Handbook of North American Indians, Volume 9, Southwest. Washington, D.C.: Smithsonian Institution.

———. 1985. The Kachina and the White Man: The Influence of White Culture on the Hopi Kachina Cult. Albuquerque: University of New Mexico Press (Revised edition of original 1954 edition.)

Donaldson, Thomas 1893. Moqui Pueblo Indians of Arizona and Pueblo Indians of New Mexico: Extra Census Bulletin. Census Report on the Population of the United States at the Eleventh Census. 1890. Part 2. Washington, D.C.: U.S. Government Printing Office.

Donovan, Bill 1971. Hopi Oppose Navajo Fence; Concentration Camp for Hopis. Gallup Independent November 24, 1971.

Dozier, Edward P. 1966. Hano: A Tewa Indian Community in Arizona. New York: Holt, Rinehart, and Winston.

Duberman, Martin Bauml, Fred Eggan and Richard O. Clemmer, eds. 1979. Documents in Hopi Indian Sexuality: Imperialism, Culture, and Resistance. Radical History Review 20: 99-130.

Durham, Jimmie 1992. Cowboys and ... Notes on Art, Literature, and American Indians in the Modern American Mind. Pp. 423-38 in M. Annette Jaimes, ed. The State of Native America: Genocide, Colonization and Resistance. Boston: South End Press.

Eggan, Dorothy 1943. The General Problem of Hopi Adjustment. American Anthropologist 45(3):357-73.

_____. 1956. Instruction and Affect in Hopi Cultural Continuity. Southwestern Journal of Anthropology 12(4):347-70.

Eggan, Fred 1950. Social Organization of the Western Pueblos. Chicago: University of Chicago Press.

_____. 1967. From History to Myth: A Hopi Example. Pp. 33-53 in Dell H. Hymes and William Bittles, eds. Studies in Southwestern Ethnolinguistics: Meaning and History in the Languages of the American Southwest. The Hague: Mouton.

_____. 1974a. Letter to Senator Henry M. Jackson, February 9, 1973. Pp. 189-195 in U.S. Senate Committee on Interior and Insular Affairs, 93rd Congress, Second Session. Hearing on Navajo-Hopi Land Dispute, July 24, 1974.

_____. 1974b. Letter to Senator Henry M. Jackson, July 6, 1974. Pp. 172-180 in U.S. Senate Committee on Interior and Insular Affairs, 93rd Congress, Second Session. Hearing on Navajo-Hopi Land Dispute, July 24, 1974.

_____. 1974c. Letter to John S. Boyden, July 18, 1974. Pp. 170-171 in U.S. Senate Committee on Interior and Insular Affairs, 93rd Congress, Second Session. Hearing on Navajo-Hopi Land Dispute, July 24, 1974.

Eggan, Fred, Richard O. Clemmer and Martin Bauml Duberman 1980. Hopi Indians Redux. Radical History Review 24: 177-187.

Eliade, Mircea 1954. The Myth of the Eternal Return. New York: Pantheon.

Elston, Catherine Feher 1988. Children of Sacred Ground. Flagstaff: Northland.

_____. 1990. Bahnimptewa wants Navajos to move. Navajo-Hopi Observer. August.

Enloe, Cynthia H. 1972. Ethnic Conflict and Political Development. Boston: Little, Brown.

Fenton, William N. 1957. Factionalism at Taos Pueblo, New Mexico. Anthropological Papers 56. Bureau of American Ethnology Bulletin 164: 297-344. Washington, D.C.: Smithsonian Institution.

Ferguson, T.J. and E. Richard Hart 1985. A Zuni Atlas. Norman: University of Oklahoma Press.

Fewkes, Jesse Walter 1892. A Journal of American Ethnology and Archaeology. Volume II. Pp. 1-160. Boston: Houghton, Mifflin.

_____. 1895a. Preliminary Account of An Expedition to the Cliff Villages in the Red Rock Country, and the Tusayan Ruins of Sikyatki and Awatobi, Arizona, in 1895. Annual Report. Smithsonian Institution: 557-88.

_____. 1895b. Catalogue of the Hemenway Collection in the Hispanic-American Exposition of Madrid. Pp. 279-326 in Report. U.S. Commission to the Columbian Exposition at Madrid. Washington, D.C.: U.S. Government Printing Office.

_____. 1896. Preliminary Account of an Expedition to the Pueblo Ruins Near Winslow, Arizona, in 1896. Pp. 517-40 in Annual Report of the Smithsonian Institution.

_____. 1897. Tusayan Katcinas. Bureau of American Ethnology Report 15: 245-313. Washington, D.C.: Smithsonian Institution.

_____. 1901. An Interpretation of Katcina Worship. Journal of American Folk-Lore 14 (53): 81-94.

_____. 1902a. Minor Hopi Festivals. American Anthropologist new series 4: 482-511.

_____. 1902b. Sky-God Personalities in Hopi Worship. Journal of American Folklore 15(56): 14-32.

_____. 1919. Designs on Prehistoric Hopi Pottery. Accompanying Paper. Thirty-Third Annual Report, pp. 207-284. Bureau of American Ethnology. Washington, D.C.: Smithsonian Institution.

_____. 1921. Ancestor Worship of the Hopi Indians. Smithsonian Institution Annual Report, pp. 485-506. Washington, D.C.: Government Printing Office.

_____. 1922. Oraibi in 1893 in Elsie Clews Parsons, ed. Contributions to Hopi History. American Anthropologist 24: 253-298.

Ford, John Anson 1955. It's Wild Where the Hopis Dance. Motor Life. September: 3-5, 44.

Forde, C. Daryll 1931. Hopi Agriculture and Land Ownership. Journal of the Royal Anthropological Institute 41: 357- 405.

_____. 1947. The Anthropological Approach to Social Science. British Association for the Advancement of Science 4(15).

_____. 1949. The Integration of Anthropological Studies. Journal of the Royal Anthropological Institute 78: 1-10.

Forrest, Earle R. 1961. The Snake Dance of the Hopi Indians. Los Angeles: Westernlore Press.

Fortes, M. 1953. Social Anthropology at Cambridge Since 1900. An Inaugural Lecture. London: The Syndics of the Cambridge University Press.

Frank, Andre Gunder and Barry K. Gills 1992. The Five Thousand Year World System: An Interdisciplinary Introduction. Humboldt Journal of Social Relations 18: 1-80.

Frisbie, Charlotte 1987. Navajo Medicine Bundles or Jish: Acquisition, Transmission, and Disposition in the Past and Present. Albuquerque: University of New Mexico Press.

Fuchs, Estelle and Robert Havighurst 1972. To Live on This Earth: American Indian Education. Garden City: Doubleday.

Fynn, Arthur J. 1907. The American Indian As A Product of Environment, With Special Reference to the Pueblos. Boston: Little, Brown.

Gallup Independent 1971. BVD to Improve Employe Conditions. May 26: 6.

_____. 1972. Navajos Set Up Human Wall. Gallup Independent June 29.

Geertz, Armin 1987a. (with Michael Lomatuway'ma) Children of Cottonwood: Piety and Ceremonialism in Hopi Indian Puppetry. Lincoln: University of Nebraska Press.

_____. 1987b. Prophets and Fools: The Rhetoric of Hopi Indian Eschatology. European Review of Native American Studies 1: 33-46.

Geertz, Clifford. 1973. The Interpretation of Cultures: Selected Essays. New York: Basic Books.

Gellner, Ernest 1983. Nations and Nationalism. Ithaca: Cornell University Press.

Gerth, H.H. and C. Wright Mills 1958. From Max Weber: Essays in Sociology. New York: Oxford University Press.

Giddens, Anthony 1976. New Rules of Sociological method: A Positive Critique of Interpretive Sociologies. New York: Basic Books.

_____. 1987. Sociology: A Brief But Critical Introduction. Second Edition. San Diego: Harcourt, Brace, Jovanovich.

Gillette, Charles 1970. Wampum Belts and Beads. Indian Historian 3(4): 63.

Gilmore, Patricia and Reid Schrichte 1991. "Forced Relocation at Big Mountain" Ignores Facts in Case. Global Justice 2 (3): 15-18.

Goldfrank, Esther S. 1948. The Impact of Situation and Personality on Four Hopi Emergence Myths. Southwestern Journal of Anthropology 4: 241-62.

Grattan, Virginia L. 1980. Mary Colter: Builder Upon the Red Earth. Flagstaff: Northland.

Graybill, Florence Curtis and Victor Boesen 1976. Edward Sheriff Curtis: Visions of A Vanishing Race. New York: Thomas Y. Crowell.

Green, Jesse, ed. 1990. Cushing at Zuni: The Correspondence and Journals of Frank Hamilton Cushing, 1879-1884. Albuquerque: University of New Mexico Press.

Greenfield, Ronald H. 1986. Letter to the Editor, Technology Review. October 22.

Gregory, Herbert E. 1917. Geology of the Navajo Country. Professional Paper Number 93. U.S. Geological Survey. Washington, D.C.: U.S. Government Printing Office.

Grumet, Robert. 1975. Changes in Coast Tshimshian Redistributive Activities in the Fort Simpson Region of British Columbia, 1788-1862. Ethnohistory 22: 294-317.

Gunnerson, James H. 1979. Southern Athapaskan Archaeology. Pp. 162-69 in Alfonso Ortiz, ed. Handbook of North American Indians, Volume 9, Southwest. Washington, D.C.: Smithsonian Institution.

Gutierrez, Ramon A. 1991. When Jesus Came the Corn Mothers Went Away: Marriage, Sexuality, and Power in New Mexico, 1500-1846. Stanford: Stanford University Press.

Haas, Theodore 1947. Ten Years of Tribal Government Under I.R.A. Tribal Relations Pamphlet No. 1. Chicago: U.S. Indian Service.

Hack, John T. 1942. The Changing Physical Environment of the Hopi Indians of Arizona. Reports of the Awatovi Expedition. No. 1. Papers of the Peabody Museum of American Archaeology and Ethnology, Harvard University. Vol. 25, No. 1. Cambridge: Harvard University Press.

Hagan, William T. 1966. Indian Police and Judges. New Haven: Yale University Press.

Hansen, Klaus J. 1981. Mormonism and the American Experience. Chicago: University of Chicago Press.

Harris, Marvin 1968. The Rise of Anthropological Theory. New York: Thomas Y. Crowell.

_____. 1979. Cultural Materialism. New York: Random House.

_____. 1991. Cultural Anthropology. Third Edition. New York: Harper Collins.

Harvey, Byron III 1963. The Fred Harvey Collection 1899-1963. Plateau 36(2): 33-53.

_____. 1970. Ritual in Pueblo Art: Hopi Life in Hopi Painting. Contributions from the Museum of the American Indian. Volume 24. New York: Heye Foundation.

Haviland, William 1990. Cultural Anthropology. Sixth Edition. New York: Holt, Rinehart and Winston.

Healing v. Jones 1962 1973. Opinion of the Court, Appendix to Opinion -- Chronological Account of the Hopi-Navajo Controversy, Findings of Fact and Conclusions of Law, Judgment. Pp. 205-433 in U.S. Senate Committee on Indian Affairs of the Committee on Interior and Insular Affairs, 93rd Congress, First Session. Hearing on Partition of the Surface Rights of Navajo-Hopi Indian Land, March 7, 1973. Washington. D.C.: U.S. Government Printing office.

Hechter, Michael 1975. The Celtic Fringe in British National Development 1536-1966. Berkeley, Los Angeles, and London: University of California Press.

Hegemann, Elizabeth Compton 1963. Navaho Trading Days. Albuquerque: University of New Mexico Press.

Henry, Helen and Marc Sills 1994. Relocation: Dine' Communities Continue to Resist. Fourth World Bulletin 3(2):7-12).

Hieb, Louis A. 1979. The Ritual Clown: Humor and Ethics. Pp. 171-188 in Edward Norbeck and Claire R. Farrer, eds. Forms of Play of Native North Americans. 1977 Proceedings of the Annual Meeting. Seattle: American Ethnological Society.

_____ . 1991. Review of *Designs and Factions: Politics, Religion, and Ceremonies on the Hopi Third Mesa*, by Lydia Wyckoff. American Indian Culture and Research Journal 15: 150-52.

Hill, W.W. 1936. Navaho Warfare. Yale University Publications in Anthropology 5. New Haven: Yale University Press.

Hinsley, Curtis M. 1989. Zunis and Brahmins: Cultural Ambivalence in the Gilded Age. Pp. 169-207 in George W. Stocking, Jr., ed. Romantic Motives. Madison: University of Wisconsin Press.

Hobsbawm, Eric J. 1969. The Age of Revolution, Europe 1789-1848. New York: Praeger.

Holum, Kenneth 1961. Letter from Assistant Secretary of the Interior to Frederick Haveland, Phoenix Area Director, Bureau of Indian Affairs. May 24. Ms. copy in author's possession.

Hopi Action News 1970. Hopi Tribal Council Budget, Dec. 1, 1970-Nov. 30, 1971. November 26

Hopi Epicentre 1987. Newsletter. Spring. Flagstaff: Hopi Epicentre for International Outreach.

Hopi Hearings 1955. Conducted by a Team appointed by Mr. Glen L. Emmons, Commissioner of Indian Affairs, and composed of Mr. Thomas Reid, Assistant Commissioner and, Program Officers Joe Jennings and Graham Holmes. Keams Canyon: U.S. Bureau of Indian Affairs, Hopi Indian Agency.

Hopi Health Department 1983. Report of the Second Hopi Mental Health Conference. Kykotsmovi: Hopi Tribe.

_____ . 1984. Report of the 3rd Annual Hopi Mental Health Conference: Prophecy in Motion. Kykotsmovi: Hopi Tribe.

Hopi Tribe 1986a. Hopi Tutu-veh-ni 1 (1). Kykotsmovi.

_____ . 1986b. Hopi Tutu-veh-ni 1 (2). Kykotsmovi.

_____ . 1989. Hopi Tutu-veh-ni 2 (18) Kykotsmovi.

_____ . 1990. Hopi Tutu-veh-ni 2 (29). Kykotsmovi.

_____ . 1993. Background on the Agreement in Principle. Press Release. March 2.

Hough, Walter 1898. The Moki Snake Dance. Passenger Department, Santa Fe Route. (Topeka?): AT&SF Railroad.

Hyatt, Marshall 1990. Franz Boas, Social Activist. New York: Greenwood Press.

Indian Claims Commission 1970. Opinion of Title. 23 Ind. Cl. Comm. 277. Docket Nos. 196 and 229. June 29, 1970. Washington, D.C.: U.S. Government Printing Office.

Indian Rights Association 1898. Annual Report. Philadelphia: Indian Rights Association.

Indian Law Resource Center 1979. Report to the Hopi Kikmongwis and other Traditional Leaders on Docket 196 and the Continuing Threat to Hopi Land and Sovereignty. Washington, D.C.: Indian Law Resource Center.

_____ . 1989. Behind the Big Mountain Relocations: New Evidence About Mineral Development Plans of the Hopi Tribal Council. Press Release. March 22. Washington, D.C.

Indian Legal Information Development Service 1972. Legislative Review 1(9). Washington, D.C.

Inkeles, Alex 1966. The Modernization of Man. Pp. 138-150 in Myron Weiner, ed. Modernization: The Dynamics of Growth. New York: Basic Books.

James, Harry C. 1956. The Hopi Indians. Caxton, Idaho: Caldwell.

_____ . 1974. Pages From Hopi History. Tucson: University of Arizona Press.

Jennings, Joe 1944. Memorandum for Mr. McNickle. April 6, 1944. Indian Office File Hopi 5839-44. National Archives, Washington, D.C.

Johnston, Bernice Eastman 1972. Two Ways in the Desert. Pasadena: Socio-Technical Publications.

Johnson, Karl 1978. Enrollment Chief Seeks Records. Qua' Toqti. March 9: 1.

Johnston, Denis F. 1966. Trends in Navajo Population and Education, 1870-1955. Pp. 375-375 in David F. Aberle, The Peyote Religion Among the Navaho. Viking Fund Publications in Anthropology 42. New York: Wenner-Gren Foundation for Anthropological Research.

Jones, Volney 1938. An Ancient Food Plant of the Southwest and Plateau Regions. El Palacio 44(4-5): 41-53)

Jorgensen, Joseph G. 1971. Indians and the Metropolis. Pp. 66-113 in Jack O. Waddell and O. Michael Watson, eds. The American Indian in Urban Society. Boston: Little, Brown.

_____ . 1972. The Sun Dance Religion: Power for the Powerless. Chicago: University of Chicago Press.

_____ . 1980. Western Indians. San Francisco: W.H. Freeman.

Jorgensen, Joseph G. and Richard O. Clemmer 1978. Review Essay: America in the Indian's past. Journal of Ethnic Studies 6: 65-74.

Josephy, Alvin M . Jr. 1971. The Murder of the Southwest. Audobon 73: 52-67.

Kabotie, Fred 1977. Fred Kabotie: Hopi Indian Artist. Flagstaff: Museum of Northern Arizona.

Kahtsimkiwa 1987. Kahtsimkiwa. Flagstaff: Hopi Center for International Outreach.

Kaiser, Rudolf 1989. Die Stimme des Grossen Geistes: Prophezeiungen und Endzeiterwartungen der Hopi-Indianer. Munchen: Kosel.

_____. 1990. Gott Schlaft in Stein: Indianische und abendlandische Weltansichten im Widerstreit. Munchen: Kosel.

Kaiser, Rudolf and Richard O. Clemmer 1989. "Spinnweben uber dem Land": Prophezeiungen der Hopi- Indianer in Arizona. Pp. 63-78 in J. Beneke, F. Jarman, and D. Whybra, eds. Aspekte amerikanischer Kultur. Band 31, Studien Texte Entwurfe: Hildesheimer Beitrage zu den Erziehungs- und Socialwissenschaften.

Kealiinohomoku, Joann W. 1980. The Drama of the Hopi Ogres. Pp. 37-69 in Charlotte J. Frisbie, ed. Southwestern Indian Ritual Drama. Albuquerque: School of American Research/University of New Mexico Press.

Kelly, Lawrence 1970. Navajo Roundup: Selected Correspondence of Kit Carson's Expedition Against the Navajo, 1863-1865. Boulder: Pruett.

_____. 1975. The Indian Reorganization Act: The Dream and the Reality. Pacific Historical Review 43: 291-312.

_____. 1980. Anthropology and Anthropologists in the Indian New Deal. Journal of the History of the Behavioral Sciences 16: 6-24.

_____. 1983. The Assault on Assimilation: John Collier and the Origins of Indian Policy Reform. Albuquerque: University of New Mexico Press.

Kennard, Edward 1965. Post-War Economic Changes Among the Hopi. Pp. 25-32 in Essays in Economic Anthropology. Proceedings of the Annual Meeting. Seattle: American Ethnological Society.

Kessell, John L. 1979. Kiva, Cross and Crown. Albuquerque: University of New Mexico Press.

Kiersch, George 1956. Mineral Resources, Navajo-Hopi Indian Reservations, Arizona-Utah. Volume I. Metalliferous Minerals and Mineral Fuels. Tucson: University of Arizona Press.

Klein, Dan, Nancy McClelland and Malcolm Haslam 1986. In the Deco Style. New York: Rizzoli.

Kluckhohn, Clyde and Robert Hackenberg 1953. Social Science Principles and the Indian Reorganization Act. Pp. 29-34 in William Kelly, ed. Indian Affairs and the Indian Reorganization Act: The Twenty Year Record. From a Symposium held in conjunction with the Fifty-Second Annual Meeting of the American Anthropological Association, Tucson, Arizona, December 30. Tucson: University of Arizona Press.

Kluckhohn, Clyde and Dorothea Leighton 1962. The Navaho. Revised Edition. Garden City: Doubleday.

Kotchongva, Chief Dan and Harry Nasewytewa, interpreter 1936. Where is the White Brother of the Hopi Indian. Improvement Era 39 (2): 82-4, 116-119.

Kottak, Conrad 1991. Cultural Anthropology. New York: McGraw-Hill.

Krutz, Gordon V. 1973. The Native's Point of View as an Important Factor in Understanding the Dynamics of the Oraibi Split. Ethnohistory 20: 77-89.

Kunitz, Stephen 1971. The Social Philosophy of John Collier. Ethnohistory 18: 213-230.

_____. 1976. Fertility, Mortality, and Social Organization. Human Biology 48: 361-77.

Kunze, Albert, ed. 1988. Hopi und Kachina: Indianische Kultur im Wandel. Munchen: Trickster Verlag.

Kuper, Hilda 1986. The Swazi. New York: Holt, Rinehart and Winston.

Kuschel, Rolf 1988. Vengeance is Their Reply. Copenhagen: Dansk Psykologisk Forlag.

La Farge, Oliver 1936a. Running Narrative of the Organization of the Hopi Tribe of Indians. Typescript in Humanities Research Center, University of Texas, Austin.

_____. 1936b. Finale. September 11. Typescript attached to Running Narrative.

_____. 1937. Notes for Hopi Administrators. Typescript Department of Interior, Office of Indian Affairs Document 52687.

_____. 1950. Comment on Running Narrative. January. Typescript attached to Running Narrative.

Laird, W. David 1977. Hopi Bibliography: Comprehensive and Annotated. Tucson: University of Arizona Press.

Laitin, David D. 1985. Hegemony and Religious Conflict: British Imperial Control and Political Cleavages in Yorubaland. Pp. 285-316 in Peter Evans, Dietrich Rueschemeyer and Theda Skocpol, eds. Bringing the State Back In. Cambridge: Cambridge University Press.

Landsman, Gail 1988. Sovereignty and Symbol: Indian-White Conflict at Ganienkeh. Albuquerque: University of New Mexico Press.

Lasswell, Harold D. 1935. Collective Autism as a Consequence of Culture Contact: Notes on Religious Training and the Peyote Cult at Taos. Zeitschrift fur Sozialforschung 4: 232-46.

Lawrence, D.H. 1924. The Hopi Snake Dance. Theatre Arts Monthly 8: 836-60.

_____. 1925. The Hopi Snake Dance. Adelphi Magazine 2(8): 685-92; 2(9): 764-78.

_____. 1927. Mornings in Mexico. New York: Alfred A. Knopf.

Leone, Mark 1979. Roots of Modern Mormonism. Cambridge: Harvard University Press.

Leupp, Francis 1906. Annual Report of the Commissioner of Indian Affairs. Washington. D.C.: Government Printing Office.

_____. 1907. Annual Report of the Commissioner of Indian Affairs. Washington, D.C.: Government Printing Office.

Levine, David 1978. Economic Theory, Volume One: The Elementary Relations of Economic Life. Boston: Routledge and Kegan Paul.

Levy, Jerrold E. 1980. Who Benefits From Energy Resource Development: The Special Case of Navajo Indians. The Social Science Journal 17: 1-19.

_____. 1992. Orayvi Revisited: Social Stratification in an "Egalitarian" Society. Santa Fe: School of American Research Press.

Linton, Ralph 1943. Nativistic Movements. American Anthropologist 45: 230-240.

Lockett, H. C. and Milton Snow 1939. Along the Beale Trail: A Photographic Account of Wasted Range land. Lawrence: Education Division, U.S. Office of Indian Affairs.

Loftin, John E. 1991. Religion and Hopi Life in the Twentieth Century. Bloomington: Indiana University Press.

Lomasumi'nangwtukwsiwmani 1991. 1989-1991 Annual Report. Hotevilla: The Hopi Foundation.

Lomayaktewa, Starlie et al. 1971. Starlie Lomayaktewa and 61 other Hopis v Rogers C.B. Morton and Peabody Coal Company. Plaintiffs' Brief. District of Columbia: United States District Court. May 20. Ms. copy in author's possession.

Lowie, Robert H. 1917. Noted in Hopiland. American Museum Journal 17: 569-73.

_____ . 1929a. Hopi Kinship. American Museum of Natural History. Anthropological Papers 30 (7). New York.

_____ . 1929b. Notes on Hopi Clans. American Museum of Natural History Anthropological Papers 30 (6). New York.

Lummis, Charles F. 1968. Bullying the Moqui. Prescott: Prescott College Press.

McGuire, Randall H. 1992. Archaeology and the First Americans. American Anthropologist 94: 816-836.

Makeel, Scudder 1944. An Appraisal of the Indian Reorganization Act. American Anthropologist 46: 209-217.

Marcus, George E. and Michael M. J. Fischer 1986. Anthropology as Cultural Critique. Chicago: University of Chicago Press.

Mason, Lynn D. 1966. Hopi Domestic Animals: Past and Present. Honors Thesis in Anthropology. Dartmouth College.

Mateer, William R. 1878. Letter to Commissioner of Indian Affairs. Pp. 8-10 in Annual Report of Commissioner of Indian Affairs. Washington, D.C.: U.S. Government Printing Office.

McEllivey, Thomas 1991. Art and Discontent. Kingston, New York: McPherson and Company.

McGavock, E.H. and Gary W. Levins 1973. Ground Water in the Navajo Sandstone in the Black Mesa Area, Arizona. In H.L. James, ed. Guidebook of Monument Valley and Vicinity: Arizona and Utah. Albuquerque: New Mexico Geological Society.

McLuhan, T.C. 1985. Dream Tracks: The Railroad and the American Indian. 1890-1930.

McNickle, D'Arcy 1944. Memorandum of September 23 to Mr. Joe Jennings. National Archives File 00-1938-Hopi-054.

_____ . 1950. Memorandum of Sept. 6 to Commissioner Dillon Myer. National Archives File 15785-1938-Hopi-054.

_____ . 1971. Indian Man: A Life of Oliver La Farge. Bloomington: Indian University Press.

McNitt, Frank 1962. The Indian Traders. Norman: University of Oklahoma Press.

Means, Florence Campbell 1960. Sunlight on the Hopi Mesas: The Story of Abigail Johnson. Philadelphia: Judson Press.

Meriam, Lewis 1928. The Problem of Indian Administration. Baltimore: Johns Hopkins University Press.

Miller, Horton 1907. Letter to Commissioner of Indian Affairs. Dec. 3. Letter-press copy in files of Bureau of Indian Affairs, Hopi Indian Agency, Keams Canyon.

_____. 1908. Letter to Commissioner of Indian Affairs. January 23. Letter-press copy in files of Bureau of Indian Affairs, Hopi Indian Agency, Keams Canyon.

Mindeleff, Victor 1896. A Study of Pueblo Architecture: Tusayan and Cibola. Bureau of American Ethnology. Eight Annual Report. Washington, D.C.: Smithsonian Institution.

Mitchell, Timothy 1989. The World as Exhibition. Comparative Studies in Society and History 31: 217-236.

Mommsen, Wolfgang J. 1974. The Age of Bureaucracy: Perspectives on the Political Sociology of Max Weber. Oxford: Basil Blackwell.

Montgomery, Ross Gordon 1949. San Bernardo de Aguatubi, An Analytical Restoration. Pp. 110-239 in Ross Gordon Montgomery; Watson Smith; and John Otis. Franciscan Awatovi. Papers of the Peabody Museum of American Archaeology and Ethnology, Harvard University. Volume 36. Cambridge.

Moore, Wilbert 1979. World Modernization. New York: Elsevier.

Morris, Richard C. 1985. Memorandum to William P. Clark (concerning the Hopi-Navajo Land Dispute.) Copy in author's possession.

Morris, Glenn T. 1986. In Support of the Right of Self-Determination for Indigenous Peoples under International Law. German Yearbook of International Law 29: 277-316.

_____. 1992. International Law and Politics: Toward a Right to Self-Determination for Indigenous Peoples. Pp. 55-86 in M. Annette Jaimes, ed. The State of Native America: Genocide, Colonization and Resistance. Boston: South End Press.

Murdock, George Peter 1949. Social Structure. New York: Macmillan.

Murphy, Robert F. 1971. The Dialectics of Social Life. New York: Basic Books.

Nadeau, Maurice 1965. The History of Surrealism. New York: Macmillan.

Nagata, Shuichi 1968. Political Socialization of the Hopi "Traditional" Faction. Paper presented at the 8th Annual Meeting, Northeastern Anthropological Association, Hanover, Massachusetts.

_____. 1970. Modern Transformations of Moenkopi Pueblo. Urbana: University of Illinois Press.

_____. 1971. The Reservation Community and the Urban Community. Pp. 114-59 in Jack O. Waddell and O. Michael Watson, eds. The American Indian in Urban Society. Boston: Little, Brown.

_____. 1978. Dan Kochongva's Message: Myth, Ideology and Political Action Among the Contemporary Hopi. Pp. 73-87 in Erik Schwimmer, ed. The Yearbook of Symbolic Anthropology I. London: Hurst.

_____. 1979. Political Socialization of the Hopi Traditional Factions: A Contribution to the Theory of Culture Change. Journal of the Steward Anthropological Society 11: 111-137.

Nash, Dennison 1977. Tourism as a Form of Imperialism. p. 37-54 in Valene Smith, ed. Hosts and Guests: The Anthropology of Tourism. Philadelphia: University of Pennsylvania Press.

National Academy of Sciences 1974. Rehabilitation Potential of Western Coal Lands. Washington, D.C.: Environmental Studies.

Native American Studies Center, University of New Mexico 1993. Commentaries: When Jesus Came, the Corn Mothers Went Away: Marraige, Sex, and Power in New Mexico, 1500-1846, By Ramon A. Gutierrez. American Indian Culture and Research Journal 17:141-77 Board, National Research Council.

Navajo Times 1990. Tribal officials not pleased with census reservation figures. August 30.

Nequatewa, Edmund 1936. Truth of a Hopi. Museum of Northern Arizona Bulletin 8.

_____. 1943. Nampeyo, Famous Hopi Potter (1859? To 1942). Plateau 5(3): 40-2.

Nibley, Preston, ed. 1944. Three Mormon Classics. Salt Lake City: Stevens and Wallis.

O'Kane, Walter C. 1953. The Hopis: Portrait of a People. Norman: University of Oklahoma Press.

Ortiz, Roxanne Dunbar 1984. Indians of the Americas: Human Rights and Self-Determination. London: Zed Books.

Ortiz, Alfonso 1969. The Tewa World. Chicago: University of Chicago Press.

Page, Amy 1990. Indian Wars: Hopis hope for return of sacred mask. Art and Auction 12: 20-21.

Pahona, Duke 1972. Statement of Duke Pahona, Hopi Indian Tribe Member. Pp. 175-77 in U.S. Senate Committee on Indian Affairs, 92nd Congress, Second Session. Hearings, Authorize Partition of Surface Rights of Navaho-Hopi Indian Land, September 14 and 15, 1982. Washington, D.C.: U.S. Government Printing Office.

Paige, Margo 1958. Indian Tells Plight: "We Can't Live Like the White" Los Angeles Citizen-News. November 14.

Palkovich, Ann M. 1985. Historic Population of the Eastern Pueblos: 1540-1910. Journal of Anthropological Research 41: 401-426.

Parlowe, Anita 1989. Peabody would sent Hopiland coal to Japan. Gallup Independent. April 27.

Parman, Donald L. 1976. The Navajos and the New Deal. New Haven: Yale University Press.

Parsons, Elsie Clews 1921. The Pueblo Indian Clan in Folk-Lore. Journal of American Folk-Lore 34 (132):209-216.

_____. 1922. Contributions to Hopi History. American Anthropologist 24: 253-298.

_____. 1923. The Hopi Wowochim Ceremony in 1920. American Anthropologist 25: 156-187.

_____. 1926. The Ceremonial Calendar of the Tewa in Arizona. American Anthropologist 28: 209-29.

_____. 1927. Witchcraft Among the Pueblos: Indian or Spanish? Man 27 (6): 106-112; (7): 125-128.

_____. 1932. The Kinship Nomenclature of the Pueblo Indians. American Anthropologist 34: 377-89.

_____. 1933. Hopi and Zuni Ceremonialism. Memoir 39. Menasha, WI: American Anthropological Association.

_____. 1939. Pueblo Indian Religion. Chicago: University of Chicago Press.

Peabody Coal Company 1970. Mining Coal on Black Mesa. St. Louis: Peabody Coal Company.

Pendley, Robert E. and Charles D. Kolstad 1980. American Indians and National Energy Policy. Journal of Energy and Development 5(2): 221-251.

Peterson, Charles S. 1971. The Hopis and the Mormons 1858-1873. Utah Historical Quarterly 39: 179 - 194.

Philp, Kenneth 1977. John Collier's Crusade for Indian Reform, 1920-1954. Tucson: University of Arizona Press.

_____ . 1983. Fifty Years Later: The Indian Reorganization Act of 1934 in Historical Perspective. pp. 7-9 in Kenneth Philp, ed. Indian Self-Rule: Fifty Years Under the Indian Reorganization Act. Sun Valley: Institute of the American West.

Phoenix Gazette 1961. Hopis Give out First Mineral Prospecting Permit. September 15.

_____ . 1964. Hopis' Lawyer to Get $1 Million. December 8.

Polanyi, Karl 1957. The Great Transformation: The Political and Economic Origins of Our Time. Boston: Beacon Press.

Pollock, Floyd 1984. A Navajo Confrontation and Crisis. Tsaile: Navajo Community College Press.

Powell, John Wesley 1895. Canyons of the Colorado. Meadville, PA: Flood and Vincent.

Qoyawayma, Polingaysi 1964. No Turning Back. As told to Vada Carlson. Albuquerque: University of New Mexico Press.

Qua' Toqti 1979. Editor-Publisher Passes Away. Sept. 13.

_____ . 1980a. Hopi police recover sacred ceremonial artifacts. May 1.

_____ . 1980b. Notice To All Hopis. Hopi Range Management Plan and Hopi Range Code. September 4.

_____ . 1980c. Hopis Condemn Smokis for performing dances. September 11.

_____ . 1982. Navajo Not Law Abiding, Hopis Testify. July 22.

Quintana, Frances Leon 1991. Pobladores: Hispanic Americans of the Ute Frontier. Los Ojos, New Mexico: Ganados del Valle.

Raymond, Chris 1990. Dispute Between Scholar, Tribe Leaders Over Book on Hopi Ritual. The Chronicle of Higher Education. October 17: A6,8.

Reif, Rita 1991. Buyer Vows to Return Masks to Indians. New York Times. May 22.

Reno, Philip 1981. Mother Earth, Father Sky and Economic Development: Navajo Resources and Their Use. Albuquerque: University of New Mexico Press.

Rhodes, Robert 1985. Hopi Education in the 20th Century. Revised ms. of a paper presented at the Advanced Seminar on the Hopi. School of American Research, Santa Fe.

Rinehart, Mary Roberts 1923. The Out Trail. New York: The George H. Doran Company.

Rivera, Eladia Valentina 1990. Unwelcome Guests: Hopi Resistance to Tourism. M.A. Thesis, Department of Anthropology, University of Denver.

Rivers, W.H.R. 1910. The Genealogical Method. Sociological Review 3:1-11.

Robbins, Rebecca 1992. Self-Determination and Subordination: The Past, Present, and Future of American Indian Governance. Pp. 87-122 in M. Annette Jaimes, ed. The State of Native America: Genocide, Colonization and Resistance. Boston: South End Press.

Robinson, Robert 1986. Hopi Employment -- Observations and informal personal interviews, December 1985, January 1986, February 1986, April 1986. Memorandum, Denver Research Institute. Denver: University of Denver.

_____. 1988. Black Mesa-Kayenta Mine Socio-economic Analysis and Final Technical Report. Denver: U.S. Office of Surface Mining Reclamation and Enforcement, Western Field Operations.

Roessel, Robert 1983. Navajo History 1850-1923. Pp. 506-23 in Alfonso Ortiz, ed. Handbook of North American Indians. Volume Ten. Southwest. Washington, D.C.: Smithsonian Institution.

Roscoe, Will 1991. The Zuni Man-Woman. Albuquerque: University of New Mexico Press

Rose, Wendy 1992. The Great Pretenders: Further Reflections on Whiteshamanism. Pp. 402-22 in M. Annette Jaimes, ed. The State of Native America: Genocide, Colonization and Resistance. Boston: South End Press.

Rosen, Sonia and Dana Weissbrodt 1988. The 39th Session of the UN Sub-Commission on Prevention of Discrimination and Protection of Minorities. Human Rights Quarterly 10: 487-508.

Rosman, Abraham and Paula Rubel 1971. Feasting with Mine Enemy. New York: Columbia University Press.

Rudolf, Lloyd I. and Susanne Hoeber Rudolf 1967. The Modernity of Tradition. Chicago: University of Chicago Press.

Rushforth, Scott and Steadman Upham 1992. A Hopi Social History. Austin: University of Texas Press.

Sackler, Elizabeth, Martin Sullivan, and Richard Hill 1992. Three Voices for Repatriation. Museum News. September/October: 58-61.

Sanders, Douglas 1989. The UN Working Group on Indigenous Populations. Human Rights Quarterly 11: 406-433.

_____. 1991. Collective Rights. Human Rights Quarterly 13: 368-386.

Schlegel, Alice 1977. Male and Female in Hopi Thought and Action. Pp. 245-69 in Alice Schlegel, ed. Sexual Stratification. New York: Columbia University Press.

_____. 1992. African Political Models in the American Southwest: Hopi as an Internal Frontier Society. American Anthropologist 94: 376-397.

Schoolcraft, Henry 1853. Information Respecting the History, Conditions and Prospects of the Indian Tribes of the United States ... Volume 3. Philadelphia: Lippincott.

Scudder, Thayer, with the Assistance of David F. Aberle, Kenneth Begishe, Elizabeth Colson, Clark Etsitty, Jennie Joe, Mary E.D. Scudder, Betty Beetso, Gilbert Tippeconnie, Roy Walters, and John Williamson 1979. Expected Impacts of Compulsory Relocation on Navajos with Special Emphasis on Relocation from the Former Joint Use Area Required by Public Law 93-531. Binghamton: Institute for Development Anthropology, Inc.

Seaman, P. David, ed. and Edmund Nequatewa 1993. Born A Chief: The Nineteenth Century Hopi Boyhood of Edmund Nequatewa as told to Alfred F. Whiting. Tucson: University of Arizona Press.

Seeger, Anthony 1991. Singing other Peoples' Songs. Cultural Survival 15(3): 36-39.

Sekaquaptewa, Emory 1972. Preserving the Good Things in Hopi Life. Pp. 239-260 in Edward Spicer and Raymond Thompson, eds. Plural Society in the Southwest. Albuquerque: University of New Mexico Press.

Sekaquaptewa, Helen 1969. Me and Mine. As told to Louise Udall. Tucson: University of Arizona Press.

Shepard, Ward 1946. Our Indigenous Shangri-La. Scientific Monthly February: 158-164.

Shimkin, Demitri B. 1953. Minerals: A Key to Soviet Power. Cambridge: Harvard University Press.

Sidney, Ivan 1989. Testimony of Chairman Ivan L. Sidney for the Subcommittee on Interior and Related Agencies of the Committee on Appropriations, U.S. House of Representatives. April 12. Transcript in author's possession.

Sills, Marc 1986. Relocation Reconsidered: Competing Explanations of the Navajo-Hopi Land Settlement Act of 1974. The Journal of Ethnic Studies 14 (3): 53-83.

_____ . 1991. Adhering to the Facts and Reaching Another Conclusion. Global Justice 2(3): 18-20.

_____ . 1992. Ethnocide and Interaction Between States and Indigenous Nations: A Conceptual Investigation of Three Cases in Mexico. Ph.D. Dissertation, Graduate School of International Studies, University of Denver.

Sills, Marc, Tanya Mote and Loring Bush 1990. USA: Forced Relocation at Big Mountain: A Case of Ethnocide? Global Justice 1(3): 11-13.

Simross, Lynn 1981. A Government Dispute Divides Navajo and Hopi Tribes; Indians in Arizona Resisting Forces Move From Their Land. Los Angeles Times. May 24. (IV, 1,6,9).

Skocpol, Theda 1985. Bringing the State Back In. Pp. 3-37 in Peter Evans, Dietrich Rueschemeyer and Theda Skocpol, eds. Bringing the State Back In. Cambridge: Cambridge University Press.

Solis-Cohen, Lita and Samuel Pennington 1989. Sacred Hopi Mask Seized by FBI at Fall Antiques Show. Maine Antique Digest. December: 18A-19A.

Spicer, Edward 1961. (Editor) Perspectives in American Indian Culture Change. Chicago: University of Chicago Press.

_____ . 1962. Cycles of Conquest: The Impact of Spain, Mexico, and the United States on the Indians of the Southwest, 1533-1960. Tucson: University of Arizona Press.

SSRC=Social Science Research Council, Summer Seminar on Acculturation 1953. Acculturation: An Exploratory Formulation. American Anthropologist 55: 973-1002.

Stephen, Alexander M. 1893. Description of a Hopi Ti-Hu. Folk-lorist 1(2-3): 83-8.

_____ . 1929. Hopi Tales. Journal of American Folk-Lore 42 (163): 1-72.

_____ . 1936. Hopi Journal. Columbia University Contributions to Anthropology 23. Edited and annotated by Elsie Clews Parsons.

Stephens, Charles H. 1961. The Origin and History of the Hopi-Navajo Boundary Dispute in Northern Arizona. M.Sc. Thesis, Department of History, Brigham Young University, Provo, Utah.

Steward, Julian H. 1955. Theory of Culture Change. Urbana: University of Illinois Press.

_____ . 1969. The Limitations of Applied Anthropology: The Case of the Indian New Deal. Journal of the Steward Anthropological Society I, 1: 1-17.

Stocking, George W. Jr. 1968. Race, Culture, and Evolution: Essays in the History of Anthropology. New York: The Free Press.

Talaihaftewa and others 1949. Letter to The President. Typed copy in author's possession.

Talayesva, Don C. 1942. Sun Chief. Edited by Leo Simmons. New Haven: Yale University Press.

Thompson, Laura 1945(?) The Hopi Crisis: A Report to Administrators. N.P. (processed ms.).

_____ . 1950. Culture in Crisis: A Study of the Hopi Indians. New York: Harper and Bros.

Thompson, Laura and Alice Joseph 1944. The Hopi Way. Chicago: United States Indian Service.

Thornton, John. 1992. Africa and Africans in the Making of the Atlantic World, 1490-1680. Cambridge: Cambridge University Press.

Thrupp, Silvia, ed. 1962. Millennial Dreams in Action. Comparative Studies in Society and History. Supplement 2. The Hague: Mouton.

Titiev, Mischa. 1943. Notes on Hopi Witchcraft. Papers of the Michigan Academy of Science, Arts and Letters 28: 549- 57.

_____ . 1944. Old Oraibi: A Study of the Hopi Indians of Third Mesa. Papers of the Peabody Museum of American Archaeology and Ethnology, Harvard University 22 (1). Cambridge: Harvard University Press.

_____ . 1958. Review of *The Great Resistance*, George Yamada, ed. American Anthropologist 60: 620-21.

_____ . 1972. The Hopi Indians of Old Oraibi: Change and Continuity. Ann Arbor: University of Michigan Press.

Turner, Christy G. II and Nancy T. Morris 1970. A Massacre at Hopi. American Antiquity 35: 320-331.

Twitchell, Ralph E., editor and annotator (with Lansing B. Bloom) 1931. Campaign Against the Moqui Pueblos. New Mexico Historical Review 6: 158-226.

Ulin, Robert 1984. Understanding Cultures: Perspectives in Anthropology and Social Theory.

UN Sub-Commission=United Nations Economic and Social Council, Commission on Human Rights, Sub-Commission on Prevention of Discrimination and Protection of Minorities. 1989a. Forty-first session. Agenda item 13. Discrimination Against Indigenous Peoples. The Relocation of Hopi and Navajo Families. Report submitted by Mr. John Carey.

_____ . 1989b. Forty-first session. Agenda Item 13. Discrimination Against Indigenous Peoples. Hopi-Navajo Relocation. Summary of Information submitted by Ms. Erica-Irene A. Daes.

_____ . 1992. Forty-fourth Session. Agenda Item 15. Discrimination Against Indigenous Peoples. Relocation of Navajo and Hopi families. Resolution Adopted.

U.S. Department of Commerce 1964. A Survey of Tourist Potential and Adequacy of Water Supply for Tourism on the Hopi Indian Reservation. ARA Casebook Number 10. Washington, D.C.: Area Redevelopment Administration.

U.S. Department of the Interior. 1978a. Memorandum Audit Report. Office of the Inspector General. June 28. Lakewood: Central Region.

_____ . 1978b. Memorandum Audit Report. Office of the Inspector General. November 28. Lakewood: Central Region.

_____ . 1980. Memorandum Audit Report. Office of the Inspector General. February 5. Lakewood: Central Region.

_____ . 1985. Report to the Committee on Appropriations, U.S. House of Representatives, on the Navajo and Hopi Indian Relocation Commission. Surveys and Investigations Staff. January.

_____ . 1989. Proposed Permit Application, Black Mesa-Kayenta Mine, Navajo and Hopi Indian Reservations, Arizona. Draft Environmental Impact Statement. Denver: Office of Surface mining Reclamation and Enforcement.

U.S. District Court=United States District Court for the District of Arizona 1989. Opinion and Order Denying Preliminary Injunction and Dismissing Action (Jenny Manybeads, et al., v. United States of America, et al.).

U.S. House of Representatives 1953. Report with Respect to the House Resolution Authorizing the Committee on Interior and Insular Affairs to Conduct an Investigation of the Bureau of Indian Affairs, Pursuant to HR 698. House Report 2503. 82nd Congress, 2nd Session. Washington: U.S. Government Printing Office.

U.S. Ninth Circuit=United States Ninth Circuit Court of Appeals 1991. Transcript. "Manybeads." May 14. Copy in author's possession.

U.S. Senate 1948. Hearings before the subcommittee on Indian Affairs. Senate Committee on Interior and Insular Affairs. Eightieth Congress, Second Session. Rehabilitation of Navajo and Hopi Indians. March 29-April 29.

_____ . 1972. Hearings before the subcommittee on Indian Affairs. Senate Committee on Interior and Insular Affairs. Ninety-second Congress, Second Session, on H.R. 11128. Authorize Partition of Surface Rights of Navaho-Hopi Indian Land, September 14 and 15.

Vayda, A. P. 1974. Warfare in Ecological Perspective. Annual Review of Ecology and Systemics 5: 21-31.

Voegelin, C.F. and Florence M. Voegelin 1957. Hopi Domains: A Lexical Approach to the Problem of Selection. International Journal of American Linguistics Memoir No. 14. Indiana University Publications in Anthropology and Linguistics. Baltimore: Waverly Press.

Voget, Fred 1975. The History of Ethnology. New York: Holt, Rinehart, and Winston.

Voth, Heinrich R. 1901. The Oraibi Powamu Ceremony. Field Columbian Museum. Anthropological Series. Vol. 3, No. 2. Chicago: Field Museum.

_____ . 1905a. Traditions of the Hopi. Field Columbian Museum. Publication 96, Anthropological Series 8 Chicago: Field Museum.

_____ . 1905b. Typescript, Voth Collection, Bethel College, Newton, Kansas. Copy in author's possession.

_____ . 1912. The Oraibi Marau Ceremony. Field Columbian Museum. Publication 156, Anthropological Series 11(1). Chicago: Field Museum.

Wade, Edwin L. and Lea S. McChesney 1980. America's Great Lost Expedition: The Thomas Keam Collection of Hopi Pottery from the Second Hemenway Expedition, 1890-1894. Phoenix: The Heard Museum.

Walker, Willard and Lydia L. Wyckoff, eds. 1983. Hopis, Tewas and The American Road. Middletown, CT: Wesleyan University.

Wallace, Anthony F. C. 1956. Revitalization Movements. American Anthropologist 58: 264-281.

Wallerstein, Immanuel 1974. The Modern World System: Capitalist Agriculture and the Origins of the World-Economy in the Sixteenth Century. New York: Academic Press.

Washburn, Wilcomb 1975. The Indian in America. New York: Harper and Row.

_____ . 1979. On the Trail of the Activist Anthropologist. Journal of Ethnic Studies 7: 89-99.

_____ . 1984. A Fifty-Year Perspective on the Indian Reorganization Act. American Anthropologist 86: 279-289.

_____ . 1985. Response to Biolsi. American Anthropologist 87: 659.

_____ . 1989. Anthropological Advocacy in the Hopi-Navajo Land Dispute. American Anthropologist 91: 738-743.

Waters, Frank (with Oswald White Bear Fredericks) 1963. Book of The Hopi. New York: Viking Press.

Watkins, Arthur V. 1957. Termination of Federal Supervision: The Removal of Restrictions over Indian Property and Person. Annals of the American Academy of Political and Social Sciences 311: 47-55.

Weigle, Marta and Kyle Fiore 1982. Santa Fe and Taos: The Writer's Era 1916-1941. Santa Fe: Ancient City Press.

Whipple, A.W. 1941. A Pathfinder in the Southwest: The Itinerary of Lieutenant A.W. Whipple During His Explorations for a Railway Route From Fort Smith to Los Angeles in the Years 1853 and 1854. Edited and Annotated by Grant Foreman. Norman: University of Oklahoma Press.

White, Leslie 1943. Energy and the Evolution of Culture. American Anthropologist 45: 335-356.

White, Richard 1983. The Roots of Dependency. Lincoln: University of Nebraska Press.

Whiteley, Peter M. 1986. Unpacking Hopi "Clans": Another Vintage Model Out of Africa? Journal of Anthropological Research 41(4):359-374 and 42(1):69-79.

_____ . 1987. The Interpretation of Politics: A Hopi Conundrum. Man 22 (4): 696-714.

_____ . 1988a. Bacavi: Journey to Reed Springs. Flagstaff: Northland

_____ . 1988b. Deliberate Acts. Tucson: University of Arizona Press.

Whiting, Alfred F. 1936. Hopi Indian Agriculture: I, Background. Museum Notes 8, 10: 51-53. Flagstaff: Museum of Northern Arizona.

_____ . 1937. Hopi Indian Agriculture II: Seed Source and Distribution. Museum Notes 10, 5: 13-16. Flagstaff: Museum of Northern Arizona.

_____ . 1939. Ethnobotany of the Hopi. Bulletin No. 15. Flagstaff: Museum of Northern Arizona.

Whitson, Hollis and Martha Roberge 1986. "Moving Those Indians into the Twentieth Century". Technology Review. July. 47-57.

Whitson, Hollis 1985. A Policy Review of the Federal Government's Relocation of Navajo Indians Under PL 93-531 and PL 96-305. Arizona Law Review 27: 371-414.

Wicoff, Mary 1993. Dennis family builds energy-saver home. Hopi Tutu-veh-ni 2 (89):2. May 27.

Wilson, Stephen 1988. Feuding, Conflict and Banditry in Nineteenth-Century Corsica. Cambridge: Cambridge University Press.

Winslow Mail 1969. B.V.D. Makes First Shipment -- To Serve 11 States. June 12.

Wolf, Eric R. 1982. Europe and the People Without History. Berkeley: University of California Press.

Worsley, Peter 1984. The Three Worlds: Culture and World Development. Chicago: University of Chicago Press.

_____. 1968. The Trumpet Shall Sound. Second, augmented edition. New York: Schocken.

Wright, Margaret Nickelson 1972. The History and Hallmarks of Hopi Silversmithing: Hopi Silver. Flagstaff: Northland Press.

Wright, Barton 1982. The Shalako. Paper presented at the Advanced Seminar on the Hopi, School of American Research, Santa Fe, New Mexico.

Wyckoff, Lydia 1990. Designs and Factions: Politics, Religion, and Ceremonies on the Hopi Third Mesa. Albuquerque: University of New Mexico Press.

Yamada, George 1957. The Great Resistance. Mexico, D.F.: Editorial LLamada.

Yava, Albert 1978. Big Falling Snow. Edited and Annotated by Harold Courlander. New York: Crown.

Young, Robert W. and William Morgan 1954. Navajo historical Selections. Phoenix: U.S. Bureau of Indian Affairs.

About the Book and Author

Despite one hundred years under the dominant American culture, Hopi culture today maintains continuity with its aboriginal roots, while reflecting the impact of the twentieth century.

A compelling study of "fourth worlders" coping with a powerful nation-state, this book depicts Hopi social organization, economy, religion, and politics as well as key events in the history of Hopi-U.S. relations.

Hopis have used their culture and their sociopolitical structures to deal with change. Clemmer focuses on six major events in Hopi history: a factionalist schism that split the largest Hopi village, Oraibi, into three villages; the impact of the federal Indian Reorganization Act of 1934; the rise of a political movement known as "traditionalism"; the story behind far-reaching oil and coal leases of the 1960s; the Hopi-Navajo land dispute; and the disappearance of ceremonial objects into private collections and museums.

Richard O. Clemmer is associate professor of anthropology at the University of Denver.

Index

Arny, William 88

1882 Reservation 88-90, 97, 162, 163, 168, 190, 196, 211, 212, 214, 234-240, 247, 258, 265

Aboriginal land boundaries, Hopi 3, 13, 16, 19, 29, 30, 32, 40, 53, 60, 138, 163, 164, 189-191, 194, 196, 197, 200, 211, 216, 233, 234, 235-238, 241, 252, 257, 260, 261, 263, 266, 267, 276, 279, 283, 284, 294, 295, 322

Acculturation 31, 85-87, 91, 106, 108, 111, 112, 114, 120, 123, 125, 127, 132, 133, 144, 167, 171-174, 176, 187, 273, 286, 319

  resistance to 172, 174, 198, 200, 273, 300

Acoma 3, 35, 67, 72, 80, 81, 168, 311

Adams, E. Charles 282

Adaptation 101, 204

Affines, affinal 56, 68, 73, 181, 190, 241

African Model 80, 117

Agave (Kwan) (One-Horn) Society 58, 81

Agency (BIA), Hopi. See Hopi Agency.

Agents, Indian 36, 308

Agreement in Principle (AIP) 252, 264-266

Ahl (Two-Horn)

  chief 61

  Society 58, 78, 79, 127, 181, 182, 186

Aholi 103, 291, 292

AIM (American Indian Movement) 9, 114, 176, 178, 248, 250, 303

Akin, Louis 98, 99

Albuquerque, NM 35, 99, 110, 140, 182, 217, 238, 279, 288, 308, 310, 312, 313, 315, 316, 318-321, 324, 325, 330

Alcatraz 109

Alcoholism 171, 210, 247, 278, 294, 317

All-Indian Pueblo Council 133, 282, 286, 299

Alliances

  political 23, 32, 40, 81, 114, 164, 278

Allotment policy 87, 91, 108, 120, 122, 127, 132, 174

Alosaka 76

Alvarado Hotel, Albuquerque 99, 140, 288

Ambler, Marjane 219

American Association on Indian Affairs 147

American Indian Ritual Object Repatriation Foundation 292, 330

Anasazi 63

Ancestors 15, 24, 64, 67, 75, 227, 305

Anderson, Wallace 192

Anglos 86, 97

Antelope 61, 62, 186

Antelope Mesa 28-31, 63, 102, 114, 284, 298

Anthropology 2, 7, 30, 43, 47-49, 51, 54, 69, 71, 73, 106, 145, 147, 169, 170, 191, 208, 233, 273, 288, 299, 308, 309, 311-319, 321, 322, 324, 325, 326-328

Apaches 31, 33, 35, 37, 65, 86, 94

Applegate, Betty and Frank 286

Applied Anthropology 169, 170, 326

Archaeological Resources Protection Act 292

Archaeology 4, 30, 33, 64, 282, 286, 292, 308, 310, 314, 316, 320, 321, 327

Architecture 3, 32, 41, 51, 54, 55, 99, 140, 148, 206, 209, 210, 257, 305, 306, 321

Area Redevelopment Administration (ARA), U.S. 274

Arizona State Museum 282

Armed forces, Hopi participation in 185, 188, 198, 207, 327

Army, U.S. 28, 30, 35-37, 43, 60, 78, 91, 98, 108-111, 123, 131, 174, 188, 192, 204, 250

Arrest and imprisonment of Hopis 88, 90, 110, 119